UPSET AT OAKMONT

UPSET AT OAKMONT
HOW DAVE HERRON BEAT BOBBY JONES IN THE 1919 U.S. AMATEUR

STEVEN SCHLOSSMAN & KARI THOMAS

University of Georgia Press | Athens

© 2025 by the University of Georgia Press
Athens, Georgia 30602
www.ugapress.org
All rights reserved
Designed by Melissa Buchanan
Set in Garamond Premier Pro and Alternate Gothic

Most University of Georgia Press titles are
available from popular e-book vendors.

Printed digitally

EU Authorized Representative
Easy Access System Europe—Mustamäe tee 50, 10621
Tallinn, Estonia, gpsr.requests@easproject.com

Library of Congress Cataloging-in-Publication Data
Names: Schlossman, Steven L., author. | Thomas, Kari (Katherine), author.
Title: Upset at Oakmont : how Dave Herron beat Bobby Jones in the 1919
    U.S. Amateur / Steven Schlossman & Kari Thomas.
Description: Athens : University of Georgia Press, 2025. | Includes
    bibliographical references and index.
Identifiers: LCCN 2024053245 | ISBN 9780820373478 (hardback) |
    ISBN 9780820373485 (paperback) | ISBN 9780820373492 (ebook) |
    ISBN 9780820373508 (pdf)
Subjects: LCSH: United States Amateur Championship (1919) | Herron,
    Dave, 1897– | Jones, Bobby, 1902–1971. | Oakmont Country Club—
    History. | Golfers—United States—Biography.
Classification: LCC GV970.3.U75 S35 2025 |
    DDC 796.352/66—dc23/eng/20250129
LC record available at https://lccn.loc.gov/2024053245

To Caitlin, Sean, and Alisha, without whom I would not be here to write this book.
—K. T.

To Steffi, whose sunshine radiates more brightly today than ever.
—S. S.

CONTENTS

Foreword and Acknowledgments   ix

Introduction. The Megaphone Didn't Do It   xiii

PART I. "NOW, HOW DO THEY DO IT—THOSE YOUNGSTERS?"

Chapter 1. Dave Herron: Gentleman Caddie and Pittsburgh Prodigy (1897–1914)   3

Chapter 2. The Kid Wonders of Atlanta: "Little Bob" Jones and Perry Adair (1902–1915)   23

Chapter 3. Grinding toward Stardom: Dave Herron at Oakmont and Princeton (1915–1916)   40

Chapter 4. "Georgia Has Golf Marvel": Jones Overtakes Adair (1916)   60

Chapter 5. The 1916 U.S. Amateur at Merion: Herron and Jones Cross Paths   71

PART II. THE WAR YEARS

Chapter 6. Still Grinding: Dave Herron and Disappointment at Oakmont (1916–1917)   85

Chapter 7. Becoming a Celebrity: Bob Jones and the Red Cross Circuit   99

Chapter 8. "An Opportunity to Witness the Game": The New Spectators of Wartime Golf   118

Chapter 9: A Gentleman Laborer: Dave Herron Finds His Game (1919)   127

Chapter 10. The "Golden Tornado" and the Summer of 1919   139

PART III. THE 1919 U.S. AMATEUR CHAMPIONSHIP AT OAKMONT

Chapter 11. "True to the Ultimate Wiggle": Discovering Oakmont   149

Chapter 12. The Terror of Oakmont   164

Chapter 13. Surprises, Upsets, and Just How Sick Is Francis Ouimet?   173

Chapter 14. A Youth Takeover   187

Chapter 15. The Championship Match   200

PART IV. AFTERMATH

Chapter 16. The Boy Wonders Go Home   243

Chapter 17. Dave Herron versus the Press   258

Epilogue. Herron and Jones: "Ten-Tenths" the Heroes of Pittsburgh and Atlanta   273

PART V. APPENDICES

Appendix 1. William Abbott, Hole-by-Hole Overview of Each Hole at Oakmont Country Club on the Eve of the 1919 U.S. Amateur Championship (August 16–23, 1919)   281

Appendix 2. Driving Distance Comparisons, Herron v. Jones in Championship Match   284

Appendix 3. Ball-Striking Comparisons, Herron v. Jones in Championship Match   285

Appendix 4. Herron v. Jones—Hole-by-Hole Scores in Championship Match Compared to Prior Scoring Averages   287

Appendix 5. Putting Comparisons, Herron v. Jones   290

Notes   295

Index   341

FOREWORD & ACKNOWLEDGMENTS

A century ago, in 1925, twenty-three-year-old Bob Jones demolished his opposition to win the U.S. Amateur Championship at Oakmont Country Club (outside Pittsburgh) by an average match-play score of 8 and 7. It was probably the greatest golf he had ever played and the second most dominant performance of his illustrious career. Perhaps the victory assuaged his disappointment of three months earlier when he bogeyed the final hole to lose the U.S. Open in a thirty-six-hole playoff to Willie MacFarlane. After Jones's 1925 victory, no one could seriously doubt that he was the rightful successor to Harry Vardon as the greatest "stylist" golf had ever witnessed.

Upset at Oakmont focuses not on 1925 but on the U.S. Amateur in 1919, when at age seventeen Bob Jones first encountered Oakmont. In one of the most controversial championships in American golf history, Jones lost in the finals to twenty-one-year-old Dave Herron, a native Pittsburgher. We tackle this somewhat obscure event not out of a misguided sentiment that every national golf championship deserves its own book. Nor do we believe that anything and everything that involves the great Bob Jones or the legendary Oakmont course warrants detailed re-creation. Trivia for trivia's sake is not what this book is about.

Instead, *Upset at Oakmont* brings new questions, new data, and a new lens to understanding the early stories of Jones and Herron and their pathways as junior golfers to Oakmont in 1919. Through their dual biography, we seek to capture that remarkable late nineteenth- to early twentieth-century era when golf in America spread at remarkable speed, took its modern competitive form, increasingly appealed to families, not just upper-class men, and—before Jones was even part of the conversation—spawned its first famous golfing heroes (Travis, Egan, Travers, Ouimet, Hagen).

Upset at Oakmont seeks to re-create the excitement that American championship golf, still in its fledgling stages, evoked over a century ago by employing a variety of new historical data and investigative and interpretive approaches. Much of our historical data are sourced from newly digitized newspapers across the United States, including multiple newspapers from Pittsburgh and Atlanta, the two hometowns of our protagonists, Dave Herron and Bob Jones. But we also tracked their careers as junior competitors in newspapers from Birmingham, Memphis, New Orleans, Altoona, Philadelphia, Detroit, Baltimore, Chicago, and New York. Golf was a hot topic in the early twentieth-century United States, and editors frequently sent sports journalists to cover both local tournaments and major championships in person (it helped that many golf writers were competitors themselves). In an age before radio or television, these reporters provided detailed coverage of each round and match to an extent that boggles the mind today.

Thus, there is a wealth of data about early twentieth-century golf sitting in newspaper archives.[1] The data are also messy, contradictory, often biased, quite hyperbolized, and riddled with typos and scoring inconsistencies. Golf writers often did not agree on what they saw (or heard), and there was no recorded footage to check who was right. We try to resolve these factual questions through a careful comparative analysis of individual newspaper reporting. For the 1919 U.S. Amateur at Oakmont, we took the extra step of comparing what reporters claimed to have seen with maps of the course to determine if what they were describing was really possible.

In many ways, Oakmont is another character in our drama—a physical space that shaped Dave Herron in mind as much as body and ultimately frustrated Bob Jones. For the first two decades of its history, Oakmont was changing and growing into the legendary course it would become, but misconceptions of its static timelessness obscure this early period. This, too, is part of our story.

In addition to immersing ourselves in newspapers and maps, we systematically collected and analyzed scoring data for every round of the 1919 U.S. Amateur Championship. Much of this statistical analysis is simply woven into our narrative, but for any reader who is interested in how we arrived at our conclusions or the data itself, we have included our methods and more detailed data sets in the appendices. Sorting out truth from fiction and opinion from fact would have been nearly impossible without this analysis, so we hope that this type of value-added information becomes more common practice in writing championship golf history.

With all of that said, we inevitably encountered puzzles that at a distance of one-hundred-plus years were challenging to resolve. Sometimes, we succeeded in untangling a particularly knotty problem, which we discuss in the footnotes. Other times, we had to rely on our best interpretive judgment. There are some things that even with the advantage of fuller evidence we will simply never know. We hope, however, that all readers will enjoy the truth-seeking journey we take them on, and will judge, as we do, that Dave Herron was the rightful victor at Oakmont in 1919.

A data-driven project such as this one would not be possible without a lot of helping hands along the way. We are fortunate indeed to benefit from Oakmont Country Club's commitment to excellence and grace in all it does to sustain the golfing vision of the Fownes family and the highest aspirations of American championship golf. Our deepest thanks to Bob Ford and Barry Hackett, who embody these traditions. They have been friends of this project from the start and, in so many ways—including countless walks in search of history over the fairways of Nos. 12, 15, and 16—have enabled its completion. Much appreciation, too, to Devin Gee, Oakmont's head professional; to former course superintendents John Zimmers and Dave Delsardo; and to club historian Dave Moore for helpful guidance at numerous points.

Our friends at the USGA, especially its museum and library staff, have also supported our scholarship from the start, and this book would have been impossible without them. Many thanks to Nancy Stulack, Patty Moran, Victoria Nenno, Mike Trostel, Susan Wasser, Shannon Doody, Stacy Schiff, Rosemary Maravetz, and Katie Boyce for their work in the trenches.

Golf history buffs today, as in the past, are a varied bunch, and we have been lucky to receive guidance from exemplars of the field. We are grateful for the stimulating historical conversations and insightful readings of our work provided by Rand Jerris, Ron Rapoport, Craig Disher, Bob Crosby, John Capers, Jon Schmerling, David Burstin, Jay Burton, Carol Semple Thompson, and David Fay, as well as the late George Kirsch, Lyle Slovick, Rhonda Glenn, John Fitzgerald, and Robert Hackett.

Carnegie Mellon University is the academic home of both authors, and several undergraduates and staff members have assisted our research as much with their passion for knowledge as their scholarly values. Special thanks to former students Phoebe Ng, Jon Murcek, and Nick Mlakar for their superb research assistance in gathering and organizing primary sources, and to our colleagues Emma Slayton and George Cann for applying their refined skill sets to help make our data analyses intelligible. And, in the History Department, colleagues and staff continue to provide essential day-to-day support for our multiple professional endeavors; deep thanks to Amy Wells, Natalie Taylor, Nico Slate, and Christopher Phillips.

Librarians, of course, have been key every step of the way. Special thanks to Carnegie Mellon University librarians Sue Collins, Andrew Marshall, Charlotte Trexler, and Gloria Henning; to Sierra Green, Margaret Hewitt, Anne Madarasz, and Andy Masich at Pittsburgh's Senator John Heinz History Center; and to Gary Rogers at the Oakmont Historical Society.

Finally, but hardly least, we are grateful to Hal Cherry, a grandson of Dave Herron, for his gracious hospitality and for allowing us to view and publish in our book numerous selections from the wonderful photo collection and mini-archive he has assembled of his grandfather's life and golf career. Hal's continuing passion for the game added much to our appreciation of early twentieth-century amateur golf ideals. And we thank him sincerely.

▶ INTRODUCTION
THE MEGAPHONE DIDN'T DO IT

Golf matches have been won before with drivers, brassies, mashies, niblicks, and putters, but this is the first time one was officially and finally decided with a megaphone.

—Grantland Rice, "Big Golf Match Was Decided on 12th Hole by Megaphone," *New York Tribune*, August 25, 1919

THE MEGAPHONE INCIDENT

Incontestably, Bob Jones and Arnie Palmer—for each, his preferred nickname—are the two most beloved figures in the history of American golf. Neither man holds the records for most victories, most majors, lowest scoring, longevity, and so on—those feats belong to other historical greats: Snead, Nicklaus, Sorenstam, Woods—but their careers are celebrated as if they did. Why?

Mainly, we think, because Americans (and Brits too) embraced Bob and Arnie for much more than their athletic triumphs. Both men were worshipped as heroes of their age. As athletes, Jones and Palmer openly bled passion and sincerity, and fans responded with love. Their victories brought personal joy to fans, women as well as men. And their failures, no less impressively, evoked sorrow, commiseration, even anger: the good guy was cheated, or the fates were against him. Their losses were our losses; history's losses, too.

Failure is a defining and endearing feature of how we recall both Jones and Palmer. Palmer won the U.S. Amateur, sixty-two professional tournaments, seven major championships (including four Masters), and ten Champions tournaments (Palmer created the Senior PGA Tour, its predecessor, almost single-handedly). Yet his failure to win the Grand Slam because he never won a PGA Championship always dogged him, and his epic collapses on television—at the 1961 Masters, the 1962 U.S. Open, the 1966 U.S. Open, and the 1973 U.S. Open—endeared him to us all the more. We suffered his collapses as much as he did, the angst on his face etched indelibly in our minds and hearts.

Jones had several "lean years" when he failed to win anything, despite experts' certainty he would eventually win everything. Bob was cast as Destiny's favored child from age fourteen onward, when he rocketed to national fame in the 1916 Amateur at Merion. Yet his first notable victory, inexplicably, did not come until 1923, at age twenty-one. A year earlier, twenty-year-old Gene Sarazen (nineteen days older than Bob) had already won both the U.S. Open and the PGA Championship. To non-golfers: Gene who?

Oakmont Country Club, located approximately fourteen miles northeast of downtown Pittsburgh, was where two of Jones's and two of Palmer's most painful losses occurred. To the over-sixty-five crowd today, the upsets at Oakmont that Latrobe, Pennsylvania–born Palmer suffered—first, to the upstart, overweight Jack Nicklaus in 1962 and, then, to the stylish, arrogant Johnny Miller in 1973—still seem profoundly unfair. Arnie deserved to win them both. Bob barely broke a sweat in winning the U.S. Amateur at Oakmont in 1925, but his two failures there remain among the most puzzling of his career: an upset at the hands of an unknown local youth, Samuel Davidson Herron, in the 1919 U.S. Amateur, and then, in 1927, his worst performance at a major championship, where he tied for eleventh place in the U.S. Open and finished eight strokes behind.

In the early twentieth century, the U.S. Amateur, not the U.S. Open, was the premier golf championship in America. It had been canceled in 1917 and 1918 because of America's late entry into World War I. The reigning Amateur champion in 1919 was Charles "Chick" Evans Jr., of Chicago, whom most considered the greatest golfer America had ever produced. In 1916, after years of dominating golf in the "West" (i.e., the Midwest), Evans was the first man to win both the National Amateur and the National Open (as, respectively, the U.S. Amateur and U.S. Open were then called) in a single year.

Still, many thought that Francis Ouimet—the Boston boy who had defeated Harry Vardon and Ted Ray in the U.S. Open at Brookline in 1913, and who erased any doubts as to his greatness by winning the U.S. Amateur the following year—was at least Evans's equal. In 1919, after three years' absence, Ouimet was eligible to play at Oakmont because the United States Golf Association (USGA)—correcting its greatest blunder ever—had finally restored his amateur status after revoking it because he sold sporting goods (including golf clubs) for a living. Golfers everywhere prayed for an Evans-Ouimet finale at Oakmont to determine, at long last, who really was the greatest American golfer.

But the final field at Oakmont was much more than Evans and Ouimet—indeed, it was the greatest field ever assembled for an Amateur championship. A record number of former champions were playing, including two Pittsburghers, Eben Byers (1906) and W. C. Fownes Jr. (1910). From New York came four-time U.S. Amateur champion Jerry Travers (1907, 1908, 1912, 1913), three-time Metropolitan Amateur champion Oswald Kirkby, and two-time U.S. Amateur finalist John Anderson. The Chicago contingent was equally strong, featuring not just defending champion Chick Evans but also Robert Gardner, a two-time Amateur champion (1909, 1915), and Daniel (D.E.) Sawyer, a Western Amateur winner and U.S. Amateur finalist. In other words, if Evans and Ouimet did not live up to expectations, there were plenty of seasoned veterans who came to Oakmont intent on winning.

The South, for the first time, also had significant representation in the U.S. Amateur. Seventeen-year-old Bob Jones and his childhood friend, twenty-year-old Perry Adair, joined veteran star and five-time Southern Amateur champion Nelson Whitney of New Orleans, and excited considerable interest at Oakmont. Jones and Adair were intriguing not only because of their youth, but also because they were already familiar names in national golfing circles. Everyone recalled the shock of hearing that, at age fourteen, Jones had reached the quarterfinals of the 1916 Amateur at Merion before losing to Robert Gardner. And he and Adair had played numerous, widely publicized golf exhibitions in the East and Midwest to raise money for the Red Cross during World War I, in 1917 and 1918. Interest now centered on Jones's recent tournament play in Canada in July 1919, where, despite his youth, he had competed spectacularly against amateurs and professionals alike in the "International" matches. The U.S. Amateur field at Oakmont, to be sure, was much "faster" than anything Canadian golf could offer. But those who had seen "Little Bob" in action declared him a long-shot winner at Oakmont if he was on his game and if the veteran players faltered.

Pittsburgh golfers were also unusually well represented at the 1919 Amateur, and not just because they were the locals. Over two dozen golfers in the Pittsburgh region qualified for the Amateur championship because they had earned USGA-approved handicaps of 5 or less. As noted earlier, Fownes and Byers were former national champions, and both were still quite competitive in their late thirties and early forties. Joining them was George Ormiston, also in his forties, who had twice won the West Penn Amateur, twice lost in the finals of the Pennsylvania Amateur, and was still considered as good as anyone at stroke play.

A fourth notable Pittsburgh golfer was definitely *not* on the national golf radar screen in the summer of 1919: S. Davidson Herron, as he was formally known, or Dave, as he preferred. Very few people outside Western Pennsylvania knew anything about Herron, although he had competed at Princeton and represented Pennsylvania in a couple of interstate matches against New York and Massachusetts (the Lesley Cup) before the war. He had only recently returned from military service, and until the virtual eve of the Amateur championship in August, he was rising at 5 a.m. every morning to labor in an ironworks, with no time to play golf. Pittsburghers, however, knew that Herron, if he could find time to practice, had both the power game and calm personality to make him a contender at Oakmont. Having caddied there for many years, played it often as the son of a club member, competed well for Princeton University in 1916 when the National Intercollegiate was held at Oakmont, and been mentored for years by Fownes, Eben Byers, and Ormiston, Herron just might catch the more experienced golfers by surprise.

That said, even locals did not really know if Dave Herron would play or what the state of his game might be. And surely all would have acknowledged—even Fownes, who played with Jones in Canada—that if any younger player had a chance to defeat the likes of Evans, Ouimet, Travers, Gardner, Sawyer, Kirkby, Whitney, or Fownes himself, it would surely be "Bobby," the "boy wonder" from Atlanta, not Herron or any number of former or current collegians who were registered to play.

The course itself, Oakmont Country Club, provided as much cause for speculation as the galaxy of star players assembled there. H. C. Fownes, W. C.'s father, had laid out the Oakmont links in 1903 without any professional guidance. While many declared the course a masterpiece from the start, W. C., an MIT-trained engineer, had ideas of his own for upgrading the difficulty of the course in order to attract a national championship. The USGA granted Oakmont the right to host the 1917 U.S. Amateur—Merion had gotten to host in 1916 despite opening just a few years earlier, in 1912—but the war intervened and the championship was postponed. Top golfers around the country were forced to wait patiently for two-plus years until the war's end before traveling to Pittsburgh to learn firsthand what all the fuss surrounding Oakmont was about. W. C., in the meantime, used 1917 and 1918 to make the course tougher than ever. And different, too.

When the nation's best amateur golfers gathered at Oakmont in 1919 in the days leading up to the qualifying rounds, they were alternately delighted and flabbergasted. Some knew almost immediately that their style of game would not work at Oakmont, and they left town quickly. Others, like Jones, Adair, and Whitney, who were accustomed to slow Bermuda greens in the South, had to quickly adjust their putting strokes lest they three-putt every other hole. Everyone recognized that their scores at Oakmont would be substantially worse than their usual. Even Chick Evans, who'd played several rounds at Oakmont before and during the war, was startled to see how much more difficult the course now was in 1919.[1]

Oakmont, in short, would take some getting used to. The practice rounds therefore took on considerable urgency; "crack" players with 2 and 3 handicaps, who assumed they would easily advance to the top thirty-two, realized they would have to adapt, and quickly, if they were going to qualify for match play. The betting odds favoring Pittsburgh veterans like Fownes, Byers, and Ormiston improved daily because of the presumed advantages of local knowledge—even though, in fact, no "local" had ever come close to winning in the twenty-two prior National Amateur championships. Many out-of-towners dreaded what they were going to tell their friends at home when they could not break 90 at Oakmont while sporting a handicap of 5 or less. As the players gathered for the official tee-off on Saturday, August 16, 1919, everyone agreed that Oakmont was the most demanding course on which the Amateur championship had ever been held.

WHAT THIS BOOK IS ABOUT

Upset at Oakmont has two focal points: (1) the unknown story of twenty-one-year-old Dave Herron, the "surprise" winner of the 1919 U.S. Amateur; and (2) the rise to fame of seventeen-year-old Bob Jones, the runner-up to Herron at Oakmont and soon to become the most celebrated golfer in the world.

More fully than ever before, we tell the story of Bob Jones's coming of age as the most precocious child and adolescent golfer the world had ever seen. For all that has been written about Jones, it is remarkable how many significant factual gaps remain in the historical record about his early years as a golfer, not to mention mythologies and inaccuracies that corrode fair interpretation of Jones's ascent to greatness. Certainly, Jones and O. B. Keeler, his first and most prolific biographer, must take some responsibility for later misunderstandings, given how assiduously they protected Jones's private space and shaped public understanding of who he was, what he thought, and what he did. But by failing to interrogate these early "tall tales," later biographers and historians played a role, too.

Bob Jones lucked out in having a doting father, "Big Bob," as he was amiably called. (Bob was "Little Bob" until his early teens; indeed, to his annoyance, some writers still called him Little Bob at Oakmont.) From the time Little Bob was nine years old, Big Bob predicted his son's place in the pantheon of golfing greats, and he did his fatherly best to publicize his son's early triumphs and make their mutually shared, father–son dream a reality. Bob had another surrogate father, George Adair, the wealthy father of his friend and golfing buddy Perry, who watched Bob's back and chaperoned both boys whenever Big Bob could not (because of business constraints or sheer nervousness) accompany his son to events. But doting and coddling often go hand in hand. Bob Jones, as we shall see, bore all the earmarks of a spoiled child as he came into and moved beyond adolescence. While his adulthood—from age eighteen onward—is not part of our story, we highlight several of his defining behavioral traits as they took root in his first seventeen years, on the road to the 1919 Amateur at Oakmont.

Many basic facts about Jones's junior golf career have not previously made it into the historical record. This lack of information has lent an air of inevitability to his ultimate success—"from age nine, we knew . . . ."—that obscures his actual path to greatness. Historians' limited understanding of Jones's junior golf career makes his ultimate success seem too inevitable—too exclusively a matter of innate talent and God's will, and too little a tale of slow progress, backward steps, and intermittent failure.

Additionally, most writers on Jones have so wanted to believe in his "immaculate conception" as a golfer that they've failed to explain the extraordinary set of social circumstances, in Atlanta and elsewhere, that facilitated his rise to fame, especially during World War I, when no championships were being played and yet Jones's game and reputation grew enormously. We have so wanted to believe in his startling precocity as a preteen that we take at face value the fact that he shot an 80 at age eleven, without acknowledging that he still had many rounds in the 90s in him, and that he would not shoot consistently in the 70s until several years later. We so want to believe that Jones learned the game instinctively, magically, stealthily—hiding behind trees to secretly observe Stewart Maiden's smooth Carnoustie swing—without acknowledging that Harry Vardon, Walter Hagen, Gene Sarazen, and even Oakmont's W. C. Fownes Jr. also became champion golfers without benefit of formal lessons.

In short, we need to raise new questions and probe new sources to explain Bob Jones's ascent to stardom as something more than Divine Providence or Fate—a favorite term of Jones, Keeler, Grantland Rice, and the entire generation of hyperbolic sportswriters who first told Jones's compelling story in the pre– and post–World War I eras.

The second main task of this book is, quite simply, to "discover" Dave Herron and establish that he played the best golf of any U.S. Amateur champion in the first quarter-century of American golf. Herron's victory received exceptional praise at the time that has long since been forgotten, but that was fully earned. First, Herron's play throughout the competition was vastly superior to anyone else's. Although the official scoring for the event was hole by hole (i.e., match play), Herron was the only player whose stroke-play scores were consistently in the 70s. His scoring in the championship match against Jones—who played his best golf in the finals—was the best ever seen in the history of the

Amateur, including some extraordinarily rare under-par golf on the outgoing nines in both the morning and afternoon rounds.

Second, Herron defeated Jones decisively, 5 and 4 (that is, he was five holes ahead with only four holes left to play, so Jones could no longer catch up). Starting all square in the afternoon, Jones played the best championship golf of his life during the first eleven holes—before the infamous "megaphone incident" (more on that shortly!)—yet still found himself 3 down on the tee at No. 12.

And third, Herron was the first player to finish at the top in each of the three discrete components of the U.S. Amateur Championship: winning all five rounds of match play, tying for first place in the 36-hole qualifying competition, and winning the team-based *American Golfer* Trophy. Herron's performance was, from start to finish, the most dominant in U.S. Amateur history—he played 32 holes in 2 over par on America's toughest golf course—and vaulted him to serious comparison with Chick Evans, Francis Ouimet, and Jerry Travers. As Joe Davis, the veteran English-born golf reporter of the *Chicago Tribune*, put it: "Herron's play throughout the tournament stamps him as one of the leading players of the country. Today he would have given Chick Evans, Francis Ouimet, or Jerome Travers quite as good a battle as he gave Jones and probably would have beaten any of this trio."[2]

In light of Herron's stunning performance—second only, arguably, to Ouimet's surprise victory over Vardon and Ray at Brookline in 1913—it is remarkable how little recognition he has received from the leading historians of American golf. Indeed, "no respect" describes most assessments of his victory. It is almost as if the unknown Pittsburgher's conquest of the legendary Jones embarrasses golfing lore and must be explained away as a fluke upset in order to preserve the game's true heroes.

For example, Herbert Warren Wind, in what remains the greatest history of American golf ever written, dismissed Herron as merely "a competent golfer" and ignored his domination of all aspects of the event that week. Instead, he questioned whether Herron "was in a class with those of the other rising amateur stars, such as Jesse Guilford, Max Marston, Fred Wright, and especially the youthful veteran whom Herron had whipped in the final of the Amateur, Bobby Jones."[3]

Like most commentators, Wind turned Herron's victory at Oakmont into a story about why Jones lost, not why Herron won so decisively against Jones at his best. Wind ignored that Herron had developed a game throughout his own adolescence that could compete equally against Jones's. No, the only reason Herron won, Wind implied, was because Jones still had the temper of an overdetermined teenager: "rub-of-the-green incidents continued to upset Bobby more than a tournament golfer could afford." And that was why a loud megaphone blast on the thirtieth hole while Jones was taking his second shot so disturbed him that he topped his ball into a deep bunker and failed to escape. "Jones not only mis-hit his shot but allowed himself to become so irritated by the official's stupidity that he never got back in the match."[4]

That Jones's chance to defeat Herron was undone by the overenthusiastic megaphone tooting of a marshal trying to keep the crowd quiet is one of the most infamous and frankly overblown tales in American golf history. Considerable nonsense has been written about what actually happened on the twelfth hole, and in the match as a whole, that has reinforced prejudice against Herron as an undeserving champion. Jones was cheated by Pittsburgh partisans, the claim goes, and that is the only reason he didn't win the Amateur in 1919—perhaps, even, the reason he didn't win his first major championship until he turned twenty-one, four years later.

It is time that Dave Herron gets his due for his decisive victory at the 1919 National Amateur (known today as the U.S. Amateur, the name we will use from here on). To that end, it is first necessary to examine how Herron learned the game and developed his competitive skills while growing up in Pittsburgh, and to explain his achievement in 1919 in ways that illuminate why he was able to defeat Bob Jones so definitely—not as a historical aberration; *not just why Jones lost, but also why Herron won.* Both matter. Second, it is essential to revisit the facts regarding Herron's victory over Jones and, indeed, Herron's play throughout the championship. Unfortunately, golf historians have ignored, misrepresented, and misinterpreted those facts in ways that denigrate Dave Herron's victory and portray it unfairly as a fluke "upset."

Separating truth from fancy regarding "the megaphone incident" and what actually happened on the last few holes of the Herron-Jones match is no simple matter; the basic "facts" remain hotly disputed, and ultimately there is no inarguable proof one way or another. But we shall do our best, combining the press coverage of dozens of newspapers with statistical analysis, to show why the true surprise in the 1919 Amateur would have been if Bob Jones, not Dave Herron, had won. Though no one ever called Dave Herron "wonder boy," he did follow up his 1919 victory by winning two Pennsylvania state amateur championships in the 1920s—one at Merion, the other at Oakmont. Charting the paths of both competitors to Pittsburgh in 1919 seems to us a dual story of adolescent precocity that is very much worth telling a century later.

PART I

"NOW, HOW DO THEY DO IT—THOSE YOUNGSTERS?"

▶ CHAPTER 1
DAVE HERRON
GENTLEMAN CADDIE AND PITTSBURGH PRODIGY (1897–1914)

Samuel Davidson Herron—Dave to his friends and sometimes Davie or Davey in the press—was named for his grandfather, San D. Herron, and born October 16, 1897, to Andrew W. and Jane Jardine Herron in the North Oakland neighborhood of Pittsburgh, a short distance from the University of Pittsburgh. He was the third of three sons, his brothers Andrew Jr. and Pomeroy being six and three years older, respectively. The Herron family was old-stock American, its roots in Pennsylvania traceable to the post–Revolutionary War era, at least.

In 1900 Andrew Sr., at age thirty-five, listed his occupation in the U.S. Census as "cashier in bank," just as his own father, San D. Herron, had listed his occupation in the 1880 Census. But this occupational classification was deceptive. Within a few years Andrew became president of the Fort Pitt National Bank, located on Fourth Avenue in the heart of Pittsburgh's financial district, and it is clear that he was already a man of considerable wealth. Their substantial residence included space for two young live-in women to help care for the family: twenty-two-year-old Lizzie Muderaus, a servant from Hungary who had emigrated to the United States six years earlier; and Eleanor Neuroth, a sixteen-year-old nurse born in Pennsylvania to German parents, who presumably tended to two-year-old Dave.

His father's wealth and social standing shaped Dave's childhood in obvious ways, not only his education but how he spent his leisure hours as well. For example, Andrew sent all three of his boys to nearby Shady Side Academy, an all-boys day school founded in 1883. The academy quickly became *the* school of choice for the sons of Pittsburgh's new-money industrial tycoons, most notably the Fricks and Mellons. The academy soon moved from its original tiny quarters on Aiken Avenue to more spacious grounds on Ellsworth Avenue. The goal of the move was not merely to expand in size but, in line with the "muscular Christianity" and amateur athletic ideals that were reshaping American Protestantism in the late nineteenth century, to make athletics central to a broadened school curriculum. This change imitated the tony public—that is, private—

The three Herron boys, from left: Andrew Jr., Dave, and Pomeroy. Cherry/Herron Family Archives.

schools in England (Eton, for example) that catered exclusively to children of the aristocracy and viewed sports as key to training true Christian gentlemen.

To be sure, Shady Side boys were prepared well to succeed academically and to attend elite colleges, especially Princeton. But one dare not understate how central athletics were to the school's evolving mission in training young gentlemen. Team sports participation was a requirement for graduation. William Crabbe, the academy's headmaster from 1883 to 1913, devoted great energy not only to structuring numerous sports teams within Shady Side, but to formalizing school athletics among the public and private secondary schools in and around Pittsburgh. Crabbe was the spearhead behind the formation of the Western Pennsylvania Interscholastic Athletic League (WPIAL) in 1907, a collaboration of public and private secondary schools to establish "a level playing field for interscholastic athletic competition among the schools in western Pennsylvania."[1] Not incidentally, Shady Side Academy's inclusion in the WPIAL also maximized competitive opportunities for this relatively small, white elite group of boys against the best young athletes in the region.

Golf, which first arrived in the Pittsburgh region in the mid-1890s (Allegheny Country Club was the first course), was soon included among Shady Side's sports offerings, and all three Herron boys played in high school for the Shady Side golf team.[2] Like many Shady Side graduates, they became skilled enough to compete at the college level as well; all three eventually played on Princeton's golf team.[3] But the Herron boys drew on more than William Crabbe's "muscular Christianity" when they chose competitive golf. Their father was already one of Pittsburgh's most avid golf enthusiasts. He had the financial means and the social and business connections to join Oakmont Country Club shortly after it was built in 1903. The course was just over ten miles from his home and easily accessible by automobile and commuter train. And the Schenley Park golf links, the city's (and one of the nation's) first public golf course, was within walking distance once the Herrons moved to the Shady Side neighborhood.

Oakmont was by far the most challenging golf course in the Commonwealth of Pennsylvania as the Herron boys were coming of age (Merion in suburban Philadelphia would not open until 1912). Even more notably, Oakmont was the training ground for the state's best golfers. The Philadelphia suburbs would spawn far more golf courses than Pittsburgh and its surrounding region in the 1890s and early 1900s; many of them (even before Merion opened) were truly first-class. But for some inscrutable reason, Western Pennsylvania nurtured a far more distinguished group of golfers. William Fownes Jr., George Ormiston, and Eben Byers (who held joint memberships at Oakmont and Allegheny) were clearly the best of this elite group, but they were followed closely by J. Frederic Byers (Eben's brother), J. B. Crookston, and, by the mid-1910s, Dave Herron. Eben Byers (1906) and Fownes (1910) were the only Pennsylvanians to win the U.S. Amateur Championship. Western Pennsylvania hosted six of the first eight Pennsylvania State Amateur championships, and Fownes himself won four of these.

Andrew Herron, to be sure, was not in the class of W. C. Fownes Jr., Byers, Ormiston, or several other Oakmont members who boasted low single-digit handicaps. These were the elite players who represented Oakmont at interclub matches and qualified each year to represent Pennsylvania against the best of New York and Massachusetts in the prestigious, highly competitive Lesley Cup matches. All the same, Andrew became a quite proficient golfer, playing as often as he could on weekends and occasionally during the week. By his forties, he sported a handicap under 10. And he had both the skill and leisure time to compete in a handful of multi-day invitation tournaments sponsored by the most distinguished golf clubs each summer. He also played in hotly contested intra- and interclub matches each weekend.

Andrew made sure his boys learned the game, instructing them on his own and perhaps securing occasional lessons from Oakmont's professionals. More importantly, he played golf regularly with all three of his boys, both informally and in club events at Oakmont. The Herrons (at least the men) were a happy golfing family, and golf was the center of their active leisure life (though the boys also played other sports at Shady Side Academy). Andrew was skilled enough to provide reasonably good competition for Andrew Jr., Pomeroy, and Dave, until Dave began to move to a higher skill level than either of his brothers in his mid-teens.

Andrew Herron, though very actively involved in facilitating his youngest

Andrew Sr. supervises his three sons as they practice their golf. Cherry/Herron Family Archives.

son's golf career, stayed entirely behind the scenes and entirely out of the press. One will search the newspapers of the time in vain for any comments by Andrew on Dave's game or competition plans. There is literally no quotation from him about Dave's ascent in the Pennsylvania amateur golf ranks, his triumphs at Shady Side Academy, his victories (including his captaincy) at Princeton, or, most conspicuously, his victories and other strong finishes in tough local and state competition en route to winning the U.S. Amateur in 1919. Not a peep.

This stands in sharp contrast to Bob Jones's father ("Big Bob"). Bob's golf game advanced dramatically in the same years, the early to mid-1910s, and Big Bob was everywhere to be seen and heard in national golf journals, Atlanta newspapers, and other Southern newspapers in publicizing his son's accomplishments and promoting his fortunes, effectively branding him for the future, even as a preteen. While Bob, like Dave, was a quiet and shy adolescent (except for Bob's hot temper on the golf course), Big Bob most definitely was not. If he was in town, whether in Atlanta or in other Southern cities where he accompanied his son to play golf, you could be sure to read what he had to say about Bob and his game. Eventually, in 1920, O. B. Keeler took over this public relations role, but before then, Big Bob—with only one child to oversee—pioneered the role of brand manager from the moment Bob began to show precocious talent.

Perhaps Andrew was more to the manor born, socially and economically, than Big Bob, and consequently more reticent to advertise his son's sports victories. Or perhaps the two proud dads were just fundamentally different personalities. But Andrew Herron, no less than Big Bob Jones, was absolutely instrumental in laying the foundations for his son's ascension to the pinnacle of American amateur golf.

Perhaps the most important thing Andrew did to develop Dave's golf talent was to encourage him to caddie from age seven onward, even though Dave, as the son of a bank president and an Oakmont member, obviously didn't have to—he had guaranteed access to the course and no need for pocket change. Bob Jones, with his father's blessing, never caddied; indeed, he never held a job of any kind until he was an adult. But Andrew, in tune with most Pittsburgh industrial barons, thought it was a good idea for his son to learn the value of manual labor. Plus, Dave, the third brother in the chain, had the advantage of being able to accompany his family to Oakmont while he was still considered too young to play the course. Dave started caddying at Oakmont in 1905, just one year after the course opened. He was only seven, going on eight, and barely as tall as a golf bag, but the club members' willingness to be kind to little Dave helped keep the Herron boys plus dad together on weekends. It also provided Dave with access and an intimate introduction to Oakmont's nuanced design while enticing him to learn the game himself—with the goal, of course, of beating his two big brothers.

It's not clear exactly when Dave Herron began to play golf himself, or whether he was given formal "lessons" by Oakmont's professionals. Some Eastern scribes later claimed that he either took lessons or modeled his swing on the one-time Oakmont professional and legendary early twentieth-century golf stylist MacDonald Smith. But this claim was mistaken; Dave actually began playing regularly at Oakmont several years before Smith arrived on the scene, and it is not clear that he ever took formal instruction from anyone. In fact, very few good male golfers of the time received formal lessons—Bob Jones was not unique in this regard. With two older brothers and a father who sported single-digit handicaps, Herron had fine role models to observe and seek guidance from, in addition to an ample supply of hand-me-down clubs.

In the summer of 1905, seven-year-old Dave Herron started playing regularly at Oakmont with his good friend and Shady Side Academy classmate H. C. Fownes II, son of Oakmont's second-in-command, W. C. Fownes Jr. E. E. Giles, a 5-handicapper at Oakmont and the area's most expert golf journalist, suggested: "I have a fancy that W. C. Fownes, Jr."—who would win the

W. C. Fownes Jr. at the 1910 U.S. Amateur (The Country Club, Brookline, Mass.). Oakmont Country Club Archives.

U.S. Amateur in 1910—"and his game appealed" to young Dave and H. C. II alike.[4]

But Dave Herron was also learning from his fellow caddies, not just the Fowneses. No role model and confidante was more important than Emil Loeffler Jr., son of the club machinist, who was two years older than Dave. Loeffler spent virtually his entire life formally connected to Oakmont, and he came to know the course intimately, at ground level, probably better than anyone else. He and his family literally lived there during his childhood; he enjoyed free access to play as long as he didn't interfere with the members. And he quickly became a favorite caddie of the best Oakmont members—W. C. Fownes Jr., Eben Byers, and George Ormiston—learning the game along the way by watching them. While still a young boy, Emil Loeffler Jr. was appointed the club's caddie master. And eventually, according to no less a judge than Gene Sarazen, who played regularly at Oakmont before winning the PGA championship there in 1922, Loeffler was Oakmont's best player—superior to both W. C. and the club professional, Charlie Rowe (whom Loeffler replaced later in the decade).[5]

While still a preteen, Dave Herron took over Loeffler's role as caddie of choice for the club's best players. Herron also, by age twelve, became the youngest member of Oakmont's caddie team, which competed intermittently against its counterparts in other clubs.[6] Before long, as Herron's game began to mature, he rose from caddie of choice to partner in intra- and interclub team matches for Fownes, Ormiston, and Byers. Whether Herron or Loeffler was the better player during the early 1910s is unclear—it was probably Loeffler, who was two years older and had more time and opportunity (he lived on the course, after all) to develop his skills. But Herron, as the son of a club member, enjoyed much higher social status than Loeffler could ever claim. Though Loeffler received plenty of quiet encouragement and technical golfing advice from W. C., it was Herron, not Loeffler, the son of a hired hand, who became the budding star that the club's top players sought as their partner for competitions.

We can gain some insight into the development of young Dave Herron's golf game from the very first time his name appeared in a Pittsburgh newspaper: the summer of 1909, when he was age eleven. He was by now a regular caddie at Oakmont, old enough to play without sneaking on, and on the verge of becoming good enough—or so he and his father thought—that he should start seeking formal competition at a higher level. The first occasion was a junior golf tournament at the Edgeworth Club—its golf course long since plowed under—a short, nine-hole track adjacent to the booming, affluent suburb of Sewickley, eighteen miles from the Herron residence in Pittsburgh. As was happening throughout the northern and eastern sections of the United States, suburban development and golf-centered country clubs expanded rapidly on the outskirts of both large and small cities, and it was not uncommon for clubs to encourage participation and offer professional instruction for youth.[7] The event at Edgeworth was for boys eighteen years of age and under, several of whom had already established a local reputation against adults in club-sponsored invitation tournaments. Dave's brothers, Andrew Jr., age seventeen, and Pomeroy, age fifteen, were both entered in this tournament, along with a dozen other aspiring youngsters from four Pittsburgh suburban golf clubs: Edgeworth, Oakmont, Allegheny Country Club, and the Pittsburgh Field Club (then located in Regent Square).

As in adult competitions at the time, a medal (i.e., stroke play)–qualifying round preceded the match-play phase of the tournament. In this era, amateurs almost never competed in medal-play tournaments alone. Match play—one-on-one—had long been considered a better test of golfing mettle than stroke play (which was for the pros) in the British aristocratic golfing tradition. (Hence, the British Amateur was a match-play championship, preceded by medal-play qualifying rounds to reduce the field and determine who would play against whom;

the British Open, in contrast—geared to professionals with only a handful of amateurs entered—was solely a medal-play championship.) The USGA essentially copied this tradition when organizing its national championships in the mid-1890s. The junior event at Edgeworth was designed to fit this mold.

W. A. Hays, age unknown, of the Edgeworth Club won the medal-qualifying round with a 76. Hays's score is hard to interpret because we know neither the length nor par score of the nine-hole course (the competitors played nine holes twice). That said, Andrew Herron Jr., who was a fine overall athlete at Shady Side Academy and a good golfer, shot just one stroke more, 77, to finish second, and Pomeroy, who had already caught up to his older sibling in golf ability, shot 78. Add a dozen or so strokes to each round and we probably have a good idea of what both Andrew and Pomeroy were then shooting at the much longer and more difficult Oakmont course, which then played to a par of 77.

Eleven-year-old Dave Herron did not score nearly as well as his older brothers. Because of his young age, his game was well behind that of his brothers, and he was surely shooting over 100 at Oakmont. But his 89 was a fine score for his first formal tournament.

Match play is (by design) quite unpredictable in rewarding those who play the best golf; it all depends on the accidents of the "draw" (who your opponent is) and how you play against him on a hole-by-hole basis (not total strokes). The "best" golfer doesn't always win; in different one-on-one matches, a hole might be tied by players who both scored 4 on a par 4 hole, but in another match the same hole might be tied by players who both scored 7, three over par. We do not know if young Hays, the medal winner, eventually won the tournament, but both Andrew Jr. and Pomeroy were eliminated early in match play by opponents they had bested in the qualifying round. Presumably they stayed around (as did their father) to watch their younger brother compete.

Dave Herron drew less-skilled opponents in his first two matches and won them both, gaining important competitive experience in the process. In the semifinal round, he lost a close match, 1 down, to a boy who had bested him in the qualifying round with an 82. Two victories and a close loss inspired new confidence in Herron and encouraged him to practice harder, so he would do better next time his father allowed him to enter a junior tournament. The following year, in 1910, twelve-year-old Herron competed again at Edgeworth against fifteen boys of age eighteen or under. Several boys from three brand-new clubs entered the event that year—Sharon Country Club, Thornburg Country Club, and Stanton Heights Golf Club, the largest private golf club the city of Pittsburgh would ever host (opened in 1909, it closed after World War II and was redeveloped for housing). Stanton Heights, which the Herrons played fairly often, would come to play a central role in Dave's ascent to local golf stardom. Two of the fifteen-year-old boys from Stanton Heights, J. B. Rose and William Lowrie, became important parts of Dave Herron's junior golf network over the coming years, and he would eventually join them on the Princeton golf team.

Overall, the quality of golf played by the juniors in 1910 was better than the year before. The winning score was 73, but Dave Herron tied for second only a shot behind. Impressively, he lowered his qualifying score at Edgeworth a full 16 shots between ages eleven and twelve. He again advanced far into the tournament, eventually losing a tight match, 2 and 1. And he was still the youngest entrant. His ability to compete effectively against older players was clearly advancing rapidly. He was soon competing on nearly equal terms not just against his father and brothers but also against Emil Loeffler Jr. and the other caddies at Oakmont.

The junior tournament at Edgeworth does not appear to have been played in 1911, and Dave Herron's name was mentioned only once that year in the newspapers—but the reference was telling. At age thirteen, he competed with the Oakmont caddies against the caddies of two nearby clubs to the east of Pittsburgh, Edgewood and Westmoreland. We do not know how well he scored in this event, but we do know that he carried a handicap at Oakmont of 9, around the same as his father and brothers. We also know that the Oakmont caddies destroyed their counterparts, winning 63-2 against Edgewood and 30-0 against Westmoreland. Clearly, Herron was integral to the caddie corps for interclub tournaments. And given the lopsided outcome of these matches, he held his own.

Dave Herron's breakthrough year on the Western Pennsylvania golf scene came in the summer of 1912, when he was fourteen years old and already playing high school golf on the Shady Side Academy team. However, the start of the season was not particularly auspicious. Both the West Penn Open (mainly professionals) and the West Penn Amateur were held at Oakmont in 1912, one championship immediately after the other. This meant that the course would be toughened considerably beyond what the club members usually played. The course was then playing at 6,407 yards, longer than all but a few golf courses in the United States. Par was 77, which included seven par 5s and only two par 3s.

Andrew Sr., Pomeroy, and Dave were all entered into the first qualifying round of the West Penn Open, but only Andrew Sr. turned in a scorecard (91). As was common for those who did not want to embarrass themselves by scoring over 100, Dave and Pomeroy failed to turn in scorecards, and their father decided not to continue playing the championship. Around two weeks later, Dave tried again in one of the more prestigious invitation tournaments in Western Pennsylvania, the Butler Invitation. Butler (thirty-plus miles north of Pittsburgh) was only a nine-hole course, as were many of the earliest golf courses in the United States. But Butler was well-conditioned and, at a lengthy 3,023 yards, par 37, unusually difficult, too.

Dave Herron's thirty-six-hole qualifying score of 179 was sixteen strokes behind the leader. Still, as one of the tournament's two fourteen-year-olds, he received special recognition for making the match-play cut at all. Indeed, of the sixteen qualifiers, six were still in their teens, demonstrating the growing opportunity for adolescent boys to play competitively. That was the highest fraction ever to qualify for match play, and a clear indication of how much demographics would soon matter in shaping the future of American amateur golf. As youth in the early 1900s began to learn the game at significantly earlier ages than their fathers (the pioneers), they would soon provide tough competition to the thirty- and forty-somethings who still dominated the top tiers of the sport. American golf's first youth revolution was clearly underway.

Though Dave Herron had not finished high among the qualifiers, his play improved as the tournament went on. He beat one of the stronger young players, E. J. State, in the second round, and then surprised everyone by beating W. C. Thompson, "playing a clever game" to "outclass . . . his older and more experienced opponent."[8] He stood little chance in the finals against R. L. James, who defeated the medalist in the semifinals and was the clear favorite of the large local gallery.[9] But the Herron-James match was nip and tuck and played at a high level. Herron calmly thrived in the moment's excitement, driving and putting as well as he had ever done. He was 1 down on the seventeenth hole and in danger of losing the match when, from a long distance away, he laid James an unplayable stymie to win the hole and keep the match alive. He and James tied on the eighteenth hole and forced the match into extra holes.

On the nineteenth hole, James missed a ten-footer that would have won, and as the *Pittsburgh Post* reported, "The gallery at this point was in a high pitch of excitement." Then this otherwise well-played match ended bizarrely on the twentieth hole:

> Herron drove from the tee first, but he drove his ball out of bounds. James followed suit. Their second shots were almost alike, straight down the middle of the course. James on his next shot, was a little to the left of the green. His approach was 10 feet from the pin, while Herron made a clever shot, laying his

ball within two feet of the cup. James then missed his long putt for a five and the hole and the match went to Herron, who sunk his two-foot putt for a five. A loud cheer went up from the gallery and congratulations were showered upon the youth.

According to the *Pittsburgh Post*, the Butler event was the first adult tournament that Dave Herron had ever competed in. "He has not been permitted to play in any of the larger tournaments held here this season, being a junior. . . . The boy was practically unheard of until the present tournament." But Herron showed himself "a fighter," and his victory against as strong a player as James marked a major advance in his game. "The work of this youngster is remarkable and his showing in the tournament . . . ranks him despite his immature years, one of the best golfers in this vicinity."[10]

Having made a name for himself at the Butler Invitation, Herron entered two weeks later into the invitation tournament at New Castle Country Club, an hour north of Pittsburgh. The fourteen-year-old easily qualified for match play and again surprised his elders by beating two home-course favorites in the opening rounds, including the tournament medalist. Herron especially impressed with his short game—no small feat on the exceptionally fast and tilted New Castle greens. "It was on the putting greens that he displayed his mettle, running down long putts from difficult angles."[11] Though he lost on the eighteenth hole of the quarterfinals, he and several other teen players demonstrated that they were skilled enough to compete against established stars—a notch or two below Fownes, Byers, and Ormiston, to be sure, but regular contenders in local club tournaments nonetheless.[12]

Just before the 1912–1913 school year at Shady Side Academy began, Dave and his brother Pomeroy traveled ninety-five miles east to play in an invitation tournament at Altoona Country Club, a rugged nine-hole course that some golfers considered the most difficult nine in the state. What made this tournament particularly interesting was the presence of J. B. Crookston, arguably the best player in Western Pennsylvania (and perhaps the entire state) who was not closely affiliated with Oakmont. No one at Altoona was surprised that Crookston's 157 handily won the medal-play qualifying rounds by a remarkable 14 shots over Dave, whose score of 171 was good for second place on the difficult course.

Unfortunately for Dave, he drew Crookston as his opponent in the opening round. Details of the contest do not survive, but in his first head-to-head match against a top-tier player outside of Oakmont, Herron lost only 1 down.[13] He was surely disappointed to be eliminated from the tournament so early, but there was every reason to be proud. His first summer of competitive golf against the best adult non-Oakmont players in Western Pennsylvania had yielded his first victory and established that he was the best fourteen-year-old golfer in the region.

While coming of age, Dave Herron had been fortunate to observe and compete regularly at Oakmont and in events at nearby clubs against many of the best players in the state—and some of the very best in the nation. He was well situated to develop and exploit his talent to the fullest without straying far from home. His caddying days at Oakmont were now over, but his stature among Oakmont's elite players had only risen.

But just how good was Dave Herron in comparison to the best of his age peers in the 1910s? Alas, data are not available to address this question on a nationwide basis. Nor do we know how competitive Herron was at this stage with the very best players at Oakmont. But it seems fair to conclude from his several summer events in 1912 that though he had won at Butler and competed well against solid adult competition at New Castle and Altoona, he was not in the league of the two greatest fourteen-year-old male golfers of the 1910s: Philip Carter of Bridgehampton, Long Island (b. 1896), and Bob Jones of Atlanta (b. 1902).

Carter had earned a national reputation in 1910 by defeating the best New York golfers in the prestigious invitation tournament at Shinnecock Hills before losing to former New York Giants baseball star John Montgomery Ward in the finals. Carter then went on to win three consecutive Metropolitan Golf Association junior championships, in addition to several invitation tournaments against many of the best players in the East. Those achievements went well beyond what Herron achieved in 1912 and the years immediately following. Nor, even more clearly, as we shall see, was Herron in the same league as fourteen-year-old Bob Jones.

Although Herron's concrete achievements still paled against those of Carter and Jones at the same age, and he lacked their national reputation, at age fourteen he had proved himself an imperturbable competitor. It would take seven more years before he transformed himself into a bona fide golf superstar and defeated Bob Jones for the U.S. Amateur title in 1919. But by 1912, in the cocoon of Oakmont Country Club and in the fire of intense club competition—at a level that, arguably, no other club in America (save the National Golf Links in Long Island, N.Y.) could match—Oakmont's best players would continue to nurture Dave Herron, their former caddie, into becoming Oakmont's third national champion.

Herron faced the summer 1913 amateur golf season with great enthusiasm

Emil Loeffler Jr., Oakmont's long-term caddie master and later greenkeeper, leans over a rail next to Oakmont's club manager, Bill Stitt. Oakmont Country Club Archives.

and probably harbored dreams of qualifying for the U.S. Amateur Championship at the historic Garden City Golf Club on Long Island. However, he focused on preparing for a different event of greater significance for the Herron family: Oakmont was sponsoring its first invitation tournament. Virtually by definition, this would become the most prestigious golfing event in the region.

Two years earlier, W. C. Fownes Jr. had taken over course operations at Oakmont from his father and club founder, H. C. Fownes. With his newly appointed greenkeeper in 1913—none other than his former caddie, eighteen-year-old Emil Loeffler Jr.—W. C. had begun the process of increasing the course's difficulty in order to realize his father's dream to host multiple USGA championships, the U.S. Amateur first and foremost.

The Oakmont course was already the longest and most challenging golf test in Western Pennsylvania and probably the entire state. But W. C. had ambitions to escalate the course's difficulty considerably as a strategy to build a national reputation as a championship-caliber course and as a training ground for elite golfers. The Oakmont Invitation in 1913 would kick-start that process.

Original plans were to hold a thirty-six-hole qualifying test to qualify for

H. C. Fownes, Oakmont's legendary founder and course designer, standing outside the clubhouse adjacent to the ninth green. Oakmont Country Club Archives.

match play, especially because Fownes determined that only sixteen players would be allowed in the championship flight. But every decent golfer in Western Pennsylvania begged for the chance to compete in Oakmont's first invitation tournament, and Fownes decided to accommodate: the top sixteen would be determined after only a single round of medal play. This decision placed enormous pressure on the region's top players who lived outside the Pittsburgh area and did not have regular opportunity to play Oakmont because Oakmont's par of 77 would not easily be breached. As the local newspaper observed, "To break 'eighty' on the Oakmont Country Club course is a test of any player's golf."[14]

Predictably enough, the man who everyone, including Fownes, considered the best medal player in Pennsylvania, Oakmont's George Ormiston, easily captured the qualifying round trophy with a score of 75. Ormiston's drives consistently found the fairway, and his irons, even for him, were especially brilliant that day.[15] The gallery applauded Ormiston heartily as he walked off the eighteenth green with a four-shot lead over Eben Byers and J. B. Rose, a young player from Stanton Heights who also played for Princeton. Fownes, the reigning State Amateur champion, finished with an 81. Dave Herron's 83 qualified easily and tied him for sixth place. Oakmont, a truly arduous test of skill, had identified virtually all of the area's best players—precisely what a championship golf course is supposed to do.

Despite his youth, Herron was fully competitive in this elite tournament. But even though he reached the semifinals, his matches received almost no press attention, especially in comparison to the hole-by-hole detail devoted to the other matches.[16] Perhaps this was because he was the youngest contestant in the field; though he clearly belonged in this group of competitors, public interest still naturally focused on the seasoned, better-known veterans. That said, the press expected a close semifinal match between Herron and his opponent, a top player from the Pittsburgh Field Club, L. C. Liddell. But Liddell played exceptionally well that day and clobbered Herron, 6 and 5.

In the end, the veteran Eben Byers handily won the first Oakmont Invitation, but the play of several junior golfers in addition to Herron on such a tough venue boded well for the future of Western Pennsylvania golf. As the *Pittsburgh Post* summed up: "There were more young players entered in this tournament than any ever held here before. For the last twelve years Byers and Fownes have been in a class by themselves, but in the tournaments so far this year it begins to look as if there are some other players coming up who will give them a good run."[17]

The Fourth of July weekend of 1913 brought more players to Pittsburgh's golf courses than ever before. In a "holiday cup" tournament at Oakmont, Dave Herron played well with his father in fourball and shot a fine 80 to win the individual handicap event. Fifteen-year-old Dave sported a 4 handicap at Oakmont, which made him the top junior player at the club and a competitive equal to the course founder, H. C. Fownes. But there was still considerable separation between Dave and the other top Oakmont players; Ormiston played to a 0 ("scratch") handicap, for instance, and W. C. Fownes Jr., considered the best player in the region and the state, had a plus-2 handicap. In other words, in a match between Fownes and Herron, Fownes would have to give Herron one stroke on each of the six most difficult holes to "equalize" the competition between them.[18]

A week after the first Oakmont Invitation, the second major tournament in the area got underway, at Stanton Heights. A three-day affair with a thirty-six-hole qualifier, there were a hundred entries, a large enough group to lead tournament organizers to ask players from local clubs to bring their own caddies so that out-of-towners would have enough caddies to hire. Fownes and Byers did not play in this event, so Herron, as the previous year's champion at Butler, entered the tournament hopeful that he might win. But the Stanton Heights Invitation boasted a better overall field than at Butler the previous year, and the quality of Herron's golf would have to be better to have a chance at winning in this "faster" field.

In truth, Dave Herron almost didn't qualify for the championship flight of thirty-two players, but he then surprised everyone in the opening match by winning the seventeenth and eighteenth holes to defeat the medalist and tournament favorite, J. B. Crookston.[19] He followed that up with an awesome display of golf and found himself again in a championship finale against none other than R. L. James, the victim of his tournament victory breakthrough a year earlier at Butler. A large gallery turned out for a repeat Herron-James match, and the newspapers reported it in loving detail. On the front nine, Herron's outstanding score of par 37 gave him a 2-up lead. He then shot even 4s on the back nine and easily defeated James 5 and 4 to win his second invitation tournament in the region, this one at the private club closest to his Pittsburgh home. Journalists highlighted how extraordinary it was for a fifteen-year-old to hold up so "imperturbably" against "much older and more experienced players.... Herron played some remarkable golf during the three days of the tournament and his victory was very popular among the spectators." The reporter took his evaluation of Herron a step further and made a bold prediction: "Although now only 15 he has been playing golf for seven years and it is the opinion of all critics who have seen him play in a few years he will be a figure in the national championships."[20]

As Herron's summer of tournament golf continued, he spent most of his time competing at Oakmont, often as a partner of Ormiston or Fownes or Byers in intra- and interclub matches, or with his father and twenty-one-year-old brother Andrew Jr., whose games continued to improve. Dave's scores indicated that he was, at the least, contributing equally in all team competitions, and certified that his 4 handicap at Oakmont was real. He clearly remained the best junior player of his age in the state, and the best junior player of any age in Western Pennsylvania.

As the summer of 1913 drew to a close, two nearby invitation tournaments remained, both of which Herron had played before and was now hopeful of winning. Since the previous season, he had matured considerably, and his capacity to withstand high-level pressure was evident; the main word used to describe his game under fire was "imperturbable." The first invitation was at nearby New

Castle, but Herron's golf there was mediocre and he lost in the second round.[21] A couple of days later, he set out for the Altoona Invitation, which featured the most geographically diverse field the tournament had ever drawn. Conditions were very tough, with winds high and the greens "lightning fast, making pitch shots impossible." The course, like most in Western Pennsylvania in summer 1913, was baked dry from a lack of rain. Only one player shot exceptionally well on the first day of the two-round qualifier, W. S. Sargent of Merion, whose 78 bested Herron and another player tied for second place at 83. But the next day Herron raised his game to the highest level he had ever reached, particularly given the difficulty of the course. Shooting the lowest score of his life in competition, 73, he beat Sargent for the medal trophy, 156 versus 158.[22]

Herron maintained his momentum during match play. "Playing almost perfect golf," he scored near par and overwhelmed his first two opponents. In the finals he was 3 up after eighteen holes, 4 up after twenty-seven holes, and 5 up after thirty holes. But then, on the verge of a lopsided victory, his usually confident putting stroke suddenly left him, and he missed several very short putts to lose three of the next four holes. He finally returned to form on the seventeenth hole and secured a halve, which won him the match, his second title of the 1913 summer season, and his third regional title in an adult golf competition.[23]

Herron's victory in both the medal- and match-play portions of the Altoona Invitation strengthened his emerging reputation as the best precollegiate player in all of Pennsylvania. He returned to Shady Side Academy for his senior year, playing golf throughout the fall at both school and Oakmont-sponsored events. A significant sign of his continuing improvement was that in fall 1913 his handicap at Oakmont was reduced from 4 to 2. No doubt, his progress was being closely watched at Princeton University, as he prepared to join its golf team, which already included two of his close friends from Oakmont, W. A. Lowrie and G. A. Peacock, as well as J. B. Rose of Stanton Heights. With a player of Herron's caliber on board, Princeton hoped to challenge Yale's long-term supremacy as the top collegiate golf team in America.

For unknown reasons, Herron's golf exploits in the summer of 1914 were not chronicled as fully as in the past by the local press. Only two things are certain: for the first time in two years, he did not win any competitions, and he did not play in two of the events he had previously won: Butler and Stanton Heights. That said, there is no evidence that the quality of his golf was declining; rather, there is some evidence to suggest that, at least at Oakmont, his game was improving.

Although his summer golf season started inauspiciously—he failed to make the first flight of sixteen players in the invitation tournament at Allegheny Country Club and had to settle for romping over his opponents in the second flight—Herron fared much better at the second annual Oakmont Invitation, where he had performed well the previous year. Oakmont's stellar reputation was growing as W. C. Fownes Jr. and Emil Loeffler Jr. began to systematically toughen the course—most recently, by adding thirty-two "pits and bunkers" and adding still more length.[24] The result was that the 1914 Oakmont Invitation drew more entrants than any previous golf tournament in Western Pennsylvania. Every serious golfer in the area clearly craved an opportunity to play Oakmont, which was in its best condition ever. As one reporter noted that June, "The Oakmont course tests the mettle of the player and he usually gets what he plays for."[25] In the case of the second Oakmont Invitation, that included several dozen players whose scores in the medal-qualifying event were over 100 and well beyond.

Dave Herron made his presence known immediately by winning the qualifying round with a 1-over-par 78—the lowest score he had ever recorded at Oakmont. As generally happened, the challenge of playing Oakmont brought the very best golfers to the top of the leaderboard; two strokes behind Herron were Eben Byers and George Ormiston, and Fownes was two shots behind them at 82. Herron was in good and familiar company, only now he had bested his mentors in a forum where all the club members could easily witness how much his game had improved.

Under the heading "Herron Plays a Remarkable Game of Golf," the *Pittsburgh Gazette Times* reported the next day on Dave's victories in his first two match-play contests.[26] He came back from behind in both—including a grudge rematch against L. C. Liddell, who had beaten him badly the previous year in the inaugural Oakmont Invitation. "Herron showed remarkable nerve for so young a player," the reporter observed, also noting that Herron's matches were drawing the largest gallery. Herron continued to play exceptionally well the next day, defeating Fownes for the first time ever in the semifinals match, and advancing to the finals against another of his mentors, Eben Byers. A notoriously fiery competitor, the 1906 U.S. Amateur champion was at the top of his game. He broke par on the front nine and shot 1 under for the additional three holes it took to wallop Dave, 7 and 6, and win the second Oakmont Invitation.

Herron wanted badly to win the Oakmont Invitation before his family and friends. Winning at Oakmont would cement his statewide reputation in ways that his victories at Butler, Stanton Heights, and Altoona could never do. Still, it would have taken a Chick Evans to beat Byers at his very best. And Herron, despite his failure to win, had reached the finals against the best field of golfers he had ever faced—indeed, one of the "fastest" fields that could be assembled anywhere in the United States in 1914. His performance attested to the continued growth of his skills, his nerve under pressure, his composure before crowds (especially before adoring local crowds), and his special aptitude at Oakmont. And his performance did much to secure his popularity among golf fans throughout Western Pennsylvania.

Oakmont remained at the center of Herron's golf life as he prepared for the 1914 Pennsylvania State Amateur Championship, which would be held mid-July at his home course. He practiced daily at the club, hoping to break through in his first try at the state's premier golf title. After his near-success at the Oakmont Invitation, local experts granted him an outside chance to win, despite his youth. Not surprisingly, the *Pittsburgh Gazette Times* took the occasion to do a feature article on him—just in case he won.

Noting that from the time he was a young boy he had spent almost every day of his summers on the Oakmont links (for several years, the Herrons maintained a summer home near the course),[27] and that he was a regular beneficiary of "pointers" from Oakmont's "crack players," the reporter assessed Herron quite favorably against other top junior golfers in the area. "Of the many Pittsburghers who have taken up the game of golf in the past five or six years, Davidson Herron . . . is the only one who gives promise of developing into a really first-class player. Herron is now only 16 years of age, but he has already defeated a former national champion and has won several tournaments from a field of the best golfing talent Western Pennsylvania can produce."

The reporter also reviewed the evolution of Herron's rise to fame in Western Pennsylvania golfing circles:

> Herron first came before the public golfing eye two years ago, when at the age of 14 years, he won the Butler Country Club invitation tournament. Last year his game was much improved and he went through the invitation tournament of the Stanton Heights Golf Club, defeating R. L. James in the finals. He also won the annual invitation tournament of the Altoona Cricket Club from a field of golfers from all parts of the state. His play so far this year has been exceptionally good. It is true he failed to land in the first 16 at the Allegheny Country Club invitation tournament, but he had little trouble winning out in the second flight. In the Oakmont Country Club invitation tournament two weeks ago he created a surprise by winning the qualifying round from one of the largest and fastest field of golfers ever entered in a tournament in Western

Pennsylvania. He defeated Ned Allis, II, champion of Minnesota, in the first round and then defeated L. C. Liddell of the Pittsburgh Field Club in the second round. In the semi-finals he went against former national champion W. C. Fownes, Jr. and won out. He then went down to defeat before E. M. Byers. He has been practicing daily for the past week and should give a good account of himself in the state championship at Oakmont which begins tomorrow.[28]

Alas, Herron got off to a poor start in the two-round qualifier for the State Amateur title. Not surprisingly, his three mentors led the field, Ormiston at top with an impressive 1 under par 153, and Fownes and Byers close behind. But Herron shot a 171, far worse than he'd been shooting at Oakmont in recent weeks, despite his daily practice. He nonetheless snuck into the championship flight and won his first match, 3 and 2. Unfortunately for him, in the second round he ran into a hot player from Philadelphia, C. B. Buxton, who had stunned everyone in the first round by shooting par figures to defeat Eben Byers. Neither Buxton nor Herron played especially well, but Buxton putted well enough to win.[29]

Dave Herron did not participate in any more events until the end of August, when he returned to defend his title at the Altoona Invitation. He was favored to win the medal competition but shot 80 and finished four shots behind Lawrence Canon, the young Altoona star who would leave shortly for Harvard. He then had the misfortune to draw Canon as his first-round opponent in match play and lost to Canon's demonstrated mastery of his home course.[30]

Although Herron was clearly far from a dominant player at the age of sixteen, he was on the radar of anyone familiar with Western Pennsylvania golf. He was the best junior player in the region and one of the best Oakmont players. He had developed his game by watching and caddying for the old hands and honed his skills by testing them repeatedly against national stars. He was not nearly as famous as Bob Jones would soon become, but he was among the very best precollegians in the East. And, just like his mentors, he knew Oakmont like the back of his hand.

► CHAPTER 2
THE KID WONDERS OF ATLANTA
"LITTLE BOB" JONES AND PERRY ADAIR (1902-1915)

Like Dave Herron and Emil Loeffler Jr., Bob Jones grew up with a friendly archrival, Perry Adair. Adair's father, George, was a key figure in both the Atlanta golf scene, where he served on the board of the Atlanta Athletic Club (AAC) and as director of the Druid Hills Club, and more widely in the South, where he was elected to multiple terms as vice president of the Southern Golf Association. George Adair was also a good friend of Jones's father, "Big Bob." So naturally, Perry Adair and Bob Jones grew up playing together despite the fact that Perry was almost three years older and, therefore, naturally developed his game a bit sooner than Bob did.[1]

At first, the boys' only home course was the East Lake Golf Club (a course first completed in 1907 and then redesigned by Donald Ross in 1913). Bob Jones stated in his popular autobiography, *Down the Fairway* (co-authored with O. B. Keeler), that he was "shooting down around 90 and occasionally a stroke or two below at the time of the [East Lake] club championship in 1912" when he was ten years old.[2]

However, it was more likely that Jones was still shooting in the high 90s, whereas Adair had started to shoot consistently in the low 90s and high 80s. In fact, a year later, in 1913, Jones shot a 90 in the President's Golf Trophy tournament in July, a 101 in the Davis & Freeman Cup in August, and a 95 in the Atlanta Athletic Club Championship later in the season. Occasionally, though, a flash of his future game dazzled galleries. Jones wrote in *Down the Fairway* that—to his great delight and perhaps surprise—he shot his first 80 in 1913, at age eleven. That is certainly not a stretch, considering he shot an 86 at the T. A. Hammond Tournament in late September, the last notable event of the 1913 Atlanta golf season (Perry Adair shot 93). But Jones, at age eleven, usually scored considerably above 80, contrary to later legend.

Despite Jones's natural abilities—he broke 90 in competition before Adair did, after all—he was still an inconsistent player. Thus, in 1913, the Atlanta Athletic Club's handicap committee considered Perry Adair the clearly superior golfer of the two boys. Adair boasted a club handicap of 8 (his father's

Reading from left to right: Howard Thorn, runner-up in championship; Robert Jones, Jr., the champion; Frank Meador, winner of defeated four; H. C. Moore, runner-up in defeated four.

Bob Jones competed on equal terms with several older boys, not just Perry Adair. Here he is shown on the left standing next to an older and much taller opponent, whom he beat in the finals of the Junior Championship of the Atlanta Athletic Club at the age of nine. Francis E. Price, "Winners in Boys' Golf Tourney," *Atlanta Constitution*, 15 June 1911.

club handicap was 3), whereas Jones's handicap of 15 was nearly double his friend's (Big Bob's club handicap of 9 was also substantially better than eleven-year-old Bob's). But age was not the only factor in the discrepancy between Adair's and Jones's games. In 1914, Adair undertook a vastly different tournament schedule from Jones's, competing in more prestigious Southern events—taking advantage of Atlanta's well-developed regional rail connections—and even competing outside the South, whereas Jones competed exclusively in Atlanta.

For example, Perry Adair's first event of the 1914 summer golf season was the Southern Amateur, played at the Memphis Country Club in Memphis, Tennessee.[3] After qualifying with an 83, two strokes better than his dad, the young Adair made it all the way to the finals in his first regional event—which also happened to be the most prestigious amateur championship in the South. Of the Atlantans that competed in the Southern Amateur, he "created the most comment. Young Adair by his good form, caused talk of a high place for him in the week's play. He appears to be an excellent medal player and will likely show well in match play, which begins tomorrow."[4] And after Adair defeated G. H. Davis of Birmingham in the first round, "It began to be noised about that it was going to take some real golf to beat 'the kid,' as he [i.e., Perry Adair] was referred to by everybody."[5]

In the second round, in front of a gallery of "at least three hundred people," Perry just barely defeated his father on the nineteenth hole by laying him a dead stymie with his second shot.[6] "The elder Adair failed, only driving his son's ball nearer the cup and the boy won with an easy putt."[7] The *American Golfer's* Southern correspondent, "The Colonel," wrote: "It was the first time the boy had ever beaten his father in a match and the father took him in his arms and kissed him."[8] George was clearly an affectionate and caring parent, and deeply involved with his son's training.

In the third round, Perry Adair defeated Whitney Bowden of New Orleans in a very tight match that ended on the eighteenth green.[9] The quarterfinals proved to be another close match. Adair again won on the eighteenth, this time against Scott Probasco, "the left-handed wizard of Chattanooga." "Though a mere wisp of a boy," the *Atlanta Constitution* wrote of fourteen-year-old Perry,

> He has been playing the steadiest golf of any of the contestants in the tournament. Every one of his matches has been most trying. They would test the nerve of the more experienced golfer than he, but though this is [his] first tournament, the young golfer has shown wonderful nerve and ability. Everyone at the course and the golfers of the south in general are pulling for the youngster to come through and win the title. They are admiring his pluck, his ability, and his golfing temperament.[10]

The rhetoric used in 1914 to characterize Perry Adair in his first "big competition" was remarkably similar to how the press would write about Bob Jones in 1916 at the U.S. Amateur at Merion. No doubt the growing legion of golf enthusiasts in the South found it charming to watch a young boy of average size compete against adults who were not only much bigger but also more experienced in competitive play. What writers and spectators could not get enough of was the ever-optimistic spirit of youthful persistence. Adair's matches were close, but he kept on pluckily fighting until he won, even if it meant taking the match regularly to the last hole or more.

Such pluck was not necessary in Adair's semifinal match against Texas State Champion George V. Rotan. "The playing of the youthful Georgian over Rotan today was sensational. He drove with the accuracy of a veteran, his approach shots were almost perfect, and his putting was consistent," the *Atlanta Constitution* reported. When the match ended on the fifteenth hole, Rotan took "the boy [Adair] on his shoulders and the crowd gave lusty hurrahs for the plucky youngster, the women leading in the cheering."[11]

Nelson Whitney, who would be Adair's opponent in the finals of the Southern Amateur, was "not only one of the best golfers in the south, but a player who apparently has no nerves, one of the longest drivers in the south and a great iron player." In the third match, he defeated Louis Jacoby—a notable victory because in the match before, Jacoby had played nearly flawless golf and shot a 6-under-par 68.[12] Whitney's experience and stellar play stacked the odds against Adair. "Golfing students here say if Adair wins, it will be on the putting greens, where his work has been regarded as remarkable. His putting has been the best of any one in the tournament." Nevertheless, all of Atlanta was rooting for Perry. According to the *Atlanta Constitution*, "Atlantans are pulling for Perry Adair, the youthful golfing prodigy, who has them by the ears by the brand of golf he is playing in the Southern championship at Memphis. The youngster has won four matches under trying circumstances—circumstances sufficient to test the nerve of the most experienced golfer."[13]

For all the hype, Perry Adair got pummeled in the finals of the 1914 Southern Amateur, 14 and 13. "Playing the same steady game that won him the championship in 1907 and 1908 and again in 1913, Whitney was master of the situation at all stages of today's play, while the fifteen-year-old Georgian, whose play in the preliminary matches has been the sensation of the tournament, was nervous and upstrung from the start."[14] At the end of the day, Adair was just "unable to stand the strain of the grueling tournament play," concluded the *Atlanta Constitution*.[15] The *American Golfer*'s Southern correspondent, The Colonel, concurred: it was an embarrassing loss but one largely explainable by Adair's youth.

> A defeat of fourteen up and thirteen to play on paper looks like the youngster went to pieces and blew up, but such was not the case. He was just worn out. On the morning of the final before the beginning of the match he told the writer that he was tired out and all in and that he felt like he couldn't walk nine holes much less thirty.

The Colonel concluded that "the strain of the grueling matches" was "too much" for Adair and the grind of championship play "was simply more than a fifteen year old boy, who doesn't weigh over a hundred and five pounds, could stand."[16] Highlighting a precocious young golfer's age and his novice status within a competition became an important trope in explaining both Perry

Adair's and Bob Jones's ascents to stardom as well as any missteps they experienced along the way. All agreed, however, that "the experience [Adair] gained will stand him in good stead in the next tournament he enters."[17]

Indeed, a month later, he won the 1914 Montgomery Invitation Tournament in Alabama.[18] Over the summer, he also competed in two Western Golf Association events. "If anybody from the South," The Colonel noted, "expects to make any kind of a show in the Western they have got to be well under eighty every round. Get as bad as eighty and someone you never heard of will give you a trimming before you know it."[19] Although Adair only qualified for the third flight in both competitions, he clearly gained valuable experience playing on more difficult championship courses outside the South.

In addition, the Adairs joined Druid Hills Club, a new and private club in Atlanta, in 1914, several months before the Joneses did. In all likelihood, the opportunity to play at two different courses gave Perry Adair a leg up on Bob Jones. Tournament records suggest that Big Bob and Little Bob did not gain regular two-course access until much later in the year, in October. Still, young Bob demonstrated that he did not need much time to adjust to the new Druid Hills course. He shot an 89 at the Druid Hills Invitation in 1914—the same score as George Adair, four strokes better than Perry, and five strokes better than Big Bob.

In the AAC Championship, both Bob Jones and Perry Adair improved their scores from the year before (Bob by three strokes to a 92 and Perry by one stroke to an 88). Interestingly, and testimony to why the two families loved to compete together, both boys shot lower than their fathers did in the 1914 AAC championship. However, the adults reasserted themselves at the Druid Hills Invitation, when, in direct competition, George Adair soundly defeated Bob Jones, 5 and 4.

So, while twelve-year-old Bob's scores in the 1914 season still fluctuated wildly, he seemed to be shooting most regularly in the low 90s and high 80s. His remarkable earlier score that year of 80 at East Lake remained a clear aberration. Meanwhile, Perry Adair's qualifying scores in the 1914 season ranged much more widely, from the low 80s to the high 90s. Dave Herron, in contrast, was shooting consistently in the 70s and low 80s on more difficult courses, but he was also the oldest of the three boys (age sixteen during the summer of 1914, compared to Adair's fifteen and Jones's twelve).

The year 1915 marked the first time that Bob Jones's father let him compete in competitions outside of Atlanta—as he recalled, "[George Adair] persuaded Dad to let me go along with them"[20]—so he joined the Adairs for "the first big event of the year," the Montgomery Invitation, "always a great event in Southern golfing circles."[21] First played in 1910, the Montgomery Country Club Invitation in Alabama was a party as much as it was a golf tournament. The *Montgomery Advertiser* announced that club manager Ross Hinds would be making lavish preparations for "table d'hote dinners" to be served Friday and Saturday night—and that there would be dancing and music each evening. "The social side of a Montgomery tournament is a big drawing card with the visitors for with a town full of pretty girls who are 'just crazy' about the Country Club, there isn't a chance for anybody not to have a good time."[22]

But sixteen-year-old Perry Adair was there to defend his championship title, not to socialize, and the *Montgomery Advertiser* singled him out as one to watch: "This young golfer was the center of interest at last year's tournament. . . . His brilliant and steady playing, his youth and affability won him many admirers." Bryan "The Commodore" Heard was the medalist, with a 76 in the qualifying round; paired with The Commodore, Adair scored an 81.[23] Bob Jones wrote later that his own score was a complete letdown, as he didn't nearly play up to his own expectations. "It seems I had forgot all about the kick I got from the first 80 at East Lake. I qualified in the second flight, which disgusted me immensely. Probably I was pretty cocky in those days."[24]

The next morning, Adair played extremely well and won the right to face Commodore Heard in the afternoon. Naturally, the contest between the medalist and the teenage prodigy drew the tournament's largest gallery, and it was a close match, "nip and tuck all the way round."[25] "When the play went to the extra hole to decide the winner," reported the *Montgomery Advertiser*, "there was [sic] perhaps three hundred following the play with the keenest interest." Although the veteran golfer from Texas had "clever approaches and putts," Adair triumphed over Heard with his "great driving."[26] George Adair, Perry's father, also won his morning and afternoon matches, putting two Adairs in the semifinals. Bob Jones, playing in the second flight, wasn't mentioned at all by the press. Perry Adair was the Southern "wonder boy" of the moment in June 1915, not Bob Jones.[27]

After taking down The Commodore, Perry Adair's next opponent in the semifinals was John Brame of Montgomery Country Club. In 1914 Brame only "lost by a narrow margin" to Adair, and "[Brame's] friends are quite confident that he will redeem himself in the play this morning."[28] In reality, Adair easily dispatched Brame. The other semifinal match was between George Adair and Harry Jernigan, which Adair won on the final hole. Meanwhile, in the second flight, Bob Jones lost his semifinal match to a little-known player, C. F. Hickman.[29] Jones later wrote that when he was beaten by "Hickman who played left-handed, I wanted to throw my clubs in the river and give up the darned game. After getting into the second flight, it some way seemed adding insult to injury to be trimmed by a man who stood on the wrong side of the ball."[30]

In an emotional finale to the championship, George Adair defeated his son in a nip-and-tuck match, gaining "revenge for the trouncing [his] son gave him last year at Memphis." It was a match in which, as the *Montgomery Advertiser* put it, "old experience and steadiness won over youthful tendency toward nervousness." After George won, "Perry Adair walked across the green to his father and shook hands."[31] But Bob Jones suspected that "Mr. Adair didn't find revenge very sweet," since after winning the Montgomery Invitation, George went around "looking as if he'd lost his last friend."[32]

The Southern Amateur was next on the schedule for both the Adairs and the Joneses. The year 1915 was the third time in the span of less than a decade that the Southern Amateur was held at East Lake—the second in 1910 and the first in 1907, when Nelson Whitney won his first Southern Amateur title. In the qualifying round of the 1907 Southern Amateur, only two players were able to make their way around the East Lake course in 90 or better. But the East Lake course had undergone significant changes over the past two years. The Colonel wrote, "The tournament this year is going to be the severest test of golf that the players have ever had to face in any Southern championship and the man who emerges at the end of the week undefeated will well deserve the title of Southern Champion."[33]

For several years, Big Bob had told his son that he could enter the Southern Amateur only after he turned fifteen, "provided [he] made sufficient progress." But to Bob Jones in 1915, especially after his disappointing performance at the Montgomery Invitation, the chance to compete in the Southern Amateur seemed like it would never come. As he recalled in *Down the Fairway*: "It seemed I never was going to be 15, and the progress I made in the Montgomery invitation tournament certainly was not of a character to warrant me in making any impassioned plea this year—1915—despite the favoring circumstances that the Southern was to be played at my home course, East Lake."[34]

Jones was therefore "surprised and a little abashed" when his father told him he could enter the Southern Amateur that year, two years ahead of schedule. And not only would he be playing for the title, Big Bob informed him, but he had also been selected as one of the four golfers—along with George and Perry Adair and Will Rowan—to represent the AAC for the team match of the qualifying round. "I was overwhelmed," Jones recalled.[35]

Of course, Bob Jones was still an unknown to anyone outside of the AAC.

The Colonel identified several Southern golfers in his column "From the South" in the *American Golfer* that he felt stood a good chance of capturing the title: Texans George Rotan, C. L. Baxter, and Commodore Heard; Reuben Bush; and, of course, three-time Southern Amateur winner Nelson Whitney. However, the *Atlanta Constitution* broke the news a week before the competition that Whitney, the defending champion, had been hit in the eye by a golf ball and was too badly injured to play at East Lake.[36] And with Whitney supposedly out, forecasting which golfer would capture the title was "an open issue."

However, Perry Adair's chances, not Bob Jones's, looked especially good to the press. "Perry Adair, the youthful local player, who was runner-up last season, will probably carry the bulk of the patronage of the sports inclined to pick a winner in advance," declared the *Atlanta Constitution*. Adair "not only played sensationally in the Southern Amateur the year before but also held the record for the new East Lake course—a 79."[37] The Colonel in the *American Golfer* similarly encouraged readers to keep an eye out for Adair as one of the younger players "who have been coming into prominence during the last year or two."[38]

During the eighteen-hole qualifying round (happily, at the last minute, Nelson Whitney "sprang a surprise" and came to Atlanta despite his eye injury), Bob Jones recalled that he was so "scared and burdened with responsibility" that he had to keep on "looking at the ground to keep from falling over."[39] Despite his feelings of anxiety, Jones turned in a card of 83—not only the lowest score on the AAC team, but just one stroke higher than the co-medalists, defending champion Nelson Whitney and Charlie Dexter of Dallas. "I seemed to be having a terrible round; but once more I was at grips with Old Man Par, and not thinking about beating anybody else," he wrote later. But, as happy as he was to help the AAC win the team competition, Jones was dissatisfied with his performance: "I kept on thinking of this shot I had pulled, and that putt I had missed. . . . It might so well have been an 80 or even better."[40]

C. H. Munger of Texas, the medalist of the 1914 Southern Amateur, had predicted that on a course as difficult as East Lake a score of "93 would get in the first 64." The course proved him correct. Indeed, ten scores of 94 qualified for the championship division. The *Atlanta Constitution* reported, "Nearly everyone was a unit in declaring that the course is some five to ten strokes harder than any other course in the south."[41] Big Bob was one of those who qualified with a 94 to play alongside his son. The newspaper was duly impressed by Bob's remarkable start, writing, "R. P. Jones, Jr., the 13-year-old son of Mr. and Mrs. R. P. Jones, led the entrants with a splendid score of 83 . . . [and] is today the hero of the Atlanta delegation." Big Bob also qualified for the championship flight, although only after a playoff since he shot a 94.

Both Joneses and Adairs survived the opening morning round, but Big Bob and George lost in the afternoon. Perry steamrolled his afternoon opponent, 7 and 6, while Bob again faced Bryan "The Commodore" Heard in "a match between the oldest and the youngest player in the field." Bob described Heard as a "short, stocky man with iron-gray hair and he wore a sun-helmet, and hit the ball with a short, flat swing that gave the ball a low flight and a tremendous run."[42] He recalled thinking that Heard couldn't "possibly keep the ball straight with that sort of poking swing, and next that he couldn't possibly get it *off* the proper line. And how he did putt!" Although the veteran golfer didn't "pay much attention" to his opponent during the match, according to Bob, Heard told him after the match that he was "a tough customer" and said the young golfer "had made him shoot a 73 for seventeen holes to beat me."[43] In what was described by the *American Golfer* as a "brilliant match," Heard defeated Bob Jones at the seventeenth hole.[44]

The next morning, Perry Adair, whom "Atlanta's hopes rest on" now that his father and both Joneses had been eliminated, defeated fellow Atlantan golfer C. B. Mott. Next, he faced none other than The Commodore himself. Everyone lucky enough to witness it agreed that the match between Adair and Heard was unusually intense and well played—a "screamer" according to the *American Golfer*'s correspondent.[45] Bob Jones was one of "nearly four hundred golfing bugs" in the gallery. The *Atlanta Constitution* noted that this was already the second event of the season where The Commodore and Perry had squared off. As the newspaper reported: "In the invitation tournament at Montgomery held just a week previous to the present tournament, they engaged in just the same kind of match, with the results exactly the same, 1-up and 19 holes in Adair's favor."[46]

After being eliminated from the championship flight, Bob Jones continued competing in the second flight, where he defeated the six-foot-three, 220-pound Clarence "Moose" Knowles of Atlanta in 19 holes.[47] He then went on to defeat two other golfers, "the shortest of whom was six feet two," and thereby made it to the second-flight finals. Jones later reflected, "I must have made a funny contrast with these great musketeers—a stumpy, tow-headed schoolboy of 13, extremely red in the face, and playing golf in long pants because I was too proud of having assumed them to go back to knickers."[48] However, the *Atlanta Constitution*'s photo of the AAC team, published in the newspaper's post-championship coverage, shows Jones as the solitary team member wearing knickerbockers (with the rest of the team wearing long pants). The photograph especially highlights his youth and smaller stature, even in comparison to Perry Adair, who was not especially tall but was almost three years older.⁴⁹

In the semifinal of the championship flight, C. L. Dexter defeated Perry Adair in what the *American Golfer* described as a "strenuous one all of the way in the morning."⁵⁰ The *Atlanta Constitution* decreed: "Young Adair's short game was his undoing. He seemed to be never up on his pitches or approach putts, while during the two rounds he missed by actual count no less than eight putts that ranged from three to five feet."⁵¹

In the second-flight finals, thirteen-year-old Jones was pitted against F. T. Clark of Nashville. At the end of the morning round, Clark was 3 up, and al-

"They Captured the Team Golf Trophy,"
Atlanta Constitution, 20 June 1915.

Frank E. Price's photo of thirteen-year-old Bob Jones appeared in the *Atlanta Constitution* on 27 June 1915.

though Jones rallied to win four holes in the afternoon, Clark won while setting a new course record of 75. The *Atlanta Constitution* reflected that it was "a good thing that Mr. Clark turned in such a card in the morning, for in the afternoon the Atlanta youngster struck his stride and turned in a card of 78, equaling Mr. Clark's score on the second nine at thirty-four."[52] The loss was a deep disappointment to Jones, and his irritation was likely heightened by the admiration and praise heaped on his friend Perry Adair for his performance in the region's most prestigious championship. Jones later wrote, "Mother and Dad said they were proud of me, but I didn't feel a bit proud of myself. Here I was, 13 years old (I reflected), and, darn my time, I hadn't won anything yet!"[53]

Obviously, Jones was being unduly hard on himself. Dick Jemison of the *Atlanta Constitution* pointed out the significant obstacles that Jones faced during the Southern Amateur:

> Little Bob Jones drew the hardest luck of any one in the tournament. He was put out of the running by Commodore Heard of Houston, the veteran pulling an eighty, the best score at that running. Then when he had worked his way to the finals in the second flight, Frank Clark, of Nashville, had to go and break the course record against the youngster. If that isn't having them break bad, we'd like to know what it is.[54]

Jones's summer schedule following the Southern Amateur was packed with events in the immediate Atlanta area and a few a bit farther from home. He played at least one event each month in July, August, and September, in addition to a variety of special matches here and there. He was indeed "leaving the cocoon" in 1915 and establishing himself as a regular competitor in formal tournament play throughout the South. The up-and-coming golfer's appearance at the Montgomery Invitation speaks not only to Big Bob's confidence in his son's playing ability but also to his close friendship with and deep trust in George Adair, letting the elder Adair chaperone his only child and guide little Bob's athletic trajectory. When charting the paths of young Bob and Perry, it becomes obvious how key a role George Adair played in facilitating the growth of the South's (and arguably the nation's) two best junior golfers in the pre-war years, by encouraging them to compete outside of Atlanta. Bob's performance at the 1915 Southern Amateur—held fortuitously at East Lake—proved to both George and Big Bob that Bob, at age thirteen, had huge potential, more so than even Perry.

At the same time, Big Bob and his wife, Clara, struggled as parents to set boundaries for their golf prodigy: how far should Bob be allowed to go, geographically and competitively, to advance his golfing prowess at just thirteen years old? No matter how capable he proved to be in competition, there were maturational factors—physical, emotional, social, cultural—that couldn't be safely accelerated. Even with George Adair accompanying, it was not clear that Bob should trail alongside Perry each time a new out-of-town, outside-the-South competitive opportunity arose. These natural parental reservations were reinforced by a sober recognition that the higher levels of Southern golf were not on par yet with Eastern and Western golf, where the nation's most prestigious amateur and junior competitions were held. And Big Bob and Clara were reticent to expose their son to potentially discouraging results on unfamiliar courses against intense competition outside their Southern cultural home. As a result, Bob's parents largely confined his competitive experiences to the South until he was a little older. But that did not keep him from expanding his regional horizons and competing frequently as a thirteen-year-old.

For instance, in the first week of July 1915, Bob, Perry, and their childhood friend Alexa Stirling (who was five years older than Bob) traveled to the small industrial town of Rome, Georgia, roughly seventy miles to the northwest and easily accessible by train, to play in a special benefit tournament at a nine-hole country club opened five years earlier.[55] Perry, who shot a 40, came within one stroke of breaking the course record. Bob shot a 41, and Alexa, following a 43 during the morning practice round, shot 48 in the tournament.[56]

Shortly after returning from Rome, on July 7, Bob Jones turned in a remarkable card of 77, "the lowest score of any Atlanta golfer on the difficult East Lake course," and came within one stroke of matching the course record of 76.[57] Less than two weeks later, he broke George Adair's course record at Druid Hills by shooting a 73 in the qualifying round of the club's Davis & Freeman Trophy Cup, "the most remarkable performance, as every putt on the round was 'sunk.'"[58] The golfers that qualified for the competition were "so enthused" with Jones's breakthrough that they presented him with a special medal to honor his achievement—further demonstration of the strong encouragement and competitive access that young golfers received throughout the South.

Although Bob was the event medalist, he did not compete for the match-play trophy at Druid Hills; instead, he and his father boarded a train the next day for Alabama to compete in the more regionally prestigious Birmingham Invitation. Meanwhile, George and Perry Adair had opted to travel to Cleveland, Ohio, to play in the 1915 Western Amateur, but when Perry failed to qualify for match play, George, who did qualify, withdrew somewhat suspiciously "owing to illness."[59] Whatever may or may not have ailed George disappeared quickly, however, because George and Perry soon joined Big Bob, Little Bob, and several other Atlanta golfers in Birmingham for the invitation tournament at the recently renamed Roebuck Golf and Automobile Club.[60]

Southern invitation tournaments at the time were just as much about "Southern hospitality" and the social scene as about the golf. Similar to the lead-up to the Montgomery Invitation in June, special arrangements were made in Birmingham to ensure that out-of-town golfers would be shown a good time.[61] Many of the country club women in Birmingham, wives and daughters alike, were assigned the role of keeping the atmosphere light and festive, the bourbon under control, and providing evening dance partners. The members of the Roebuck Club were even generous enough to place "their motor cars at the disposal of the visiting golfers."[62]

This was the second invitation golf tournament at Roebuck, and the *Birmingham Age-Herald* called special attention to both Bob Jones's and Perry Adair's presences.[63] "Dad said I might enter the big invitation tournament at the Roebuck Country Club in Birmingham," Jones wrote in his autobiography, "and I'll always love Roebuck, because that's the first important tournament I won."[64]

Heavy winds drove qualifying-round scores quite high. A local player managed to score 80 for medalist honors, as compared to a 90 for Jones, a 91 for Adair, and a 95 for Big Bob to secure the last qualifying spot. Notable Southern player Reuben Bush, the defending champion, shot an 88, with scores for the field topping out at 128. "Expert forecasters on the links predict that Reuben G. Bush will repeat his success of last year.... However, it is expected that ... the Adairs, and the Joneses will force Mr. Bush to extend himself."[65] The next day, in match play, Bob Jones—incorrectly identified as age fifteen, rather than thirteen—beat Perry Adair, "the far-famed youngster of Atlanta," on the sixteenth hole. However, the "distinct surprise" of the afternoon was when Big Bob eliminated Reuben Bush.[66] In the semifinals, Little Bob beat Scott Probasco while William Badham beat Big Bob, denying the gallery a father-versus-son match in the finals. But the younger Bob, demonstrating "real golfing temperament and grit," won the Roebuck Golf and Auto Club's Invitation Tournament against Badham 1 up on the twenty-first hole. His "several exhibitions of nerve in making recoveries on holes where he seemed hopelessly beaten" thoroughly won over the crowd.[67] In fact, he quickly became the favorite of "one of the largest galleries that has ever turned out in a golf match in Birmingham, giving him a distinct advantage—even though Badham was a local player."[68] The gallery became so excited that tournament organizer John M. Inglis had to caution the spectators several times "not to be too enthusiastic."[69]

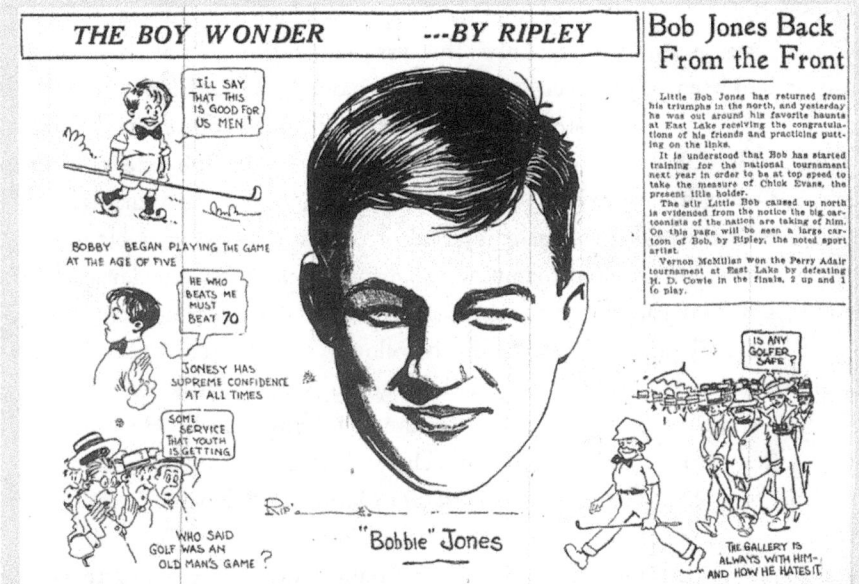

By 1916, "Bobbie" Jones had become "The Boy Wonder" as Perry Adair slowly drifted out of the limelight. Ripley, "The Boy Wonder," *Atlanta Journal*, 11 September 1916.

In "a grueling match for both contestants," Bob Jones's "wonderful approaching" earned him the victory—even though "Badham's driving and putting excelled the Atlanta youngster." The gallery "rushed to the youth with congratulations," although Badham got to Jones first, saying: "Bob, you're the best man and that was the hardest fight I have ever tackled." The thirteen-year-old modestly replied: "Mr. Badham, you're the best driver I have ever seen, and I was very fortunate to win."[70] Jones's playing ability throughout the Birmingham Invitation was enough to convince veteran golfers not only that the young man had a "brilliant future," but also that "with a little more experience, he is looked upon to give any golfer in the south a close run."[71]

With his first regional victory at Birmingham, Bob Jones was, at last, starting to emerge from Perry Adair's long shadow. Following his win, the *Atlanta Constitution* began to report more fully on Jones's play and to laud him as a prodigy: "Young Jones is easily one of the best golfers in Atlanta, and, with a little more seasoning, will make them all hustle." He now clearly shared the reputation as Atlanta's "boy wonder" that had belonged only to Perry Adair when the 1915 summer season began.

Two weeks later, after beginning his freshman year at Technological High

School, Bob Jones tied for the low qualifying score of 82 in the Atlanta Athletic Club's Championship at East Lake. This was the first time that a club championship had been played over East Lake's new course—remodeled in 1913—so the local press was interested to see how tough this new course would play.[72] Tough, indeed: Perry Adair's 87, George Adair's 88, and Big Bob Jones's 89 were all good enough to place them in the championship flight.[73] In a surprise turn of events that would become a regular occurrence as the boys grew older, Bob outlasted Perry in the AAC championship. More dramatic still, he defeated his father, 4 and 3 in the finals, to become the youngest AAC champion ever.

The AAC Championship was quickly followed by the Atlanta City Championship at Druid Hills. Bob "added to his golfing reputation" by turning in "a splendid score" of 80, the low score for the qualifying round.[74] He and Perry then sailed through their first two matches, which set up the possibility that "Atlanta's two boy wonders," as the *Atlanta Constitution* dubbed them, might meet in the finals if they both won their semifinal matches.[75] But Bob's next opponent was George Adair, whom the Atlanta oddsmakers—despite Bob's notable recent victories—still favored to win. George did defeat Bob.[76] And after Perry won his semifinal match, the Atlanta City Championship at Druid Hills ended the same way the AAC Championship had: with "another 'father-and-son' affair, for which Atlanta is becoming famous."[77]

George easily defeated Perry, 6 and 5, to become the first and only two-time "champion golfer of the city."[78] His victory at the Atlanta City Championship, at age forty-one, closed out the most successful golf season in his amateur career to date. At age sixteen, Perry had not fully eclipsed his father yet. But 1915 was a pivotal and transformative year for Bob Jones. It was the first year he competed outside of Atlanta, and he won three events: the Roebuck Invitation in Birmingham and the Druid Hills Club Championship and AAC Championship, both in Atlanta. Now, he had three invitation tournament victories to his name, whereas Perry Adair had just two (the 1914 Montgomery Invitation and the 1915 Davis & Freeman Cup at East Lake). Additionally, over the summer, Jones established two new course records—a 77 at the newly renovated East Lake course and a 73 at Druid Hills. His tournament qualifying scores leapt well beyond his average of the previous summer; Jones was now shooting consistently in the 80s—a ten-stroke improvement.

Bob Jones's game was also clearly catching up with Perry Adair's, although it had taken several years. Despite the almost mythic stories of Bob's early golf career, he did not, in fact, just burst onto the scene in 1915, instinctively playing championship-caliber golf. And really, of Atlanta's two "wonder boys"—Bob

Jones and Perry Adair—Bob was the less remarkable at first. But his competitive game naturally evolved as he gained more experience, beginning in 1913 when he first started playing regularly in Atlanta events and, more often than not, turned in rounds of 90-plus. Still, he was watching and learning and honing his game under the guidance of East Lake professional Stewart Maiden. By 1916, Bob Jones was ready to step out onto the national stage to show off just what he could do.

▶ CHAPTER 3
GRINDING TOWARD STARDOM
DAVE HERRON AT OAKMONT AND PRINCETON (1915-1916)

Bob Jones's ball-striking, even at thirteen years old, often appeared to onlookers as a God-given, once-in-a-lifetime talent. He did not seem like the kind of boy who had to work hard at the game, although he did. Dave Herron, in contrast, was a more obvious grinder, practicing diligently every day it was warm enough to improve his game just a little bit more. In late 1914, as he turned seventeen, Herron was still playing in the shadow of Oakmont's greats, including Eben Byers, William Fownes Jr., and George Ormiston. He could not yet match their games, as evidenced by the ups and downs of his shortened final competitive season at home before he left for Princeton. Yet, there was no reason to believe his talent had already peaked.

For one, in November Herron was declared the winner of Oakmont's season-long McCurdy-Trees "ringer" trophy, which went to the player with the lowest "ultimate round" best score per hole record of the entire 1914 campaign. The "ringer" event was one way of approximating who had the best potential to "go low" at Oakmont, that is, to eagle or birdie the highest number of individual holes at some point during the entire season. That Herron came out on top of this intriguing test, especially on the longer holes where his length off the tee increased the chance of making eagles and birdies, testified to his ability to score low at Oakmont when he was playing his best. And the fact that George Ormiston, by consensus the best medal-play scorer in the state, finished second in the "ringer" competition demonstrated how good a gauge it was for measuring the suitability of one's game for playing a uniquely long and difficult course like Oakmont.

A second indication that Herron's game was sharp and still improving was that he won the 1914 Princeton town championship (the "President's Cup") in October. By intercollegiate sports rules of the day, freshmen were not allowed to compete on varsity athletic teams, the aim being to ensure they had a chance to adapt to the new demands (academic and otherwise) of college life before devoting time and travel to intercollegiate athletics. The Princeton town championship thus became something of a proxy intrasquad match for all Princeton

Princeton's golf team in 1916. Standing at far left is Pomeroy Herron; Dave Herron stands on the far right. D. C. Corkran, seated on the left, was Princeton's most notable player at the time. Princeton University Archives, Seeley G. Mudd Manuscript Library.

golfers, including freshmen. It was an event of considerable prestige and bragging rights.

Dave Herron's brother Pomeroy, who started at Princeton the same semester as Dave, also competed in the President's Cup. But Dave knew he could easily best his brother. The real competition would come from other Western Pennsylvania members of Princeton's golf team, specifically senior and captain J. B. Rose, sophomore W. A. Lowrie, and junior G. A. Peacock. Even more challenging would be L. M. Washburn of Merion, who was runner-up in the singles competition of the 1914 Intercollegiate, and D. C. Corkran of Baltimore, a freshman who had qualified for the 1914 U.S. Amateur. Herron, at age sixteen, was relatively young to start college, and this group of collegians—though not of the stature of Fownes, Byers, and Ormiston—was the toughest group of age peers he had ever competed against.

Dave Herron scored solid victories in the first three rounds of the town championship and made it to the finals, where he faced the senior, L. M. Washburn, who, in addition to finishing second in the National Intercollegiate Championship, had also been previously selected to represent Pennsylvania in the interstate Lesley Cup matches. The Herron-Washburn match was close all the way and ended in a tie after eighteen holes; two extra holes later, Herron won. Pittsburgh's *Gazette Times*, proud of its local star, exaggerated a bit, claiming that Washburn was the reigning intercollegiate champion when he had actually been the runner-up. But the newspaper rightly saluted Herron for winning "his first appearance in a big tournament outside of Western Pennsylvania" and for hanging tough to defeat an accomplished upperclassman like Washburn. Herron's victory, the newspaper added, "was pleasing to his many friends in Pittsburgh" who were anxiously waiting to learn if his game would reach new heights at Princeton.[1]

Dave Herron was not nearly as well-known outside his hometown as Bob Jones quickly became in the South. But, attesting to the growing audience for golf news, the *Gazette Times* kept Pittsburghers informed about Herron's performance throughout the spring of 1915:

> Word comes from Princeton that Bernard [J. B.] Rose, Grant Peacock and Davidson Herron, all Pittsburgh boys, are playing a great game this year and should prove strong factors in the intercollegiate team matches. Herron recently competed in several matches at the Baltimore Country Club, playing with Clyde Cochran [i.e., D. C. Corkran], a fellow student, against Warren Cochran [i.e., Corkran, D. C.'s brother, a high-profile amateur] and Nipper

Campbell who is now [a] professional at Baltimore. The Princeton students were victorious in both matches.[2]

Obviously, Herron received special attention in the Pittsburgh press as the city's youngest premier junior player. When he traveled later in the semester to compete in the Baltimore club's prestigious spring invitation tournament—America's most famous golfer, Francis Ouimet, was also entered—readers were updated on his achievements and the fact that the Baltimore press were carefully observing him. Alas, Herron did not fare well in his individual matches in Baltimore: he first lost a close match to a physician from Atlantic City, and then lost on the nineteenth hole to another good player from Philadelphia.

In recounting Herron's mistakes in Baltimore, the *Pittsburgh Gazette Times* called special attention to a notable aspect of his game that had never before received notice. Herron eagled a 450-yard, par 5 hole by hitting a driver and a cleek (1- or 2-iron) to within a foot of the cup—the main point being that he'd hit an iron into what was then seen as a long par 5.[3] Few good players could hope to reach this green using a fairway wood on their second shot there, much less an iron. In the past, it was the overall excellence of Herron's game, most particularly his irons and, on occasion, his putting, that had made him stand out as a junior player in Pittsburgh. That, plus his unusually mature temperament—his unflappability. No one had ever singled out his power off the tee before for special comment. But as golf team photos of him as a freshman and sophomore at Princeton reveal, he was becoming taller, heavier, thicker, and, in general, a formidable looking athlete. Quite naturally, he became a more powerful golfer as well. In time, as we shall see, his strength would become a signature feature of his brand of golf. Signs of those bodily changes and subsequent improvements to his game were already emerging before the end of his freshman year at Princeton, and before he even became eligible to compete for the golf team as a sophomore.

A third clear-cut sign of just how much Dave Herron's game had improved by 1915 was his Western Golf Association (WGA) handicap rating. Each year in April, the WGA released an updated list of the best players in the "West" (i.e., the Midwest), including the "Pittsburgh region." In the 1910s, the WGA stood only a half-step below the USGA as a respected national authority in overseeing the game's future. Likewise, in the pre-war era, the two major championships the WGA sponsored, the Western Amateur and the Western Open, carried prestige just below that of the U.S. Amateur and the U.S. Open. No Pittsburgh players were rated as high as Chicago's Chick Evans and Robert Gardner in the

WGA's 1915 handicap list. But there would have been no quibbling in Western Pennsylvania about the identification of W. C. Fownes Jr. and Eben Byers as the region's finest players, with handicaps of 2, or of George Ormiston—who was significantly older and no longer as competitive—with a handicap of 4. At Oakmont, as well as nationally, these three players had long been considered the Steel City's best, and Dave Herron had been lucky to come of age as a golfer under their collective guidance.

However, it was the two Pittsburgh golfers whom the WGA rated at handicaps of 5 who received the most attention because their games had improved so dramatically in the past few years: Stanton Heights veteran J. B. Crookston and Oakmont's seventeen-year-old Dave Herron. Crookston and Herron had already fought on equal terms against each other on several occasions. With both their games on a clear upward trajectory, it was hard to predict who might be the better golfer in the short or long run. But Herron's WGA rating—which tied him for fourth-best golfer in Western Pennsylvania and ranked him higher than his Western Pennsylvania teammates at Princeton—testified to how rapidly Dave's reputation was growing on a national level. Though only a freshman, Herron was clearly regarded as a future star of the Princeton team, which was the reigning intercollegiate champion.[4]

Herron spent the summer break in 1915, following his freshman year, playing on Oakmont's team in the Western Pennsylvania Golf Association League. The team's first match was against Allegheny Country Club at its home course, and the Oakmont teams squeezed out a narrow two-point victory in both fourball and individual matches. Herron played exceptionally well and was the only Oakmont player to win both his fourball and singles matches. The match provided an important tune-up for the upcoming West Penn Amateur Championship, which would be played that year at Oakmont. One hundred players were entered, and some members of the public viewed Dave Herron as a potential winner. At the same time, he knew that, almost inevitably, he would have to defeat Fownes, Byers, or Ormiston en route to the title. Collectively, they had won thirteen of the past fourteen West Penn Amateurs.

Conditions were ripe for good scoring in the two medal-qualifying rounds. But Fownes was increasing Oakmont's difficulty each year, sometimes in subtle ways, and the qualifying scores were higher than anyone expected. For the fourth consecutive time in a local competition of note, George Ormiston won the qualifying medal with a score of 159, five over par. Fownes finished one shot behind, and Herron finished two behind Fownes at 162—clearly demonstrating to everyone that he was playing well.

After an easy opening-match victory, Herron was pitted against Fownes, and his game was not as good. Fownes was 2 up at the turn with a score of 39, and he continued to play better than Herron on the inward nine, closing him out on the fifteenth hole. "The lad [Herron] put up a plucky performance," the *Pittsburgh Gazette Times* wrote in affectionate terms, "but he succumbed to the superior play of his older and more experienced opponent."[5] By this stage, Herron was outhitting Fownes and the other Oakmont veterans off the tee. But even though Oakmont was an unusually long course, there was obviously a lot more to scoring than sheer power. And probably no golfers in the United States knew how to scramble better than Fownes, Ormiston, and Byers did. (Byers would go on to win the 1915 West Penn Amateur; Fownes would win in 1916 for the eighth time.)

That Dave Herron possessed the all-around skill set to play well on both short and long courses was already evident from his previous victory at Stanton Heights in 1914. In anticipation of defending his title over the summer, he prepared for the 1915 Stanton Heights Invitation by practicing regularly there (it was the closest course to his home, apart from the Schenley public links) and playing an assortment of team matches at Oakmont. As good as he was on Oakmont's course, his game thrived just as well at Stanton Heights.

So, for the second time in his career, he won both the qualifying medal- and the match-play competitions in the same event (he had accomplished that feat the previous summer at Altoona). Even though the field at Stanton Heights included all of the area's best golfers, Herron's score of 148, two over par, handily won the medal competition.[6] And his local opponents in the match-play rounds were as formidable as could be. Four held ratings under 5 on the Western Pennsylvania Golf Association's handicap list (which was not as stringent as the Western Golf Association's handicap system). On the first day he beat J. B. Rose, his teammate at Princeton, and then R. C. Long of Stanton Heights (who was rated a 6 by the Western Golf Association). On the second day, he eliminated George Ormiston in the semifinals before defeating J. B. Crookston in the championship round.

Herron was now coming into his own. And his game seemed in great shape to take the next big step in his career: competing for the first time in the U.S. Amateur, to be held in 1915 at the Detroit Country Club—the top course in the nation, according to the famed British golfers Harry Vardon and Ted Ray. "This will be [Herron's] first appearance in real fast company and just where he will finish is hard to determine," the *Gazette Times* noted. "That he will qualify in the first 64 is more than likely, and his chances of surviving in the 32 which will remain after the second day's play are also bright."[7]

Dave Herron had thought about competing in the Western Amateur in

Cleveland as a tune-up for the U.S. Amateur, but ultimately decided against it and chose instead to practice intensively at Oakmont. The summer was drawing to a close, and everything he had done to this point was geared to prime him for the "fast company" he would face in Detroit. To be sure, he had faced a comparably stellar field on a smaller scale in the Lesley Cup matches the previous year in New York. But that was in a much more supportive and intimate team setting. The U.S. Amateur, by contrast, was every man for himself: the biggest and most highly publicized individual golf championship in the world in the early twentieth century, save for the British Amateur and the (British) Open.

In fall 1914, Herron had played in a tournament in Baltimore that featured the legendary Francis Ouimet (though they did not meet during that event). But he had never played against the other top Americans who had built towering national reputations over the past decade: golfers like Jerry Travers, Chick Evans, Robert Gardner, D. E. "Ned" Sawyer, John Anderson, and the South's best player, Nelson Whitney. The U.S. Amateur was what Herron had been preparing for since starting the game at age seven. In truth, he had been groomed for championship golf as well as any young player in the early twentieth century by playing and caddying at Oakmont. And his game in the summer of 1915 was as sharp as it ever had been. But he was still only seventeen years old, a product of Western Pennsylvania, with only one year of college golf and one Lesley Cup experience to draw on in competing against the nation's most experienced veteran players. Was he ready for the biggest stage possible in American amateur golf? It was time to find out.

Playing in the U.S. Amateur in the 1910s was a drawn-out affair that equally emphasized team competition and individual performance. The USGA, founded in 1894, was an organization rooted in elite, country club golf that promoted team-based, interclub competition. Before the individual contest began in the Amateur, there were two highly publicized team events that took two full days to play and that accentuated the virtues of team play. First was the East-West match, ten men on a side, which would decide which region earned bragging rights for the following year. Second was the *American Golfer* team trophy competition, sponsored by the legendary Walter Travis, which paired members of individual clubs in a fourball, best-ball competition. Fifty pairs would compete in Detroit—an all-day affair the day prior to the start of the individual championship, with elaborate ceremonies afterward.

These two day-long, team-based events would then be followed by two separate days of medal qualifying—a new practice introduced in 1915 because of the record number of entrants, 138 in total, who held USGA-approved handicaps of 5 or less. The first day of qualifying (eighteen holes) would reduce the field to the top sixty-four scores and ties; the second day (another eighteen holes) would then reduce the field in half to thirty-two contestants, after which the match-play championship would finally—at long last!—begin.

Obviously, true gentlemen golfers, that is, true amateurs, had to have a fair amount of time free from everyday job-related responsibilities to travel to and compete in the U.S. Amateur—not to mention the funds to cover costs. Excepting Francis Ouimet, early twentieth-century amateur golf at the highest level was not a working-class or even a lower-middle-class sport. Generally, only the wealthy had the resources and time to compete at the national level.

Six players from Oakmont entered into the championship. They left for Detroit by automobile on August 25, two days before the "sectional" East-West competition would begin, leaving the participants who had not previously played Detroit Country Club, such as Dave Herron, just a single day to practice. Initially, Herron was not selected for the East-West team competition. W. C. Fownes Jr. was captain of the East, Ned Sawyer captain of the West, and each announced eight of the ten players on their teams a week before the event. Fownes initially selected only three Western Pennsylvania players: Byers, Ormiston, and himself. He chose an additional five players of high renown from the East Coast states—Travis, Travers, Ouimet, Anderson, and Max H. Behr of New Jersey (the state amateur champion who had founded *Golf Illustrated* the year before). Oswald Kirkby, the star New York player of the moment (along with Anderson), had other pressing business and could not compete in the 1915 championship. Fownes decided to choose the final two players after he consulted with the other team members on site.

Ultimately, and to the disappointment of many, Travis (a semifinalist in the previous year's U.S. Amateur, at age fifty-two) chose not to attend the 1915 U.S. Amateur, and so Herron was added to the East team at the last minute. Thus, four of the East's players came from Western Pennsylvania and none came from Philadelphia—perhaps something of a political choice, given the Philadelphia-Pittsburgh rivalry, but also reflecting the reality that Merion and other elite Philadelphia clubs had yet to spawn a truly first-rate set of golfers comparable to those from Oakmont. In the end, Fownes's choice of Herron, his former caddie, to play on the East team paid off royally.

Fownes paired himself with Herron against E. P. Allis III and Allan Swift of the West team, and the two Oakmonters won decisively by 6 and 5. Then, in singles, Herron played very well to win a close match against the former Western Amateur and Intercollegiate champion, Albert Sockel. Herron was not the only East team player to win both of his matches, but he was the youngest. His stellar play silenced the doubts of anyone who dared question his place on a team filled with superstars like Ouimet and Evans (who played against each other in Detroit for the first and only time prior to the 1919 U.S. Amateur; Ouimet won in nineteen holes). Dave Herron proved yet again that he was mature beyond his years and an intrepid competitor in "fast company." Although the East and West teams ultimately played to a draw, seventeen-year-old Herron emerged as one of the East's rising stars.

The following day, Fownes again chose Herron to compete as his partner and clubmate in the *American Golfer* team trophy match. To everyone's surprise, Herron putted poorly, and the twosome's best-ball score of 77 was seven shots behind the leaders. Herron may have been dauntless, but he was not nearly as consistent a player as Fownes, particularly in his putting and iron play. In Pittsburgh, he sometimes lost matches he had been expected to win, and he experienced periodic off days even when he had performed superbly the day before. In Detroit, at this most important moment in his young golf career, it remained to be seen whether he could quickly fix what was wrong and get off to a good start when the "real" championship—that is, the first qualifying round for the individual competition—began.

Whatever he did, the fix worked: amazingly, he tied Ned Sawyer with a score of par 73 at the top of the leaderboard in the first qualifying round for the individual championship. Sawyer's performance was no surprise; year in and year out, along with Chick Evans and Robert Gardner, Sawyer was one of the West's most consistent premier performers (hence his selection as captain of the West team). But Herron's score was truly a "Davidson who?" shock because most of the assembled "cracks" had never heard of him. The *Pittsburgh Gazette Times* nicely captured the surprise: "Oakmont Lad Startles Oldest Followers of Game by His Remarkable Demonstration in First U.S. Championship in Which He Ever Played." This was Herron's first truly big championship "outside of his home city," and though "Herron's name is well known to all Pittsburgh golfers . . . he caused quite a sensation here today."[8]

Herron's par 73 at the difficult Detroit Country Club was the best round of championship golf he had ever played. His performance at Stanton Heights two weeks earlier had been impressive, but this was the U.S. Amateur, and Detroit Country Club was the course Vardon and Ray had singled out as the most challenging in America. Furthermore, the USGA, after observing that a few players were shooting around 75 in the East-West and *American Golfer* Trophy matches, had pushed back the tees for the first qualifying round, creating severe driving angles on many holes and extending the course's length to over 6,600 yards. Many of the top players struggled with these last-minute changes and finished nowhere near par; Fownes shot 80, as did Anderson.

Indeed, John Anderson, who was also one of the early twentieth century's most respected golf journalists (a regular contributor to Travis's *American Golfer*), could not get over the shock of Herron's 73. Detroit Country Club, in his judgment, was a course on which it was no disgrace to shoot 86 or 87. Before the championship began, Anderson was quite confident that this tough of a venue would catapult only the very best players to the top of the leaderboard—proven stars like Ouimet, Evans, and Fownes. But Herron's round had undermined all of his predictions, and he would no longer even hazard a guess about who would qualify. Under the subheading "Herron Puzzles Experts," Anderson wrote: "Time was when the matter of qualifying was a foregone conclusion, for most of the golfers who got into the match play, for there was a great discrepancy between the play of the participants.... No longer can reliance be placed in having extreme steadiness."[9]

In topping the leaderboard in the first qualifying round, Herron certainly showed that he had no fear and could rise to the occasion. Somehow, he'd solved his serious putting problems of the day before because he putted spectacularly in his opening qualifying round.[10] Beyond that, he also had unusual good fortune. On the 380-yard, par 4 thirteenth hole, things did not start well when he hit only a "fair drive." But his second shot was anything but fair: Herron holed his midiron for an eagle! In addition, the last-minute lengthening of the course may have played to his advantage, or at least to others' disadvantage. As noted earlier, he'd been adding power to his game as his body matured. An action photo of Herron in Detroit revealed a trim, athletic-looking young man with a full, well-balanced follow-through. And because Oakmont was his home course, he was also more accustomed than most to playing a lengthy championship layout, where it was common to hit a fairway wood or long iron into a par 4 green.

All that said, he learned quickly that fame is indeed fleeting. For all the attention that he received on day one, he received barely a mention after shooting 86 for a total of 159 in the second qualifying round, even though he easily qualified for match play. He succumbed to miserable weather conditions, as did Chick Evans and other stars who scored well into the 80s. In the end—confirming that young players were confounding the "experts"—Yale sophomore Dudley Mudge won the qualifying medal with a score of 152 (79, 73). Somehow, Mudge, who had recently won the Minnesota state championship, had no trouble shooting par figures in the second round's rain and wind. And Mudge's performance made clear that Herron still had a ways to go to be recognized as one of the top players in American college golf.

The first day of match play in Detroit was a stunningly bad day for Pittsburghers; all of them lost in the first round (contested at thirty-six holes). Dave took the harshest thumping, losing 7 and 6 to the South's ace player, Nelson Whitney, who was well known among the Eastern elite because he summered on Long Island and played regularly at the National Golf Links.[11] Whitney played exceptionally well against Herron, scoring in the mid-70s. After the first eighteen holes, Herron was 6 down, mainly as a result of poor iron play. He steadied himself on the back nine, but Whitney matched him all the way before winning on the twenty-ninth hole.

Ultimately, as predicted, veterans dominated match play at Detroit, with Robert Gardner defeating John Anderson in a close match for the championship title. For Herron, his first U.S. Amateur was a decidedly mixed bag. He was of course thrilled to be chosen to compete on the same team as Ouimet, Anderson, and Fownes in the East-West match, and more thrilled still to earn two victories and perform as well as anyone on the team. But his game was erratic throughout the week: great one day, horrid the next, with no single part of his game clearly to praise or blame. He putted lights out in the first qualifying round, sank a long iron shot from the middle of the fairway, and shocked the pundits by shooting par and tying Ned Sawyer for the opening-day lead. The next day, he dropped thirteen shots, and while he still qualified for match play, he never knew what might go wrong from one day to the next. A tough first-round draw against Whitney, a seasoned veteran, further doomed his chances. It must have been a very quiet ride home for the three Oakmonters, who had every reason to believe that at least one of them would shine at an exceptionally tough venue like Detroit Country Club.

Shortly after returning home from Detroit, Herron left again for his sophomore year of college. Within a week, the entire Princeton golf team—four of the eight members hailed from Pittsburgh—traveled to the annual Intercollegiate Championship in Greenwich, Connecticut. After Princeton's success in 1914 dethroning Yale for the first time (Yale had previously posted nine consecutive wins), and then defeating Harvard for the championship, Herron had good reason to believe Princeton would win the Intercollegiate again as the team was even stronger in 1915–1916. Even so, he knew that Yale's squad was equally strong with Dudley Mudge at the top.

Herron started out well in the fourball competition in Greenwich, making a birdie for his team on the first extra hole to win the match. In the afternoon singles he lost decisively to Franklin W. Dyer, the New Jersey star of the University of Pennsylvania team. But Princeton still beat Penn soundly in the overall team match, meaning the team title came down to Princeton and Yale. Against Yale, Herron played quite well in both fourballs and singles, winning 4 and 2 and then 4 and 3, respectively. Unfortunately, D. C. Corkran, playing in Princeton's top spot, lost to Mudge, in both singles and fourballs, giving Yale the win and the 1915 Intercollegiate team championship title.

But that was really only the start of the Intercollegiate Championship (which required students to miss a full week of school at the very start of the fall semester). In the multi-day singles competition that followed the team championship, Herron finished fifth in the qualifying round with 159, six shots behind the winning medal score of 153 by Yale's Frank Blossom. In his first singles match, he trounced his opponent from Illinois, but then, to his dismay, lost in the second round to his teammate and fellow Oakmonter, Grant Peacock. Blossom ultimately went on to win the match-play as well as medal-play titles, thus giving Yale a sweep in the 1915 Intercollegiate and returning the team to its traditional place atop American collegiate golf.

Perhaps for personal reasons, Herron did not immediately return to Princeton after the Intercollegiate Championship; instead, he returned home to compete in a mixed foursomes competition at Oakmont. A couple of weeks later he was honored (if not surprised) to learn of his selection to represent Pennsylvania for a second time on its Lesley Cup team. Conveniently, the 1915 matches would be played not far from Princeton, at Merion; Pennsylvania would initially compete against Massachusetts, with the winner playing the defending champion team from New York. Herron was the only one of his Princeton teammates to be chosen for the Lesley Cup. Though the U.S. Amateur was still the most prestigious event in which Herron had ever competed, the Lesley Cup was arguably the most challenging because many of the New York and Massachusetts players carried national reputations, and nearly all were wily veterans. It was one thing to play on the same team in the East-West match with such national legends as Travers and Ouimet and such local legends as Anderson and Kirkby of New York and Jesse Guilford of Massachusetts, but it was quite another to compete directly against them.

The match between Pennsylvania and Massachusetts was quite exciting, as the Quaker State players fought back from a sharp deficit in the morning team matches to clinch seven of the eight afternoon singles matches and win the overall contest, 8 to 7. The match, played in early October, featured un-

Pennsylvania first fielded a team for the 1909 Lesley Cup at Huntingdon Valley Country Club north of Philadelphia. E. Ellsworth Giles (third from the left in the back row), W. C. Fownes Jr. (front row left), and George Ormiston (front row right) all played in that cup. "First Pennsylvania Lesley Cup Team," *Pittsburgh Gazette Times*, 6 October 1919.

seasonably cold temperatures, harsh winds, and persistent rains—more like St. Andrews than Philadelphia. Dave Herron and his partner were among the losers for Pennsylvania in fourball competition, and at a deficit of 4 to 1, prospects for a Quaker State victory looked grim. But the singles players for Pennsylvania were tenacious: five of the afternoon matches went to the eighteenth hole and beyond, including Herron's, and the Pennsylvanians won each one. The premier match was between Fownes and Ouimet and ended in a tie, with both men managing to shoot in the low 80s in the terrible weather. Only Ouimet's pulling his approach shot into deep wet grass on the first play-off hole gave Fownes the victory.

The Pennsylvanians had now earned the right to face off against New York in the finale, but this match did not go well, for Herron or the team. The New Yorkers demolished the Pennsylvanians, 12 to 3, although John Anderson emphasized how close all of the matches actually were, and how much more competitive each team was from top to bottom in comparison to earlier years—"a leveling of the players," he called it, with lopsided victories a thing of the past. Dave's doubles match carried unusual excitement, as he and Fownes were paired against the two aces of the New York team, Travers and Kirkby. The New Yorkers closed out the match on the seventeenth hole. Certainly, Anderson's own singles match against Herron could not have been closer, with Anderson eking out a victory on the first extra hole.

Anderson's column describing his victory over Herron in the *Pittsburgh Gazette Times* highlighted just how well Herron was playing, while also capturing the gentlemanly tone that the Lesley Cup match was supposed to embody.

> My own match with Davidson Herron, who it will be remembered led the field at Detroit with 73 on the first day, was one of the hardest I have had this year. Herron's medal card was 74, probably five strokes better than almost anyone else either yesterday or today, and his game was a treat to watch. I happened to be in a good scoring vein myself, with a 75, due to some long putts, and this time the low medal score did not win. Herron was 2 up at the turn, 1 up with 7 to play, and then it was my turn to win. We were all square at the last hole and it was my good fortune to win with par four at the nineteenth. The standard of play may well be judged by the scores of the last 12 holes, which Herron made in 49 and I in 47.[12]

The Lesley Cup brought to a late-season end Dave Herron's extraordinary golf performance in 1915, on the eve of his eighteenth birthday. The season was filled not with victories or runner-up finishes, but rather with periodic displays of excellence that were superior to any golf he had previously played. He had also competed in more high-profile venues outside Western Pennsylvania than ever before, and against players who equaled—occasionally, even went beyond—the best he'd ever experienced growing up at Oakmont. Herron demonstrated that he could win, but most of all he showed that he was afraid of no one and, furthermore, that he could "go low" at venues as difficult as Merion and Detroit Country Club. In truth, he was not doing anything spectacularly newsworthy yet, and he was not winning with regularity, but he was building a reputation as a young man with tremendous potential. He was certainly well known by both the Eastern and Western golfing elites. And by common consensus, he had the physical, mental, and emotional strengths to someday become a winner at the game's highest levels.

Conveniently, as secretary of the Intercollegiate Golf Association, Dave Herron had the authority to choose the venue for the next Intercollegiate Championship. In mid-December, he announced his decision: Oakmont![13] Yale and Princeton would still be the two teams to beat, but Pittsburgh was located centrally enough to make the trip feasible for nearly all teams and all players of "national reputation" who might choose to play at Oakmont even if their teams could not. And, further, because the competition would be scheduled a week after the U.S. Amateur at Merion, Oakmont would be within easy travel for the most talented collegiate players who would play in both championships.

In spring 1916, unsurprisingly, the USGA deemed Herron eligible to compete again in the U.S. Amateur. More interestingly, the Western Golf Association—which continued to embrace Pittsburgh as "West" even though the USGA labeled it "East"—reduced his handicap from 5 to 4. This placed him in an elite group of only thirty-two men from "Western" states with handicaps of 4 or less. Only nine of these thirty-two "Western" golfers were rated at 3 or better. At the top, rated "scratch," were the Chicagoans—Robert Gardner, the defending U.S. Amateur champion, and Chick Evans, widely recognized (along with Boston's Francis Ouimet) as America's greatest amateur golfers, even though Evans had not yet won a U.S. Amateur title. Ned Sawyer, with whom Herron had tied for the lead the year before in the opening qualifying round in Detroit, was the only golfer to receive a handicap rating of 1. At 2 were three individuals: W. C. Fownes Jr. and Eben Byers, both from Pittsburgh; and one from Chicago—H. Chandler Egan, a two-time U.S. Amateur champion in 1904 and 1905. Rounding out this super-elite group of nine golfers, three received a 3 rating: J. D. Standish Jr. of Detroit, Paul M. Hunter of Chicago, and H. K. B. Davis of San Francisco.

Of course, the Western handicap ratings did not include any of the top players from the East, so it was impossible to determine where Dave Herron stood on a national basis, or even in relation to his college peers. Complicating the matter was the USGA's decision not to offer its own handicap ratings in 1916 but to instead merely list, alphabetically, all those it certified eligible for the U.S. Amateur. Still, two things were clear: first, Herron was not yet considered one of the nation's truly elite golfers, that small group with handicaps of 3 or better; second, he was still in very good company. Nelson Whitney, who'd defeated him so decisively at Detroit, was also rated at 4, as was Dudley Mudge, the Yale player who'd won the qualifying medal at Detroit after Herron had taken the first-day lead.

In mid-June 1916, Herron got a chance to show just how much his game had improved over the past eighteen months at the twenty-second Allegheny Invitation, the oldest golf tournament in Western Pennsylvania, played at the region's oldest golf course, Allegheny Country Club. Just returned from Princeton, he had only played in this event once, when he was a junior at Shady Side Academy, and to his embarrassment he had failed to qualify for the first flight of sixteen (though he handily won the "beaten eight" medal). Now, at age eighteen, he was determined to make a better showing, although the size of the field (over a hundred entries) and the level of competition were higher than ever. The course, too, now playing at over 6,000 yards to a par 73, presented more interesting challenges than in earlier years, including several new holes that Donald Ross had recently designed.

The event began with a fourball competition. Dave Herron, paired with his brother Pomeroy, shot 73—good enough for third place behind the powerhouse team of Fownes and Ormiston. His game was sharp, and the fourball event gave him a good chance to learn the redesigned course. Learn well he did: despite horrific rain, he won the qualifying medal by matching par with a 73 (three shots better than Fownes), which astonished most participants.

> The players were drenched, and a heavy downpour which set in at noon made the putting greens miniature lakes, some of them ankle-deep. The adverse conditions played havoc with the scores. It was not an infrequent happening to take four or five putts on the green. The putter was discarded and instead the players used their mashies and their niblicks to hole out. . . .The mettle of the players was subjected to a test, their endurance and perseverance being tried to the extreme.[14]

Herron won his first match easily but then had to confront Fownes in the second round. Fans understandably considered this the premier match, the two top medalists going head-to-head, and most of the gallery followed it. "It was anybody's match all the way until the seventeenth hole," the *Pittsburgh Post* reported, until Herron badly botched his approach and gave the hole away with a double bogey.[15] He should have squared the match at the eighteenth hole, with Fownes in trouble, but he three-putted from 25 feet to tie with bogey and lose the match 1 down. Fownes, "at the top of his game," went on to defeat Byers the following day to win the Allegheny Invitation.[16]

In the weeks preceding the next big regional championship, the West Penn Amateur at Oakmont, Dave Herron maintained an active inter- and intraclub golf schedule and accustomed himself to the course's latest innovations that Fownes and Loeffler had introduced for the 1916 season. This preparation was doubly important because of the upcoming Intercollegiate Championship at Oakmont in September. Herron's play at Oakmont was sharp, although the competition sometimes was not. In a league match scheduled at Oakmont by the Western Pennsylvania Golf Association (WPGA), the Oakmont team demolished its Field Club counterparts, winning every match—"the worst defeat in the history of local team matches."[17] Herron contributed his share to the thrashing, handily taking down the top Field Club player, L. C. Liddell, who had beaten him badly three years earlier in the first Oakmont Invitation. He then paired with his friend and former Shady Side Academy teammate H. C. Fownes II to win a doubles match as well.

That Herron was raising his game to a new level, especially at Oakmont, became clear a couple of weeks later, when he defeated Fownes in an epic contest to win the club-sponsored W. W. Flanegin Cup. In retrospect, these intraclub competitions seem of little historic interest—social events, like their Southern counterparts, with a big dance to follow. But at Oakmont the golf was *always* deadly serious; H. C. Fownes and W. C. Fownes Jr. never took a one-on-one match lightly in their lives. Instead of the more stringent WGA handicaps, the Flanegin Cup used Oakmont's own handicap system, which in 1916 placed Fownes one shot better than Herron.[18] Thus, Fownes had to give Herron one stroke for eighteen holes, which they agreed would come on the par 4 fifth hole; Herron ended up winning that hole because of the handicap even though he and Fownes both scored par 4s. As a result, the two tied the match, even though Fownes would have won 1 up on his own card. That said, it was how the match unfolded that so captivated local attention and revealed much about Herron's growing mastery of Oakmont.

Fownes played perhaps the best nine holes of his life on the outward nine, shooting a 34—a simply unheard-of number at Oakmont at the time. Herron did his best to stay with him, but still found himself five holes down at the turn—presumably an insurmountable lead against one of the steadiest players in American amateur golf. But he came back in a rush on the back nine, winning six of the holes and shooting an astonishing 33—his best nine holes ever on any golf course, let alone at Oakmont. As they ascended the eighteenth tee Herron was down only one hole.

It was here that he pulled off the most remarkable comeback of his young career. Fownes drove down the middle of the fairway, as he almost always did, while Herron hooked into a shallow water hazard (a trench) adjacent to the left of the eighteenth fairway. His ball lay in a marshy patch in long grass. The crowd that gathered around him assumed he had no choice but to first escape the hazard with a niblick (9-iron) and then hit a long iron from the fairway onto the green. But Herron, feeling that he needed a 4 to have any chance of overtaking Fownes, decided on a different strategy: to use all of his considerable strength to power the ball from the water directly onto the green. Hitting "a shot that few except young Herron could play," he did just that: he somehow propelled the ball far enough, and high enough on the steep uphill climb, to place his ball not only on the green but beyond the flagstick.[19] Fownes, after seeing this unexpectedly great shot, pulled his approach into a bunker to the left of the green and lost the hole to Herron, thus tying the match. The final scores of the day were a 4-under-par 73 for Herron, his best ever at Oakmont, and a 2-under-par 75 for Fownes. It was perhaps the greatest match ever played in Oakmont's already storied twelve-year history.

The Flanegin Cup could not end in a tie, so Fownes and Herron, now clearly the two best golfers at Oakmont, played off the tie in another eighteen-hole contest. Herron beat Fownes, shooting a 76 to Fownes's 77. He was now, in the summer of 1916, playing the best golf of his life and, when he was playing his very best, he could compete on equal terms with Fownes at Oakmont. Furthermore, he was now scoring in the 70s with far greater regularity than ever before. In other words, he was ready and capable of competing head-to-head with anyone at Oakmont, in match or medal play.

The Flanegin Cup ended just before the West Penn Amateur began. Those who'd had the good fortune to watch Dave Herron shoot 33 on Oakmont's back nine were placing their bets on him. Quite naturally, expectations for Herron to finally win a "big" event, especially on his home course, were growing. "Herron has never won a big tournament," observed the *Pittsburgh Post*, but "during the past few years he has been fast coming to the front and is being picked by many as the winner of the present tournament."[20] Continuing their great play and reinforcing the close personal relationship they had developed over the past decade, Herron and Fownes teamed together for the fourball match that preceded the official championship. On an unbearably hot day where the scoring was higher than expected, they shot the low gross score of 74, three shots better than anyone else.[21] Both players seemed primed for victory in the West Penn Amateur. That said, it would have been foolish not to bet on Fownes given his remarkable prior success in this event, his mastery of Oakmont, and the reality that—perhaps pressed by competition against Herron—he too, at age thirty-nine, was probably playing the best golf of his life.

In enervating heat and humidity, with the course toughened to high championship standards, Fownes won the qualifying round the next day with 160, far above the scores that he and Herron had recently been shooting. Herron finished in fifth position, at 163, a very good showing that actually looked like it would be much better. He was only one shot behind Fownes after the morning round, and he shot a terrific 37 on the outgoing nine in the afternoon to take a commanding lead with only three holes to go. But everything fell apart for him on the sixteenth and seventeenth holes, scoring 8 on No. 16 and 6 on No. 17, where his ball "sunk in the earth . . . in a cavernous bunker."[22] By the end, Herron was just happy to finish and qualify for the championship flight.

Herron continued to play well in the early rounds of the 1916 West Penn Amateur, easily advancing to the quarterfinals, where he faced his familiar Pittsburgh friend and now collegiate rival from Yale, Dwight Armstrong. Both young men spurred each other on, shooting around par but with Herron making a birdie on the seventeenth hole to win 2 and 1. Unfortunately, this match was the end of his run of truly sparkling golf. Against his long-term mentor, Eben Byers, in the semifinals, his game fell apart in the early holes—he bogeyed twice and was 3 down after just three holes—and when Byers birdied No. 10 to go 5 up, the match was essentially over.[23]

In this West Penn Amateur, as in most others played over the previous decade, the finalists included Byers, Fownes, and Ormiston. Dave Herron had emerged by 1916 as the fourth of a new "Big Four" in Western Pennsylvania golf, surpassing J. B. Crookston for the honor. But the old-timers continued to play consistently well, and they all knew the intricacies of Oakmont at least as well as Herron. He was easily the longest hitter of the four, and getting stronger every day. But that was not enough to make the difference on as challenging a course as Oakmont—in sharp contrast to even the best Southern courses, including Atlanta's East Lake and Druid Hills—that rewarded straightness and pinpoint accuracy at least as much as raw power.

The day after Herron lost to Byers, Fownes won the West Penn Amateur for the eighth (and last) time in his career. By all measures, Herron was now good enough to win the most prestigious regional events, and Western Pennsylvania fans began to expect it of him. But, for all his imperturbability, he obviously still had not mastered the full set of mental and physical skills needed to win a major championship, even at his home club.[24]

Nor could he yet compete on even terms at Oakmont against the best professionals in the region, which included several of the best in the country. The West Penn Open immediately followed the West Penn Amateur at Oakmont and was only a two-round event, which reflected the lower stature of professional versus amateur golf in the pre-war era. Fred Brand of Bellevue Country Club won with a mind-bending score of 148, 6 under par for the two rounds. Fownes finished third in the event, five shots behind Brand with a 1-under-par 153. By contrast, Herron, competing in his first West Penn Open, scored 162 for the two rounds—a mediocre performance in comparison to how he had been recently faring. For all his improvement in the past year, shooting consistently in the 70s at Oakmont still remained a great challenge.[25]

In addition to Oakmont, Herron had grown up playing Stanton Heights Country Club on a regular basis. As the event's two-time champion, he enthusiastically entered the 1916 Stanton Heights Invitation, for which a record 170 players registered to play (not including Fownes or Byers; like many wealthy Pittsburghers, they left town for vacation in early August, prior to returning to prepare for the U.S. Amateur in early September). Stanton Heights was a shorter and hillier course than Oakmont, and Herron's prior victories at its invitation tournament attested to his comfort-level playing there. His growing power provided advantage on only a few holes, especially now that the summer drought baking the fairways was transforming everyone into a boomer off the tee.[26] The greens were abundantly watered, however, so that approach shots would hold and no major embarrassments in putting would occur. In the absence of Fownes and Byers (though Ormiston was entered), Herron and J. B. Crookston of the home club were the favorites to win.

Herron sparkled in the qualifier, which had to be cut to a single round in order to accommodate the large field. He had always scored well on this course, and he did so again, shaving one stroke off par with a 72. But the opening match-play rounds brought many upsets. He barely survived his first match against *Pittsburgh Gazette Times* golf journalist E. E. Giles, with neither player on his game. Herron played well enough to win his second match and advanced to the semifinals against little-known P. H. Preston, who was playing well above his usual game and had already defeated the Princeton captain, W. A. Lowrie. Against Preston, in a massive rainstorm, Herron's short and long games both faltered badly; he could neither hit the fairways nor chip predictably. That led to an embarrassing 5 and 4 defeat for the tournament favorite—a big disappointment for Herron. Despite the continuing maturation of his game and his unflappable demeanor, he still lacked what it took to win on a regular basis.[27]

Herron had one last chance in the summer of 1916 to iron out the inconsistencies in his game, and it was a major one: the U.S. Amateur at Merion, whose field included the two most widely celebrated teen phenoms in the nation, Atlanta's seventeen-year-old Perry Adair and fourteen-year-old Bob Jones. It would be Dave Herron's best opportunity yet to insert himself in the conversation about who was America's best young amateur golfer.

▸ CHAPTER 4

"GEORGIA HAS GOLF MARVEL"
JONES OVERTAKES ADAIR (1916)

By 1916, Bob Jones and Perry Adair were competitive equals, and they started their tournament season in Alabama at the Montgomery Invitation just as they had in 1915. Jones hoped to redeem himself after what he perceived to be a dismal showing the previous year, and Adair looked to take the title from his father. "The golf course of the Country Club of Montgomery, considered by experts to be the best in the South, [is] in perfect condition for the tournament," the press reported. So perfect, in fact, an unnamed Southern golfer blamed his "big score" on the distractingly beautiful conditions: "The greens were so smooth and soft that I just completely forgot all about my game for thinking about how I would like to play on such a course all the time."[1]

Promising a "gallery of stars" in addition to pristine conditions, the *Montgomery Advertiser* announced, "Undoubtedly, this year's tourney will be far and away the best attended of any ever held here, as indicated by the big advance entries."[2] Nearly two hundred golfers ended up competing in the qualifying round on June 8, a huge increase over the 112 players who competed the previous year.[3]

Golf news, it seemed, continued to sell papers in Alabama: Perry Adair and his father dominated press coverage as they had the year before. Under a section titled "Famous Golfers Here," the *Advertiser* proclaimed, "George Adair and his son, Perry, both of Atlanta, Ga., the finalists of the fifth annual Invitation Tournament, held here last June, were among the early arrivals of Wednesday. . . . Both of the golfers have large followings which predict that the championship lies between them again this year."[4] But, this time, Jones's own accomplishments during the 1915 season earned him a special nod from the paper. "Much interest is taken in the youngsters Perry Adair and Bobby Jones. . . . These two will give a lot of trouble to older and more seasoned golfers."[5]

Like most tournaments of the time, the Montgomery Country Club Invitation also featured team contests that were reported on in depth. Bob Jones was listed under the Atlanta Athletic Club team, along with Perry and George Adair.[6] In the eighteen-hole qualifying round, "Young Adair played a steady game throughout, his drives being long and his approaches especially accurate," and turned in the low score of the day: a 76. The *Advertiser* noted that George Adair, in contrast, was "badly off his game" and took 91 strokes to maneuver around the course.[7]

The newspaper's prediction that the "boy wonders" would outplay the more seasoned veterans was so far holding true. On Friday, Perry Adair and Bob Jones won all of their matches, setting up a teenage showdown.[8] The young Atlantans' victories stirred "great interest in the semi-final round" because Jones and Adair would finally face one another in a competitive match. "Mr. Jones has a large following, each member of which is confident that he will succeed in winning the match from Perry Adair," declared the *Advertiser*. "On the other hand, Mr. Adair has his friends who are equally as confident that he will be the one to get into the final this afternoon."[9]

Adding to the excitement was the fact that Jones had played the course in 70 in his morning match. To put that score in context, the *Montgomery Times* included in its coverage an account of Louis Jacoby—formerly of Texas, now of New Orleans—who had turned in a card of 68 several years before, when Montgomery's course didn't have any bunkers. "Experts Friday afternoon declared that Jacoby would have taken at least ten more strokes to make the course as it now is, with the same shots made when he made the record for the course." Thus, Jones's amazing 70 combined with "the steady playing of Perry Adair, who again turned in a card of 76," promised the galleries a tense and exciting match.[10]

The boys did not disappoint. Jones later wrote that his semifinal match against Perry was

> the most spectacular of all the matches we played. I went out in 33 and was 3-up, and figured I had the match in hand. Then Perry broke away with a burst of golf that seldom can have been equaled. He came home in 33, including a stymie on the sixteenth green, and beat me on the last hole, 1-up. . . . It was the hottest blast of really hot golf I had yet encountered; and I knew then why Perry was called the Kid Wonder of Dixie."[11]

O. B. Keeler concurred, writing later: "It very likely was the greatest golf match played up to that time in the south—and it was played by boys of fourteen [Jones] and seventeen [Adair]."[12]

By this point in their careers, Perry Adair had been enjoying press adulation for almost two years, and his celebrity had definitely helped raise golf's profile in the South. Now, Bob Jones had taken some of that spotlight for himself, and his mere entrance into an event merited press attention. As the two arrived in town in late June for the prestigious Birmingham Invitation Championship, reporters singled out both boys as standout players. "Adair is recognized as one of the greatest players in the south. Although a youth in his teens, he has won more trophies, probably, than any other player in the country at his age," the *Birmingham Age Herald* decreed. Jones, meanwhile, in the newspaper's opinion, was "in some respects as good a player as Adair, though he lacks experience in tournament contests."[13] More than 140 players attempted to qualify for the Birmingham Invitation. Jones shot a 73, one shot behind the winning medalist score.[14] Somewhat ironically, Adair missed the cut, carding a 78, and was relegated to the second flight.[15]

In the championship flight, Jones's first two matches were close, but he then easily won his semifinal match. The final contest between him and 1915 Alabama state champion Jack Allison featured exceptional golf, with Jones finally winning on the eighteenth hole by shooting an estimated medal score of 70.[16] With this victory, he regained his lead over Adair in terms of the number of championship trophies each "boy wonder" had won. Still, even though Jones was the 1916 Birmingham Invitation champion and Adair hadn't even qualified for the championship flight, the *Atlanta Constitution* went out of its way to heap praise on Adair as "Atlanta's crack young golfer."[17] It would only be later in 1916 that Jones's reputation truly began to eclipse his best friend's in the South.

East Lake's Invitation Golf Tournament began in early July, and weather conditions for the 128 contestants in the qualifying round were terrible. Still, despite "a downpour of rain," George Adair turned in the lowest score, a "splendid card" of 81.[18] Bob Jones was three shots behind while Perry Adair could do no better than 88. As Jones relaxed during the first match-play round—he won by default—Perry Adair persisted through a close match and managed to win 1 up.[19] Both boys then easily defeated their next several opponents to set up a rematch between the two "kid wonders," this time in the finals rather than the semis.

In the eighteen-hole finale, Jones was "in splendid form" and beat Adair, 4 and 3. He played out his bye holes for a "wonderful" score of 77. Considering "the rain, the mud, and the general adverse conditions," Jones had played remarkably well.[20] This achievement caught the eye of the *New York Times*, one of the first newspapers outside the South to report on Jones. In an article subtitled "Georgia Has Golf Marvel," the publication incorrectly identified Jones as a thirteen-year-old prodigy (instead of fourteen), who shot a blistering 68, which was also badly incorrect.[21]

A few weeks later, still in Atlanta, Jones played in and won the qualifying round of the Davis & Freeman Cup tournament at Druid Hills. But he then abruptly withdrew so that he could travel to Tennessee to compete in the Knoxville Invitation. The new Cherokee Country Club course in Knoxville was 6,112 yards. "Every improvement has been made to place this course in the best possible condition," the *Knoxville Sentinel* reported, but it had yet to be tested by any of the best golfers in the South.[22] The club made every effort to impress, recruiting J. H. Ingalls, the "famous professional of Birmingham," to take charge and fulfill Knoxville's quest for recognition as one of the South's rising urban jewels. "There is little question but that this will be one of the most brilliant social events ever held in Knoxville."[23]

The *Sentinel* celebrated the news that Adair and Jones would enter the contest and took extraordinary care to detail the boys' movements en route from Atlanta to Knoxville.[24] Chaperoned by George Adair, Bob Jones and Perry Adair arrived in town the Tuesday before the match. Unsurprisingly, the local press paid more attention to Perry Adair. Under the title "Perry Adair Most Unassuming Young Man Imaginable," the *Sentinel* painted a portrait of a winningly humble rising star. In response to the question "How does it feel to be the best known golfing youngster in the United States," he replied, "I don't think anything about it.... But I do appreciate the kind things that many people have said about me."[25]

With pride, the *Knoxville Sentinel* also reported a compliment that George Adair—whom the paper identified as "one of the leading business men" of Atlanta—paid to Knoxville. "You seem to have a very hustling city," he said. "I have been here only a short time, but I have already been impressed with your magnificent hospitality. Furthermore, I believe this tournament will be one of the biggest invitation meets held anywhere in the south this season."[26]

Perry Adair and Bob Jones, as a pair, struck Knoxvillians as rather quiet despite all the attention they were receiving: "Perry Adair and Bob Jones Jr., of Atlanta, conceded the gest [*sic*; i.e., "greatest"] golfers in the south according to age were also the cynosure of all eyes. Both youngsters are reticent to the extreme. They have very little to say but they always seem to be in the best humor, and always ready to listen to a good joke."[27] This portrait of Jones contrasted strongly with his widespread reputation for having an explosive temper and a penchant for throwing clubs after a missed shot. Years later, in 1940, sportswriter Grantland Rice described young Jones as "a short, rotund kid, with the face of an angel and the temper of a timber wolf." "At a missed shot," Rice wrote, "his sunny smile could turn more suddenly into a black storm cloud than the

Nazis can grab a country. Even at the age of 14 Bob could not understand how anyone ever could miss any kind of golf shot."[28]

The Cherokee Club Invitation initially went quite well for Bob, Perry, and George. But in the second round, George and Perry, "the two stars of Southern golfdom," were both eliminated, with Perry losing in twenty holes to another rising star from Georgia, seventeen-year-old J. Simpson Dean.[29] "It has been a noticeable, as well as notable, feature during the present tournament that youth has held the day," commented the *Knoxville Sentinel*. Indeed, only one player over the age of eighteen made it to the semifinals.[30]

In the eighteen-hole finale, Jones won the Knoxville Invitation Golf Tournament easily by closing out Simpson Dean on the fourteenth hole. He was incorrectly identified as a seventeen-year-old, not a fourteen-year-old; the source of the newspaper's confusion may have been that seventeen was Dean's age—youth held the day indeed. The large gallery was "disappointed" by the lopsided match, as Jones "made perfect drives and puts [sic], but Dean made a number of poor ones, which resulted in his defeat."[31] Although Jones "clinched" the match at the fourteenth hole and "Dean wanted to quit there, . . . the gallery yelled for full play." Dean agreed to play out the bye-holes so that Jones, the youngest competitor in the entire field, could have a chance to set a new course record. In the end, Jones's 73 came within a shot of the recently established course record of 72.[32]

Still, despite the anticlimactic nature of the final match, commentators declared the newly minted event a huge success. "The late invitation tournament, pronounced one of the most successful meets of its kind held in the south this season," the *Sentinel* assured its readers, "went a long way toward stimulating interest in golf in this city."[33] And no small part of that success was due to Bob Jones's spectacular golf.

Even more impressively, Jones played the Cherokee Club Invitation despite being afflicted with lumbago.[34] Somewhere in between his streak of tournament triumphs, which so far included the Birmingham Invitation, the AAC Invitation at East Lake, and the Cherokee Club Invitation, he made time to fit in two weeks of violet ray treatment to forever rid himself of the lumbago that had made walking difficult at Knoxville (clearly it had not affected his ability to win). To cement his expanding regional domination, Jones entered the inaugural Georgia State Amateur that would be played in Atlanta the first week of August.

From the start of the 1916 Georgia State Amateur, it was clear that younger competitors would triumph. For the qualifying round on August 2, Jones posted the low score: a clean 76. Fellow youngster Simpson Dean, whom Jones had just defeated in Knoxville, was tied at second with a 79, while Perry Adair scored a respectable 81.[35] Additionally, the Atlanta Athletic Club, comprised of Adair, Jones, V. R. Smith, and C. V. Rainwater, copped the team competition medal with the low score of 322.[36] "Infant prodigies continue to rule supreme," the *Atlanta Georgian* wrote.[37]

Jones breezed through his first two matches, but his rematch against Simpson Dean was much closer and received considerable press attention.[38] The *Atlanta Georgian* noted that this was the first time that Bob Jones had truly been tested since the championship began—and arguably, since his defeat at the hands of Perry Adair in Montgomery much earlier in the 1916 season.[39] Simpson Dean rallied hard on the thirteenth hole in what the *Georgian* called the "hottest battle of the tournament" thus far. With a chance at the state title on the line, Dean exhibited "the most spectacular burst of speed" by winning three holes in succession. Jones's lead from his excellent play on the first nine, including three scores of 2, rapidly diminished.[40] On the seventeenth green, Dean needed only to knock down a five-foot putt to win the hole and extend the match. "He had the line exactly but the ball stopped one turn short," recalled Jones. "Gosh—he was disgusted!"[41]

While Simpson Dean was battling gallantly against Bob Jones, Perry Adair was struggling to defeat an older Atlantan of some renown, Milton Dargan. The pair went all the way to the seventeenth green, where Perry finally won. At the end of the day, the *Atlanta Georgian* reported back to its readers that Jones, the "youngest of the 'boy wonders,'" would meet Adair—for the third time this summer—in the finals of the Georgia State Amateur championship. The match turned out to be the highlight of Atlanta's 1916 golf season.

So far, Jones and Adair were tied in head-to-head matches. This week, Adair was playing better golf tee-to-green, and Jones's putting was still erratic. By the noon lunch-break on Saturday, Adair was 3 up on Jones. The *Georgian* relayed this information through a banner headline, "Perry Adair 3 Up on 'Little Bob' Jones."[42] The newspaper also printed a photo of Jones—his determined, almost grim, gaze reflecting an age much more mature than his fourteen years.

Play was scheduled to resume at 2:30 p.m. After drinking a glass of milk and eating a light sandwich, Jones marched out to the eighteenth green. Furious with his putting in the morning round, he chipped and putted for the next hour—"a terrible thing to do," he reflected years later, "but a kid can stand anything."[43]

He may have started the afternoon round 3 down, but by the fourteenth

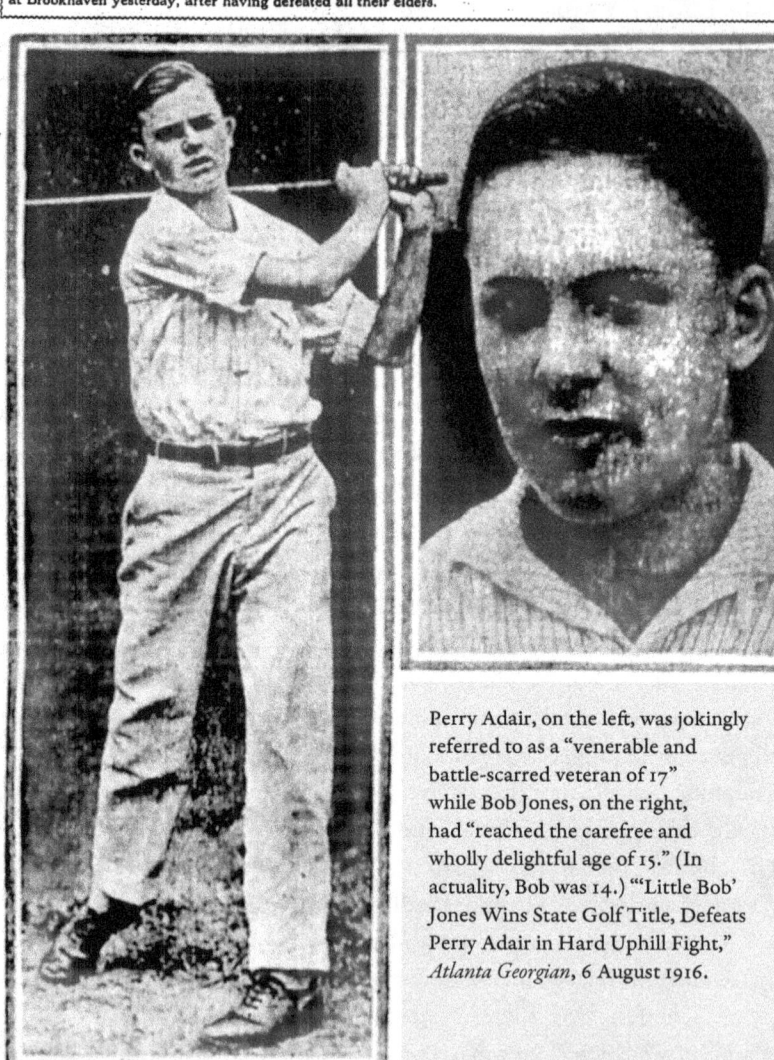

Perry Adair, on the left, was jokingly referred to as a "venerable and battle-scarred veteran of 17" while Bob Jones, on the right, had "reached the carefree and wholly delightful age of 15." (In actuality, Bob was 14.) "'Little Bob' Jones Wins State Golf Title, Defeats Perry Adair in Hard Uphill Fight," *Atlanta Georgian*, 6 August 1916.

hole he had taken the lead and given many spectators the impression that he was superhuman. When he sank a twenty-foot putt for "a magnificent 3" on the sixteenth hole, O. B. Keeler, following along in the gallery with the rest of the press, said he heard a spectator say, "If you stuck a knife in that kid he'd bleed ice water."[44] Jones would later write that he felt a "strain I never was conscious of before."[45] The match finally came to a close on the eighteenth hole when "Perry putted, his ball stayed out, and he walked over and shook hands with the State champion."[46]

With his victory at the 1916 Georgia State Amateur, the legend of Bob Jones as a golfing automaton truly began. The *Atlanta Journal*'s write-up on the final match included a quote from an unnamed veteran golfer: "I don't believe any golfer living could have beaten Bob Jones the way he was going on that last eighteen holes. It was weird, something that went outside the realms of human endeavor and became supernatural."[47] In a similar vein, O. B. Keeler reflected,

> It's a dour game, tournament golf. It's a grim, bitter, relentless grapple of nerve and sinew and soul. I started to add heart, but that isn't it. Where you get weak isn't in your heart. It's right back of your belt buckle—and the word for what you have when you DON'T weaken is only four letters long, but they won't let me put it in this home paper. That's golf.[48]

Keeler then posed the question: "Now, how do they do it—those youngsters?" With an eloquent "I dunno," Keeler launched into a glowing review of Adair and Jones's hard fight to the finish, writing on every aspect of the match with his trademark flair for the fantastic. He described the boys' tee shots at the par 3 eighth hole as an "unbelievable brace of shots that couldn't have been placed there with a rifle," and wrote of Adair's face so "set in lines that you wouldn't look to see in the face of a man under 40, and ready and eager for the last and ultimate tilt with the hardest battle in life." Regarding the stats for the afternoon cards, Keeler wrote that they were "nipping a brace of strokes off Old Man Par, and sending Colonel Bogey reeling from the links to the Nineteenth Hole, to drown the memory of a murderous defeat."[49]

Reflecting later on the match in *The Boys' Life of Bobby Jones*, Keeler wrote that the match not only made Jones the first-ever amateur state champion of Georgia, but "it rearranged the order in which golfers were wont to mention Atlanta's favorite sons. Up to this match it always was Perry and Bob. After that classic struggle at Brookhaven it became Bob and Perry."[50] In 1916, seventeen-year-old Dave Herron could only claim to be one of the best amateurs in Western Pennsylvania, whereas fourteen-year-old Bob Jones was indisputably the best amateur in the entire state of Georgia.

No less important for Bob's rising celebrity as golf's greatest child prodigy was the fact that USGA committeeman Ralph Reed had witnessed Adair and Jones battle it out on the links. Thoroughly impressed with both boys' skills, Reed enthusiastically encouraged their parents to give them permission to compete in the upcoming U.S. Amateur at Merion Golf Club outside Philadelphia.[51] Keeler documented the exchange between Reed, George Adair, and Big Bob Jones: "After the Georgia championship Mr. Reed insisted, to Big Bob, that Bob had earned the right to play in the national amateur, at Merion." Big Bob was initially hesitant, citing his son's young age. "And then George Adair said: 'I'm taking Perry. You let Bobby come along with us!'" "So Big Bob nodded," wrote Keeler.[52] A few weeks later, the *Atlanta Georgian* announced on August 17 under the headline "Boy Cracks Enter U.S. Golf Meet" that Little Bob Jones and Perry Adair would be heading to Philadelphia for the U.S. Amateur. "Not that they haven't been in some pretty hot competitions since this good year was born, but this time they are going up against the best amateur players of the nation," the newspaper noted.[53]

The caliber of competition across the entire United States, not just within the South, was an item of hot debate for both local and national newspapers in the months preceding the 1916 U.S. Amateur. Golf in the South was certainly not equal to that of the East or Midwest, but writers for the *American Golfer* highlighted the improving quality of Southern golf, among both men and women. Alexa Stirling's recent win at the Women's Southern Championship, they argued, provided clear evidence that "the average play in tournament golf in the South is gradually improving and that the number of golfers who are likely to win any tournament held in the South are more in number than they were in the last two or three years."[54] The *American Golfer* also observed of Bob Jones, "It is freely predicted that in the course of a few years in which he can gain the necessary experience that he will develop into one of the very best golfers in the country." And "the kids are setting the pace," O. B. Keeler observed in the *Atlanta Georgian*. He ended his article with this prophecy: "In ten years from this well known date you will see a crop of crack golfers under 30 batting around 70 in this town; and they will be the still young Perry Adairs and L. B. Joneses [i.e., "Little Bob"] who grew up with their clubs and absorbed from them the Spirit of Wood and Iron that makes a golfer."[55]

For Keeler, the array of Southern golfers at Merion in 1916 was unquestionably the strongest contingent the South had ever sent to challenge on the national stage: "Little Bob Jones and Perry Adair and George Adair, from Atlanta; Nelson Whitney and Rube Bush, from New Orleans; George Aldredge, Charlie Dexter, and George Rotan, from Texas—they make up the more or less intrepid octet who will march driver to driver to the first tee next Saturday, ready to do or die for Dixie (loud cheers)." Perry Adair told Keeler that he and Bob Jones had put their heads together for a battle plan to ensure that they both qualified for match play. "I never have seen the course but they say it's no harder than East Lake. We'll get all the practice we can, of course, and then pray for the weather and an even break with the luck." And "watch Whitney," Adair told Keeler, who in turn told his readers: "Myself, I'm going to watch Perry a bit. Also Little Bob. Those kids are dangerous in anybody's tournament."[56]

Not long after Jones was crowned the Georgia state champion, newspapers across the nation readied their predictions for the U.S. Amateur. William H. Evans, writing for the *Philadelphia Public Ledger*, prefaced his article "Can You Pick the Next Amateur Golf Champion?" with this statement: "There is no sport of the sport loving Americans quite comparable with that of prognostication." And being habitually wrong was not a deterrent to participating: "The dopesters certainly had things wrong last year in discussing the amateur golf championship for not one of them thought for a moment that either of the finalists [Robert Gardner and John Anderson] had a chance under the sun."[57]

Heading into the 1916 Amateur at Merion, William Evans identified Jerry Travers (a four-time Amateur champion), Bob Gardner (the 1915 Amateur champion), Chick Evans, Oswald Kirby, and Max Marston as the most likely winners.[58] When making its predictions the *Atlanta Georgian* listed ten names that were "credited with being able to go through the field," including the same names selected by Evans, with the additions of John G. Anderson (who was a finalist in 1915), Nelson Whitney, L. B. Paton, Ned Sawyer, and young Philip Carter.[59]

At the U.S. Amateur, regional rivalries were historically a matter of East versus West—since the U.S. Amateur started in 1895, not a single Southern golfer had appeared in a final. In fact, it was not until 1913 that a Southerner advanced to match play, when Nelson Whitney of New Orleans and Alfred Ulmer of Florida made it through the qualifying rounds, only to lose their opening matches. In 1914, no Southern golfers made an appearance, but in 1915, "not only did Mr. Whitney make a good showing in this tournament but the South was able to send two other players into the championship division." According to "The Colonel," who wrote the "From the South" column in the *American Golfer*, "The fact that three Southern players were able to get into the match play of the [1915] championship [in Detroit], where in the past the

South has been able to get not more than one and very often not even that one through the qualifying round, is gratifying to the golfers of the South as it demonstrates that the game is steadily improving in the South and that little by little we are getting players who are nearer in the class of the players of the North, East, and West."[60]

As for a future where the South possessed an Amateur champion in its ranks, The Colonel wrote that "such an expression as this may seem like a pipe dream but with the number of new courses being built and with those which are already built being made more difficult all of the time and thus demanding greater accuracy from all of the players, who can tell that we may be able to develop in the South some golfer, who may be able to weather the storm of a championship."[61]

"Little Bob Jones"—"who is not so blamed little, at that, being constructed along the general lines of a piano mover," wrote O. B. Keeler—had emerged as the most likely candidate to fulfill this pipe dream.[62] At the beginning of 1916, he and Perry Adair had been equals, but now Jones had started to surpass his older friend. Materially, Jones had won three notable events compared to Adair's one, and of the three times they met in competitive matches in 1916, Jones won twice. He had overcome the three-year age gap, and now both young men were playing the best golf of their teenage lives. Jones had proven that, at least on Southern golf courses, he was now capable of shooting rounds in the 70s and low 80s with considerable regularity. And he was quite capable of persevering through tough matches until the very last hole. In short, even at age fourteen he could compete with the very best golfers from the West and East. Including golfers older than he, such as Pittsburgh's eighteen-year-old Dave Herron.

▸ CHAPTER 5
THE 1916 U.S. AMATEUR AT MERION
HERRON AND JONES CROSS PATHS

As always, the last big golf event of the 1916 summer season was the U.S. Amateur, held that year at Hugh Wilson's four-year-old masterpiece, Merion Golf Club. It was the first competition where Dave Herron and Bob Jones would cross paths. By now, Herron was a known commodity in the U.S. Amateur because of his solid play in the East-West matches in Detroit prior to the 1915 championship, and because he had shot 73 to tie Ned Sawyer for the lead after the first qualifying round. But Jones was still largely unknown outside of the South. And, certainly, neither teenager was expected to contend for the title.

It remained to be seen whether Herron could sustain the level of excellence he'd achieved in the first half of the summer now that expectations for him had started to rise. In the weeks leading up to the Amateur, he chose to practice entirely at Oakmont, performing credibly in a number of intraclub events. He rode in the same car with W. C. Fownes Jr. and George Ormiston to Merion, where they were joined by eleven other players from Western Pennsylvania. The Pittsburgh press largely ignored Herron, but they were quite hopeful that either Eben Byers or Fownes, who had played spectacularly all summer, might win the U.S. Amateur for the second time and bring another major championship trophy back to Pittsburgh.

How the press characterized Fownes's competitive prowess is of considerable interest, for Fownes was not only Herron's long-time mentor but also his most frequent playing partner in recent club events. At Merion, they did not team up for the *American Golfer* Trophy competition as they had in Detroit, but Herron rightly viewed Fownes as his main role model for learning the mindset of a champion and of a leader. Fownes epitomized these qualities—which is why he had been selected to captain the East-West team in 1915, and why the USGA would later tap him for major leadership roles (including captaining the first Walker Cup team and serving as president of the USGA in the mid-1920s). On the eve of the 1916 championship at Merion, the *Pittsburgh Sunday Post* nicely sketched Fownes's key qualities that Herron himself—though now a more physically powerful player than Fownes—had been internalizing since his youth. "What should serve Fownes well in this coming tournament," the *Post* observed, "is his temperament."

> If there is a player with golfing temperament it is the Oakmont player. He has the faculty of playing just a little better than his opponent. Francis Ouimet, the former titleholder, in an article which appeared in a leading golfing magazine, commenting upon Fownes, referred to him as "the golfer with the iron nerves." Fownes had been able to withstand the nerve-racking strain of golf, and is a player of wide experience in tournament play. Fownes has schooled himself through many years of play to meet all tests. Even in a friendly match he concentrates his efforts upon the proper playing of every shot. One never sees him playing a shot carelessly.
>
> Another valuable asset in Fownes' makeup is his imperturbability and his resourcefulness. His play is disconcerting to an opponent. He can play out of a trap or a bunker as well as he can from out on the fairway. He is a terror when it comes to sinking the long putts when they are needed.[1]

For the 1916 Amateur, the USGA would experiment with a new format for the qualifying rounds by splitting the competitors between Merion's East and West courses. William Evans of the *Philadelphia Public Ledger* (incorrectly) predicted "that lower scores will be made over the east than the west course, largely because the golfers will underrate the various holes, singly and collectively. The play over the west course is likely to be more careless, because of the absence of bunkering and the many short holes."[2]

Evans's prediction ignored a key fact: starting in 1915, Hugh Wilson and William Flynn, Merion's eminent custodians, had dramatically increased the course's difficulty in anticipation of hosting the 1916 Amateur. They had done so by constructing numerous subtly positioned but visibly intimidating "traps and bunkers"—the "White Faces"—that added a new punitive dimension to an already exceptionally tough layout. "Bold in design and bold in their visibility," historian Jeff Silverman wrote, "Wilson's bunkers began to populate the course like an advance of new settlers, making immediate statements." Flynn elaborated the underlying philosophy behind "the White Faces": "A concealed bunker has no place on a golf course. When concealed, it does not register on the player's mind. . . . The best looking bunkers are those that are gouged out of the faces or slopes, particularly when the slope faces the player. They are much more effective in that they stand out like sentinels beckoning the player to come on."[3]

Bob Jones had never seen a golf course that looked like Merion, especially since even the toughest Southern golf courses, including East Lake, had few bunkers. But it was Merion's greens on the East and West courses that truly puzzled him. "They looked like billiard tables to me and I was crazy to putt on them," he reflected years later.[4] But the beautiful greens were deceptively fast—in a practice round, on the West course, Jones forgot about the "bewildering" speed of the greens, knocked his ball hard with his Travis putter, and watched it roll past the hole and right into a brook. He had traveled out of Atlanta with the Adairs before, but never this far north. The entire experience was a wonderful, thrilling adventure. Jones later wrote that he was "simply pop-eyed with excitement and interest."[5] The party checked into the new swanky Bellevue-Stratford Hotel in downtown Philadelphia, where many of the other competitors were also staying because it was a short commuter train ride to the course.

Before the qualifying rounds began, participants played in the *American Golfer* Trophy competition, which was a fourball team event. Instead of partnering with Fownes, Herron teamed with Oakmont's R. G. Morrison. They finished three shots behind the leaders with a 73 on the more difficult of Merion's two venues, the East course (Herron shot a 74 on his own card and was helped by his partner on only one hole). Thus, as the qualifying rounds began for the 1916 U.S. Amateur, there was every reason to believe that Dave Herron would remain at the top of his game, as he had been virtually all season. At the very least, everyone expected him to qualify among the top thirty-two for match play just as he had done the previous year in Detroit.

But for whatever reason, Herron played his worst golf of all of 1916 (indeed, worse than all of 1915 too) in the two qualifying rounds at Merion. So, too, curiously, did several other major young stars at Merion, notably Phillip Carter of Long Island (a pre-tournament favorite in some experts' eyes) and Norman Maxwell of Philadelphia, neither of whom qualified for match play. Herron's putting was the most obvious culprit, but it took much more than that to explain why he scored two rounds of 85, or 170—three shots higher than the cut for match play and a whopping sixteen shots worse than the medalist, none other than Fownes. To add to the sting of disappointment, Byers and Ormiston finished third and fourth, respectively, marking a truly phenomenal performance in the qualifying rounds by all the top Pittsburghers, except Herron.

What could explain his unexpected failure? On the one hand, the greens at Merion were exceptionally fast, especially in the high winds that buffeted play all day. But Herron was familiar with fast greens at Oakmont. And he had mastered Merion's greens quite well during the *American Golfer* Trophy event two days earlier (he took the day off in between). Of course, both Merion courses were significantly lengthened before the qualifying rounds, just as they had been the previous year at Detroit. But that, too, should not have caused him particular difficulty because Oakmont was still a longer venue than Merion.

Perhaps the best explanation for his failure to qualify, even as his overall game continued to improve, was a recurring laxness in focus of the sort that Fownes never suffered. Though imperturbable under stress, Herron could not always cope with the sustained mental strain of championships, nor could he make the most of his "B-game." These were long-term problems that he had been resolving with considerable success during the past two golf seasons, but they remained recurring issues during his Princeton years. Just because his game seemed to be on a roll in the weeks and days preceding the Amateur did not mean that he could maintain the mental sharpness and resilience needed to score consistently.

Meanwhile, Bob Jones, one of the last players to start on the West course, coolly shot a 74—the lowest score recorded in the morning on either qualifying course. By that afternoon, everyone was watching Jones as a realistic prospect for the Amateur title. The *American Golfer* reported afterward that "no less than 1,400 automobiles were parked near the clubhouse"; everyone wanted to check out the "kid wonder" for themselves.[6] Jones wrote about his newfound fame in *Down the Fairway*. "After luncheon, when I got over to the East Course, word had got about that the new kid from Dixie was breaking up the tournament, and almost the entire gallery assembled to follow me. Gosh—it scared me to death!"[7]

After Jones's stunning score in the morning, reporters scrambled to find information on the young newcomer. Desperate for details to add color, they included incorrect information provided by dubious, unconfirmed sources such as neighbors "just across the way from the Joneses."[8] To address the mixed information written about him in the newspapers years later, Jones provided a candid, self-deprecating appraisal. "I was 14 years and six months old, five feet four inches tall, and weighed 165 pounds—a chunky, rather knock-kneed, towheaded youngster playing in long pants."[9]

Under the headline "Age and Youth Tee Off Together," the *Philadelphia Inquirer* wrote that the concept

> that golf is a game not only for old age but for youth was cusiously [sic] demonstrated.... In the morning the fifteen-year-old [sic] child wonder, who holds the Georgia State title, R. T. Jones, Jr., of Atlanta, turned in the low score of the day for the west course of 74. The boy went poorly in the afternoon over the east course, his card showing a total of 89 against par of 70. But his total for the day of 163 put him among those qualifying for the match play.[10]

The *Inquirer* described the excitement surrounding the qualifiers: "In the morning most of them followed Evans and Gardner, in the afternoon, Marston, Guilford, Sawyer, and young Bob Jones had hundreds in their wake. Jones, who is only fifteen [actually 14] and who is the Georgia champion, interested the crowd more than the bigger stars.... When his name was posted among those who had qualified the huge crowd that stormed the score board vigorously applauded."[11] Jones was not the only Southern golfer who had made it through to the next day. The *Atlanta Georgian* proudly reported, "It certainly can be said that the South came into its own yesterday, for R. T. Jones, Jr., Atlanta; Nelson M. Whitney and Perry Adair, Atlanta, secured coveted places in the 32."[12]

In the meantime, disappointingly, Herron was reduced to cheering for his fellow Pittsburghers from the gallery.[13] Higher expectations, his own and those of others, may have factored into his poor performance during the medal rounds. A Dr. Nelson from Altoona, who had observed Herron play superbly at Merion on a number of past occasions and who was also on site during the Amateur, pointed precisely in this direction. "If there can be such a thing, Herron regards his game too seriously," the doctor stated. But he also "was outspoken in saying Herron is the best player of his years in this country."[14] Furthermore, shooting an 85 on the more difficult East course in the morning round, after shooting a 74 there two days earlier, may have unnerved Herron. Almost everyone was having trouble scoring decently at Merion. A two-round total of 167, the same as at the difficult Detroit course the previous year, proved sufficient to qualify for match play. Thus, it would only have taken a round of 82 in the afternoon, on the easier West course, for him to make the cut. But surprisingly, he scored as poorly in the afternoon on the West course as he did in the morning on the East. Herron was simply not yet psychologically ready to compete consistently at his best on the national scene—not at Detroit in 1915 or Merion in 1916.

Bob Jones, however, had arrived, and the press and galleries were expecting quite the performance from him in match play. Yet when he drew Eben Byers, the 1906 U.S. Amateur champion and Pittsburgh's favored son, for his first match, he recalled, "Everybody in our party began to condole with me. Tough luck, they said, catching a big one in the first round." Byers had won the Amateur when Jones was just four years old, in 1906. Stepping in as the supportive surrogate father, George Adair clapped Jones hard on the back and told him not to listen. "Remember what old Bob Fitzsimmons used to say," he apparently told Jones. "'The bigger they are, the harder they fall!'"[15]

Bolstered by George Adair's encouragement, Jones won his very close match against Byers the next day on the thirty-fifth hole. But he "felt no elation whatever over my successful debut in a national championship." Both the veteran champion and the youthful marvel had a habit of expressing their emotions the same way—for each shot they mis-hit, they threw their clubs. The playing group behind them remarked that it looked like a "juggling act." And Jones joked for many years afterward that he only won because Byers ran out of clubs first. "I knew I was lucky to win, the way I had played, and that I ought to have been well drubbed."[16] Regardless, he had won, and the South survived to see another day of championship play with one of its ranks still in contention. The *Atlanta Constitution* commented rather obviously that "the defeat of Byers by young Jones was regarded as a distinct upset."

The next day, Jones went up against Frank Dyer, the state champion of Pennsylvania. He was 5 down by the sixth hole, and the outcome seemed bleak. So bleak, in fact, that John Anderson, covering the match for *Golf Illustrated*, wrote that "if there had been a train leaving for Atlanta that moment which he could have caught he would have taken it at once." Jones, perhaps still in the mode of playing against crusty, club-throwing Byers, or perhaps simply indulging his youthful temper, "smote the air with his clubs." According to Anderson's account, George Adair walked up to him and said to the boy, "Bob, you are playing bad golf because you are not in the right mood. Now you just get your mind on the game and play for all you are worth or I'll send you right back home. You may get beat 15-down, but you have got to take it in the right spirit or you won't get the best out of your game. Now go right at him."[17]

Five holes later, Jones had won back three holes and reportedly said to George Adair: "I'm only 2-down now and I think I'll get those back. I'm much obliged for your advice."[18] Although he ultimately pulled himself together, the *Philadelphia Inquirer* didn't let Jones's passionate displays of temper slide by unnoticed. "He puts all he has into his shots and, boy-like, he worries a lot over mistakes and at times shows by little outbursts of temper that things are not going right with him."[19] In contrast, the more sympathetic *Atlanta Georgian* (where O. B. Keeler was on staff) praised Jones's ability to tamp down his temper, writing, "It is truly wonderful that so young a player has such complete control, at least outwardly, over his feelings."[20]

In that evening's edition of the *Atlanta Georgian*, readers were notified that Little Bob Jones was "the South's sole survivor" and would be facing Robert Gardner, the reigning titleholder, in the quarterfinals the next day. "Golf experts," continued the newspaper, "considered Jones' play nothing short of marvelous, due to the fact that he was 5-down in the first 6 holes of his match and still had the fighting spirit and reserve force left to even up the match on the first 18 holes and then win out handily in the afternoon round."[21]

The *Atlanta Constitution* reported that those betting heavily on the matches at Merion had been so impressed with Jones's quality of play that "they could not give better than 5 to 4 on Gardner's chances of victory."[22] The Philadelphia newspapers were also impressed with Jones's grit; one proclaimed him the "precocious hero of the hour." Another wrote of "Robert Jones Jr. of Atlanta, the Georgia champion who, with assurance and confidence worthy of a veteran, proceeded to pull the chestnuts out of the fire after losing five of the first six holes."[23] The *Philadelphia Public Ledger* even went so far as to draw comparisons between the fourteen-year-old and golfing legend Harry Vardon.

Jones was well aware of the weight riding on his shoulders. He heard not only from well-wishers on the course at Merion, but also from admirers all over the country. An influx of telegrams reached him before his match against Gardner—he thought some of them were tremendously funny, including one from a man who apparently wired him, "Beat Gardner and you can have my whole darn lumber yard." And an admirer from Detroit messaged: "Will be at Merion Saturday and expect to see you and Gardner fighting for the title. You've put Atlanta on the map."[24]

Before Bob Jones, there was Robert (Bob) Gardner. In 1909, Gardner became the youngest winner of the U.S. Amateur at nineteen years and five months when he defeated Chandler Egan in the finals at Chicago Golf Club. Seven years later, Bob Jones was looking to break Gardner's record by a full five years. The *Philadelphia Inquirer* joked, "A giant for his age, Jones appeared almost like a midget alongside the tall and slender Gardner. His shoulders, though, were powerful and their strength rivaled Gardner's for the long drives."[25] Jones was the underdog because of his lack of experience, but he was also the fan favorite. According to the *New York Times*, "hardly a person in the great crowd that followed the match around the links was hoping that Gardner would defeat the game little Southerner, who has proved the sensation of the tournament."[26] Interest was so intense that following the match was, according to the *Atlanta Georgian*, "the largest gallery (easily numbering in the thousands) that has ever watched a golf match in this city."

After the first eighteen holes in the morning, Jones was 1 up, much to Gardner's bewilderment.[27] When the competitors broke for lunch, Gardner confessed, "It's too much for me to figure out," in response to Jones's proficiency on the course. "I can't see how he does it."[28] The morning round had been wildly back-and-forth, and the press was duly impressed that Jones managed to hang in, and better yet push Gardner to play better golf: "For a 14-year-old lad to lose four holes in succession, to take three putts on three successive greens, to stand 2-down to the national amateur champion at the sixth hole, and to square it at the ninth bespoke a stout arm and a bold heart."[29]

Indeed, "A mere child has arisen to confound the greatest of the country's golf stars," proclaimed the *Atlanta Georgian*. The *Los Angeles Morning Tribune* added, "Beating past and present champions is a fad with the latest golf sensation from the land of Dixie."[30] James R. Crowell, writing in *The Spur*, praised the city of Atlanta for being "particularly productive of golf prodigies." "For in addition to Robert Jones," he wrote,

> there are Perry Adair, eighteen years old [actually 17], whose luck it is that a brilliant performance in his first championship should be overshadowed by his companion's more sensational accomplishment, and Miss Alexa Stirling, also eighteen [actually 19] years old, who jumped into national prominence in her first try for the title in the 1914 tournament at Nassau, and who went through to the final round at Onwentsia last year.... Adair, like Bobby and Miss Sterling, is a finished golfer, having an excellent command of every club in his bag and trained to possess the proper temperament.

Furthermore, Crowell felt that Jones's incredible performance in his first U.S. Amateur was evidence "that any schoolboy who trains properly for the ordeal is worthy of pitting his skill against that of his more experienced elders. And it is the last word to prove that golf is just as much a game for the young as it ever was for the old boy."[31]

Pundits may have viewed Bob Jones's ascendance as a herald of the youth movement to come, but he reflected, years later, that his evident fearlessness was most likely a result of naiveté: "I hadn't sense or experience enough to be afraid."[32] After returning from lunch, he got off to a bad start and was 2 down by the sixth hole. He wrote in *Down the Fairway* that for all the certainty he felt that he would retake the lead, Gardner's seemingly endless supply of recoveries said otherwise. Youthful optimism had him telling himself that Gardner couldn't keep it up: "I'll get him yet!" He wrote: "I had felt all along that I could beat Bob Gardner, but there was something besides him that was big and hard and invincible.... That was what kept the pressure on me; that was what beat me."[33] The *Louisville Courier-Journal*, reflecting the far-reaching interest in this match, reported that its back-and-forth rhythm turned definitively in Gardener's favor on the sixth hole of the second round.

Both players drove long balls going to the sixth hole, but Jones put his second ball fifteen feet short of the flagstick, whereas Gardner was off the green and placed very badly for his approach. He was forced to play to a green that sloped away from him and was very fast. Gardner, however, laid this difficult shot dead and thus picked up his par 4. Jones had expected to win, and the half disappointed him. On the seventh and eighth holes the conditions were exactly the same, Jones getting his par 3 and 4 by playing every shot perfectly, whereas Gardner got his pars in weird fashion.[34]

The night after the match, Jones gave a similar account of the day's proceedings at the Bellevue-Stratford Hotel. "When he made those shots on the sixth, seventh, and eighth holes I just naturally went dead and lost ten pounds right there."[35]

After the ninth hole, Gardner was never really in any danger of losing. The match ended on the thirty-third hole, with a twenty-foot putt that ended Jones's dream of winning the 1916 U.S. Amateur. "It looked as if 'the Kid,' as the gallery called Jones, would carry the champion another hole," the *Louisville Courier-Journal* stated, "but Gardner's second drive was a whale, just short of the green. His approach was hashed and left him twenty feet from the flagstick, but he sank it, thus getting a three with the second ball, which enabled him to halve Jones' perfectly-played par four and end the match."[36] Despite Jones's defeat, the *New York Times* noted, "It took a full-grown national champion to overcome the prodigy of the links."[37]

Probably never in the history of American golf journalism had a quarterfinal match received so much national attention. The newspapers wrote admiringly of Bob Jones's mature and sportsmanlike conduct during the quarterfinal match—the vanquished was the first to rush over and offer the champion a hearty handshake and earnest congratulations. The *Philadelphia Inquirer* provided a wonderful image of the exchange: "It was necessary for Gardner to stoop slightly on account of the great difference in height." The *New York Times* wrote that Jones made his way back to the clubhouse while whistling a comic song. "Twirling his golf club in his hand, and greeting sympathetic words with a smile, he strolled off the links where in the last few days he has made for himself a reputation which will long endure in the history of American golf."[38] Gardner praised his young competitor, saying, "He put up a better game than I had expected. He's a real one, that is sure."[39]

For the reporters probing him for juicy quotes, Jones had a no-frills response: "Yes, I am very much disappointed. I was not sure that I could beat Mr. Gardner, but I did expect to make a better showing against him. He beat me in the sixth, seventh, and eighth holes this afternoon through the wonderful manner in which he recovered. I am going to Pine Valley tomorrow and after that match I am going right home. School starts next week, you know."[40]

As disappointed as Jones was, Atlanta was ecstatic. It was hard to tell that he had lost from the way the *Atlanta Constitution* raved over the young golfer's performance at Merion, with a nod for Perry Adair as well. Calling Jones the "golf hero of the year," no, "of the decade," the newspaper concluded, "Atlanta needs more Bob Joneses and Perry Adairs. They are the kind of stuff that build good cities and keep them to the forefront."[41] Not that excitement over Jones's golfing prospects was limited to his home city. The *Philadelphia Public Ledger* concluded its post-championship reflection with the prophetic sentence: "Here is a secret, 'the little Jones boy' is going to play right along until he becomes America's amateur champion golfer."[42] *Golf* magazine added that "'Bobby' is an Atlanta product and we go on record with that as a reason for his good golf. They are producing other wonders there."[43]

And according to George Adair, Walter Travis, the winner of multiple U.S. Amateurs and the British Amateur, believed that Jones possessed "the best control of his body in his swing of any player at the tournament."[44] H. B. Martin, the president of the New York Newspaper Golf Club, corroborated George's claim. Doubling as a writer and cartoonist for the September 1916 edition of *Golf* magazine, Martin drew a cigar-smoking Travis and an unidentified spectator, his mouth open in amazement, watching a chubby-cheeked Jones above the caption "W. J. Travis admired Bobbie Jones' Driving." While it was unanimously agreed that Bob's future was bright, Martin took it one step further. He mused, "Some one remarked to me the other day that this little Bobbie Jones would some day make a very fine golfer if he kept on. In my opinion, the boy has already arrived."[45]

The *Atlanta Georgian* reported that by Monday, the boys were back in Atlanta for class—Jones to the Boys' Technological High School and Perry Adair to Marist College. Jones rode the East Lake train into town surrounded by a group of his classmates. "'So, you are going back to school today, eh, Bob?' someone called out to him. 'Tough luck, ain't it?' the 'Kid' answered with a smile." While Perry Adair busied himself with school, George Adair and Bob Jones both gave short interviews to the *Atlanta Georgian*. When the reporter asked about the difference between Merion and the courses in the South, Jones had a lot to say. "'The championship course is harder,' he said. 'It is twenty yards shorter than East Lake, but it is better trapped, the traps are deeper, and the greens are much faster. The grass on the greens is short and thick and as smooth as a billiard table.'"[46]

The *Atlanta Georgian* also got an honest answer out of George Adair as to whether there would be a chance to see a national competition in Atlanta: "Not the slightest. . . . We haven't got the courses—the traps on the Merion course make East Lake look like it hasn't any traps—and we haven't got the grass. Our Bermuda greens are mere substitutes for the greens they have up East."[47]

Although George Adair dismissed the idea of hosting a national championship in the South, the "Old Sport's Musings" column in the *Philadelphia Inquirer* acknowledged that a national championship *player* must soon come from the region: "The fact that the youngest players coming from the South made such gallant stands against the more mature and seasoned golfers, makes it appear that some day, in the very near future may be, the championship will be carried to the Southland from the East and West."[48] Notable golfer and journalist John G. Anderson agreed. As he wrote in *Sporting Life*: "The arrival of Bob Jones and Perry Adair have given the South a real place in golf which will not be lost until these players have grown quite old." He continued, "What with Bush, Whitney, Adair, and Jones the south has a quartette of golfers who could vie with any other quartette in the land, taken from any particular section of the country."[49]

The national press made sure to include Bob Jones, the sensation of the competition, in all of its write-ups. Lauding Jones as the "Infant Terrible from Atlanta," *World of Sports of All Sports*, a weekly editorial digest, informed readers that "the precocious fourteen-year-old child packed up his tops and marbles" and that he had gotten so close to winning that "elder golfers are still quaking over the shock they got." *Golf* magazine declared:

> Fortunately for the game of golf, Gardner showed Bobby in the afternoon that he must try again. It sounds unfriendly to say "fortunately," but if young Jones had managed to put Gardner out we should have been flooded, not without reason, perhaps with inquiries as to "What kind of game is this here golf when kids can lick champions?" So, in a measure, the sacrifice of Robert, junior, was necessary for the dignity of the game.[50]

In the end, Chicago's Chick Evans, age twenty-six, won the 1916 U.S. Amateur by defeating Gardner, the defending champion, 4 and 3. With this victory, Evans completed his unprecedented quest to win the U.S. Open and U.S. Amateur in the same year—a feat, by any reckoning, that matched Francis Ouimet's wondrous victory over Vardon and Ray at Brookline three years earlier.[51] Still, all eyes had been on Bob Jones at Merion—perhaps even Dave Herron's. Jones made a deep and lasting impression that convinced many that he was the future of not just Southern golf but American golf as well.

PART II
THE WAR YEARS

▶ CHAPTER 6

STILL GRINDING
DAVE HERRON AND DISAPPOINTMENT AT OAKMONT (1916–1917)

There was little time to waste after the U.S. Amateur finals at Merion since the National Intercollegiate Championship at Oakmont began a week later. Both Dave Herron and his teammate D. C. Corkran wanted to maximize Princeton's practice time in the hope of reclaiming the Intercollegiate team title from Yale. As part of W. C. Fownes Jr.'s long-term plan to attract higher-caliber national championships to Oakmont, he and his greenkeeper and confidante, Emil Loeffler Jr., worked steadily behind the scenes—just as Hugh Wilson and William Flynn had done at Merion—to increase the course's difficulty before the collegians arrived. While the Intercollegiate did not hold nearly the prestige of a USGA event, the best college players of the time were mainly wealthy Ivy Leaguers, and many of their families had close USGA ties. Impressing the collegiate authorities was a shrewd first step in enticing the most prestigious championship prize in early twentieth-century American golf, the U.S. Amateur, to Oakmont.

The local press in Pittsburgh, not surprisingly, paid as much attention to the Intercollegiate at Oakmont as it did to the Amateur at Merion, and especially to its two homebred stars, Princeton captain William Lowrie and "the brilliant young Oakmont player," Dave Herron. The local press fully expected Herron to win the individual Intercollegiate title on familiar turf.[1] Outside of Pittsburgh, however, Princeton was not favored to win the team title.[2]

Neither the Princeton team nor Herron disappointed their fans in the team competition. Harvard surprised everyone (especially Yale) in reaching the finals against Princeton, but the Crimson Tide (Harvard) were helpless against the Orange and Black (Princeton). "The Cambridge players were completely outclassed and never had a chance, being swamped by the brilliant golf displayed by" Herron and his teammates. Princeton shut out Harvard, 9–0, which was a surprise given how well Harvard had been playing to that point. Herron and Corkran, The *Pittsburgh Post* noted, were playing particularly well, and Herron most especially, "who has been playing par golf since the tournament opened."[3] He had shown earlier in 1916 that when he was on his game, he could match par at Oakmont (still set at 77) and even defeat Fownes in head-to-head competition. After the let-down at Merion, it was surely a great relief to Dave and the entire Herron clan to see him fully confident, at home, in an event of such importance.

Herron played superbly in the team competition, but it was the magnitude of his individual triumphs against the other teams' top players that most impressed onlookers. Playing in the No. 1 slot and pitted against Dudley Mudge, captain of the Yale team and medalist at the 1915 U.S. Amateur, Herron simply destroyed him, winning 8 and 6. He also routed the Harvard captain, Lawrence Canon (the young star from Altoona that Herron had competed against several times), by shooting under par.

Dave Herron and the entire Princeton team were on a roll at Oakmont, and the press hoped that his surge would carry over into the several days of individual championship matches that began the following morning. Herron "was playing brilliantly ... and his approaches were straight for the pin. He was also putting well." The press pointed out his obvious advantage at Oakmont: "If he continues to play up to his form he has the best chance to win, as he has the advantage of playing over his home course, with which he is thoroughly familiar."[4] Another possible advantage, some writers noted, was that the "fair sex" comprised a not-insubstantial share of the large gallery cheering Herron's every move. It was an advantage indeed to be playing a high-profile event before an adoring hometown crowd on one's home course.

Herron continued to dominate the nation's forty-three best collegians, first by winning the medalist competition that preceded the individual championship. Up to this point the weather had been perfect, but dropping temperatures and increasing wind sent everyone's scores skyward, even Herron's. "It was hard to drive straight down the course, the ball often being caught by zephyrs and carried wide from its intended course, landing in trouble."[5] The best he could manage under the conditions was an 80, which was still three strokes better than his closest competitor.

The unfortunate assignment of Dave Herron and D. C. Corkran—Princeton's two best players, with the edge arguably going to Corkran based on his fantastic play at Merion—to the same bracket made it inevitable that one of the nation's best collegiate players would not make it to the semifinal round. And after Yale's Frank Blossom, a previous Intercollegiate champion, unexpectedly lost to one of Princeton's lesser players, all eyes were focused on Herron and Corkran, both of whom continued to play great golf.

Weather conditions remained challenging, but in his first match of the individual championship Herron swamped a player from the University of Illinois, 6 and 4. Corkran, however, was playing even better than Herron: "Since coming to Oakmont, Corkran has been a terror on the greens, seldom missing a putt, and he has been displaying ability to sink his long ones when they are needed."[6] In addition, Corkran was driving the ball tremendous distances, regularly 275 to 300 yards, rifling his irons to the flagstick, and using his strength to rebound from the rough whenever he found it. Given how exceptionally Corkran was playing and how quickly he had adapted to Oakmont, his only serious obstacle to winning the Intercollegiate Championship was his teammate and close friend Dave Herron.

As predicted by both contestants' outstanding play all week, the Herron-Corkran match was a vivid display of high-caliber golf. Both played near par figures on the front nine, and Corkran emerged with a 1-up lead. Disappointingly, the quality of their play deteriorated on the back nine when the duo made three 6s and a 7 between them; Herron lost the par 5 twelfth hole, for example, a 6 to a 7. But, uncharacteristically for Oakmont, the Princeton teammates were also able to make quite a few birdies, and the match remained close to the end. Both birdied the sixteenth hole (then playing as a short par 4) and tied the seventeenth with pars as Corkran closed out Herron to win, 2 and 1. Having watched his friend play every step of the way a week earlier at Merion, Herron understood just how much in the zone Corkran's game was, but he still took the defeat hard. "Herron had his heart set on winning the championship, and it was his cherished ambition to capture it over his home course. He played good golf, but Corkran played better," the *Pittsburgh Post* reported, and Corkran's under-par score of 76, despite carding three 6s, was more than Herron could overcome.[7]

Unfortunately for Corkran, the strain of playing such a tough match against Herron depleted everything he had left to give. The rest of Princeton's team (and Harvard's) went home, confident that Corkran would utterly destroy J. W. Hubbell—a lesser player on the Harvard team whom Corkran had previously defeated in the team championship. But to everyone's astonishment, Hubbell came back from 6 down (it was a thirty-six-hole match) to beat Corkran on the final hole. Not even Herron's earnest effort to help Corkran stem the bleeding—he emerged from the gallery on the fifteenth hole to caddie for his teammate—could straighten out Corkran's wild tee shots, which were the kiss of death at Oakmont. As the *Pittsburgh Post* observed, Hubbell rather heroically succeeded "without the moral support of his teammates, although he won the large gallery over to his side by his brilliant work and grim determination."[8]

Herron and Corkran soon joined their teammates back at school in New Jersey. Meanwhile, the Fownes family received the good news it had long awaited: Pennsylvania would host two championships back-to-back. The USGA had selected Oakmont for the 1917 U.S. Amateur. Having observed several collegians score close to par (77) at the Intercollegiate, and knowing that the Amateur would attract a more talented field, Fownes and Loeffler quickly set to work stiffening the course's difficulty to justify its selection as a national championship site.[9]

No sooner had Dave Herron returned to Princeton to begin his junior year then he left for Boston to compete for the Pennsylvania team against Massachusetts in the 1916 Lesley Cup matches, the winner to face the New York team (the defending champions) the next day. Business obligations prevented W. C. Fownes Jr. from competing in the Lesley Cup this year, but five of the nine men chosen for the team still came from Western Pennsylvania: Eben Byers, designated the No. 1 player, followed by Herron, No. 2, and in descending order, J. B. Crookston, Dwight Armstrong (Oakmont/Yale), and (substituting for Fownes) Lawrence Canon (Altoona/Harvard).

On the first day of competition, Massachusetts decisively defeated Pennsylvania, with only Byers and Dave posting victories for the Pennsylvania team. The winds blew fiercely and the scores were high; Herron was the only singles player to break 40 on the front nine. In a hard-fought match where the players were never separated by more than a single hole, Byers outlasted the Bay State's top player, the long-hitting Jesse Guilford (the USGA having recently revoked Boston's Francis Ouimet's amateur status). By contrast, in his singles match Herron opened up a four-hole lead after six holes, only to give back two holes before making the turn. From that point on, though, "Herron was hunting him again like a terrier following a rat and there was no such thing as the Bostonian (Rodney Brown) gaining after that."[10]

Herron, paired with Crookston, also posted the sole doubles victory for the Pennsylvania side. They played well enough together to break 40 and take a commanding lead on the front nine, only to lose the first three holes coming inward before retaking control and closing out the match on the sixteenth green. Other than these three wins, however, Pennsylvania lost every other singles and doubles match, and the Pennsylvania players returned home or to school the next day as Massachusetts went on to face New York. The Western Pennsylvania press, it should be noted, went out of its way to place the blame for the loss squarely on team members from Philadelphia: "It was no fault of the players from this end of the state, as they all showed up well in both the foursomes and single matches."[11]

To the obvious disappointment of everyone, Pittsburgh's top collegiate players including Herron, citing their school studies, chose not to return to Allegheny Country Club in mid-October to compete in either the Pennsylvania State Amateur or Pennsylvania State Open championships. But although he was a serious student—Herron won a top literary prize when he graduated from Princeton—and had already missed a fair amount of the fall semester to play competitive golf, he remained a true Oakmont stalwart and made time during early October to return to Pittsburgh to compete in inter- and intra-club matches. In the former, he contributed to a trouncing of the Pittsburgh Field Club, 31 to 6, winning his singles match very decisively, and then teaming with his brother Pomeroy to defeat their opponents 5 up. In an intraclub match a few days later, Dave Herron finished second, with Fownes and Ormiston well behind.[12]

Clearly, even while at Princeton, Oakmont remained a centerpiece of Herron's life; whatever his school obligations, he regularly found time to return home and reconnect with his mentors and family (his father still played regularly in these club matches). We suspect that if the 1916 State Amateur and State Open had been played at Oakmont instead of Allegheny Country Club, he might have come up with an excuse to interrupt his studies and return home to compete in front of his family and friends. He remained that much of an Oakmont loyalist.

However, there was an additional incentive for Herron to return periodically to Oakmont: to keep abreast of yet more changes that Loeffler and Fownes were introducing to the course in anticipation of the 1917 U.S. Amateur Championship. As the *Pittsburgh Post* explained:

> Emil "Dutch" Loeffler, the ground-keeper, has a force of men making changes on the course. Five of the greens will be changed, the first greens being converted into undulating greens. Work on the ninth green is already completed. Loeffler has achieved quite a reputation in America over the excellence of the Oakmont course. The dry season this year has caused the groundkeeper no end of trouble. Admiration has been expressed by all the visitors of the fine condition of the Oakmont course this fall. It now ranks among America's leading courses.[13]

These changes were well underway by the time Herron returned home to play in October, so he had a chance, quite literally, to watch the changes unfold and begin to adjust to the course's new demands well before the summer of 1917. Clearly, and contrary to architectural legend, Oakmont continued to be a dynamic work-in-progress in the eyes of its chief overseers, W. C. Fownes Jr. and Emil Loeffler Jr.

As spring returned to Pittsburgh in April 1917, the Western Pennsylvania Golf Association (WPGA), noting the humming local economy and newspapers' expanding golf coverage, anticipated the region's greatest season ever. The number of players continued to increase at a rapid pace, and likewise the number of courses, with differing levels of difficulty. The better courses were also investing large sums in improvements, both to satisfy the rising expectations of their members and to increase their chances of hosting regional championships. Chick Evans's dual victories in both the U.S. Open and U.S. Amateur championships in 1916 had enhanced the game's country-wide popularity more than anything since Ouimet's victory over Vardon and Ray in 1913. In fact, Evans turned out to be an even better popularizer than Ouimet because of his outgoing, carefree personality both on and off the course. But most exciting of all, for Pittsburghers, was the fact that the region's first major championship would soon be held at Oakmont—the greatest championship of them all, the U.S. Amateur.

Evans had already come to town to practice at Oakmont, as well as a few other leading courses in the area, and had his eye on winning back-to-back Amateur titles. The WPGA had long felt that, apart from Metropolitan New York and New Jersey, Western Pennsylvania was the most golf-centric region of the United States; now everyone would have a chance to witness that for themselves. The Amateur would also demonstrate that Oakmont was comparable to the most challenging links anywhere in the United States and perhaps the world. The National Intercollegiate Golf Championship had given Pittsburghers just a small taste of the excitement that would come when the world's leading golfers traveled to Oakmont for the 1917 U.S. Amateur.

Pittsburgh's golf enthusiasts were always a bit resentful that the Steel City's leadership in American golf was never fully acknowledged by the elites in New York, Boston, and Philadelphia. The city took great pride in the fact that it had already produced two Amateur champions, Eben Byers (1906) and W. C. Fownes Jr. (1910). And Pittsburghers were ever on the alert for the latest snub; this year it was the New York Metropolitan Golf Association's handicap list. As a rule, Pittsburghers were never included on the MGA's list; the WPGA published its own handicap list, as did the other regional golf societies. But Byers held a club membership at the National Golf Links on Long Island, and he, along with a few other notable golfers who held secondary memberships in New York clubs, usually received an MGA rating. They therefore had been allowed to play in the MGA's annual amateur championship—the most distinguished regional golf championship in the United States. That year, however, the MGA voted to bar all but full-time residents from its rating lists, and to bar them also from its annual championship. Pittsburghers smelled a political rat: "The amendment to the bylaws was framed principally to hit Byers, who about 10 years ago proved runner-up for the New York honor, and Nelson Whitney of New Orleans, whose prowess last season scared the Gothamites."[14]

The MGA's rating system in 1917 was quite stringent. For the previous season, Byers had been rated a 3 by the MGA (Nelson Whitney a 4). The only scratch (0) rating the MGA issued was to Jerry Travers, and the only rating of 1 was issued to Oswald Kirkby (previously a 2), winner of both the MGA and New Jersey amateur championships in 1916. Many in New York viewed Kirkby as second only to Evans at the national level. No other golfer received a rating of 2 from the MGA, and only three golfers received a rating of 3: Max Marston, John Anderson, and Gardiner White. After that, the floodgates opened quite a bit, as seventeen golfers in the New York area were rated at 4.

Interestingly, Dave Herron was among those who in 1916 were given an MGA rating of 4, along with his Princeton compatriot D. C. Corkran. Both earned an MGA rating only because Princeton Golf Club was an MGA member. The MGA's rating was by far the highest recognition that Herron had ever received in national golf circles. Despite failing to qualify for match play at Merion, the nation's most elite regional golfing association still considered him to be among the top twenty-five amateur golfers in the New York metropolitan area.

Soon after, the WPGA secretary, George Ormiston, sent his ratings to the USGA in order to qualify eligible golfers for the 1917 U.S. Amateur at Oakmont. For the first time, rather momentously, Herron was given a scratch handicap (0), which placed him at the same level as Fownes and Byers. Obviously, the WPGA and MGA lists were not truly comparable; no one would place Fownes or Byers or Herron at the exalted level of Travers or Kirkby (or, for that matter, Evans or Ouimet, each of whom was rated by his own regional golf association). But within Pittsburgh, Herron's great season at Princeton and during the summer of 1916—excluding his failure to qualify for match play at Merion—merited him this formal recognition as equal to Oakmont's finest.[15]

Alas, everyone's high hopes for the 1917 golf season in Western Pennsylvania were dashed when President Woodrow Wilson asked Congress for a declaration of war against Germany on April 2. The United States officially made Germany its enemy a few days later, and the entire American golf world—as had happened three years earlier in the United Kingdom—turned topsy-turvy. Both the USGA and the United States Tennis Association (USTA) sought guidance from the War Department about whether it would be appropriate to stage their national championships while the nation was at war. In general, athletics for building strong youth were given the federal government's imprimatur, but the USGA and USTA, representing the two highest-profile sports linked to social elites, quickly came to the conclusion that holding their national championships during wartime would be perceived as unpatriotic (and elitist) by the general public.

Until late April, Pittsburghers nursed a faint hope that the USGA would still hold the scheduled U.S. Amateur at Oakmont, just later in the summer of 1917, because, they rationalized, most of the nation's top golfers were too old for inclusion in a military draft. "Conscription would deal a staggering blow" to football, track, rowing, and other intercollegiate sports aimed at men in their late teens and early twenties "who would be subject to draft in case of conscription," pundits argued, "whereas golf would go almost untouched." Some also contended that golf would render a major public service by keeping "middle-aged men in good physical condition should it be necessary to call upon them for service later in the war. Golf serves to bring business and professional men out of their offices into open air." Whatever the merits of these arguments, the USGA decided not to take a chance on the game's long-term public reputation. In the name of patriotism, it canceled the U.S. Amateur, U.S. Open, and other golf championships it sponsored for the duration of the war.[16]

The USGA had made its decision, but what about competitive golf at the local level? The WPGA continued planning its usual regional championships for the summer of 1917. At the same time, in what appeared to be mainly a symbolic gesture, three acres of the Pittsburgh Field Club were given over to raising chickens and growing potatoes, corn, and other crops "to help solve the food problem of the country." But "agitation" soon bubbled to the surface throughout the region "in favor of abandoning the first league matches." In this confused moment, regional golf leaders still found time to argue publicly about smaller matters, for example, whether competitive parity among the clubs could be maintained now that Crookston and Richard C. Long, two of the top players at Stanton Heights, had switched club allegiances to Oakmont.[17]

As late as the end of May, some Pittsburghers still believed that the USGA would allow Oakmont to host the 1917 Amateur: "Because of the war clouds it seems probable that the actual battle for championship honors may be postponed to 1918, but it is not unlikely that an August [1917] tournament will be held at Oakmont on the dates previously chosen, unless the war should take on grave aspects for America."[18] The *Pittsburgh Sunday Post* continued to boost

Pittsburgh as an epicenter of American golf, claiming that apart from New York, only Chicago compared "favorably" in "golfing levels" with Pittsburgh. Bashing Philadelphia was standard hype for Pittsburgh's sports press, but the *Pittsburgh Sunday Post* still granted that, as a whole, the Keystone State "has no counterpart the world over."

Oakmont, of course, stood out especially in the booster rhetoric for Pittsburgh. It was "one of a half dozen giants among the country clubs that new conditions have brought into being within a decade . . . no other American courses seem as interesting just now." H. C. Fownes, the argument went, had dared to be radically different in 1903 by extending the course's length to over 6,000 yards, a move for which he was roundly condemned in some golf quarters at the time. But Fownes was prescient: 6,500 yards or more had become the new standard for championship play by the late 1910s, and the Fowneses were lionized as pioneers in raising the standard for excellence at the championship level.[19]

The historical record is unclear about how often Princeton's or other college golf teams actually competed in spring 1917. America entered the war in early April, shortly before the formal college golf season usually began. The *Daily Princetonian*, the highly detailed student newspaper, contains no mention of the team having competed at all in 1917 (nor is a 1917 yearbook available to otherwise record the team's activities). No doubt the Princeton team practiced at its local club, which is walkable from campus, and the members surely competed against one another in intra-team matches. But formal intercollegiate matches, or even a match between Princeton and nearby Trenton Golf Club (the team's only loss in spring 1916), may not have occurred. Throughout the country, war and golf were not considered a good political mix, especially in the first few months. The entire college spring golf season may have been canceled due to public (and USGA) ambivalence about golf as a wartime sport.

By the time Dave returned home to Pittsburgh in June, the USGA had officially canceled the 1917 U.S. Amateur, with the understanding that it would be held sometime in 1918 if the war was over by then. The decision to cancel the National Intercollegiate Golf Championship—which Dave, as captain-designate of the 1917–1918 Princeton golf team, was surely looking forward to—was also finalized around this time. Throughout the country regional golf associations and individual clubs began to sponsor "patriotic" matches of various kinds during the summer, often with the participation of well-known amateurs and professionals, in order to raise money to assist the war effort.

From the start of the war, Pittsburgh golfers were determined to put their patriotism on full display. They eagerly promised to raise more money via these patriotic tournaments (to subsidize the Red Cross and other war-related charities) than just about any other city, and some evidence suggests that they were successful. At the same time, in the interest of wartime frugality, the tournament sponsors eliminated the expensive cups and trophies that, along with fancy dances, had been mainstays of early twentieth-century amateur golf.[20]

The first seasonal tournament of note in Western Pennsylvania, the invitation tournament at Allegheny Country Club in June 1917, took the form of a "patriotic tournament," with the Pittsburgh chapter of the American Red Cross as its beneficiary. A fairly extravagant sum, ten dollars, was charged for entry, but many of the entrants—130 in total—contributed much more than that (including many who had no intention of playing). In fact, most of Pittsburgh's best golfers declined to participate in this inaugural patriotic tournament. Dave Herron and Dwight Armstrong stayed away, as did Herron's former Princeton teammate, J. B. Rose, whose family were Allegheny Country Club members.

The reality was that almost no younger golfers showed up, in part because so many of them had enlisted to fight the Germans, but also because those who had not were reluctant to be seen playing golf. "The Allegheny Country club alone has lost 30 of its younger players through enlistments. Even the players yesterday in their journey over the course were brought to the realization that the country is at war by the war gardens scattered over the course. Part of the course is plowed up and planted." Beyond that, America's entry into war had severely dampened local interest in golf. "There is not the enthusiasm of former years, and some of the players who participated yesterday were out on the course for the first time." Even Fownes and Byers declined to play in the tournament, although they doubtless paid the entry fees to enable the event to take place.[21]

Reflecting this dampened interest in the months following America's entry into the war, regional and state golf associations varied in enthusiasm for hosting their customary annual tournaments. In some places it was golf as usual on the local level, albeit with a patriotic overlay, but in other places regular events were quietly canceled. At the WPGA, much enthusiasm remained for continuing on as normal, and for challenging the USGA's decision to discourage formal golf championships during wartime. In early July, building on the welcome given to a recent professional tournament held at Beaver Valley Country Club, the association confirmed its intention to hold both the West Penn Amateur and West Penn Open at the Pittsburgh Field Club. Most of the top players—

Herron as well as Fownes, Byers, Ormiston, Richard C. Long, J. B. Rose, and others—agreed to play.

The *Pittsburgh Post* took this opportunity to single out Herron and Byers. Byers had neglected golf after the war broke out, and his game had definitely suffered. But he started playing seriously again in late June, and by early July he was regularly breaking par at Allegheny Country Club. "He will be a factor in the amateur tournament next week at the Pittsburgh Field Club," the newspaper assured local fans. Of Herron, it said: "If Dave Herron, the Oakmont Country Club youth, enters in the tournament he will have to be reckoned with. There is not a better player in this district than Herron. Of course his play needs tightening up and there are some shots he will have to master, but he is still young and his defects can easily be remedied by hard practice."[22] For all of the hype, however, the WPGA ultimately decided at the last minute to cancel its two major championships. Neither the West Penn Amateur nor the West Penn Open took place in 1917 or 1918.

Later in July 1917, however, Stanton Heights did hold its annual tournament. Though the eighty entrants were significantly fewer in number than those who participated in 1916, the sponsors considered it successful because it helped keep interest in Western Pennsylvanian golf alive and raised significant money to help the troops. Financially, the Pittsburgh area was contributing well more than its share via golf patriotism, having "achieved a record no other city can boast of. To date the contributions amount to more than $9,000, and it is likely this will be exceeded before the close of the season." Plans were in the works for the biggest patriotic tournament of all to be held at Oakmont more or less when the U.S. Amateur had been scheduled in September. And the region's women golfers, though they had canceled their competitive season, were also actively at work to sponsor a benefit tournament of their own.[23]

For all this activity, however, there were fewer and fewer top-level young amateurs competing because most of them—realizing that a draft was in the works by Congress—chose to enlist in the military. By late July 1917, Dwight Armstrong, "one of Pittsburgh's most promising young golfers," was already on active duty in the U.S. Navy. J. B. Rose and P. H. Preston had enlisted in the United States Signal Reserve Corps and were no longer playing as they prepared to leave for training camp.[24] Thus, even the country clubs that wanted to continue hosting events started to cancel them because of the shrinking number of entrants.

Even the young men, such as Dave Herron, who did not enlist gave up playing—perhaps out of a sense of shame and a desire to be inconspicuous as one of the few young men not fighting in the war. Herron had tried unsuccessfully to enlist in the armed services, several times, after the war broke out. But although he did not look particularly heavy or out of shape in his golf team photos in 1916, he apparently gained significant weight afterward, or at least was too heavy to meet the strict physical fitness enlistment standards in effect in 1917. He tried to follow Dwight Armstrong into the navy "but was rejected on account of his excessive weight." Before that, "he tried for the officers' reserve corps, but was rejected on account of his age, being only 19 years old." Thus Herron, even though he was still living in Pittsburgh during the summer of 1917 and free of military obligation, was "playing little golf this season." He did not even play in Oakmont's regular intraclub events, though his older brother Andrew and father did. However, the *Pittsburgh Sunday Post* assured its patriotic golf fans that Dave Herron "has not abandoned hope of entering the service."[25]

Rejection by the armed services stung Herron deeply. After all, he was the most prominent athlete among his friends, and he very much wanted to fight for his country, yet no branch of the military would accept him because of his weight. As the summer progressed, he continued to be a no-show in Oakmont events—just at the time that his game reached a new level of excellence and recognition from the MGA and WGA. Although Congress was now putting in place a draft, he already knew that he would not be able to pass the physical examination, so he had no choice but to return to Princeton for his senior year in the fall, without even the Intercollegiate Championship to look forward to. Whether there would be a college golf season in 1917–1918 at all was questionable, but Herron was selected as Princeton's team captain regardless.

Perhaps out of a sense of duty toward his teammates, he finally played in a single-round tournament at Oakmont in late summer, shooting a respectable round of 82. Meanwhile, the summer golf season of 1917 dragged to a quiet close, and only two of the usual invitation tournaments—at Allegheny and Stanton Heights—were played. Herron did not play in either of these tournaments, nor did more than a handful of the top players in the region. These were fundraisers, pure and simple, not truly competitive golf events as in the past. "The war played havoc with golf this year," observed the *Pittsburgh Sunday Post*, "and what looked as if it was going to be a big year for golf turned out to be a poor one."[26]

After Herron returned to school and began playing regularly at Princeton Golf Club, he quickly returned to form. In early October, he set a new course record of 72, beating the prior record of his former teammate and Oakmonter, Grant Peacock, by one stroke. A couple of weeks later, on the same course, he won the club's President's Cup for the third time in four tries. The student newspaper called special attention to his drive of 280 yards on one hole—suggesting that he was a bigger and stronger person than in his freshman and sophomore years, and he was also getting longer off the tee. And to cap his improvised fall golf season, he traveled to the Jersey Shore in late October 1917 to play in the Atlantic City Invitation. After finishing second in the medal competition, he won the tournament on a course he'd never played before. Thus, even without a National Intercollegiate Championship in which to prove his merits, he showed that he was a worthy captain and the dominant player on the Princeton golf team. He was scoring lower than ever before on the Eastern courses and, within his limited range of opportunity, was starting to win local tournaments with some regularity.[27]

Thankfully, for the sake of the many avid golfers still in Pittsburgh, plans finally took shape in early October 1917 to bring Chick Evans and Ned Sawyer from Chicago to square off against two local professionals, Charlie Rowe of Oakmont and Peter O'Hara of the Field Club, to play a match at the Field Club that would hopefully raise substantial funds for wartime charities.[28] Of course, this was not nearly the event everyone hoped it would be; the original plan was to bring in Francis Ouimet to play against Chick Evans, which Ouimet had agreed to do but could not in the end because he had already been drafted and was called to training camp before his scheduled date in Pittsburgh.

Nevertheless, Evans and Sawyer were big names in early twentieth-century golf, and while their appearance could not hope to match the previous big golf exhibition in Pittsburgh—when Vardon and Ray lost to Fownes and Byers in 1913—the exhibition would help keep golf enthusiasm alive in Western Pennsylvania. "The appearance of the distinguished players will ring down the curtain on one of the most apathetic golf seasons in many years. If the sport is to flourish here something must be done next season to remedy conditions such as existed during the present season."[29] Pittsburghers were elated that Evans conducted himself in a joyful and gregarious manner during his exhibition match, making "such a hit with the gallery that there was immediate agitation for a second appearance here."[30]

However, in another great blow to Pittsburgh golf, Oakmont lost its greenkeeper, Emil Loeffler Jr., to the U.S. Army. The *Pittsburgh Sunday Post*, recognizing that Loeffler was, in fact, "one of the best professionals in the vicinity" (indeed, he had turned down offers from other clubs to become their professional instead of Oakmont's greenkeeper), emphasized just how vital Loeffler was to refining the course to host a U.S. Amateur.

> His departure will be a distinct loss to the Oakmont club, and the excellence there will be a monument to him as a greenskeeper [*sic*].... For several years he had been working to get the course in condition for the national amateur championship and was about to have his ambition realized... when it was called off on account of the war.... There is not a better kept course in the United States than the Hulton course, and many of the improvements that have been made on the links in recent years have been under his supervision.[31]

Though Loeffler had already left for training camp when the good news arrived, he was doubtless happy to learn that the USGA had formally committed to holding the next Amateur at Oakmont—in 1918, or 1919, or 1920, whenever the war was finally over.[32]

Spokesmen for golf in Pittsburgh and many other cities spent much of the winter of 1917–1918 wringing their hands over the terrible malaise in American golf after so many years of rapid advance. That "the past season saw a remarkable decrease in interest in the golfing game" because of the war was undeniable, but had the USGA made the right moves in canceling all the major championships? After all, the Western Golf Association had ignored the USGA's request and continued to encourage many more formal golf competitions than in the East. Who was in the right?

> At the first the plan of calling off all championships struck all golfers as a patriotic move, a move that showed respect for the boys in khaki, but as the season grew older and the other side of the move became broader, many golfers openly expressed the opinion that the action was unnecessary and a blow at the great Scotch game. It was argued that, instead of calling off all championships, they should have been played, if for no other reasons than to divert the minds of the people, temporarily from the pressing problems of the day, and thus prepare them for the battles when they came.
>
> But, on the other hand, it was also argued that to continue championships during the war was to deprive the golfers who had enlisted of a chance to display their prowess. And that is just how the matter now stands. Some golfers figure that another season like the one that is passing will be a great blow at the foundations of the game, and argue that the first action of the United States Golf Association at its next annual meeting should be to rescind the action of the last meeting in calling off championships for the duration of the war, thus enlivening the game.... There will be considerable opposition to a like move next spring, the events of the past summer to be used as an argument.[33]

Obviously, the future of wartime golf in Western Pennsylvania remained uncertain.

▶ CHAPTER 7

BECOMING A CELEBRITY
BOB JONES AND THE RED CROSS CIRCUIT

Bob Jones's regional tournament victories in 1915 and 1916, in addition to his Georgia State Amateur title, had established this newly minted teenager as one of the very best golfers of the South. And besides bringing his name to national light, his stunning play at Merion solidified his celebrity status in the national press at the ripe age of fourteen. Unlike Dave Herron, however, the war did not bring Jones's career to a screeching halt. In fact, quite the opposite: golf's wartime hiatus provided him an unprecedented opportunity to play one-on-one against the top professionals and amateurs in the United States and beyond. As the war progressed, so did Bob's skill set, competitive experience, and celebrity profile.

The 1917 Southern Amateur, which was held as scheduled, was "about the only fixture of any importance that got itself played in the first war-year," Jones (with his co-author, O. B. Keeler) contended years later in *Down the Fairway*.[1] That is, in the South. Jones and Keeler were understandably not keen to mention the considerably more prestigious Western Amateur Championship, which was held in Chicago a month after the Southern Amateur. Both Bob Jones and Perry Adair finished far behind the qualifying medalist and lost in the first round.[2]

Despite the wartime ambivalence toward golf, the Birmingham press proudly heralded the Southern Amateur (and the city's premier venue, Roebuck Golf and Automobile Club) since it was the first time the city had hosted the region's most important championship. Headliners included Nelson Whitney and returning champion Reuben Bush of New Orleans, "The Commodore" Bryan Heard from Texas, and C. L. Dexter, the winner of the 1915 Southern Amateur at East Lake. Among the "list of noted Southern golf celebrities," the *Birmingham News* pointed out that there was a large delegation from Atlanta—a veritable "bee-hive of golfers"—that included "Bob Jones, Sr. and Jr.," George and Perry Adair, Tom Prescott, Victor Smith, and C. V. Rainwater.[3] Columnist Henry Vance highlighted Bob Jr.'s and Perry's youth. "Perry and Bob Jones found it easy to break away from Atlanta on [draft] registration day as neither are old

Bob Jones finishes his swing in perfect balance, circa 1917. Wikimedia Commons.

enough to register. In fact, these two wizards of the R. and A. game should be in the boy scout movement, instead of the trenches in Europe."[4]

Meanwhile, the *Birmingham Age-Herald*, the local competing newspaper, also celebrated the presence of the "cream of the game's production in the south."[5] But the *Age-Herald* seemed to favor Nelson Whitney and featured a drawing of him surrounded by smiling cartoon facsimiles that displayed his achievements. "It wuz a cinch!" one of the caricatures of Whitney proclaimed regarding his first Southern Amateur title in 1907. Since then, Whitney had been crowned a Southern Amateur champion three more times, winning the title again in 1908 and back-to-back in 1913 and 1914.[6]

In spite of the war, the *Birmingham News* promised the Southern Amateur would bring to the city "the greatest assemblage of golfing talent ever assembled south of the Mason and Dixon Line" and "the biggest golf-week, in fact, the old town has ever enjoyed."[7] Accordingly, officials at Roebuck busied themselves with making sure their club was in prime condition. Noting that workmen had been fine-tuning the greens for two weeks leading up to the championship, the paper stated: "The Roebuck course is in better shape than it has ever been and this is saying a great deal for it has long been recognized as one of the best in the South."[8] The Roebuck club also worked hard to ensure that Birmingham itself would be enjoyable for the influx of out-of-town visitors and ready for the "galaxy of stars" the city was excited to show off.[9]

"A number of new faces are seen about the clubhouse, men that are getting their baptism of fire in the Southern, and it may be that the tourney this year will bring surprises," the *Atlanta Georgian* reported. But "the wise men around the clubhouse" were predicting that the final would be between one of "Atlanta's terrible infants"—Bob Jones or Perry Adair—and Reuben Bush.[10]

In a practice round on Sunday, Jones scored a 74, one stroke off the amateur record set in the fall of 1916 by Chick Evans. "The performance of Young Jones," commented the *Birmingham Age-Herald*, "caused many of the local colony to believe that the Atlanta lad will cop the honors in the tourney. His play shows a great improvement since he was last seen in action here in 1915, when he won an invitation tourney at Roebuck."[11]

A generously estimated 150 golfers made their way around the Roebuck golf course the next day, including Bob Jones, his father, Perry Adair, and George Adair.[12] Young Bob and Perry played a foursome match against Reuben Bush and Louis Jacoby, soundly defeating the reigning title-holder and Jacoby, 4 and 2.[13] And for best ball, the two teens shot 71 to Jacoby and Bush's 75.[14] Fred Bodeker of the *Birmingham Age-Herald*, calling Jones's play "of the sensational variety," reported that veteran golfers thought he "would have no trouble in winning the title should he perform throughout the tourney as he did" throughout the practice rounds.[15] Jones's place as frontrunner was cemented by Southern Golf Association President Smith's disheartening announcement that although Nelson Whitney had traveled to Roebuck and even turned in a card for Sunday's practice rounds, he had formally withdrawn from the event at the last second "due to business obligations" in New York.[16]

Despite the loss of Whitney, galleries still turned out to see Jones in action. The first official day of the championship "was a perfect day for golf and the entries hit the course at Roebuck in the best of spirits."[17] The pairing of Jones and Heard drew the largest gallery after the *Birmingham News* published side-by-side photos of them under the title "The Youngest and Oldest Men in Golf Tourney Are Meeting Today."[18] Jones played well and advanced to the championship flight along with ten other Atlantans—Atlanta was "even better represented than Birmingham."[19]

On the first day of match play, Jones easily beat two Birmingham players by lopsided scores of 7 and 6. Adair also "trimmed" his opponents. "Shining as bright and somewhat particular stars of the first day of elimination play were Perry Adair and young 'Bob' Jones, both playing like champions," the *Atlanta Georgian* reported, "and neither apparently worried in the slightest by the huge and often demonstrative galleries that followed the matches in which they took part."[20] But if spectators were not a concern, the weather was. Competitors had complained since the championship began that the hard-baked surfaces were causing their balls to roll unpredictably into unexpected places at unexpected speeds. The hard fairways exacerbated Adair's erratic driving, and his putting form was off, too, such that in the second round, he fell to C. H. Munger of Dallas on the sixteenth hole. Meanwhile, Jones annihilated a local favorite and moved immediately into the quarterfinals against Reuben Bush, the defending champion.

A sizeable gallery quickly developed to watch Jones and Bush tee off. Bush had handily won his match earlier in the day, but against Jones his putting—always the suspect part of his game—deteriorated in the afternoon, and he missed one short putt after another. In contrast, wrote the *Atlanta Constitution*, Jones's performance remained "remarkably consistent and the ordeal of facing the champion failed to waver him."[21] Similar to how the Pittsburgh press emphasized Dave Herron's imperturbability, Southern reporters highlighted Jones's nonchalant attitude when competing head-to head against proven veterans. The match was decided on the sixteenth hole, with Jones winning, 3 and 2.[22]

The golf writers who had skeptically viewed Jones's performance at Merion as "a flash in the pan" were forever silenced by his victory over Bush. "Had the same gentlemen witnessed 'Little Bob's' triumph over Reuben Bush, of New Orleans, title holder of the South . . . they would have wondered where they got that 'flash' stuff," the *Atlanta Georgian* wrote under a bold title: "Bob Seen as Sure Champion."[23] More clearly than ever before, Perry Adair became Bob Jones's sidekick, not the other way around.

So far, Jones was indeed the standard to beat. He had won his first three matches by large margins and closed out the reigning champion on the sixteenth hole. But his opponent in the thirty-six-hole semifinal match, seventeen-year-old Thomas "Tommie" Wheelock of New Orleans, had handily beaten Jones's father in the opening round and was "the dark horse" of the competition.[24] Not to worry: Bob Jr.

Louis Jacoby, on the left, was a consistent contender in early twentieth-century Southern golf. "Contestants in Today's Title Match," *Atlanta Journal*, 9 June 1917.

quietly went about his business and was 7 up after the morning round.[25] His easy victory set up an intriguing final match between the smooth-swinging fifteen-year-old from Atlanta and the fidgety, crotchety, wily Southern veteran, Louis Jacoby.[26]

Fuzzy Woodruff of the *Atlanta Georgian* threw caution to the wind in predicting an easy win for Jones: "If Bob Jones doesn't win the championship of the South over the golf course of the Roebuck Club at Birmingham today, then Wilson isn't President and Roosevelt isn't anxious to fight, and Bryan is."[27] The noted New York amateur John G. Anderson, writing for *Golf Illustrated*, felt that revenge would be sufficient motivation to spur Bob to victory. "Youth as a general thing keeps in mind the defeats registered[,] and perhaps the previous beating given to Jones by Jacoby was in the latter's mind when he started off on the first few holes of the thirty-six-hole final," Anderson mused.²⁸ He was referencing Jones's and Jacoby's "feature match" earlier in the year at the Druid Hills Invitation in Atlanta, where Jacoby had triumphed over Bob.²⁹

The weather during the championship match was wild: gusts of wind in "almost hurricane proportions" and "driving, blinding rain." Jacoby and Jones made it to the sixteenth hole, only to be forced to seek shelter after hitting their drives until the rain let up. When play resumed, the torrential downpour had washed away Jacoby's ball. Jones told his competitor to just drop another, but the disruption may have affected Jacoby's concentration. By the end of the morning round, Jones held a 5-up lead and "there wasn't a man or a woman or child in the great gallery that followed the play who didn't see victory perched on the banner of the Georgia youngster."³⁰

Birmingham sportswriter Henry Vance wrote a column earlier in the week about Jones's strict tournament regimen. "One of the secrets of young Bob Jones' success is this: Bob never tires of golf and is never idle a moment during a tournament. When he gets in from the morning round he takes a light lunch, goes on the green, and practices putting until time for the start of his next match."³¹ This was not the case before his match with Jacoby, though. As Jones would write years later about his not-so-light lunch: "According to my stupid juvenile custom, I filled my system with pie-a-la-mode at luncheon, toddled out on the course in a semi-comatose condition from a superabundance of calories, and proceeded to lose the first three holes of the afternoon round."³²

Despite his food-induced stupor, Jones maintained his lead and won the fourth hole in spectacular fashion, scoring a tap-in birdie two after rifling an iron that hit the flagstick.³³ Throughout the match, he "displayed the sangfroid and the modest demeanor that won for him reams of praise from Eastern experts and players." This was in sharp contrast to the "snappy, tense and highly strung game" played by Jacoby, whose jittery manner and severely crouched stance made the game look like a painful burden. "The boy's game was more than wonderful—it was a revelation. No such golf was ever played here before," claimed the *Birmingham Age-Herald*.³⁴ As Frank P. Glass frankly put it, Jacoby was "simply outclassed in every department of the game" to the tune of the score, 6 and 5.³⁵

Breaking "the monopoly that New Orleans players have been having on the title for years," Bob Jones was only the second Atlanta golfer in seventeen years to capture the Southern Amateur.³⁶ When he sank the putt that won, loud cheers broke out from the gallery and Jacoby congratulated Bob with a warm handshake. "Whereupon Bobby," the *Atlanta Georgian* reported, "grinned a shy sort of grin, said 'Much obliged,' and looked exceedingly pleased and uncomfortable." However, even before Jacoby could shake his hand, someone else got to him first.

> The champion's mother isn't a strong woman, nor a large one. In fact, she looks to weigh only about 105, but she was watching her son at every tee, through every fairway and on every green. She didn't miss a shot, and when that putt on the fourteenth said "ker-plunk," as it announced the birth of a new champion, the little woman forgot everything else, and, as swift as a swallow, sped across the green, and gathered her son into her arms, kissing him squarely on the mouth, and Little Bob, red and sheepish, grinned.[37]

The *Birmingham News* reused a photo of Bob the newspaper had printed earlier in the week for its Sunday edition—Perry Adair had been in the original, but he was cropped out to leave just a headshot of Jones, smiling and wearing a natty bowtie. The Southern Amateur was symbolically important: it was Jones's first regional title. Reminiscent of his lament that he was a failure at age thirteen because he hadn't yet won anything, his later recollection of this important victory in Birmingham emphasized luck and how erratically he had played, not the outstanding performance that onlookers witnessed: "Still I was playing golf, and not learning anything about the game. I remember I had lost control of my pitches at Roebuck, and couldn't make them bite and sit down, so I just accepted it as a visitation of Providence or something and went on trying to chip back close enough to hole a putt."[38] Even when he was beating opponents by wide margins, fifteen-year-old Bob always found fault with his game.

Up North, the *Chicago Daily Tribune* excitedly announced after Jones's victory that Chicagoans would soon have the opportunity to see Jones and Adair in action on "western" turf. As the war continued and the media drummed up nationalist support for the boys across the ocean, enthusiasm for golf naturally began to wane, making star athletes more important than ever to attract galleries to local exhibitions and tournaments. "Flossmoor Country club golfers have arranged one of the banner Red Cross events of the local season for next Sunday afternoon, when Bob Jones and Perry Adair of Atlanta, Ga., will meet Champion Charles Evans Jr. of Edgewater and Warren K. Wood of Flossmoor in a fourball match at eighteen holes." Jones, the newspaper wrote, "is probably the most phenomenal golfer of his age the game has seen."[39]

The Chicago press ran several articles about Jones in order to increase anticipation for the event, such as "Some Kid! Fifteen Year Old Boy, in Golfing Limelight, Is coming to Chicago to Play." "Jones is the most forceful player of his age in the world and in the amateur championship at Merion made one drive of 350 yards," the *Chicago Daily Tribune* claimed.[40] Opposing the young golfers from Atlanta was Chicago's own formidable local talent. Chicagoan Warren Wood had won the North and South Amateur in 1906, won the Western Amateur in 1913, and was the runner-up (to W. C. Fownes Jr.) at the 1910 U.S. Amateur. However, in a surprise twist, Wood's nephew suddenly passed away and Wood could not play on Sunday.[41] Luckily for organizers, no less a star than two-time U.S. amateur champion Robert Gardner, who had beaten Bob Jones in the quarterfinals at Merion, replaced him.

Since Jones was totally unfamiliar with the Chicago area, he and Adair practiced at the South Shore Country Club on the morning they arrived, then played another practice round at Flossmoor in the afternoon. Both boys played exceptionally well, with the golfing press observing every stroke. The *Chicago Daily Tribune* observed that "the boys should give Evans and Gardner a fine match."[42]

By all accounts, they did; the match was a total success, with one caveat. Chick Evans wrote, "The Atlanta boys were a great magnet for the golf fans," drawing an estimated 2,500 spectators and raising the considerable sum of $1,000 to benefit the Red Cross.[43] Unfortunately, some fans became unruly and compromised the golfers' ability to play their best. As Joe Davis semi-joked, "The gallery moved in open skirmishing order, occasionally breaking into a gallop. Several trenches were captured and at the short seventh water hole a war scribe slipped and sprained his elbow, the injury putting him out of commission."[44]

As for the caliber of play, "The Southerners started out as if to make a record," winning the opening two holes with birdies, but those were the only holes that Jones and Adair won. "Their best ball count of 40-41-81," commented Davis, "indicates they were not going too well." In the end, "Chicago's two Brobdingnagian golfers, Charles Evans Jr. and Robert A. Gardner, proved too strong a combination for the invading midgets from Atlanta, Bobby Jones and Perry Adair."[45]

The next major competition that Jones and Adair played was the 1917 Western Amateur, which had been mired in controversy from the beginning of the year, when the Western Golf Association rejected the USGA's redefinition of amateur status. The USGA had earlier voted to restrict amateur status to exclude anyone who "engag[ed] in any business connected with the game of golf wherein one's usefulness or profits arise because of skill or prominence in the game of golf." This decision barred Francis Ouimet, who co-owned a

Chicago Tribune, 18 June 1917.

From left: Robert Gardner, Chick Evans, Perry Adair, and Bob Jones. Photo International, "Here Are the 'Big Four' of Golfing World Crack Amateurs as They Looked at Chicago," *Atlanta Georgian*, 26 June 1917.

sporting goods shop, from amateur competition until further notice. Now, the USGA had expanded its ban to include course architects and consultants as well, which meant that Walter J. Travis was also considered a professional, even though neither he nor Ouimet, two of the best golfers in the world, played golf for a living.[46]

The Western Golf Association felt these decisions were unfair to Ouimet, Travis, and to the game itself. Charles Thompson, the president of the WGA in 1917, said on record, "Personally, I am not in accord with the amateur ruling of the United States Golf Association. I think it hits a number of players who [are] amateurs in spirit and action, even if earning their living in sporting goods establishments."[47] In the end, the WGA voted against adopting the USGA's new rules regarding amateur status and, just to make clear where the WGA stood on the issue, invited Ouimet to play in the Western Amateur.

Of course, Ouimet was grateful for the invitation, but he also wasn't going to let his disbarment by the USGA stand without a fight. On June 18, 1917, he and his business partner John Sullivan submitted a request to the USGA to be reinstated as amateurs. Before the USGA executive committee, Ouimet presented proof that he had turned down offers that would have benefited him financially, produced affidavits detailing his duties and salary as a Wright & Ditson employee, and demonstrated how golf would be less than a quarter of the Ouimet & Sullivan store business for the next year. "The committee intimated that if Ouimet and Sullivan would eliminate golf from their business they might be reinstated," reported the *New York Times*. "Neither of the partners has any present intention of eliminating golf from their business, and neither believes that it is any crime against amateurism to retain that branch of supplies."[48]

In a unanimous vote, the members of the USGA's executive committee rejected Ouimet's application for reinstatement. Ouimet, "by many considered as the greatest golfer of the world," hadn't played in a major championship since. In securing his entry into the 1917 Western Amateur, the *New York Times* wrote, the WGA "has played a trump card."[49]

This was all happening at a time when many golf associations were canceling their championships all together, but the WGA decided to stay its course because golf, WGA President Thompson argued, kept men "pleasantly and perpetually prepared."[50] Of course, the WGA received an onslaught of criticism for defying the USGA and holding a regional championship despite the international situation. Try though Thompson did, it was impossible to deny that an actual title was being played for—it was not just a Red Cross fundraiser.[51] In fact, there was such an uproar that Thompson felt the need to release an article in the August edition of *Golfers Magazine* titled "The Reason for the Western Championship." Thompson cited President Woodrow Wilson's hope "that sports would continue as far as possible" during the war and revealed how the WGA had donated entry fees and additional money to the Red Cross.[52] And the prizes, he assured the public, would be limited to bronze war medals.[53]

Not satisfied with stirring up the golf world by holding a prestigious championship during wartime or rejecting the USGA's rule change or inviting a professional (i.e., Ouimet) to an amateur championship in order to snub the USGA, the organizers of the Western Amateur also invited several golfers from other regional associations whose organizations had canceled their own championships. These invitations were highly unusual—"the first time in history of the WGA [that] Easterners were invited to enter"—and highly controversial, too, as the prerogative of assembling a national field had traditionally been reserved for the USGA's annual championships.[54] But the USGA had canceled its events, so the WGA seized the opportunity to strengthen its own championship field, which now included Francis Ouimet, John G. Anderson of New York, and Jesse Guilford of Massachusetts. Ironically, Heinrich Schmidt, the Western Amateur's defending champion, could not defend his title as he had already enlisted for military service.[55]

And yet, the WGA was not yet finished upending tradition. In late May, a little over a month before the Western Amateur began, the WGA abolished "stymies." "The new rule," as the *New York Times* reported, "upsets one of the cardinal rules of the ancient Scottish game by providing that the ball nearest the hole shall be played first when both balls are on the putting green," Apparently, the WGA's president, Charles Thompson, did not consult any of golf's other governing bodies before instituting the change, even though it affected how competitive golf was played in "three-quarters of the United States and all of Canada."[56] Essentially, the Western Golf Association had gone rogue.

Despite the flack (especially from Eastern golfers) that the WGA continued to receive, the *New York Times* believed the Western Amateur Championship would be "the banner event of the golfing year," especially considering that there were "no other events of like nature" during 1917. "If not in name," the newspaper wrote, "it [the Western Amateur] is in fact comparable this year to the late lamented [U.S.] amateur championship." Since Bob Jones's national debut at Merion, the national press had more reason to look below the Mason-Dixon Line and was keen to comment on the caliber of competition that Jones grew up playing around and against. "There are going to be many contestants who will try [Ouimet's] skill to the utmost," the *Times* commented. "For instance, Bobby Jones, the sensation of a year ago, is on his way from Atlanta, accompanied by a formidable array of golfing talent. Among the others, most of them youngsters of pronounced skill like Jones, are Perry Adair, Tom Prescott, and Richard Hickey."[57]

Although the press declared that the field in Chicago would be rich with decorated players, there were certainly some notable absences. "The West will be represented by a galaxy of stars, even though Bob Gardner and Chick Evans will not compete. Just what influences have been brought to bear so that these two will not play in a tournament within their own city is not quite clear," wrote the *New York Times*.[58] An examination of other publications illuminates why they were absent: World War I! *Golf Illustrated* had published a picture of Robert Gardner the month before in its July 1917 edition with the accompanying caption: "Robert A. Gardner: Will enter officer's training camp next month." And Chick Evans explained in a later book that "when, in the spring of 1917, war was declared with Germany, the national tournaments were postponed. I at once announced that I would enter no tournaments and play no public golf except 'for the benefit of the Red Cross.'"[59]

The *Atlanta Constitution*, unsurprisingly, predicted a strong Southern showing. "While most of the local and out-of-town clubs had several representatives in the tournament, it was noticeable that none of them was able to maintain the cohesion of the Georgia players. Oracles of the game predict that a Southern golfer will reach the penultimate, if not the final round."[60]

Alas, it was not meant to be. Bob Jones succumbed in his first-round match to the Midwestern ace D. E. "Ned" Sawyer, the defending Western Amateur champion.[61] Jones scored well, despite errant tee shots that often landed in bunkers, but Sawyer's ball-striking from tee to green was pristine; the *Los Angeles Times* went so far as to call it "the best golf of the first round."[62] In fact, to everyone's surprise, none of the Georgia delegation survived the first round of match play. But in the end no one was disappointed as Francis Ouimet claimed the title after an exciting 1-up victory (giving rise to the *Los Angeles Times*'s tongue-in-cheek headline: "Francis Ouimet, Professional, Captures the Amateur Championship").

The newly minted champion called special attention to the excellence of Jones's performance in Chicago. "The Southern quartet," Ouimet wrote in *Golf Illustrated*, "landed nicely in, though Bobby should have done much better. He had the misfortune of bumping into 'Ned' Sawyer[,] that campaigner with a world of experience and hard-fought matches in back of him. . . . He covered himself with glory however, and forced the stolid Sawyer to produce magnificent golf before he would acknowledge defeat."

The magazine printed a wonderful photograph of the Southern delegation to accompany the championship coverage. The caption read, "The Young Southern Brigade and Their Mentor." George Adair was in the middle of the photo, flanked by Perry Adair on his right, Bob Jones on his left, and Richard Hickey and Tom Prescott on the far right and left, all giving the camera their most take-me-seriously juvenile gazes.[63]

The war added a strange dimension to the 1917 Western Amateur. So far, the war had not really hindered the progress of Jones's game or escalating fame—certainly not like how it had reduced Dave Herron's ability to play competitive golf. Indeed, in the coming months of 1917 and 1918 as well, war relief efforts would significantly advance Jones's celebrity by granting him unique opportunities to compete against some of the most talented golf professionals in the world.

In late July 1917, a few weeks after the Western Amateur, the recently formed Professional Golfers Association (PGA) decided to sponsor a War Relief Fund tournament that proved to be a tremendous success. The tournament had a unique format: four teams—Scottish Professionals, English Professionals, American Professionals, and American Amateurs—competed in a series of team matches at prominent New York and New Jersey golf clubs to raise money for charities that were integral to the war effort. Four-time U.S. Amateur winner Jerome Travers captained the Amateur team, Walter Hagen the American "homebred" professionals, Jock Hutchison the Scottish, and Jim Barnes the English professionals. Each captain not only had to select the men for his team, but also had to place each player hierarchically "in order."[64] Travers picked both Bob Jones and Perry Adair for the elite American Amateurs team.

On July 23 the "leading local feminine exponents of the game"—such as Metropolitan women's champion Mrs. W. A. Gavin and Mrs. Frank Hayes of Great Neck, New York—assisted by "professionals of international reputation," kicked off the first week of war relief competitions with mixed foursomes matches at Englewood Country Club in New Jersey.[65] Figuring that a direct competition between men and women would attract interest and therefore raise more money, the event organizers decided that all contestants, male and female alike, would drive from the same tee (as was still the custom) and play their second shots from whichever ball was better positioned.[66]

The first international team match, held at Baltusrol on July 25, set the tone for the rest of the contest. "No three-ringed circus ever offered as many attractions," commented the *New York Times*, "nor kept its spectators so busy trying to see a part of what was going on as did the opening contests of the international golf team matches."[67] The English Professionals absolutely "swamped" the American Amateurs with mortifying results (at least for the Amateurs): 15 to 1 in the fourball matches and 29 to 12 in the singles.[68] The single point for the Americans in fourball came from the two youngest members of the team, fifteen-year-old Bob Jones and nineteen-year-old Norman Maxwell of Philadelphia, who saved the amateurs from complete annihilation in the morning. "The youngsters approximated 76 after taking four putts on the first green."[69]

The slaughter continued in the afternoon, although the American Amateurs fared better in singles than in the fourball matches. Of particular delight to the spectators, Jerome Travers, "America's most famous amateur . . . returned to local competitions in a blaze of glory" by winning his singles match against the Metropolitan Open champion, Gilbert Nicholls. Jones, who the *New York Times* described as "the youthful Southern amateur champion," triumphed 1 up in his individual match against Cyril Walker of Shackamaxon, "one of England's brightest golf stars."[70] Interestingly, Walker won the first three holes from Jones, and then, Jones later recalled, "my temper came to my rescue." He "won five of the next six holes of that crazy match."[71] Even though Walker played an excellent nine holes on the way back—he shot an estimated 38—"the Atlanta wonder refused to be shook loose."[72]

For the matches at Baltusrol, Jones was listed as No. 6 for the amateur team, wedged between Norman Maxwell at No. 5 and Perry Adair at No. 7.[73] Team captain Travers's rationale for placing Maxwell ahead of Jones, despite the Atlanta youngster's excellent recent achievements, was that Jones was a title-holder only in the South, whereas Maxwell had won a prestigious multiregional championship, the North and South Amateur.

Two days after the initial four-way contest, the American Amateurs faced off against the Scots while the American Professionals played against their English counterparts at Siwanoy Golf Club in Westchester. For this match, Captain Travers raised Jones and Adair, respectively, to Nos. 5 and 6 and demoted Maxwell to seventh position. Both the amateurs and professionals rewarded the eager and sizeable galleries watching them that day with "exceptional display[s] of golf."[74]

Once again, Bob Jones stood between the amateur team and total disaster. "Jones and Adair Save Amateurs from Golf Rout," read the *Chicago Daily Tribune* headline. Identifying Jones as "the Southern champion" and Adair as "the Atlanta junior," the newspaper wrote that Jones "had the distinction" of finishing 2 up over 1908 U.S. Open champion Fred McLeod while Adair won his match against G. O. Simpson 1 up.[75] The *New York Times* agreed that Jones's score of 76 against McLeod was impressive: "Bobby Jones won everlasting fame by defeating the veteran Fred McLeod of the Columbia Country Club by two holes."[76] The *Atlanta Constitution* proudly reported that its "brilliant young Atlanta pair" had played "as well in the singles as they had done as a team in the foursomes, and had the satisfaction of bringing in the only three points scored by the amateurs."[77] Besides Jones and Adair, however, the American Amateurs were not playing very well. After the match at Siwanoy, the American Professionals were in first place with 89 points. The English and Scots were far behind but neck-and-neck with each other, with 59 and 56 points, respectively. The American Amateurs were in dead last with 24 points.

The week of international matches culminated at Garden City Golf Club, where the American-born professionals further demonstrated their superiority.[78] None of the amateur teams won their foursomes matches against the homebred professionals, including Jones and Adair, who lost by seven holes to Jack Dowling and Emmet French of York, Pennsylvania. It was the worst "match of their association," O. B. Keeler wrote years later about their experience at Garden City: "They were both wild. Bobby would follow a good drive by Perry with a scandalous hook into the deep rough, or, if Perry happened to drive off the fairway, Bobby would spank the ball clear across into trouble on the other side."[79]

Jones, however, alone among the amateurs, managed to win his singles match against French with an estimated score of 77.[80] "The Atlanta boy gained a lot of respect as a fighter and golfer who is always dangerous," commented the *New York Times*. The *Times* also reminded its readers that all the players Jones had faced were "players of rank," and that "the little Southern amateur champion deserves all the credit in the world for his achievement."[81]

Although Travers, a native New Yorker, received by far the most press attention among the amateurs, the week of matches definitively proved that Jones's performance at Merion in 1916 was no fluke. As the greatest golf prodigy in American history, he was swiftly becoming a bona fide celebrity, both inside and outside the sports world. Moreover, the wartime international matches exposed him to several of the premier golf courses in the East, ones that he would return to many times in years to come. Even more importantly, in his view, was that for the first time he "became involved with the pros in earnest."[82] So even though the war had put major amateur as well as professional championships on hiatus, Jones for the first time was able to compete on a regular basis against the top professionals in the world. As a result, his national profile, based on his fast-maturing skills, his fierce competitive mindset, and the reflected glory of the golfers he faced, grew enormously.

Overall, the new competitive format for wartime golf and fundraising proved to be extraordinarily popular. The grand totals, in holes won: Homebreds, 152; Scots, 87; English, 72; Amateurs, 28. Jones and his fellow amateurs were obviously trounced, but he had performed splendidly, reinforcing his "kid wonder" aura and, no less notably, earning the respect of top professionals and amateurs as one of the greatest sports phenoms of all time.

As he acknowledged later, at fifteen years old he did not grasp the political and patriotic ramifications behind his participation in the War Relief Fund tournament. That he was contributing financially or personally to the war effort did not even cross his mind. Instead, from his typically adolescent perspective, he was simply expanding his horizons and having the time of his life: feted at every stop by an adoring public transfixed by his precocity; traveling for free to new and exciting parts of the country; competing regularly against better golf professionals than he had ever seen close-up; and, no doubt, continuing to study the game and learn by observation, just as he had been doing since his first encounters with Stewart Maiden at East Lake.

Bob Jones's and Dave Herron's experiences of the war could not have been more different, and the root of the contrast was the 1916 U.S. Amateur at Merion. Herron's surprise failure to qualify for match play unfortunately ensured that his name was not on the list of amateurs Jerome Travers considered for his War Relief team, whereas Jones's impressive play at Merion against former champions like Eben Byers and Robert Gardner put his name at the top of the list. Few people outside of Pennsylvania knew who Dave Herron was, and that severely limited his wartime opportunities to play in high-profile charity matches; by contrast, Jones's rocketing fame generated numerous prospects for him to compete at the highest levels and cemented his place as the greatest young golfer in the world. Furthermore, Jones was not of age for the military draft, so he (unlike Dave Herron) could play in fundraising exhibitions without any hint of shame. In fact, there was no better way for teenage Bob Jones to contribute to the war effort than playing golf. Dave Herron, in contrast, quietly slipped off the radar and largely put his game on hold until the war was over.

Organized intercollegiate golf, unlike charitable exhibitions, completely fell apart during the war. Indeed, at Princeton University, as of February 1918, there were no concrete plans to field a golf team for the spring season, even though Columbia, Williams, and the University of Pennsylvania had expressed interest in doing so. Yet neither Harvard nor Yale had made a decision, and all that could be said at Princeton was that "if enough interest can be aroused among the colleges," maybe they would hold the National Intercollegiate in the spring.

Alas, these tentative plans were soon canceled; there would be no Intercollegiate Golf Championship in 1918. Beyond that, Princeton appears to have canceled its entire spring golf season (though the team likely still played intrasquad matches). It was, indeed, an unfortunate moment to be captain of one of the nation's two most prestigious college golf teams. And it was, sadly, a lost, last opportunity for Dave Herron, at age twenty, to enhance his profile as Princeton's best golfer and one of the best young players in the nation.[83]

Though disappointed, Herron was a strong all-around athlete, and he bled the Orange and Black. Starting in the latter weeks of fall semester and continuing through the spring, he threw himself into playing on Princeton's other sports teams that were short on men. In the 1917–1918 school year, he joined and regularly competed for three different teams: swimming, water polo, and track. In water polo, he became a mainstay of the team, and his contributions received regular notice in the student newspaper. Herron competed less frequently in track, although he did participate in the famous Penn Relays, and he mainly threw the hammer, a sport in which heft was a valuable asset. By participating in more varied sports, he was likely trying to lose weight and build flexibility and muscle in order to pass the military's physical exam and enlist as soon as he graduated.[84]

But Dave Herron was more than just an athlete; he was also a fine student. He graduated in the normal four years and was singled out at graduation for a literary award—one of two graduates in 1918 to share the Class of 1870 Prize in Olde English. As E. E. Giles would note in 1919, Herron "was not only captain of the golf team at Princeton during his senior year, but he took his proper place up front in his class."[85] His academic achievements suggest that he took seriously the gentlemanly ideal of a liberal education. Beyond that, what seems most to have impressed his fellow students was his personal manner—the calm, kind imperturbability that had also impressed golfers in Pittsburgh. At Princeton, Herron was voted neither the most handsome, wittiest, or "prettiest" among his fellow seniors, nor was he even voted the best senior athlete (not competing in golf during the fall or spring semesters could not have helped). But he was tied for the lead in recognition as Princeton's "Best Natured" graduate—a tag that nicely captured his personality.[86] In the exit information that Herron provided the university, he made clear that he planned, first, to serve his country by entering the "aviation service," and afterward, to make business his profession, just like his father and grandfather had done.

Though he competed in multiple varsity sports in his last semester at Princeton, Herron must have fit golf somewhere into his schedule (Princeton's golf course was near campus) because his game was reasonably good the week after he returned to Pittsburgh. In June 1918, unlike the year before, golfers decided to turn out en masse to compete in the Allegheny Invitation, which was again being conducted under Red Cross auspices. War was the new normal in American life, and sportsmen of all kinds gradually adapted. Vivid reminders of the ongoing conflict were ubiquitous: the U.S. flag hung on the club flagpole above the Allegheny Country Club flag, and the latter was embossed with "80 stars, each representing a member who answered the call to the colors." Parts of the golf course were still planted with "grain, potatoes and garden truck."[87]

At the Allegheny Invitation, Herron tied with Eben Byers at the relatively high score (for Allegheny Country Club) of 156 for the top spot in the medal qualifying rounds.[88] His game got sharper as the week progressed in the unusually tough competitive environment of Western Pennsylvanian golf. After defeating his first opponent in terrible morning weather, he played Byers in a nip-and-tuck afternoon match, their scores improving as the skies cleared and the course dried. Three-down after eight holes, Herron squared the match by the twelfth hole, and then claimed the final two holes to defeat Byers.[89]

The following morning, his opponent was the always difficult J. B. Crookston; Herron won decisively, again under trying weather conditions. The press spotlighted the part of his game that was now receiving much more attention: his raw power and length off the tee. "Conditions favored Herron yesterday. The course, as a result of the rains, was slow and a heavy wind was blowing, giving the advantage to the long player. He was getting as much as 300 yards on his drives, and in playing the long holes he seldom failed to get home with his second shot." He also putted well. His game overall, in every dimension, was "disconcerting to an opponent." With a par on the last hole, his score would have equaled the course's recently lowered par of 72.[90]

In the finals, Herron defeated John Graham of Stanton Heights to win the Allegheny Invitation for the first time. In defeating Graham he continued his exceptional scoring and gave an extraordinary "exhibition of golf. Which in the memory of the gallery followers has never been excelled here in a tournament.... Spectators said there is not a player in the state who could have defeated the kind of golf that Herron played." As usual, "he displayed his imperturbability. As one in the gallery remarked, 'He is a player without nerves.'" The newspaper account concluded: "There is no more popular player than Herron. Despite the fact that he ranks as one of the leading players of the state, he is modest and unassuming in his demeanor."[91] Or, as the Princeton students put it, "best natured."

Apart from playing with his father a week later in "the usual Saturday matches" at Oakmont, Herron's victory in the Allegheny Invitation was his send-off for

On the left is Dave Herron in his marine uniform. On the right are the three Herron boys, each in uniform. Pomeroy had enlisted in the U.S. Navy, Andrew Jr. was a Marine, and Dave was hoping to contribute to the war effort through aviation. Cherry/Herron Family Archives.

military service. Immediately upon graduation from Princeton, he reapplied to serve in the "aviation section of the Navy." Likely thanks to all of the diving, track, and water polo he had played while intercollegiate golf was on hold, he had lost enough weight and gained enough strength to pass the physical exam. He left in early July 1918 for the Naval Aviation Ground School training center at the new Cambridge campus of the Massachusetts Institute of Technology, with the goal of becoming part of the first generation of fighter pilots within the U.S. Marine Corps. The MIT program, though, conducted basic training as well as specialty training, first seeking to whip recruits into superb physical condition before they put themselves in harm's way. Reportedly, after a little over a month's training, Herron had "reduced his avoirdupois 20 pounds."

Herron's golf demeanor, the Pittsburgh press predicted, would serve him well in the U.S. Marines. "Herron has the necessary temperament to be a successful flyer, and he is imperturbable in tight places. The Boches [i.e., the enemy German soldiers] will have no terrors for him."[92]

▶ CHAPTER 8

"AN OPPORTUNITY TO WITNESS THE GAME"
THE NEW SPECTATORS OF WARTIME GOLF

For the men who were either too young or too old to serve in the military—and the women who wanted to participate in some capacity—war relief campaigns provided an excellent vehicle for openly displaying their patriotism. For sports, hosting fundraising exhibitions turned out to be the most politically acceptable way to provide competitive continuity for athletes while avoiding larger controversy. As historian Stephen Lowe has put it, "In exchange for some charity, golf remained on the sports pages and cloaked itself in patriotism, while providing its players an opportunity for competition."[1]

In 1918 the golfing community continued to contribute to the cause by playing in the name of the Red Cross. Prominent New York amateur John Anderson broke "a lifetime rule by consenting to play in Red Cross exhibitions on Sunday," despite the promise he'd made to his mother to never golf on the Sabbath.[2] Not surprisingly, after his 1916 victories in both the U.S. Open and U.S. Amateur, Chick Evans received many more invitations than he could feasibly accept to play in fundraising exhibitions at distinguished clubs. But as far as Evans was concerned, it was every well-known golfer's moral and patriotic duty to serve as a dual ambassador for golf and war relief. Not long after the U.S. declaration of war in April 1917, Evans had submitted plans for a "systematically arranged season of Red Cross golf" to USGA officials, but to his disappointment, the proposal was "tabled." However, the WGA, which Evans approached following the USGA's dismissal, proved more receptive to the idea.

Under the WGA's umbrella, Bob Jones, Chick Evans, Kenneth Edwards, and Warren K. Wood played a well-publicized Red Cross exhibition golf match in Memphis on 18 May 1918. Not only did Jones and Edwards win their doubles match against Wood and Evans, but Jones defeated Evans again in their singles match later in the contest. "Little Bob," reported the *Atlanta Constitution*, "has been playing even better golf this season than last and his accomplishment in defeating Evans 1 up in this match is being heralded by the golfers of the south as a splendid achievement for a golfer of his age."[3] Illustrating the newspaper's point, Jones turned in the low card of the day, a 74, while Evans shot 75, Edwards 76, and Wood 82. Joe Davis was especially excited by the prospect that Jones was growing stronger. "The young Southern champion has added considerably to his weight and no longer looks like a boy player," he wrote.[4]

"Atlanta's three golfing celebrities" arrived in Chicago on July 14, 1918. Bob Jones, Perry Adair, and Alexa Stirling went to Homewood, where they were staying with golfer Elaine Rosenthal.[5] The following day, Adair and Stirling narrowly beat Jones and Rosenthal by one "point." Nonetheless, on the front nine, Jones's driving stood out, "and but for a missed putt [he] would have had a 'perfect 36.'"[6] In Fort Worth, Jones recalled in *Down the Fairway*, "I remember I shot a 70 and broke the course record there."[7] In Kansas City, Jones and Adair were paired against Warren Wood and Chick Evans for an exhibition match benefiting the American Fund for French wounded. A gallery of two thousand spectators watched Jones and Adair lose to Evans and Wood, 5 and 3.[8]

A few days later, in time for July 4, Jones and Adair returned to Atlanta, where the AAC was hosting a WGA Red Cross golf match at East Lake, in addition to a "monster Red Cross parade" and numerous associated festivities.[9] "Atlanta's two boy golf wizards" were scheduled to play against Jimmy Standish and Kenneth Edwards, "two of the greatest of the western golfers."[10] Everyone and anyone was invited to the match: "Atlantans, who have been wanting to see what a golf game was really like, but who were not privileged because they were not members of any of the local clubs, will have an opportunity to witness the game."[11]

The *Atlanta Constitution*'s coverage of the impending match provided an excellent example of how golf as a sport (and golf journalism, too) benefited from the war, and how the spirit of patriotism that infused these exhibitions made golf substantially more popular and accessible to a wider public. Jones and Adair defeated Standish and Edwards in front of an enthusiastic home crowd of two thousand. Jones shot 77, Adair 82, Standish 82, and Edwards 81. Caddying rights were auctioned off, and Jones brought in the highest price: $215.[12] O. B. Keeler particularly recalled that Jones and Adair wore "bright-red Swiss Guard caps somebody had given them in St. Louis, they wore them in all their matches thereafter, until they were lost, and very brilliant and showy I thought they looked."[13]

Later in the month of July, Jones embarked on a more high-stakes and formalized fundraising tour of exhibition matches for the Red Cross with Alexa Stirling, Perry Adair, and Elaine Rosenthal.[14] The oldest of the four players, Rosenthal had come to prominence in 1914 at the U.S. Women's Amateur, where she played admirably in the finals—losing only 1 down as an eighteen-year-old competing in her second national competition. She was also the defending Western Women's Golf champion for 1917.

A year younger than Elaine Rosenthal, Alexa Stirling was the defending 1916 U.S. Women's Amateur champion (having defeated Rosenthal in the quarterfinals). Furthermore, she was deeply involved in relief work—"her best effort," the *Atlanta Constitution* reported, "having been given during the great fire in Atlanta last May, and during the coal famine this winter. Nor does she disdain the gentler service of making surgical dressings, knitting sweaters, and contributing with her violin to relief concerts."[15]

The foursomes' monthlong Eastern tour took them throughout the entire Northeast, from New Jersey to New York, Connecticut, Rhode Island, Massachusetts, Vermont, and back to Pennsylvania between July 17 and August 15, 1918.[16] Chaperoned by Elaine Rosenthal's mother and J. A. Scott, the four "kids," as Bob Jones later recalled, had the time of their young lives, "traveling all over the eastern part of the United States, playing golf almost every day, and being acclaimed as fine young patriots—a phase of the tour which never seemed to register with me. I couldn't see that we were doing anything for our country."

Bob Jones, on the far left, putts while Alexa Stirling, Elaine Rosenthal, and Perry Adair watch. Paul Thompson, "Golf Tourney for the Benefit of the American Red Cross, Montclair, N.J.," 17 July 1918. New York Public Library Special Collections.

Bob Jones "driving over a bunker" at Montclair Country Club in New Jersey. Photo by Paul Thompson. New York Public Library Special Collections.

Jones and his friends were "simply playing golf, which was what we would rather be doing than anything else; visiting new golf courses—having a grand time."[17]

The foursome kicked off their eastern tour at Montclair Golf Club in northern New Jersey, after which they traveled east to Wykagyl Country Club in Westchester County.

Jones and Rosenthal won by 5 points, and Jones had the best medal score, a 77.[18] Soon afterward, at Shennecossett Country Club in New London, Connecticut, Jones shot another 77 and was again low scorer. Emphasizing the ever-widening gap between Jones and Adair, on July 24, Jones and Rosenthal defeated Adair and Stirling by 6 points at Springfield Country Club. Jones shot a remarkable 73.[19]

Rosenthal made headlines in Boston on July 27 for her card of 84, "one of the best ever shot by a woman over the difficult fairways at Brae Burn." She and Adair beat Jones and Stirling by a decisive 12 shots.[20] For whatever reason, Jones's game fell apart at Brae Burn; he shot an embarrassing 87 and his temper flared. Walter Travis's correspondent for New England, going by the pseudonym "Bunker Hill," recounted in the *American Golfer*:

> What made the match especially disappointing was not so much the margin between the pairs as it was the failure of Master Jones to show anything of the quality of golf for which he is famed and his failure to keep under cover a fit of peevishness to which he gave free rein. However, "Bobby" is only a boy, after all, and when those who saw the match at Brae-Burn watch him again, it is to be hoped that they will see him playing the style of game that won him such approbation at Merion and with that sunny, Southern smile that makes him so likeable when he is "good."[21]

The harshest reaction to Jones's "peevishness" came from his playing partner Alexa Stirling, who wrote about the incident at Brae Burn many years later, expressing her feelings of humiliation when Jones blew up: "I wished only that the ground beneath me would open and let me sink from sight." Stirling (nearly five years his senior) chastised Jones after the match for his mortifying display of temper. She recalled, "Later, when I berated him, Bob said, 'I don't give a damn what anybody thinks about me.' After a moment he added, 'I only get mad at myself.' Suddenly I saw him as a 15-year-old boy driven to the demands of perfection he made of himself."[22]

Following Bob Jones's poor play and behavior at Brae Burn, the four young golfers traveled south to Wannomoisett Country Club outside Providence, Rhode Island, where Jones was matched against his hero—still ostracized from the amateur ranks by the USGA—Francis Ouimet. "The Southern boys" beat Ouimet and his business partner, J. H. Sullivan Jr. At least in comparison to Brae Burn, "Master Jones showed a complete reversal of form" and scored an estimated 78 in the afternoon mixed foursome matches. In the *American Golfer*'s opinion, however, Elaine Rosenthal's 80 was the feature of the match, "breaking the women's record of the course and coming within six strokes of the men's record."[23]

After playing in Rhode Island, the traveling youngsters reversed direction and headed north to Vermont. Their destination was Ekwanok, the first golf course designed by Walter Travis, which included a layout and terrain unlike any the Southerners had confronted before. Continuing their pattern of switching partners between tour stops, Jones and Rosenthal defeated Adair and Stirling by 3 points. Jones and Perry both shot 77s, but Elaine Rosenthal was again the star. "Playing from the intermediate men's tees," she scored 86 while Alexa Stirling, finding the course unfamiliar and difficult, shot 92.[24]

Two days later Jones had clearly adjusted to the idiosyncrasies of Ekwanok. "The celebrated 'Bobby' Jones of Atlanta, in playing his farewell round of a three-day visit at the Ekwanok Country Club today, established a record for the course with a card of 71," the *New York Times* reported. His score was four strokes better than the previous course record, held by notable New Jersey amateur Max Marston. And, the *Times* was careful to point out, even though all Red Cross matches were "exhibitions," Jones played Ekwanok from the back tees and holed all of his putts while demolishing the old course record.[25]

In early August 1918, as Jones and Adair began to prepare for their return to college, the four young golfers headed south for charity matches in and around Philadelphia. The quality of Adair's golf picked up, though Stirling's record-setting play continued and she garnered almost as much attention as Jones. Their exhibition match at Essex Country Club in New Jersey raised more than $1,500, proving that the "Dixie Kids," male and female alike, were indeed the kind of national draw the Red Cross had hoped they would be.[26]

Jones and Adair's return to Atlanta in mid-August was reported in the society pages of the *Atlanta Constitution*. The pair was en route "to Greenbrier, White Sulphur Springs, this week to play in a Red Cross match" against Chick Evans and Kenneth Edwards, who they defeated in a nip-and-tuck match in twenty holes, which raised an extraordinary $7,000 for the Red Cross.[27] "Bobby Jones was the chief factor [in victory]," wrote the *Constitution*, "with his phenomenal driving, and he turned in an individual card of 76."[28]

Western Golf Association president Charles F. Thompson, the *American Golfer* reported, "feels highly gratified over the achievements of the western and Southern 'youngsters.' . . . The Red Cross matches in the Middle West have had a stimulating effect on golf and undoubtedly created a much greater interest in the play of the professionals."[29] In addition to the extraordinary fundraising to which Bob Jones had centrally contributed, the Eastern Red Cross tour was incredibly important in expanding his own golf horizons. The tour exposed both Jones and Adair to the courses of the Northeast, where most future national championships would be held. And the exhibition matches were a unique set-up for intensive learning. Jones was already familiar and comfortable with his "competition." He had grown up playing against Adair and Stirling, so instead of focusing on trying to beat them, he could focus fully on trying to beat Old Man Par. To do that, he had to learn to adjust to unfamiliar grasses, topography, bunkering, and hole designs. And throughout the tour he showed yet again, as he had at Merion two years earlier, that he was a lightning-quick study. With the exception of his dismal showing at Brae Burn, he was able to shoot regularly in the 70s and consistently "outplay" his older "kid wonder" counterpart, Perry Adair.

The *American Golfer*'s published list of "Ages of Prominent Golfers," which came out in August 1918, reflected Jones's growing skill and celebrity. "Master 'Bobby' Jones" was, by far, the youngest golfer on the list as a sixteen-year-old. The list incorrectly referred to "Master Perry Adair" as a twenty-year-old, although he had only recently turned nineteen. Regardless, other than the five other golfers in their twenties—Chick Evans, Walter Hagen, Bob Gardner, Jesse Guilford, and Francis Ouimet—the fifty-two "prominent golfers" of the time were all significantly older (thirties and forties) than Jones and Adair.[30] Unsurprisingly, the list did not include Oakmont and Princeton's standout, twenty-year-old Dave Herron.

By the end of August, the "Dixie Kids" tour had come to an end, but Jones's personal golf journey in 1918 was far from over. "I got a telegram from Chick Evans," he later wrote, "saying that Warren Wood, who was to have toured the East with him for the Red Cross, was ill, and asked me to take his place."[31] In mid-September, Evans, with Jones as his partner, kicked off the eastern leg of his Red Cross golf tour with a fourball match at Baltusrol. "The Chicago wizard," paired with "the boy wonder," was "largely responsible for his side" defeating Max Marston and Oswald Kirby. Evans made his way around the already legendary course in 75, while Marston shot 79 and Jones and Kirby shot 82.[32]

The next day, Evans and Jones traveled to Scarsdale Golf and Country Club, where they were beaten, 1 down, by two notable professionals, Tom McNamara and Jack Dowling. Evans and Jones "played good golf," acknowledged the *New York Times* reporter, "considering that it was the first time they had ever been over the course." Impressively, everyone shot under 80: Tom McNamara with the best score of 74, Evans 75, Dowling 76, and Jones 77.[33]

The four players faced off again two days later at North Shore Country Club on Long Island—a "greatly improved course" that was "new to both of the amateurs."[34] Their unfamiliarity with the course may have contributed to another narrow defeat for Evans and Jones at the hands of the professionals. Jones shot 76, one stroke better than his partner, but two strokes more than the professionals, both of whom shot 74.[35]

On September 19, Evans and Jones easily defeated Max Marston and John Anderson at Shuttle Meadow Golf Club, in central Connecticut. Even though Evans played well, "The credit for the victory," the *New York Times* reported, "must go to the sensational Atlanta youngster, who carried the burden of the match on his shoulders and incidentally broke the record of the course with a brilliant 71." The newspaper speculated that Jones "might have done even better than this [course record of 71] had he not missed a few putts which rimmed the cup."[36]

The next day, Evans and Jones lost in nineteen holes to Tom McNamara, paired this time with professional Louis Tellier, at Worcester Country Club in Western Massachusetts. "It was close all the way," wrote Joe Davis, with Evans having the best score, a 71.[37] Traveling an hour to the east the next day, Evans and Jones lost to Yeoman "Mike" Brady, the famous Boston professional golfer, and Jesse Guilford, the Massachusetts State Amateur champion, at Brae Burn. Unlike the previous time Jones played at Brae Burn, he kept his temper under tight control throughout the match and improved his score by seven strokes. Still, Brady and Guilford won; Evans and Jones's best ball was 72 whereas Brady and Guilford's was 68.[38]

On September 22, Evans and Jones traveled to Whitemarsh Country Club outside Philadelphia and won 2 up against the venerable Jerome Travers of New York and local star Max Marston for the benefit of the Soldier's Tobacco Fund. "At one time it seemed that this match would have to be abandoned because of the closing of the Sabbath to automobiles," observed the *American Golfer*. Without "a suitable means of conveyance from trains, and with no automobiles running at all," match organizers feared that attendance would be limited. In the end, however, more than two thousand people "justified the committee's eleventh hour decision to go through with the proposed match." The spectators reached the course in horse-drawn vehicles or on "Shank's Mare," that is, by foot. The exhibition raised more than $5,000.[39]

Evans "was at his best" and played steadily for a score of 74. Jones, "the little lad from Atlanta," was "erratic" in both his game and emotions; "the spectators are of the opinion that he must master himself before he will be a true master of the game," commented the *American Golfer*.[40] Still, he shot 80, the same score as Travers, who was "not in his top form by any means." Although Jones had kept his scores mostly under 80 when touring with Adair, Stirling, and Rosenthal, showing how much he had improved over the past three years, his scores with Evans fluctuated between the high 70s and low 80s. But the touring schedule with Evans was also much more rigorous, as they traveled to seven different courses in six states in the span of just nine days.

The final leg of Bob Jones's patriotic golf tour, played with arguably the greatest golfer in the world in 1918—Chick Evans—was the icing on the cake for his continuing golf education. For one, the tour with Evans surely helped him understand that he was not yet, at age sixteen, as good as many other top golfers, amateurs and professionals alike. But he had always learned and improved by closely observing his elders, including his father, the Adairs, Alexa Stirling, and, of course, Stewart Maiden. By having the unexpected good fortune to play on an extended tour with Evans, he gained the special opportunity to observe the Chicagoan day in and day out to an extent that probably no one else ever had. He also got a chance to compete against many of the leading players of his time (including the legendary Travers, who was nominally in retirement except for the wartime incentive). And he observed human models of excellence that reinforced his own deep commitment to self-improvement. Adding to the intensity of this curriculum, he assimilated and applied all this new knowledge on an array of championship-caliber courses in the Northeast that forced him to elevate his game simply to survive against tougher and more experienced players.

Perhaps more than anything, Jones's intensive wartime touring toward the end of 1918 further accelerated his golf celebrity. On relatively short notice, spectators showed up in large numbers wherever he played. With Chick Evans—golf's greatest publicity magnet of the time—leading the way and playing superior golf, Bob Jones was granted a once-in-a-lifetime opportunity to observe true greatness close-up while engaging in head-to-head competition against one top player after another with a built-in audience of adoring fans. "Best of all I remember how I enjoyed battling with the professionals," he wrote years later with his customary understatement.[41]

In November 1918, the war finally ended. Dave Herron was quickly discharged from service before ever seeing action or traveling overseas. After completing his preliminary training in Cambridge, Massachusetts, he had been sent in October for schooling as a pilot at the Naval Aviation flying school in Miami, Florida. But the United States, United Kingdom, France, and Germany declared the Armistice ending the war on November 11, 1918, before Herron had completed his specialized training. Many soldiers who were already deployed and serving abroad, such as Emil Loeffler Jr., would spend several more months in the military, but recent recruits, like Herron, were simply sent home.

With his patriotic duty now discharged and his college years over, Herron had to decide just what kind of professional occupation to pursue. And, in light of how little competitive golf he had played in 1918, at either Princeton or Oakmont, he also had to decide if it was feasible—starting in November, of all months—to resuscitate his golf game in time for the next U.S. Amateur at his home course in August.

Meanwhile, Bob Jones resumed his studies in mechanical engineering at Georgia Tech University and, more or less, returned to his normally scheduled golfing events around Atlanta, having been granted an exquisite taste of life outside the South and playing golf "semi-professionally" against many of the very best players and on the best courses that American golf had to offer.

▶ CHAPTER 9
A GENTLEMAN LABORER
DAVE HERRON FINDS HIS GAME (1919)

Given Dave Herron's strong academic record at Princeton, his notable athletic achievements, and his preference for a business career—not in banking, like his father, but in the iron-and-steel industry, like the Fownes family—his first job after returning home from the navy may seem odd: he became a laborer in an ironworks on Pittsburgh's South Side—the A. M. Byers Company—run by J. Frederic Byers, Eben's brother (and a later president of the USGA). Herron left for work six mornings a week at 5:00 a.m. to take public transportation with a heavy lunch pail in hand. Not the career one might expect for a scholar-athlete whose father and grandfather were bank presidents! But Dave Herron had clearly decided not to follow directly in his father's line of work, at least not at first (he would eventually, in the 1930s, leave the steel business and become a bond salesman). At some point in the winter of 1918–1919, he began to work long, strenuous days and eat side-by-side with immigrant laborers at the Byers Ironworks. With his easy-going temperament and physical strength, he fell in quickly with his working-class colleagues—many of whom would later come to cheer him at Oakmont—whose cultural origins, schooling, and social life outside of work were radically different from his.

Before deciding to labor in an ironworks, Dave very likely conversed with his closest Oakmont mentor, W. C. Fownes Jr., who had made a similar choice after graduating from MIT in the late 1890s. At his father H. C.'s urging, W. C. had learned steel manufacture from the bottom-up, as a laborer, before climbing the ladder of the family's lucrative steel business. Indeed, learning the complexities of industry from the bottom-up was an approach that many "barons" in Western Pennsylvania considered a wise prerequisite before taking over an inherited business. Herron had already learned the game of golf bottom-up by working as a caddie, and that had obviously turned out well. Why would he not apply the same principle to his nascent business career?

Unfortunately, with his arduous work schedule, he had only limited time to practice golf, which hindered his preparations for the 1919 U.S. Amateur. Luckily, the winter season of late 1918 and early 1919 was extraordinarily mild, giving Herron a better chance to hit the links than if Pittsburgh had endured its usual harsh cold, wind, and snowfall. Local golf enthusiasts were thrilled by the temperate weather, and with the end of the war, Pittsburghers flocked to golf courses in droves—Dave Herron and his family among them.[1]

It was during this unusually warm winter that the USGA officially confirmed that Oakmont would host the 1919 Amateur in August. Two years earlier, Oakmont's membership had subscribed $20,000 to improve both the course and clubhouse to make them worthy of a national championship. When Emil Loeffler Jr. initially took over as greenkeeper in 1915, the greens were "having trouble" and the course itself did not provide as severe a test as the USGA wanted. But Fownes and Loeffler had made numerous improvements in the interim—the addition of new "pits," trenches, and bunkers seemed never to stop, the gnarly rough grew thicker each year, and the green speeds were approaching those of the best clubs on the East Coast. While Oakmont's somewhat austere clubhouse did not match the palatial quarters of many clubs in the Northeast and Chicago, it too was being expanded and refurbished to meet the USGA's elite expectations.[2]

Certainly, there was a lot riding for the USGA on the nation's first U.S. Amateur since 1916. Everything had to be "first class" because the war had "killed competitive play," and the USGA felt that the 1919 Amateur, "the derby event in American golfdom," would play a key role in "restor[ing] golf to its pre-war standing. . . . This event alone will serve to stimulate interest in the sport."[3] Or so they hoped. The Fownes family understood fully that everything about Oakmont must satisfy the closest scrutiny. Western Pennsylvania's growing reputation as a major golf center—the utopia of American golf, with (allegedly) "more people playing golf here than anywhere else"—was on the line.[4] And so was the future of American championship golf.

The biggest uncertainty at Oakmont in the early winter months of 1919—and it was no small matter—was when Loeffler would finally be mustered out of military service to take charge of the final course preparations. Loeffler had served on the front lines in France, in numerous battles, and had survived mustard-gassing. Once the USGA provided the official go-ahead, well-placed Oakmonters did their best behind the scenes to secure his return to Pittsburgh as soon as possible. But even the USGA and industrial barons from Oakmont could not secure Loeffler's discharge until mid-spring. Consequently, from the moment he returned to Pittsburgh, Loeffler had to work day and night until virtually the start of the championship in mid-August to ensure that Oakmont was in the finest condition it could be.

But what sort of a test would the new and improved Oakmont provide? In 1919, most of America's best golfers had never played (or been invited to play) the then fifteen-year-old course. The two regional centers of American golf since the 1890s were the East (New York/Philadelphia/Boston) and West (Chicago), and few American golfers were aware of the dramatic growth of competitive golf in Western Pennsylvania. To illustrate, although Merion (in Philadelphia) did not open until 1912, its nationwide reputation was boosted enormously by staging the 1916 Amateur there. And, as a result, Merion quickly became a legendary venue that wealthy Easterners sought every opportunity to play. Oakmont, in sharp contrast, was still relatively unknown and much harder to access—Pittsburgh was never an easy city to reach from the East by rail. Even Chicago golfers often integrated Merion, and not Oakmont, into their business travel plans because of numerous other championship courses along the New York/Philadelphia axis.

Few Pittsburghers knew much about Oakmont. Because it was an elite private club, nonmembers who weren't high-caliber golfers had little access to it. Most Pittsburghers who played golf in the pre-war era did so on the badly overcrowded free links at Schenley Park or at the private Stanton Heights Golf Club. Once the USGA confirmed its intention to hold the 1919 Amateur at Oakmont, however, Pittsburgh golf writers tried to convey to readers just how much tougher Oakmont was than any other golf course in Western Pennsylvania. "The course is a strictly championship course, affording a variety of golf, and is designed to test the skills of a player. It is a difficult course and a penalty is attached to every misplayed shot. Woe to the player who does not drive a straight ball."[5]

The local press also offered subtler assessments to the golf cognoscenti. For one, Oakmont was built on a clay base. This meant that its fairways could get baked hard in hot weather, and that the course might therefore not play to its full measured length—most especially, on the course's several lengthy downhill holes. True enough but, as a *Pittsburgh Post* reporter explained, that was not the whole story. In actuality, Oakmont's fairways were not quite as subject to baking as many in the East assumed. Even in sustained hot weather, the course usually played close to its considerable length—which even by Eastern standards was exceptionally long. "One thing about the Oakmont course is that you do not get any long rolls on the drives. The turf is velvety and spongy and is not hard and baked as some of the courses over which the National championship has been determined in recent years, and the players get the distance they hit for." Moreover, the reporter reminded readers, the penalties for mis-hit shots were unsparing. "Another thing the players will discover is that it is hard to get back a shot that has been wasted."[6] In other words, there was scant opportunity to play heroic recovery shots at Oakmont. This was Calvinist Protestantism applied to golf. Take your punishment was the watchword; hubris could ruin an entire round (and chance to qualify for match play) on a single hole.

On another occasion, a *Pittsburgh Post* reporter offered an equally incisive but simpler observation about the psychology of the game at Oakmont. Familiarity with the course, it seemed, did not necessarily stir love or understanding.

> The oftener you play at Oakmont the harder the course becomes. As the players make trips over the course they become acquainted with the trouble which is scattered over it and it brings home to them the severe penalty which is attached to misplayed shots. Anywhere, there is something about the psychology of these traps and bunkers and the trouble which is scattered over the course to penalize the erring ones.[7]

A month before the 1919 championship began, the *New York Times* began to drum up nationwide excitement for the championship by informing its readers about the distinct challenges Oakmont would pose to the East's "crack" golfers. It would pose a "great test," "one where accuracy is going to count tremendously." Fownes and Loeffler had added bunkers in 1917 in anticipation that the Amateur would be held then, but they had added many more since, with the result that in 1919 Oakmont was the most difficult course in America. "All of the greens are well guarded and there is plenty of artificial trouble along the fairways, together with rough that is difficult to play out of with satisfactory results." All in all, "the man who can play straight as a string and get plenty of bite to his ball on the approaches will do well at Oakmont, but there are only a few players on that order."[8]

Perhaps not surprisingly, it was the premier syndicated sportswriter of the day, the *New York Tribune's* Grantland Rice, whose columns about Oakmont best captured the shock and awe experienced by the nation's top golfers once they put in a few rounds of practice. Best to let Rice's reactions flow in his inimitable prose.

> There are nightmares and ghastly visions which are haunting the dreams of 130 of America's best golfers, assembled here for the championship test.
>
> These sombre nightmares and highly spectacled visions consist of an endless series of traps, bunkers, pits, and trouble in general for any golfer who is slogging his way around the Oakmont course and not hitting each and every shot as each and every shot ought to be hit.

We are on record now as stating that Oakmont is the hardest test that any amateur championship has ever drawn and that only the finest golf will prevail against par. There is nothing tricky, unfair, or mysterious about the course. It is merely a sheer and rugged test of golf where wood and iron must play their part in order to score.

We have never seen a course where, on an apparently simple hole, a 7 or an 8 comes with greater suddenness. . . .

The greens here are in a wonderful shape, but getting a long approach dead from 30 to 50 feet away is no easy assignment. It is extremely simple to slip six or eight feet over and then to lose your golfing nerve and stop six or eight feet short. It is so simple that the best golfers here are doing it despite the fact that the greens are true to the ultimate wiggle.[9]

In the summer of 1919, speculation was rife about who would contend at Oakmont. Two months earlier, at the U.S. Open at Brae Burn, Walter Hagen had defeated the local Brighton boy, Mike Brady, in a playoff after Brady faltered and shot 80 in the final round. Already the 1919 Open was less remembered for stellar golf (both shot 301) than for Hagen's partying all night with blackface entertainer Al Jolson before changing into golf attire at the club just in time to tee off. The upcoming U.S. Amateur, by contrast, elicited far more public interest because, quite simply, the most famous American golfers of the time were amateurs: Jerry Travers, Francis Ouimet, and Chick Evans at the very top, in no particular order, but also high-profile regional favorites like Oswald Kirkby, Max Marston, and John Anderson in "the East," Robert Gardner and Ned Sawyer in "the West," Nelson Whitney, Reuben Bush, Bob Jones, and Perry Adair in the South, and W. C. Fownes Jr. and Eben Byers in Western Pennsylvania.

The East-West rivalry was particularly keen, as Evans of Chicago was still, at the beginning of 1919, the reigning champion of both the Amateur and Open as a result of his dual victories in 1916. And the great players of the East were anxious to displace this brash, talkative, no-trace-of-a-gentleman interloper from the Windy City. But Evans made clear throughout the summer, in his customarily effervescent way, that he was "not the slightest bit inclined to politely hand over his crown and scepter to another."[10] True, some thought that the exceptional speed of Oakmont's greens would be hard for Evans to adjust to—particularly if and when he had to confront a putting savant like Ouimet.[11] But no one could deny the quality of Evans's golf "through the green" (in the lingo of the times)—simply the best of his generation, pro or amateur—which seemed as sharp in 1919 as in 1916. In terms of ball-striking skill, Evans was the closest to England's transcendent Harry Vardon that America had ever produced.

Evans has long stood at the head of the list when it comes to the actual number of shots that a golfer has in his bag. Through the green, he consistently outplayed the amateur field for years, but his putting kept him from actually grasping the title. With renewed confidence in his touch on the green, due to a change in putters and also perhaps to the winning of his two national titles, Evans will be particularly hard to defeat [at Oakmont].[12]

Of one thing every golf commentator agreed: the upcoming event

should be the finest national amateur golf championship ever held in this country. Not only are all the older favorites entered, but a host of youngsters have forced [sic] to the front in the quiet period of the sport since war killed competitive play. A bold guesser might pick two out of the four semi-finalists, but not even a fortune-teller could risk his reputation by hazarding an opinion of the final result.... The quality of the field and play will undoubtedly put golf in high favor again in this country.[13]

Although he is not well remembered today, Jerry Travers, not Francis Ouimet or Chick Evans, was widely acknowledged in 1919 as the greatest golfer America had ever produced: a four-time U.S. Amateur champion, a five-time Metropolitan Amateur champion (which almost carried the stature of a major at the time), and—duplicating Ouimet's great feat at Brookline Country Club in 1913—a U.S. Open winner against the professionals in 1915. Even Evans's dual victories in the Amateur and Open in 1916 had not displaced Travers from the top of the firmament in American golf. At age thirty-two, Travers was hardly an old-timer, but he had mostly stopped playing competitive golf after his U.S. Open victory, although he had reemerged to play against Chick Evans and Bob Jones in a few wartime fundraising matches.

In other words, Jerry Travers remained, simultaneously, a known quantity and an active mystery—a man of greater intrigue than Chick Evans who never seemed to stop talking. To the surprise of many, Travers decided to resume competition, and the USGA winked at its own guidelines in declaring him eligible for the 1919 Amateur. It would be folly to exclude him, because no past champion elicited more curiosity from American golf fans than Travers.[14]

But there was another former Amateur champion whose appearance at Oakmont stirred even greater public interest: Francis Ouimet. No longer a "boy wonder" at twenty-six years old, Ouimet had become a genuine folk hero following his victory over Vardon and Ray in 1913, and he validated that achievement by crushing Travers, 6 and 5, in 1914 to win the Amateur at Ekwanok. Ouimet's great fame, of course, derived in good part from his modest family circumstances; like virtually all professionals at the time, he had learned the game as a caddie. Unlike the caddie/professionals, however, Ouimet had made clear that he intended to remain an amateur forever and to seek his fortune in business. College was not a serious consideration, so post-1913 he naturally took advantage of his celebrity as a golfer in the Boston area and accepted a position in a sporting goods store that sold golf clubs, balls, bags, tees, and so on in addition to a wide variety of other athletic equipment. This ultimately led to the USGA's controversial decision to declare Ouimet a professional merely because he made a living selling golf equipment and thus ineligible for the 1916 Amateur at Merion.

Despite widespread opposition from the golfing public, the USGA maintained its ban on Ouimet for several years; indeed, it might well have done so indefinitely if not for World War I. Ouimet, contrary to a rumor at the time, never sought to evade military service. Instead, both before and after Ouimet was drafted, he played regularly in Red Cross benefit golf matches, and he became one of the premier golf fundraisers in the United States. After his induction into the U.S. Army, he served overseas alongside the French Army in the ambulance service and eventually rose to the rank of lieutenant, acquitting himself quite well.[15] But it was not until Ouimet was mustered out of service after the Armistice that the USGA quietly lifted its ban and restored him to amateur status.

Thus, Ouimet would be allowed to play the 1919 U.S. Amateur at Oakmont, his first since 1915. His game had remained sharp throughout the time of his ban, and those who had a chance to observe him in Red Cross exhibitions in 1918 and in Canada in 1919 said that Ouimet—known as both a long hitter and a wizard on the greens—may have been "playing the greatest golf of his career.... Francis Ouimet is the idol of the proletariat and the man in the street.... Men, women, and children who cannot tell a brassie from a sand trap remember Ouimet and his famous victory, and always will." A *New York Times* reporter, speaking of an invitation tournament in Westchester County that Ouimet was using as a tune-up for Oakmont, observed: "Lately he has been coming to the front in good style, and his play in this tournament will be watched with interest as a guide to his chances for the national amateur championship at Oakmont."[16]

The South was the least familiar region of the country to most golfers, but it would be more ably represented at Oakmont than ever before. In 1919 the South's most distinguished players were, in clear rank order, Nelson Whitney of New Orleans, Bob Jones, and Perry Adair. Whitney was already well known to Easterners because he summered regularly on Long Island and played in prestigious invitation tournaments at the National Golf Links and Shinnecock Hills. And his consistency, competitiveness, mature demeanor, and all-around game were legendary. Except for when he was in the throes of severe back pain, he was a threat to beat anyone. So, no one doubted that Whitney would finish among the top thirty-two and probably advance to the later rounds of match play even on as difficult a course as Oakmont. And Bob Jones, of course, was a nationwide celebrity because of his performance at Merion and in the wartime charity exhibitions.

However, Jones, at age seventeen, was not the youngest "boy wonder" that the USGA had deemed eligible to play at Oakmont. That distinction belonged to New York's latest prodigy, Jesse Sweetser, playing out of Ardsley Country Club in Dobbs Ferry, who was a month younger. But Jones was by far the most famous young player in the field and, by common assent, the most talented as well. Only a handful of Pittsburghers had ever seen Jones play, but they were quite ready to believe the hype after W. C. Fownes Jr. confirmed that Jones was the real deal. The *Pittsburgh Post* viewed "the Southern phenom . . . as one of the likely contenders" at Oakmont.[17] And the *Pittsburgh Gazette Times* wrote: "There is one player who will bear watching in the coming tournament, Bobby Jones, the Southern youth, who is playing phenomenal golf this year. He has every shot in his bag and despite youth he is one of the best players in this country. . . . Even some of the professionals believe the youthful Southern star will cop the championship [at Oakmont]."[18]

Yet, a few in Pittsburgh held some reservations about Jones. Rumors of his untamed temper on the golf course were rife, especially after both he and Byers engaged in epic club- and oath-hurling at Merion in 1916. But temper is a tricky emotion in sports: whether Jones's outbursts ultimately helped or hurt him, from a competitive standpoint, was far from clear. In any event, the Pittsburgh press perhaps made more of Jones's temper than the evidence at hand warranted, and they never bothered to compare his demonstrative displays with those of other high-strung players (such as native son Eben Byers, whose temper tantrums at age thirty-six were at least equivalent to Jones's).

A subtler dissection of Jones's "few faults" identified one that he might indeed have to "overcome . . . if he is to win from the classy field which will play at Oakmont." Jones was considered by most experts—including the 1919 U.S. Open winner Walter Hagen, who was in Pittsburgh in August writing a syndicated column on the Amateur—to be "the longest driver at Oakmont."[19] The only serious challenger in the amateur ranks for pure distance off the tee, Hagen thought, was Jesse Guilford, the Massachusetts champion and a no-show at

Oakmont. Regardless, Hagen argued, even if Guilford drove the ball farther, he was much less likely than Jones to be on the fairway—so, case closed.

But Jones was inclined to hubris when it came to length off the tee. At age seventeen, he was only of modest size at approximately 5 feet 7 inches and between 145 and 155 pounds. Hence, his ability to drive the ball farther than anyone else was a great source of pride to him, especially in comparison to Guilford, who was a very large man. But his pride could also get him into trouble; as one writer explained, "Principal of these faults . . . is Jones' desire to outdrive his opponent at all times. Should his opponent at some stage of a match outdrive him by as much as 10 feet . . . he may become rattled or angry and not put up his best game."[20]

However, realistically, even though Jones lacked experience and emotional maturity, many experts considered him a threat to win at Oakmont because of the sheer purity of his ball-striking and his steely mental toughness. Given the vicissitudes of the draw in match play—if Evans, Ouimet, Travers, Gardner, Fownes, Kirkby, Sawyer, or Whitney fell to lesser opponents in the early rounds—no one would truly be shocked if Jones made it to the championship match.

The number of players who would actually tee off at Oakmont remained unclear until just before the event began. The USGA remained flexible about deadlines as it sought as large a field as possible for what almost felt like an inaugural national championship after the long wartime hiatus. The USGA felt certain the success of this event was critical to reviving the pre-war momentum that had begun to push golf to the forefront of American sports. Among the 150 or so possible participants were many youths in their early twenties, often recent or current college players, upon whose shoulders the game's future would soon rest as Byers, Fownes, Travers, and several others in their thirties and forties retired from regular competition.

One golfer's name that, somewhat surprisingly, popped up in a July *New York Times* report on the upcoming Amateur championship was that of S. Davidson Herron. Dave Herron, of course, had not competed in a nationally visible competition for a very long time. But he was known to the *Times* from his play at Princeton and in the Lesley Cup. As the *Times* reporter assessed golfers from Western Pennsylvania who would compete at Oakmont, he singled out only Fownes and Herron as "distinctly formidable." He continued: "Davidson Herron, the youthful golfer who made a fine showing in the qualifying round of the national at Detroit in 1915, has been playing excellent golf." Clearly, Dave was not entirely unknown in Eastern golfing circles.

But did the *Times* reporter actually visit Oakmont and see Herron practicing during the summer? That seems unlikely, given that he had hardly played any golf since returning home from the navy in November 1918. Here is how a *Pittsburgh Post* writer summed up Herron's potential and personal situation in late June 1919, when he was "not seen much on the links these days":

> Herron has the making of a champion and above all he has the one necessary requisite essential to a champion. And that is golfing temperament. . . . He is employed at one of the local mills learning the steel business. His duties do not give him much opportunity to go out on the links, as by the time he finishes his day's toil he is too tired to go to the links.[21]

Sometime in July, Dave Herron made the final call: he could not be true to his love of the game, or of Oakmont as his home away from home, and not compete in this year's U.S. Amateur. With the support of his boss, J. F. Byers, he negotiated a deal to take a month's leave of absence in order to play golf full time, starting August 1. Yet, he decided not to stoke his competitive fires through formal competition. Instead, he focused entirely on regaining the rhythm of his swing, getting back his feel for Oakmont's greens, and improving his substandard short approach shots—the one major weakness in his game. He also needed to familiarize himself with the most recent changes that Fownes and Loeffler continued to fine-tune until the very eve of the championship.

By early August, despite intensive practice, Herron still had a way to go before he returned to pre-war form, at least in terms of consistency. The press reported that "Dave Herron was out there also. He is playing spotty golf. He is liable to turn in a 72 or 73 in one round and take an 88 on the very next. His game requires tightening up, and this is what he is seeking to do in his daily visits to the course." Still, this observer concluded, "I can see no cause for apprehension concerning his chances to qualify. Any man who can go around Oakmont in 72 strokes may be put down at once as a star. Herron has done this and can do so again."[22]

Herron devoted every available minute to preparation for the Amateur. There were, after all, ghosts to vanquish. His biggest regret at Princeton had been his failure to win the individual National Intercollegiate title in 1916 when the championship was held at Oakmont. Nothing that had transpired in his life since then—flunking the physical for the military, captaining Princeton's golf team, graduating college with honors, serving in the navy, laboring in an ironworks—had come close to satisfying his desire to win a notable championship on his home course. Winning the U.S. Amateur would be the sweetest victory of all, and he committed himself to making that happen.

In the rest of the country, Bob Jones was the "boy wonder" stirring the sports press in 1919 with his precocious golf. But not so in Pittsburgh, where Dave Herron embodied the city's dreams of a third Amateur champion. While the city had developed a number of fine collegiate golfers, there was concern that not enough was being done to steer athletically inclined youth toward golf in comparison to the city's fervid passion for baseball and college football. Dave Herron stood out as the shining exception—the one potential superstar whose growth as a golfer had been overseen by Oakmont's best, and whom Pittsburghers had been fortunate to observe every step of the way.[23]

> There are many folks here who believe that Herron will be a big factor in the coming National.... Before entering the service last summer Herron was playing a brand of golf that would have tested the mettle of any player in this country. Although a youngster, he has been playing in tournaments during the past seven years.... He won the only big tournament staged here last year, the Red Cross tournament at the Allegheny Country club [sic]. Herron has all the necessary requisites of a champion. He is strong and hits a terrific ball from the tee and, what is more, he is imperturbable in the right places. In the coming tournament he will have an advantage in playing the course over which he learned to play golf and over which he caddied before taking up the game.[24]

Two weeks before the Amateur, the *Pittsburgh Post* reaffirmed everything it had said before about Herron. Above all the veterans, the newspaper contended, he was Pittsburgh's main hope in the upcoming championship. Not Fownes, whose play had been spotty all season and whose business and other obligations kept him from practicing; not Byers, who hadn't been able to hit his tee shots straight for the past two years; not Ormiston, who might qualify for match play but "lack[ed] the fighting qualities, which are essential to a successful match player"; but Dave Herron. Pittsburgh was backing its local boy, without hesitation.

> Much is expected of Dave Herron in the coming tournament. He played his first [U.S. Amateur] tournament in 1915, when he was only 17 years old. His debut was an auspicious one. He was tied for low score at the end of the first round of the qualifying round at Detroit. This was quite an honor for the youngster. In 1916 he played at Merion, but went to pieces and failed to qualify. Since that time Herron has improved as a golfer. He has grown to

manhood, he is a physical giant, and he has been a student of golf since his boyhood days.

His career as a golfer began when as a boy he started out caddying at Oakmont. Golfers say he was one of the best caddies they ever had. Not all of his time was occupied in carrying golf bags as he played whenever he could find the time. It was back in 1912 when he made his debut on the links in a match, being entered in an invitation tournament held at the Butler Country Club. He qualified for the first flight, went through the three elimination rounds and found himself pitted against R. L. James in the final round. James is the present [1919] Western Pennsylvania amateur champion. Few in the gallery conceded that the 14-year-old-boy had a chance, but he did and what is more played a great uphill game, squared the match on the home hole after being down throughout the match, and won out on the twenty-first hole. And since that time he has played fine golf.

Herron has beautiful form, hits a terrific long ball and is a good putter. Since growing to manhood he has matured, which is very evident in his play, and his golfing temperament.[25]

▶ CHAPTER 10

THE "GOLDEN TORNADO" AND THE SUMMER OF 1919

By the time Bob Jones arrived in Pittsburgh with his father and the Adairs in August 1919, he had already enjoyed a long and successful summer golf season, starting with reaching the semifinals of the Southern Amateur in late June. On the morning of June 21, a couple of days before the Southern Amateur began—and by "crafty design the last week before national prohibition set in," Jones recalled later—he and Perry Adair, this time chaperoned by the Joneses instead of George Adair, arrived in New Orleans.[1] In the afternoon, they headed out to the country club links, and "immediately both were the center of attraction among the local golfing colony," who wanted to see the boys "try their hands over the course" for themselves.[2]

Bob Jones's nationwide celebrity had been significantly enhanced by his wartime touring schedule, but he had long been a rising superstar in the South, including in golf-crazy New Orleans. So even though the city was home to Nelson Whitney, the South's finest player, the New Orleans press treated Jones as a major celebrity coming back "home" for the Southern Amateur—the competition where his precocity had first revealed itself, long before the nation had started paying attention to either him or Southern golf.

Jones and Whitney were the predicted finalists. A little over a week earlier, Whitney had won the Trans-Mississippi Championship at the Saint Louis Country Club in an epic final match that lasted forty holes. Therefore, it was no surprise, reported the *Atlanta Constitution*, that "the greatest interest will center in the match between Whitney and Jones as they are figured the favorites in the tournament over all others."[3]

Just before the event began, Ellis Knowles of Pensacola, Florida, "threw a wrench in the calculating machinery of those who thought they had the winner picked" by tying the course record (70)—set by New Orleans's second greatest golfer, Reuben Bush.[4] "Without detracting from the performance of the local star [Bush]," wrote the *New Orleans Times-Picayune*, "it must be pointed out that innumerable bunkers have been thrown across the right-of-way since Bush went around in two less than par," which made Knowles's accomplishment all the more impressive.[5] But of even greater interest to pre-tournament spectators was the fourball match that paired Jones and Adair against Nelson Whitney and Reuben Bush. The two Atlanta boys lost to Bush and Whitney, in part because "Fighting Bob" was "slightly off the form of which he is capable," according to witnesses. Jones, Adair, and Bush compiled cards of 79, three strokes higher than Whitney's 76.[6]

On June 24, Whitney and Ellis Knowles led the sixty-four championship qualifiers with scores of 76. Bob Jones shot 78, the same score as Reuben Bush; Perry Adair shot 79, and Big Bob also qualified for match play with 95. The tie for first would have been three-way if young Jones hadn't double-bogeyed the last hole. "The Atlanta players were followed by a big string of fans, many New Orleans people joining to watch the play of Jones especially," observed Leslie Rawlings of the *Atlanta Constitution*.[7] The *Times-Picayune* pithily remarked on Bob Jones's faithful fan following that "if pulling could have done any good Bob would not have blundered into the 6 that cost him the [qualifying round] medal."[8]

All was quickly forgotten the next morning, however, when the match-play championship formally began and Bob Jones "startled the crowd with one of the greatest shots ever made on any golf course." He knocked his ball "into a shoe which was in a wheelbarrow," the *Atlanta Constitution* wrote. "Many of the Atlanta people lost heart. 'He'll never get it out,' they said. But Jones never gave up.... He looked at the ball, then at the shoe. Taking a niblick, he got the ball out of the shoe as easy as if he had driven it, and then halved the hole."[9] Jones won his match easily against a local player, 6 and 5, and then defeated his afternoon opponent by the same lopsided score.

Likewise, Perry Adair easily won his two opening-day matches but was defeated the next day by the notable amateur Louis Jacoby—"No one thought that the Dallas man, although he was the runner-up in 1916, could bump off the young Atlanta crack." The *Atlanta Constitution* included an ominous line of reasoning as to why Perry was knocked out earlier than anticipated: "Adair has been away off.... The fact that his father, George Adair, was not here was blamed for his poor showing by some of his fans."[10]

For his third-round match, Jones played against another golfer from Atlanta, Richard Hickey, dispatching him quickly at 5 and 4.[11] In the fourth round, Bob exhibited a prime "sample of his real talent"—he played par golf for thirteen holes and soundly defeated O. S. Carlton, "the sensational player from Houston, Texas." The match was "a nip and tuck affair until the fifth, when Jones shot a three on a par five hole"—an amazing feat, especially considering he drove into the rough, somehow recovered with a blast of 220 yards that landed on the green, and finished off the eagle with a thirty-foot putt.[12] Now, in the semifinals, he would face none other than Nelson Whitney.

The public eagerly anticipated the match between Jones and Whitney, as "both men so far outclassed their fields," and because the two had never met in match play despite participating in the same events for several seasons.[13] "The Atlanta scribes who came here [from] the Cracker and Coca-Cola city were down hook and line on Jones' chances," and the New Orleans press felt equally confident about Whitney.[14]

The *Atlanta Constitution* gushed the following day, "The match between Whitney and Bobby Jones was the greatest ever shot over the local course." To humorously kick off the match, "There was a great laugh from the Atlanta crowd when Reuben Bush, 1916 champion [and a native of the Queen City], took hold of the bag of Nelson Whitney and caddied for him." Jones and Whitney were square at the end of eighteen holes, but Whitney went on an afternoon tear, "like a cyclone does through Kansas," and defeated Jones, 6 and 5. While the Atlanta crowd clearly pulled for Jones, who, in the afternoon, was "wild from the tee" and "lacked his usual distance," they still "showed their real sportsmanship and congratulated Nelson Whitney" when he won the match.[15]

In its coverage of the event, the *Atlanta Constitution* tried to persuade its readers that losing the semifinal match at the 1919 Southern Amateur "was the first decisive defeat that Bobby Jones, Jr. had suffered in a golf tournament in the south."[16] This wasn't strictly true, but it did demonstrate just how much Jones's celebrity as a premier golfer had grown. Still, his head-to-head match against Whitney highlighted a simple fact: although he was already, at age seventeen, a legend inside and outside Atlanta circles, in 1919 Nelson Whitney was the South's greatest amateur golfer. Whitney went on to embarrass Louis Jacoby the next day, 12 and 11, winning his fifth Southern Amateur championship title and reinforcing his hold on Southern golf preeminence.

But Bob Jones's game was steadily gaining recognition at the national level, too. Months earlier, the executive committee of the USGA had received an invitation from its Canadian counterpart, the Royal Canadian Golf Association (CGA), to play an international match in Canada in the summer of 1919.[17] W.C. Fownes Jr. of Oakmont was chosen as captain, and he selected a true all-star list of Americans to compete: John Anderson, Eben Byers, Chick Evans, Robert Gardner, Max Marston, Francis Ouimet, Oswald Kirkby, George Ormiston, Jerry Travers, and Bob Jones. Nelson Whitney's name was noticeably absent (presumably due to business obligations). The Canadian association team was led by eight-time Canadian Amateur champion George Lyon, with his son Seymour Lyon, John Hadden, F. S. Hoblitzel, W. McLuckie of Montreal (who had just won the Canadian Amateur), E. S. McDougal, T. B. Reith, W. J. Thompson, and 1913 Canadian Amateur champion G. H. Turpin completing the lineup.

In late July, to little fanfare, players from the New York metropolitan district (Anderson, Marston, Kirkby, Travers) and Eben Byers boarded the 6:45 a.m. Cleveland Limited out of Grand Central Station to Hamilton, Ontario, for the first American–Canadian golf competition in more than ten years. (Fownes was already in Canada making final arrangements for the match.) How Bob Jones, the only Southern player on the team, made his way to Canada is unclear.

The CGA and USGA formally conducted their match on July 26, and the American team decisively beat the Canadians by a score of 12 points to 3.[18] In the morning four ball matches, the Americans completely "outclassed the Canadians, 5 points to 0," and in the afternoon, the Americans won 7 of the 10 singles matches.[19] Although the *New York Times* had reported earlier in the week that none of the metropolitan area golfers brought their Schenectady putters, the American team did actually have them and were permitted to use them, although the Canadians under R&A rules were not. Thus, contradicting itself, the *Times* reported: "The Americans used that club [the Schenectady putter] for their close work," although the newspaper still called special attention to the lone player on the American team who preferred more traditional equipment. "Proving himself an exception, Bobby Jones contented himself with a straight putter."[20]

The *Atlanta Georgian* assured its readers that Atlanta's child prodigy was performing splendidly up North. "Bob Jones of Atlanta, the youngest member of the American team," played near or under par in both his morning doubles and afternoon singles sessions."[21] The *New York Times* hailed Jones's doubles match with Fownes as "one of the prettiest matches."[22] And his 5-and-3 win over E. S. McDougall (while shooting 2 under par) was the second most lopsided victory in the singles competition. The Canadian International match proved that Jones's fame was not just hype. The *American Golfer* later published a photo of the American team. Jones sat wedged between Chick Evans and Jerome Travers, his youth quite evident among this group of distinguished golf veterans of the East and Midwest.

The Canadian Open (an entirely separate event from the Canadian International) began on July 29, so the American amateur team stayed to compete. The players were joined by several other countrymen who made the trip North. The

American Golfer called Fownes and Jones "the headliners among the amateurs, with the Western Open champion, Jim Barnes, and the runner up, Leo Diegel of Detroit, and J. D. Edgar of Atlanta leading the professional squad."[23] Jones's superb 71 led the field by one shot after the eighteen-hole morning round, but his afternoon score of 77 left him five strokes behind Edgar. Edgar had been playing spectacularly, including at the recent Western Open in Cleveland, where he finished just two shots out of first place, but to little acclaim.[24] J. Douglas Edgar was a recent transplant from Newcastle, England; he immigrated to the United States in April 1919 and started working at Druid Hills in Atlanta as a teaching professional. (He was well known for teaching Tommy Armour, the budding Scottish professional star who would later win the 1927 U.S. Open at Oakmont.[25]) Although Edgar was never formally one of Jones's instructors, Jones freely admitted that he learned a lot from the man. "He was a marvelous teacher, and while he was never my 'instructor,' I learned, of course, from observation," Bob said, years later. "[Edgar] was, I'd say, an inspirational player. He played in spurts. When his game was good, it was brilliant; when it wasn't it could be miserable, and most always it depended on his temperament."[26]

At the Canadian Open, Edgar was brilliant, shooting a 72 in the morning and a 71 in the afternoon.[27] Atlanta was quite proud of Edgar, and Walter Hagen had recently done much to improve the public's perception of golfing professionals, but the press was still biased in favor of gentleman amateurs over those who competed for money. So, the *Atlanta Georgian* made sure to tell readers that their favorite amateur, Bob Jones, "is holding third place, and must still be reckoned with."[28]

In what the *Atlanta Georgian* described as "two miraculous rounds," Edgar shot a 69 followed by a record-setting 66 the next day. The stunning scores gave him a total of 278 strokes for seventy-two holes, "the lowest score ever made in any open championship, played anywhere in the world."[29] Edgar demolished, by five shots, the all-time scoring record of 283 that Jim Barnes—who finished second in a three-way tie with Bob Jones and former champion Karl Keffer of Ottawa—had tied just a week earlier at the Western Open. Edgar's winning margin of sixteen strokes in the 1919 Canadian Open still stands over a century later as the largest in North American professional golf history.[30] "Against this play naturally, no man could stand," the *American Golfer* proclaimed. But the journal's coverage still mentioned Bob Jones: "The other Atlanta entrant, Robert Jones, fulfilled in this tourney all the good things which had ever been prophesied by scoring a 71 and sharing second honors with the two just mentioned. That was [a] feat which ranks with the best amateur performances of

J. Douglas Edgar's record sixteen-stroke winning margin at the 1919 Canadian Open still stands as of 2024. "Here's New Canadian Golf Champ," *The Georgian*, 31 July 1919.

recent date and outlines a future peril in the professionals' path for American Open honors."

Jones was the low-scoring amateur, but it was definitely Edgar's moment in the sun. O. B. Keeler wrote an article for the *Atlanta Georgian* on the professional's monumental win. He noted that the Canadian Open was the fourth big event that Edgar, a former French Open champion, had competed in since recently immigrating. "This little chap," Keeler wrote, "had a hard time getting acclimated. The putting greens worried him." And perhaps most troubling, Keeler joked—since Georgia was dry before the Eighteenth Amendment in 1920—was not being able to have his customary pint of ale to settle his nerves before starting a round. "It's a wonderful country," Edgar told Keeler, "and it's an odd country in some ways, if you'll pardon me for saying so. How should a glass of ale or a bottle of beer become a criminal offense against the laws of the land?" Regarding Edgar's performance in Canada, Keeler said: "I doubt if this generation of golfers will witness its like again."[31]

Keeler alluded to the fact that many Atlantans had expected Jones, not Edgar, to be the breakout star for the South against Canada. In his short time in the United States, Edgar and Jones had played often against each other. "Playing match after match against Bob Jones, foursomes and two ball contests, [Edgar] never beat Bobby once that I recall," Keeler observed. "Their last encounter was a match at East Lake, where Bob won, 2 up in 36 holes, after having the Englishman hopelessly beaten in the morning round."[32] However, at the Canadian Open, Edgar had vastly eclipsed everyone. So far, though, Jones's summer exploits consisted of a semifinal exit at the Southern Amateur, winning two of two matches at the Canadian International, and finishing tied for second with the great Jim Barnes (winner of the 1916 PGA Championship) at the Canadian Open. For a seventeen-year-old, he was doing incredibly well. But, of course, Bob Jones had always been hard on himself. Like many of his fans, he was genuinely expecting to win at least one notable competition in the summer of 1919. A victory at the U.S. Amateur at Oakmont would wipe away any and all disappointments.

PART III

THE 1919 U.S. AMATEUR CHAMPIONSHIP AT OAKMONT

Starting in the second week of August, roughly 150 of the country's greatest golfers, a few dozen USGA officials, and the sports writers from at least fifteen major newspapers descended on the Pittsburgh region for the first Amateur Championship in the United States since 1916. But the cloistered world of championship amateur golf could not entirely escape the harsh realities of postwar social, economic, and political life in 1919. For most Americans, the nine months since the Armistice had been among the most divisive and violent in U.S. history.

Gone were the happy economic times that most Americans had enjoyed since 1914 as wartime production ceased and the economy fell into recession. The patriotic cohesion of the previous two years that had papered over fundamentally irreconcilable moral, race, and class divisions vanished almost overnight. Fear and anger began to dominate front-page newspaper headlines, riling up public opinion and making 1919, as some historians see it, the most traumatic year the nation would experience until the fissures of 1968.

For sports history fans, 1919 stands out for the unimaginable corruption ("Say it ain't so, Joe") of the Chicago White Sox bowing to gamblers and throwing the World Series to the Cincinnati Reds, forever tarnishing America's national pastime. But that was trivial compared to other transformations wracking the United States.

Chronologically, the first major change of 1919, which overnight turned most adult Americans into lawbreakers and popularized the image of the gangster, was the enactment of Prohibition. A different kind of national crisis erupted later in the year, one that had a deep impact on

Pittsburgh: the violent collision of labor unionists and industrial titans. Hostilities that had been simmering for months finally burst out in September, resulting in the Great Steel Strike of 1919—the largest labor strike in American history up until that point.[1] Violence was not limited to labor disputes, however. In one vile episode after another, racial violence spread across the country, marking 1919 as one of most dangerous years for Black Americans since Reconstruction.[2]

Turmoil of an entirely different sort roiled the national political scene as well. President Woodrow Wilson had successfully managed America's late entry (1917) into World War I, but his idealistic peace plans were undercut in 1919 by his Allied counterparts, who demanded much harsher penalties against Germany than he thought wise. Ultimately, Wilson failed to gain American congressional approval for either the Treaty of Versailles or America's entry into the League of Nations. Beyond these diplomatic failures, Wilson's health became a topic of urgent public concern after he contracted a virulent form of the influenza virus that had propelled the pandemic of 1918 and then reemerged in spring 1919. Even worse, Wilson suffered a severe stroke several months later that, in effect, left his wife in charge of the presidency.[3]

President Wilson was, of course, only one of tens of millions of victims of the worldwide pandemic. Though the pandemic is often remembered as "the Spanish Flu of 1918," it likely did not originate in Spain and was comprised of four separate waves, the last of which did not subside until 1920. By the summer of 1919, the worst of the pandemic seemed to be over, but public health authorities could not promise that the flu would not soon return.[4]

Fear of contagion and recontagion persisted throughout 1919 and continued to drag down Americans' sense of well-being. As competitors arrived at Oakmont in early August, USGA officials had good reason to fret about the plague's (that's what they called it) potential impact on players and spectators alike. After all, Pittsburgh had witnessed a skyrocketing death toll from influenza in both 1918 and 1919.

Overall, Pittsburgh experienced the worst epidemic of any major city in the United States. The average death rate for eastern cities was 555 per 100,000 residents. By contrast, Pittsburgh's excess death rate was a whopping 807 per 100,000 people. The Steel City's ordeal with influenza was even deadlier than that of Philadelphia (748) or Boston (710), two communities where influenza ran rampant in the fall of 1918. Despite advance warning and preparation, organized local leadership, and efficient allocation of resources, Pittsburgh fared horribly during the crisis.[5]

As we shall see, no sooner had the golf begun than influenza became a real concern for USGA organizers as one of their greatest stars, the conqueror of Vardon and Ray—Francis Ouimet—fell ill.

▶ CHAPTER 11
"TRUE TO THE ULTIMATE WIGGLE"
DISCOVERING OAKMONT

Those with their eye on the 1919 U.S. Amateur expected USGA officials to arrive at the latest on the Monday before qualifying began. Headquartered at the downtown William Penn Hotel, the USGA's most important job was to regulate late entries to the championship and construct the pairings sheet for the qualifying rounds on Saturday (August 16) and the following Monday (August 18), as well as for the *American Golfer* team trophy competition on Sunday. But as of Tuesday (August 12), no one in the press had seen or interviewed any USGA officials, and the pairings for Saturday's qualifying round still had not been published.[1] According to John Anderson, the esteemed golf writer (and player) from New York, and E. E. Giles, who was playing in the Amateur while also covering it for the *Pittsburgh Gazette Times*, pairings and start times for the first round were not formally published in the local press until Saturday morning, and USGA officials didn't arrive on the course until Friday, the day before the championship got underway. Players who reasonably wanted to know their start times sooner than the morning-of had to track down Oakmont's caddie master, who was in possession of the single physical copy of the pairings sheet.[2]

Naturally, competitors arrived much earlier than Friday in order to practice. Young Joseph Crawford of Stanton Heights, who had only returned from military service in France a month earlier, had been practicing for days before the USGA officials arrived. A few weeks earlier, Crawford had surprised everyone by winning the Stanton Heights Invitation (Dave Herron did not compete), clearly demonstrating that it was possible to resurrect a first-class golf game after a long break. But despite his recent victory, Crawford was not considered a shoo-in to qualify for match play on the difficult Oakmont course. An admiring reporter who had seen him play at Stanton Heights pointed out, "Playing in a National tournament is a severe test on the nerves and the one thing Crawford will be lacking in will be experience, this being the first [national] tournament in which he has played."[3]

That said, the Pittsburgh press was confident that six, possibly more, of Western Pennsylvania's best golfers would still finish among the top thirty-two qualifiers and advance to match play. That was an extraordinary percentage, nearly one-fifth, but the press believed that local knowledge would matter more than usual because Oakmont was a tougher test than most out-of-towners had ever confronted. Even those who had played Oakmont a few years earlier didn't comprehend the new challenges that Fownes and Loeffler had planned for them. "There is not going to be any phenomenal low scoring at Oakmont," decreed one local publication. Two rounds of 82, it was thought, would easily be good enough to qualify among the top thirty-two.[4]

Eben Byers was notable by his absence in the weeks preceding the event, but that was because he was practicing diligently at the National Golf Links on Long Island, a course Easterners still considered the most difficult in the country. Recent reports had him shooting two consecutive 75s, so he seemed fully prepped for success at Oakmont even though, at age thirty-nine, he was one of the oldest golfers in the field. Doing less well in his last-minute practice sessions, unfortunately, was Pittsburgh's finest, W. C. Fownes Jr., whose business and USGA obligations had curtailed his time on the course the past few months. His performances in the only two summer tournaments he entered, the Allegheny Invitation and the International match against Canada, had been disappointing. But Fownes knew Oakmont better than anyone else—a fact the Atlanta press would later throw in his face—and no one dismissed the wily veteran's chances once the championship began. His poor play was not "causing his friends any alarm," and he was "expected to take good care of himself when the tournament opens."[5]

Chick Evans and Francis Ouimet were expected to reach Pittsburgh midweek, leaving them two or three days to practice. But six days before the championship began, the press learned that Ouimet was ill, perhaps seriously so. He had contracted influenza (some reports claimed malaria) at Camp Devens in Massachusetts while serving in the army, and, like many who succumbed to the disease, he never fully recovered.[6] Ouimet's fans were justly concerned when news of his illness began to spread.

> The announcement that Francis Ouimet was suffering from tonsillitis caused some apprehension here, but it is hoped that his illness will not interfere with his coming here. Ouimet's presence is very much desired here. Evans and Ouimet are regarded as the greatest amateurs in America. An effort was made to get in touch with Ouimet here yesterday by some of his friends, with a view of ascertaining if his illness will interfere with his coming here, but up until last night nothing was heard from him.[7]

The stars from the East and West (plus two Canadians) began to reach Pittsburgh on Wednesday, and all but Chick Evans made it out to the links for at least nine holes by Thursday, two days before the first (eighteen-hole) qualifying round on Saturday. Where was Evans? No one really knew. Evans had a habit—perhaps a bit of gamesmanship?—of promising to arrive ahead of time, but then not actually arriving until the day before, or even the day of, the qualifying rounds. This coy strategy had served him well in the past; if nothing else, it conveyed extraordinary confidence in his skills and an uncanny ability to size up a course quickly. Evans had played Oakmont several times in exhibitions as he was passing through to the East, and he felt that was enough. He would just adapt to whatever recent changes Fownes and Loeffler had introduced, at least well enough to make the top thirty-two. In the end, Evans cited business exigencies and delayed leaving Chicago (with his mother) so long that he had to telegram the USGA on Friday evening to request a late afternoon starting time on Saturday. This brashly self-centered request would inevitably affect the plans of his assigned playing partners, not to mention the accuracy of the hard-to-find pairings sheet. But Evans understood, correctly, that as the defending (1916) U.S. Amateur champion the USGA dared not turn him down.

E. E. Giles, in his daily column for the *Pittsburgh Gazette Times* covering the Amateur, expressed approval of Evans's late arrival strategy. Evans had done it successfully before, at Brookline in 1913, and Giles considered it a tactic that served the game's most elite players well. Giles's insights on the matter were intriguing.

> Many of the star players, who have nothing to worry them until the matches start, are reaching the scene later than was their former custom. Evans has played the Oakmont course and, like a dozen others, is not particularly concerned about the qualifying end of the affair.
>
> Evans, like Ouimet, could get past Saturday with three clubs, if he had never seen the course, and Monday morning [i.e., the second set of qualifying rounds, at thirty-six holes] would find him ready for a record round at the crest of his game.... Watch the foxy boys! No over-golfing for the experienced ones with a chance at the title. They don't wear the edge off before the battle opens.
>
> The great player can size up a course in his first round. Almost instinctively he knows the best line to the hole. He notes not only the points where trouble lurks, but goes the ordinary player one better by steering to the course

which best opens the highway to the pin. Ouimet can do this—and so can Evans—likewise John Anderson, Byers and Travers. Will Fownes can name the landmarks after the round and without apparently looking at them.... Great golfers possess these little traits, and they contribute enormously to their equipment.[8]

Against this backdrop, Ouimet's arrival by automobile early Thursday afternoon received considerable attention. He and his wife checked into the Schenley Hotel across from the University of Pittsburgh campus, and then headed to the course so Ouimet could play nine holes with the 1909 and 1915 National Amateur champion, Chicago's Robert Gardner. Ouimet scored a 2-over-par 39 on his first try over the front nine—the revamped and somewhat arbitrary "par" score for Oakmont had recently been reduced to a total of 73 (37-36)—then got in a full eighteen holes the following day. He was thrilled to find out in person just how good a course Oakmont was. Indeed, he gushed to any and all that the course was "the most wonderful he has ever played over," with greens even better than the best in Boston.[9]

Pittsburghers were attentive to every bit of praise the course received from out-of-towners—most especially from notables whose breadth of experience allowed comparisons with all the top courses in the United States and United Kingdom. As, for example, the former president of the Western Golf Association: "Considering everything that contributes to the making of a great course—greens, fairway turf, proper placing of hazards, length, etc., I think anybody who plays Oakmont will say that it is 25 per cent ahead of any course in this country."[10] George E. Morse, the former Vermont state champion, said that Oakmont "offers far and away the best test ever afforded in the national." John Montgomery Ward, baseball legend and veteran New York amateur golf star, no doubt offended East Coast pride in claiming that "Oakmont is even harder than the national links" on Long Island.[11] John Anderson, who would write a lengthy summary of the 1919 Amateur for the *American Golfer*, called Oakmont "the finest course on which a championship has ever been played in this country.... It is truly a championship course."[12]

Harry Keck, the *Pittsburgh Gazette Times*'s sports editor, summed up all the unsolicited praise from newcomers to golf in Western Pennsylvania: "After a practice round or two, they have unanimously agreed that they never have seen Oakmont's equal as a championship layout. It is a square and fair test; not a tricky one which might prove the undoing of the real players and provide a fluke champion. The best man will win."[13] The inherent toughness of Oakmont, for example, made it unnecessary to "trick up" the course by placing the cups in "unfair places on the green, as too often is the case in tournaments. The location of the cups will be such that the players will have a chance on their putts. Oakmont is a difficult enough course without having the cups placed in freakish spots on the greens."[14]

With Ouimet a relatively late arrival and Evans a no-show until Saturday, press coverage of the practice rounds focused on the most noted Pittsburgh players as well as the four-time U.S. Amateur champion, Jerry Travers, and "the Southern phenom," Bob Jones. Several days of intense practice had paid off for W. C. Fownes Jr., and on the eve of the Amateur he could fairly be considered a contender. "For a time it was feared that he would not be on his game, but right now he is playing as good golf as he ever did." Likewise, Eben Byers, who had just arrived in town; his drives had finally straightened out, and he was again playing like a former champion. So, too, Dave Herron, whose erratic play of the week before—low 70s one day, high 80s the next—had given way to the steady power game that had so impressed Pittsburghers a year earlier at the Allegheny Invitation. The time off for intensive practice that Herron had negotiated from the A. M. Byers ironworks was clearly paying off.

The once unbeatable Travers, in contrast, was slogging around Oakmont in the mid-80s. Though working hard to regain his swing and putting stroke, the four-time Amateur champion was a pale reminder of the golfer he had once been. His fans could only hope that he could sneak through the qualifying rounds and give himself a chance in match play, because he was still considered America's best one-on-one golfer ever. But if the qualifying scores were low, Travers had no chance because he did not have a prayer of breaking 80 at Oakmont.

The most newsworthy moment in the lead-up to the 1919 Amateur was Bob Jones's magical march onto the Pittsburgh scene. Jones and his entourage—Stewart Maiden, his "ex-mentor" (Maiden had left Atlanta and taken a job at a golf club in St. Louis); "Big Bob," his father; Perry Adair, his friend since childhood; and Richard Hickey, a young Atlantan whose game had improved rapidly the past year—arrived on Tuesday night and checked into the Schenley Hotel.

Maiden had traveled with Jones from St. Louis to Pittsburgh to help him straighten out a persistent hook. According to the *Atlanta Journal*, Jones had avoided golfing in Atlanta because he didn't want to get used to putting on slower Bermuda greens again, so very few journalists from his hometown had seen him play in person recently. And they did not want Jones's fans to grow discouraged. "No one is in better position to advise Bob than Stewart, because he knows Bob's game thoroughly. It isn't intended to leave the impression that any faults have cropped up that need correction, because they haven't," Angus

Stewert Maiden, The Silent, Snapped Before He Knew it

Stewart "Kiltie" Maiden was Bob Jones's earliest instructor in the game of golf. "Stewert [sic] Maiden, The Silent, Snapped before He Knew It," *Atlanta Georgian*, 18 September 1915.

Perkerson of the *Atlanta Journal* assured his readers. "The trip to St. Louis is simply to talk with Stewart, to play with him, to see if he can offer any suggestions that will add to the game Bob will show."[15]

Observers at Oakmont, however, quickly pieced together that Maiden was there for much more than a pep talk. On a course as well-bunkered as Oakmont, accuracy off the tee was just as important as distance. And Jones had "implicit confidence" that his old teacher, who was "a sort of golf father" and had overseen his game "since its incipiency,"[16] could fix his swing.

Like at the Southern Amateur, George Adair was again noticeably absent from the Southern entourage because he was seriously ill. In late July, the *Atlanta Georgian* relayed news about the ailing George Adair, who was on the mend according to his brother and business partner, Forrest Adair. "George is at the Mayo Hospital in Rochester, Minn., and the reason Forrest thinks he is improving is because he (Forrest) got a telegram from him (George) desiring to know why he (George) had not been more fully apprised concerning certain business transactions of the firm of Forrest & George Adair." "If he's well enough to want to talk business," Forrest told the paper, "he must be getting along all right."[17] Unfortunately, Forrest was overly optimistic. In the end, George, who had chaperoned Bob Jones and Perry Adair at so many events, did not attend the 1919 U.S. Amateur (he would die two years later, at the age of forty-seven).

With three full days at Oakmont to practice, the Atlantans chartered a car the next morning, arrived at the course at 1:00 p.m., and wasted little time before heading out to meet their caddies. As they did regularly at East Lake, their home club in Atlanta, the boys formed teams to motivate their practice as they acquainted themselves with the course—Jones played with Maiden, and Perry Adair played with Hickey. Big Bob observed every shot, as did Walter Wilkes, the sportswriter (whose main expertise was tennis) from the *Atlanta Georgian* who shadowed young Jones at Oakmont.[18]

Wilkes adored Oakmont. He identified some of the major differences between top Southern versus Eastern courses, and clarified the quick mental adjustments Bob Jones would have to make in order to meet its stringent demands.

> The course itself is a beautiful one of greater than usual length—the eighteen holes total 6,536 yards [the course actually played at 6,707 yards for the Am-

Pittsburgh's golf journalists took much interest in dissecting Bob Jones's technique and comparing it to his form three years earlier at Merion. "Bobby Jones, Golf Prodigy, As a 'Kid' and As a Grownup," *Pittsburgh Gazette Times*, 31 August 1919.

Outlined by the white square is a furrowed bunker at Oakmont in 1919. Note that the photograph's original caption drew attention to Loeffler's innovation: "Golfers will note the furrowed sand in the trap to the left, a little added touch which worried even the greatest in that wonderful field." *Philadelphia Inquirer,* 31 August 1919.

ateur]. The player is faced on practically every tee with the necessity of lacing out a ball, carefully placed as to direction, at least of respectable length. In fact, I think I have never seen a course which penalized tee shots so sternly. It is fair, however, and if a player keeps straight he has little to fear from the countless traps which guard the fairway on every hand.

Further, he noted—and this was before Fownes began to haul tons of thick, rocky sand from the nearby Allegheny River to toughen the hazards—the bunkers at Oakmont provided a challenge to which the Atlantans were not accustomed. "Once in a bunker up here, it is almost impossible to make a recovery of any great difference, as the sand is of thinner [*sic*; we think he meant "thicker"] variety than is customary in the South and is carefully arranged by a heartless greenskeeper in a success of ridges so as to make a recovery from them all the more difficult."

Wilkes's observation on the "ridges" in Oakmont's bunkers may startle golf historians, but it confirms what other first-time visitors saw as well: as least as early as 1919, some of Oakmont's bunkers were "furrowed" with ridges of sand that made escape unusually difficult. This reality is contrary to Fownes's own claim that he did not introduce the "furrowed" bunkers for which Oakmont would become infamous until the 1920s. As noted earlier, some modest "furrowing" of the bunkers was already in place for the 1916 Intercollegiate championship, but the practice apparently became more commonplace in 1919. As the *New York Times* on-site reporter described them: "The Oakmont officials have also adopted the system of raking ridges in the bunkers at right angles to the line of play. This eliminated a lot of luck where the only one-way player might find his ball neatly teed up in a bunker, while some less fortunate but more erring brother would locate his ball eight inches down in a footprint. This way everything is equal and every lie is a bad one." It was Emil Loeffler Jr.'s father, the club machinist, who manufactured the special rakes that his son employed to do the "furrowing."[19]

But during the 1919 Amateur, it was Loeffler Jr. who became infamous. Bob Gardner boasted during the first qualifying round that he had managed to find a smooth, unraked bunker. According to the *New York Times:* "'Ha,' he said as he climbed triumphantly out of the pit, 'at last I got to a trap before that fellow with his trick rake.'"[20]

All four Atlantans played well during their first practice round on Wednesday at Oakmont. They were helped by the inch of rain that had fallen the day before (August 12). The rain had softened the greens so they better held well-struck approach shots; the rain had also softened the fairways just the right amount to provide perfect lies. "The turf on the fairways was smooth as velvet and so even that crisp irons shots and clear-ups with brassie and spoon became the order of the day." The Atlantans took advantage as they were all long hitters, but Jones was consistently ahead of everyone else.

However, adjusting to the speed of Oakmont's greens was a nightmare—even for Jones, who had become familiar with the quicker greens of the Eastern courses in the New York area and Ontario, Canada. No matter how accurate their approach shots were, Atlantans could not gauge the green speeds properly, even from short distances; at Oakmont, the ball simply would not stop rolling. Thus, a three-putt possibility loomed on every hole. "The part of the game which caused the Southern players most trouble was the greens which were freshly clipped and of lightning fastness. It was amusing to the spectators and discouraging to the players to see the short putts run on four or five feet past the hole in the early part of the match."[21]

Adair and Hickey were 3 up on Jones and Maiden after the first nine. Jones played exceedingly well but needed forty-one shots since the riddle of the greens completely stumped him. In a quick moment, however, everything changed, and he suddenly tore apart the back nine. He "played as flashing golf as ever was seen on the Oakmont course. His playing was a revelation," proclaimed the *Atlanta Constitution*.[22] For example, on the par 5 tenth hole, Jones hit a brassie to the green from 225 yards and managed to stop the ball just four feet from the cup to score an eagle. He played the eleventh hole equally brilliantly, scoring a birdie 3 to go 3 under par on the back nine after only two holes. A par followed on the long, 567-yard, par 5 twelfth hole, which Wilkes regarded as the most difficult on the course (this hole would mainly play at 601 yards once the championship began). Jones then birdied the thirteenth and fourteenth holes and was thus 5 under par after his first five holes on the back nine; his team had won every hole to miraculously go from 3 down to 2 up. A par 3 ended the match on the sixteenth hole (recently changed from a par 4 to a par 3).

After that, Jones appeared to relax: following a poor drive into tree stumps, he bogeyed the short, par 4 seventeenth hole before parring the long, par 4 eighteenth for a back-nine score of 32 and a total score of 73—the new par value for Oakmont. His score was the lowest that day or any other during the practice week. (Adair shot 81, and Hickey and Maiden shot 83.) While it is uncertain, of course, whether Jones holed each and every putt during this match-play practice round, he presumably would have wanted to do so as he sought to learn the greens and prepare for the medal-play qualifying rounds. Regardless, his score of 32 on Oakmont's back nine would not be bettered in USGA competition until 1973, when Johnny Miller shot 31 to clinch his record-setting final round of 63 to win the U.S. Open.[23]

None of the Pittsburgh writers witnessed Jones's play, but all were genuinely stunned when they heard that he had shot 32 on Oakmont's back nine. Word spread quickly that the pre-tournament publicity hype about Jones was not exaggerated. He was a quick learner and could play a truly magical game. From this point on, no one doubted that, if the champions of past years fell early, Jones could win the championship despite his youth.

Early on Thursday morning—much as had happened three years earlier at Merion, when Jones set a course record in his first qualifying round—a very large gallery showed up on the first tee to watch him play, hoping for another record-setting performance. It did not happen; he played poorly the entire practice round. As at Merion, the sorely disappointed gallery began to drift away after the first nine. But there was one aspect of Jones's game that did not disappoint: his length off the tee. In 1919, Jones was a few inches taller and significantly lighter than three years earlier at Merion (between ten and eighteen pounds lighter, according to different reports). As his body took adult form, he became an even longer hitter, which pleased the crowds (and Jones himself) immensely.

By Thursday morning the fairways had dried from the Tuesday rain, and

Jones took full advantage. "The only department of the game that Jones shone in was his long game. He was getting his usual terrific drives and was getting from 250 to 300 yards from them."[24] Actually, his drives, though long, were missing the fairways on Thursday or, just as often, running through them. As a result, he had to play regularly out of damp, gnarly rough and all variety of hazards that had no counterparts on Atlanta's golf courses. The best he could shoot on Thursday was an 82, although he again scored lower on the back nine (43-39). About the best Wilkes could tell his *Atlanta Georgian* readers was that no other amateur managed to break 80 on Thursday, so Bob Jones's 82 really was not too bad. Curiously, all three Atlantans shot higher in their second rounds at Oakmont, with Perry Adair topping out at 88. As a Pittsburgh writer had observed some months earlier, greater familiarity with Oakmont didn't necessarily translate into lower scores. For some players, the psychological battle only increased as they more fully understood the course's exhausting challenges.

The Atlantans played a second eighteen-hole match against each other on Thursday afternoon. Jones reduced his morning score by only two strokes, from 82 to 80, and Adair reduced his from 88 to 85—still worse, by all predictions, than would be necessary to qualify on Saturday among the top sixty-four for Monday's additional thirty-six-hole qualifying rounds. All in all, Jones's first three practice rounds at Oakmont went well enough. True, his opening round in the low 70s seemed an accident, and on Thursday "he did not appear to be the same person who yesterday afternoon broke the amateur mark for the last nine holes." But given his youth and unfamiliarity with the course, it seemed likely that as he continued to adjust, he would qualify easily for match play and have the potential to beat just about anyone if he was truly on his game.[25]

For all the pleasure they took in watching Bob Jones play golf, some members of the Pittsburgh press could not pass up the opportunity to take a dig, particularly after Jones's game declined dramatically on Thursday. Exactly as they had heard, Jones had an on-course temper that he did not hide when his shots went awry. That temper was apparently on full display on Thursday. The "'Golden Tornado,'" not the "boy wonder," "was having his trouble in finishing near 80, much less breaking records," one reporter observed. As predicted, the problem lay not in his skill set but his impulsivity.

> Bobby has one opponent to overcome if he is going to win the championship, and that is himself. Bobby is a finished golfer, has mastered most of the shots which are necessary to become a champion, and has the fighting spirit so essential in match play, but from his playing the past few days it would seem that he has not mastered himself.[26]

Under the subheading "Bobby Easily Peeved," the reporter implied that Jones experienced a visible fit of pique: "When he misses a shot he becomes ruffled and his favorite diversion when he is peeved is to hurl away his club. This very often disturbs his mental poise."[27] Jones's supporters maintained that he never threw a club at Oakmont, and we have seen no clear evidence to the contrary. He did, however, turn the air blue and broke at least one club in anger.

On Friday, the day before the first qualifying round—when the field would be cut to the top sixty-four and ties—all competitors (except Chick Evans) were on the course, determined to get in two additional rounds of practice. The Atlanta foursome decided to split up—perhaps to push themselves into a more competitive frame of mind or maybe to excite Pittsburghers who wanted to see Atlanta's "boy wonders" compete head-to-head against the Steel City's finest; Jones and Adair were paired against Fownes and Oakmont's new pro, Charlie Rowe. It was a terrific contest from start to finish; the young Atlantans won 2 up, after Jones almost sank his second shot on the long and difficult eighteenth hole. The quality of the golf was stupendous. Adair, who had not shot lower than the mid-80s since arriving at Oakmont, returned to stride, played brilliantly, and had the best round of anyone. Like Jones in his first round at Oakmont, Adair equaled par with a score of 73 on Friday. Although Jones had largely eclipsed Adair in the public eye, Adair could still match his younger friend on the links on his best days.

And both friends had outstanding days. Had Jones not given up on the par 4 seventeenth hole—he failed in three tries to get out of its infamous front-right bunker (later named "Big Mouth")—he too might have equaled par. The press emphasized how long a hitter Jones was since he had unexpectedly reached the cavernous bunker with his tee shot. Fownes could not even come close to Jones in distance off the tee, nor was his putting as sharp as usual, but his scrambling from off the green was pure wizardry. Fownes was now scoring solidly in the high 70s, and he was of course highly motivated to win his second Amateur title on the course that he and his father had nurtured into one of America's finest.

Yet despite his fine golf and the fact that he was playing with Fownes, golf's ultimate even-tempered gentleman, Jones's emotional volatility was again on display on Friday. Reporters witnessed "a burst of temper" after he sliced one of his brassie shots and "gave bent to his anger by striking the greensward violently with his driver. In doing so he broke the shaft of this club—his favorite brassie. Last night he had to have a new shaft made."[28] This latest tantrum, combined with his hissy fit in "Big Mouth," cast further doubt on whether he was emotionally equipped to defeat (in Walter Hagen's view) "the strongest [field] I have ever seen in any amateur championship" on "by far the best course that this amateur championship was ever played on."[29]

Jones's temper tantrums only enhanced his celebrity and increased public interest in what he would do next. By the time the championship began, Pittsburghers were as much intrigued by the exploits of Bob Jones as of their homegrown wannabe, Dave Herron. And as the qualifying rounds began, Jones and Adair—not Dave Herron—were the two "kid wonders" the national golfing press identified as most likely to cross the generational divide and take down one of the "Big Four": Ouimet, Evans, Travers, and Gardner. Only they had matched the new par of 73 in their practice rounds, and Jones, in addition to shooting 32 on the back nine, had twice broken 75 (that's how on-site commentators did the calculations, in spite of Jones's pickup on No. 17 against Fownes and Rowe).[30]

In the vacuum created by the continued absence of Chick Evans, the press and fans showered loving attention on Francis Ouimet. His game was assuming true championship form—the best of his career, most felt—in spite of some signs of continuing physical weakness due to his ongoing bout with "tonsillitis." Two-time Amateur champion Robert Gardner was also finally playing well, shooting a 78 after initial rounds in the 90s on his first harrowing encounters with Oakmont. E. E. Giles was not surprised to see this: "Gardner has the habit of coming to a tournament without having had much connected play and then warming quickly to his best game and causing all kinds of trouble.... The ascending game is the winning game when players of equal ability clash."[31]

Grantland Rice also remained a devoted Gardner fan, always marveling at the former Olympian's extraordinary physique. Rice saw Gardner as a likely winner at Oakmont:

> The Chicago star is in rare physical condition, and this will count heavily over a course above 6,700 yards in length.... Gardner was driving a long ball with a high trajectory all day, and this is the shot needed here. The low tee shot with the hook for a run spells constant trouble. Gardner has the tee shot needed to get him around in low figures while there isn't a finer golfer at match play in the tournament.[32]

The *New York Times* actually considered Gardner "the longest hitter among front-run amateur golfers. [Jesse] Guilford may hit them with a bit more carry, occasionally, but for consistently straight, long shots, Gardner probably leads the field. Indeed, in his match with Guilford at Merion, he even out-drove the big New Englander from the tee by a narrow margin."[33]

Among Pittsburghers, however, "a strong 'hope'" remained that twenty-one-year-old Dave Herron could win the championship.[34] On Friday, most local fans chose to watch the Jones/Adair vs. Fownes/Rowe match. But some got to see Herron in action because George Ormiston had persuaded Francis Ouimet to team with him in a match against Dave Herron and Dwight Armstrong, Herron's childhood friend who had recently graduated from Yale. It turned out to be another great match for spectators and an indi-

Several newspapers ran this photo of Dave Herron as it became clear in later rounds that he would be a contender for the 1919 Amateur title. Cherry/Herron Family Archives.

cation that Herron's game was as good as it had ever been. Indeed, Herron, at his best, could match Bob Jones's best. The *Pittsburgh Gazette Times* reported, "Herron at times played brilliant golf and brought forth applause from the big gallery."[35] Herron and Armstrong combined to shoot a best-ball score of 71 in defeating Ouimet and Ormiston, 1 up.

Perhaps most striking to those who had not seen Dave Herron play in a while was that he easily held his own against the long-hitting Ouimet. According to the *Pittsburgh Post*, "The match developed into a long driving duplex between Ouimet and Herron. . . . Right now there is not a player who is hitting a longer ball than Herron."[36] This stark observation had never before been made about Dave Herron—not even when he won the Allegheny Invitation before entering the navy because he could only then be compared with his fellow Western Pennsylvanians. At the Intercollegiate at Oakmont in 1916, it was his fellow Princeton ace, D. C. Corkran, who had received the oohs and ahs for exceptional length off the tee, not Herron. But after he graduated from Princeton in spring 1918—having competed that year for the first time in swimming, water polo, and the hammer throw—observers began to describe Herron increasingly as a power golfer. Now, in summer 1919—following military training, where he had shed at least twenty pounds, and following several months of hard labor casting iron molds—Herron was more powerful than he'd ever been. At least by one man's observation, he was the longest hitter in the entire U.S. Amateur field.

How long a hitter Herron was mattered, because distance was considered vital for success at Oakmont. "It is a long, hard course, more suited to the tastes of the heavy hitters," observed the reporter for the *New York Times*.[37] Might he now pose a real threat, especially because he was playing on his home course, to the nation's most famous power golfers—Ouimet, Evans, Gardner, Jones, Kirkby, Marston—all of whom hit "a long, high ball with little run . . . well adapted to avoid disaster on this most troublesome of golf courses"?[38] Before the competition got underway, Pittsburghers who had witnessed the recent changes in Herron's game really had no way to answer this question. But if the *Pittsburgh Post*'s observation turned out not to be hyperbole, and with the rest of his game fully intact, his exceptional length off the tee might place him very much in the mix for the Amateur championship. "Davidson Herron is the boy," E. E. Giles of the *Pittsburgh Gazette Times* contended. "Davidson has the shots and the physique to support them. He is quite capable of upsetting the aspirations of the best of them when in his happiest scoring mood."[39] At the least, in Pittsburghers' eyes, Dave Herron stood as good a chance as Bob Jones.

▶ CHAPTER 12
THE TERROR OF OAKMONT

As the first eighteen-hole qualifying round got underway on Saturday, August 16, 1919, the general consensus was that an 87—or fourteen strokes over par—would suffice to advance to the second, thirty-six-hole qualifying rounds on Monday.[1] That prediction had been closer to 82 when the players first arrived en masse on Wednesday. But some club champions had yet to break 100 at Oakmont, and it was becoming increasingly clear that many players would not be able to adjust to Oakmont's relentless demands. True, some players of national renown, such as Bob Jones and Perry Adair, or merely local renown, like Dave Herron, had posted scores below 75 in practice. But practice rounds in fourball matches nearly always included conceded putts and pickups on difficult holes. Thus, a recorded bogey in match play might, in reality, translate into a triple or quadruple bogey in medal play, especially at Oakmont, where the hazards often required multiple slashes to escape.

"There are two heavy handicaps," Grantland Rice reflected, that make medal play more difficult than practice: the "mental" or "nervous strain" of competition and "the physical handicap of shooting from the back of the back tees with cups generally placed at elusive spots along the greens."[2] The mental toll that Oakmont's layout took on players was evident even in practice. As for tricky hole placements, the greenkeeper, Emil Loeffler Jr., was not expected to locate them in impossible corners or on sharp grades, but who really knew in advance what he would do? The fact was that the tougher the hole placements, the greater the advantage to Oakmont veterans like Fownes, Byers, and Ormiston, who were among the premier short-game artists in the game. If Loeffler was of a mind to increase home-course advantage, locating flagsticks in tricky places might be the simplest way to accomplish that.

The game's two most popular superstars, Francis Ouimet and Chick Evans, grabbed the headlines during Saturday's first qualifying round, and attracted most of the galleries too (an estimated 1,500 spectators for Ouimet alone). But it was the peripatetic Louis Jacoby—who had strong Pittsburgh roots, having learned the game as a boy on "the free links at Schenley Park"—that won the eighteen-hole medal event with a score of 76.[3] "Ouimet is traveling at a great pace these days," noted the *New York Times*. "He has the shots, the youth, and the confidence. . . . He is all the more anxious to gain this honor since it is his first appearance in a national championship since he was debarred [by the USGA] after the 1915 event. . . . With his winning personality, which makes him a favorite wherever he goes, his success would be highly popular."[4]

As he played the eighteenth hole, Ouimet looked like he would surpass or tie Jacoby as medal winner in the first qualifying round—and this even though his shot-making was erratic and his first putts regularly drifted several feet past the hole (he made nearly all the comebackers). But Ouimet had the misfortune of playing the eighteenth during a severe hailstorm that unleashed a third of an inch of rain in just twenty minutes. Some described the storm as a tornado or "miniature cyclone"—which resulted in so much casual water that one writer dubbed the afternoon "aquatic golf."[5] "Those unhappy souls still left in a struggle to qualify for Monday's final medal round were pelted with hailstones almost as large and hard as the golf balls they were playing with," Grantland Rice wrote. "Many golfers came in with big red and blue welts on their hands and necks . . . and two small caddies were knocked down."[6] Chick Evans remarked later that George Ormiston looked like he had been "through a small-pox siege" by the time he got back to the clubhouse.[7]

Under these harsh, soaking conditions, Ouimet struggled for a long time to sink his final putt for a 7 on the eighteenth green and ultimately finish one behind Jacoby at 77. But his 1-under-par 36 on the front nine, before the "cyclone" hit, was two shots better than anyone else's. Clearly, Ouimet was at the top of his game, to his fans' delight. Most of the press, and probably the galleries too, unabashedly hoped that he and Chick Evans would slug it out in the end. "Ouimet still remains the more popular of the two and has more followers than the present titleholder [i.e., Evans]," the *Pittsburgh Sunday Post* commented.

> It would seem that the long game of Evans and that of Ouimet are about the same, with little to choose when it comes to playing the iron shots. But there is one department of the game in which Ouimet excels and that is in putting. Ouimet is a better putter, and it is upon the greens that most of the matches are won or lost. It is going to be a great duel between these two luminaries and it is to be hoped that they will clash before the tournament closes.[8]

Ouimet may have been more nationally popular, but Evans had more than his share of long-time fans in Pittsburgh. Western Pennsylvanians liked his rough edges—there was nothing shy or reticent about him—and locals remembered him well for his sparkling personality during the Red Cross match at the Pittsburgh Field Club in 1917. But as Saturday morning rapidly approached with no sign of Evans, many fans started to worry that he wouldn't make it to Oakmont in time to tee off. Though Evans had requested and received a very late tee time on Saturday afternoon, everyone assumed that he would arrive at the course in the morning to at least warm up. Noon passed, however, and no one had heard a word from him. It was not until 12:30 p.m. that Evans telephoned officials to say that he and his mother were on their way to the course. He arrived only one hour before tee time, and walked quickly to hit a few balls and putts before starting his round. No one could deny that the reigning U.S. Amateur champion exuded confidence!

Evans had the advantage of being paired with his old friend Ormiston, who briefed him on the recent changes in hole length and placement of hazards that Fownes and Loeffler had made to the course. Of special concern were the locations of new bunkers that inevitably affected course strategy on both tee shots and approach shots. No one was particularly surprised that Evans's long game did not suffer for lack of practice at Oakmont. His ball-striking was simply that good, and he played "brilliantly at times." But his putting, also not surprisingly—Rice pointed out before the event began that "Ouimet is one of the best putters in the country, Evans, among the leaders, one of the worst"[9]—was inconsistent, especially with regard to speed. "There are no keener greens in America than at Oakmont," said one close observer who watched Evans struggle, "and it will require several rounds of play before he gets the touch of them."[10]

Regardless of Evans's difficulties on the greens, his score of 80 (38-42), on a day when only eight players shot in the 70s, showed just how solid his tee-to-green game was, even without practice. In fact, his round was even better than that; his late tee time trapped him at the fourteenth hole when the driving rains and hail hit the course, forcing him to deal with greens that had been "converted into miniature lakes." He and Ormiston had to seek "shelter behind one of the cavernous bunkers to escape the hail and at the end of the storm... they were covered with welts.... He was drenched to the skin, while his clubs were wet and he could not grip them properly.... It is quite possible that had Evans not been required to finish his round after the storm he might have finished first."[11]

In the end, after witnessing the excellence of Evans's round under these conditions, the *New York Times* challenged anyone who dared assume that Ouimet had eclipsed Evans as America's premier golfer, although with one obvious caveat:

> Evans is almost unanimously considered the best amateur golfer America has ever produced, but once on the putting green this mastery fails him. It is not that he is such a poor putter, but that he does not reach the level of players like Travers and Ouimet. He is playing well now, and, if any one can be a logical favorite in such a lottery as a national amateur golf championship, Evans seems to be the man.[12]

Understandably, Ouimet, Evans, and current front-runner Jacoby received the bulk of attention in the press coverage of the first qualifying round. But several other unusually good—and unusually poor—showings sparked interest. These included Robert Gardner, whose 79 demonstrated how quickly he was adapting to Oakmont after shooting in the 90s three days earlier; Jerry Travers, who shot 84 but did not care because his tee-to-green game was off and his sole concern was qualifying for match play; Eben Byers, whose driving went awry yet again but who snuck in at the limit with an 89; Bob Jones, whose play continued to alternate between superlative and mediocre as evidenced by his 82 despite a very poor start; Jesse Sweetser, who shot 78 even after catching the brunt of the hailstorm in his final holes; W. C. Fownes Jr., who shot a disappointing 86 after scoring consistently in the 70s during the practice rounds; and Dave Herron, whose 84 (40-44) was much better than the score indicated because he teed off next to last and struggled with the storm and its aftermath ("aquatic golf") from the tenth hole onward. Herron "was on his game practically all the way," a local reporter assured his family and friends. "Herron was in pleasing form and looks to be able to hold up the Oakmont end of the tourney in dogged fashion before the champions shake him off." That said, familiarity with the course did seem to be a boon in the first medal-qualifying round; eighteen Pittsburgh-area players survived to advance into Monday's thirty-six-hole qualifying rounds.[13]

Shockingly, the one headliner who failed to qualify was Perry Adair. Perry's 73 the day before was considered the best overall round anyone had played all week. But after a disastrous 49 on the front nine, including a 7 on the par 4 second hole and a 10 on the par 5 fourth hole—where he spent over half his shots in bunkers—he played mediocre golf on the first seven holes of the back nine and concluded that he could not score better than the low 90s. So, he picked up his ball on the sixteenth green. Bad weather had nothing to do with Adair's problems; he was an early starter, got off to a nightmarish start, and was unable to turn things around. Like many others in the field who found themselves in that situation—including a couple dozen players whose scores threatened to rise well above 100—he chose to discontinue play rather than post a score that would embarrass him.[14]

Perry Adair's quick departure dumbfounded the local golfing press, which had heartily embraced him as "one of the best players entered in the tournament." But his first coach and confidante, his father, who had guided his golf career with such a steady hand, was not present to help his son past his frustrations. So, after walking the final two holes as a courtesy to his playing partner, "the youth took his fate to heart and tears coursed down his cheeks as he entered the club house."[15] Unfortunately, Adair's emotional exit assured him the public notice he desperately wanted to avoid, and the press could not resist digging for a deeper story. Yet when interviewed later, he showed considerable "grace under the very disappointing circumstances."[16] That's golf, he said: "Oh, I just wasn't going right, that's all."[17] He kept it simple: he'd had a very bad day at the worst time, but remained confident that he could revive his game on Sunday, when he and Jones were obligated to represent East Lake in pursuit of the team-based *American Golfer* Trophy. And, after the hailstorm, in the early evening, he played nine practice holes with Stewart Maiden to prepare.[18]

The Atlanta press was heartbroken. The day before, the *Atlanta Constitution* declared it "a foregone conclusion" that the "formidable trio" of Richard "Dick" Hickey, Bob Jones, and Perry Adair would all qualify and "thrust [Atlanta] upon the national golfing map with a vengeance."[19] Hickey squeaked through with an 86, so two of Atlanta's great hopes survived into the second qualifying round.

But Perry Adair's struggles were indicative of the profound shock that undid many superb and steady golfers (including Grantland Rice, the ace among golf journalists) who failed to break 90 on opening day. As a columnist for the *Pittsburgh Post* forewarned, Oakmont challenged mind and spirit as no other early twentieth-century golf course did. "There is not a player entered in the tournament who will not say that it is the most difficult course in America."[20]

A less somber tone inflected the appraisal of a New York reporter whose interviews with the players detected more a sense of awe than despair.

> Expert and duffer alike agree that the links of the Oakmont Country Club... is without a shade of doubt the longest and finest test of golf that has ever been used for a national championship in this country. Kirkby, Evans, Ouimet, and other favorites are in ecstasies over the difficult shot requirements, and the average duffers stand agape at the distances to be covered against the multiplicity of yawning traps. There is not a letup from the first tee to the last green. If a shot is lost, it is gone forever. Even the foremost professionals who have played the course complain on the virtue that there is not a single hole on the course where one could mentally lean back and count on a[n] easy 4 or 5. Every shot has to

Perry Adair was still included in the *Atlanta Georgian*'s roundup of stars even though he failed to advance to Monday's qualifying rounds. Bob Jones, Chick Evans, and Francis Ouimet are the other golfers pictured. "Four Stars in National Amateur Golf Tournament," *Atlanta Georgian*, 17 August 1919.

be played surely and accurately if the golfer is to stay on the fairway or stick to the green. But no one would have it otherwise. It is a great course, a fine field is competing over it, and the golfer who emerges victorious at the final round will have well earned his laurels as national amateur golf champion of 1919.[21]

The *American Golfer* Trophy competition—the Walter Travis–sponsored fourball match with teams comprised of two players from the same club, which had first been integrated into the U.S. Amateur at Detroit in 1915—was played on Sunday, between the two days of qualifiers. Many of the veteran players elected to rest before the two qualifying rounds began on Monday, especially as it rained again late on Sunday—this time more steadily, smoothing the pristine fairways and greens (Oakmont drained extraordinarily well). At the same time, the additional rain made the course play longer than during the practice rounds. It was now difficult for some of the field to reach a few long par 4 and short par 5 holes that had been conquerable before. Furthermore, the new rains thickened the rough, drenched the sand, added water to the trenches, saturated the bunker embankments, and, generally, provided even greater advantage to the more powerful players who hit high, long-carrying tee balls, while disadvantaging veteran aces like Fownes, Ormiston, Byers, Anderson, and Travers, who relied on low, running tee shots with a sharp hook to maximize distance on the ground.

Chick Evans was one of the veterans who elected not to compete on Sunday. Instead, he played informally with Oakmont professional Charlie Rowe to gain strategic insight into Oakmont's exceptional green speeds, insight he would desperately need if the rains let up and the greens rolled keener still. After his round with Rowe, Evans offered extraordinary praise for Oakmont:

> This is the finest course I ever played over. The more I go over it the more interesting I find it. I delight in playing it, and it is a good test of golf. There is nothing fluke about the golf here and you must play for all you get. The element of luck is reduced to a minimum, and it is an ideal course on which to stage a championship.

Recognizing Oakmont's great severity—and despite the fact that he had shot 77, two more than Rowe, in their Sunday round together—Evans predicted that on Monday scores as high as 171 would qualify for match play, as compared to 167 at Merion in 1916.[22] Walter Hagen agreed with him.[23] Oakmont was at least two shots harder (per round) than Merion.

Francis Ouimet could not play at all on Sunday because he was again seriously ill—almost deathly so, initial reports implied. Ouimet had never fully recovered from his recent illness (or perhaps the influenza he contracted in 1918), and the time he had spent on Saturday in the rain and hail trying to putt-out for a triple bogey 7 on the eighteenth green had worsened his health. He became quite ill that evening, running a fever as high as 103. On Sunday morning, word reached the course that Ouimet was still quite sick. His fever had abated somewhat by Sunday evening, but his wife and two physicians urged him to withdraw immediately without competing in the final two qualifying rounds on Monday.

Ouimet defiantly refused, issuing a press release that he would show up at the first tee on Monday "if he never sank another putt in his life."[24] No one from the USGA dared interfere one way or another in Ouimet's decision-making. But his withdrawal from the first U.S. Amateur Championship since the war would doubtless diminish its prestige and also undermine the USGA's public relations effort to rectify (without admitting it had been in error) the damage done by banning its only true folk hero for four long years. Losing Ouimet to illness was a nightmare scenario for the USGA, especially after Evans had barely made it to the first tee in time for Saturday's qualifying round. So, J. Frederic Byers—Eben's brother, a fine golfer in his own right, and a leading figure on the USGA's executive committee—assured the public that "Mr. Ouimet would be shown every consideration as regards starting time tomorrow."[25]

Among the former Amateur champions, only Robert Gardner chose to compete for the *American Golfer* Trophy. While his extraordinary team—he paired with New Jersey's ace, Max Marston—played quite well and nearly won the event, more notable was that they both carded individual scores in the mid-70s. This confirmed the belief of some experts that both Marston and Gardner had as much chance as Ouimet or Evans to win the entire event. However, it was an obscure young player, Paul Tewksbury, recently of Boston but now playing out of Aronimink Golf Club in the Philadelphia area, who shot the low individual round on Sunday. Tewksbury, who barely made it into the Monday qualifier with an 89, shot a remarkable sixteen shots lower, an even par 73, on his own card for the *American Golfer* Trophy. Unfortunately for him, his equally young clubmate, J. Wood Platt, was unable to help his team on any hole. His best-ball score was also 73, and it put them in a tie for third place. Whether either of these young Philadelphians could play steady enough golf over thirty-six holes on Monday to qualify for match play was anybody's guess, but their names were now known for the first time in USGA circles.

Two teams tied for first-place honors, and, interestingly, all four golfers were either former or current Princeton players. Richard Haight of Scranton, Pennsylvania, who failed to advance to the Monday qualifying rounds with a score of 90, and J. Simpson Dean, the new, long-hitting star of the Princeton team from Rome, Georgia, combined to shoot a best-ball score of 72. So, too, did the two recently graduated native Pittsburghers, Grant Peacock and Dave Herron, both lifelong Oakmont members. Herron played the superior individual round in his twosome, shooting 76 on his own card and "doing most of the stellar work for the Oakmont team."[26]

In other words, on the eve of the all-important, thirty-six-hole qualifying rounds to determine which thirty-two golfers would advance to match play and compete head-to-head for the national championship, Dave Herron—after struggling to a back-nine 44 during the worst of the hail on Saturday—was back on track. He was scoring solidly in the 70s at Oakmont, just as he'd been doing during practice the week before. The intensive preparation he had begun less than three weeks earlier was paying off: he was scoring as consistently low at Oakmont as he ever had—perhaps even better. Even the Oakmont caddies who had known Herron most of his life felt compelled to chime in on the current excellence of his game, according to Walter Hagen. Those with a ground-level view of golf at Oakmont, and who understood Herron's "imperturbable" personality, felt confident that he could win the whole thing.

Bob Jones's scoring, in contrast, had been erratic since he and his entourage first arrived in Pittsburgh five days earlier: alternating between the low 70s and mid-80s, with no clear pattern of steady improvement even as he came to know the course better. Jones had gone far out of his way to bring his old coach Stewart Maiden from St. Louis to work one-on-one with him in practice, but as of Sunday many aspects of his much-admired game were not yet locked in. He continued to fight a sharp hook off the tee, his irons were inconsistent, and he was missing short putts.[27]

Thus, the foundations were laid for a showdown no one anticipated. Bob Jones and Dave Herron—one, age seventeen and a rising college sophomore at Georgia Tech; the other, age twenty-one and a Princeton graduate, navy veteran, and pipe-roller—each had devoted family and well-wishers on-site to cheer their efforts to win. And both young men embodied the youth revolution that was promising to change the demographics of championship golf in the 1920s. To be sure, Jones and Herron were not the only young golfers at Oakmont with the potential to overtake their elders. But with Perry Adair having self-destructed in the first qualifying round on Saturday, they were the best of those who remained. The thirty-six-hole qualifying rounds for match play on Monday would definitively prove whether they were up to the challenge.

▶ CHAPTER 13

SURPRISES, UPSETS, AND JUST HOW SICK IS FRANCIS OUIMET?

Monday morning, seventy-five players faced off for the thirty-two available match-play slots. Originally, the USGA had hoped to winnow the field to sixty-four after the first eighteen-hole qualifying round, but scoring on Saturday was so high, and it was taking so long to finish a single round, that the USGA decided it was more expedient to forgo a thirteen-way playoff and just let everyone who scored 89 or better compete in Monday's thirty-six-hole final qualifying test, a grueling all-day affair.[1]

After so much rain (six of the past seven days), some of it truly torrential, the course, already 6,707 yards long, was playing even longer on Monday, and "there was [still] practically no roll." Walter Hagen, who was covering the championship as a journalist because as a professional he could not compete, and Chick Evans predicted that 171, or two rounds in the mid-80s, would qualify.[2]

Turns out, Hagen and Evans were just one shot off; 172 was the cut, the highest in history at the U.S. Amateur.[3] Monday's continuing rain played a significant part in driving up scores. "I don't think I ever saw a worse day for a big tournament," Hagen said.[4] Grantland Rice wrote that "the driving rain, which came with the usual accompaniment of black clouds, softened the bunkers to a dangerous state." Balls embedded themselves deep in the sand and the grass embankments (i.e., "faces" or "lips" or "facades") of bunkers, which often required several shots to escape.[5] Players could not even hold their clubs, according to Walter Wilkes, writing for the *Atlanta Georgian*. "Badly hooked shots" were common, and drives got "very little roll" because of the "heaviness of wet soil."[6] Hagen warned that the bunkers were more dangerous than they first appeared:

> The traps are deep, and many of the players are greatly fooled in trying to play out of them, as the sand is not loose and flaky, and one must be content to get the ball back into the fairway, trusting to place in a spot, where he can take a full wallop at it with his next shot. This, combined with a full growth of rough and uncut grass along the side of the course, is not going to permit any player making any very brilliant recoveries.[7]

173

It was the rough that kidnapped Bob Jones's ball on the twelfth hole, not sand. Playing at over 600 yards, the twelfth was objectively the most difficult hole of the course.[8] Jones's drive on Monday was "beautiful" and "straight down the fairway." But he sliced his brassie second shot deep into the rough and, after five minutes of fruitless searching, declared the ball officially lost. In the end, he took an 8 for the hole. Still, he had a chance to tie for medal honors if his putt on the eighteenth green had not "stayed out by an 'eyelash' margin."[9] In addition to still struggling with the hook that Maiden was unable to eliminate from his drives or irons, he had not quite figured out Oakmont's greens.

But it was not Little Bob's fault. "Fate seemed to have determined that Bob shouldn't have the low qualifying honors," Angus Perkerson wrote, invoking a trope that Atlanta's golf writers had long used to explain away any difficulties the city's "Wonder Boys" encountered.[10] Earlier in the week, Perkerson claimed that the only reason Perry Adair had never broken 75 at East Lake was because "a jinx has always bobbed up on one or two holes."[11] His early exit from the championship was a result of "hard luck."[12] And Bob Jones's temper was treated more like a disability or handicap—a sympathetic tragic flaw hampering his destined success—instead of something he could and should learn to control.[13] His temper was not his fault, and neither were any misplayed shots; it was the hand of Fate at work.

Jones's two-round total of 159 was not enough for first place in Monday's qualifying rounds, but it did earn him many new admirers. "It is the general opinion of the players and the gallery," Hagen reported, "that he would be fighting in this tournament as long as anyone else."[14] He was now considered a safe bet for the semifinals.

However, for most commentators, Chick Evans was still the favorite to win, for several reasons. One, he was the defending champion. Two, he was known for playing with a chip on his shoulder and would therefore want to defend his title that much more, especially after losing the U.S. Open crown (to Walter Hagen) at Brae Burn Country Club several weeks earlier. Three, the Red Cross exhibition matches throughout the war had kept Evans's game sharp while less-connected golfers lost their edge. As proof, Evans turned in a score of 161 after two steady and laid-back rounds. Evans "seems to have the best game," Hagen speculated, though he added, "Chick is such a bad putter that he might find his Waterloo before the end of the week in a most unexpected way."[15] And four, the man most likely to be his Waterloo, Francis Ouimet, the one man capable of "cudgeling" Evans out of the competition, was supposedly on death's doorstep.[16]

The *Atlanta Constitution* claimed that Ouimet was "too weak to pick up his shoes" on Monday morning. All the same, despite nearly collapsing three times, he shot 79 in the morning and 84 in the afternoon for "one of the gamest exhibitions ever witnessed." However, Ouimet's second round left him so weakened that several strong men had to literally carry the six-foot-tall golfer back to the clubhouse, where he spent the entire night under the watchful eye of a physician, unable to travel back to his hotel room.[17] Ouimet's fever had returned, and he'd spent most of the day playing in hard rain. Fans feared that Ouimet's "indomitable pluck" might not be enough to propel him through another thirty-six holes of golf come morning.[18]

A few other stars made the cut: W. C. Fownes Jr. of Pittsburgh, Nelson Whitney of New Orleans, Robert Gardner of Chicago, and Max Marston of New Jersey. But many who were expected to qualify with ease failed: Pittsburgh's Eben Byers and George Ormiston, New York's Jesse Sweetser, Atlanta's Richard Hickey, and perhaps most surprisingly New Jersey's three-time Metropolitan champion, Oswald Kirby, to name just a few.[19] In a championship expected to be dominated by old hands—the *Atlanta Georgian* had predicted a few days earlier that the new champion would "come from among the little group of high-class players who have stood at the head of American golf for several years," not "a dark horse" who "would have little chance with the class represented here"[20]—the leaderboard was instead topped by a new crop of young men few had heard of. Tied for first at 158 were Paul Tewksbury, Jimmy Manion, and Dave Herron. Tewksbury hailed from Philadelphia (though he was actually a recent transplant from Massachusetts). Manion was a public links golfer from St. Louis. And Walter Hagen seriously thought Pittsburgh's Dave Herron was going to win low medal honors—he "looked to have the best chance," but Herron encountered the fiercest weather of almost anyone on his last nine and had to settle for a tie. The three were scheduled to play off for the honors sometime later in the week after their matches concluded.[21]

Collegiate golfers Simpson Dean, Dwight Armstrong, and Grant Peacock also qualified. The field was disproportionately local—six Pittsburghers made the cut for match play.[22] The field was also disproportionately young and untested. "I noticed names of at least sixteen who have not qualified in an amateur championship before. This is half of the field, and most of the players are new material that has come to the front in the past three years," Walter Hagen wrote.[23] "Three years has made a great deal more difference with the amateur golfers than it has with the pros."[24]

John Anderson disagreed with Hagen that the sudden youth takeover had anything to do with amateur golf's wartime hiatus. "Why should experienced golfers fail, and fail miserably?" he asked in a syndicated special report.

> The answer is not an easy one, but we are inclined to believe that it is wholly a mental reason, and that memories of past failures count heavily in the score against the man who is expected to secure a place in the coveted thirty-two. ... It must be remembered by the rank and file of sportsmen that golf is the most exacting of games. From the mental point of view the player has much time at his disposal to think and to anticipate what may happen.... The black cloud of uncertainty looms over one's head until the golfer yields to its blackness and loses faith in himself.[25]

Oakmont confronted players with an unfamiliar and unrelenting psychological challenge, and many experienced golfers perhaps did crack under the mental strain. But to dismiss the youngsters' success as beginners' luck was to ignore the profound demographic shift happening in American golf. A natural result of golf's growing popularity in the 1910s, and the rapid proliferation of courses across the country, was that children were beginning to pick up the game from their parents earlier and earlier. To preserve this momentum during the war, the USGA wisely promoted golf as a way for all male Americans to get into shape for military service. And many country clubs across the United States waived membership fees for men who enlisted.[26]

Still, adult male players, who were either overseas fighting or avoiding being seen on a golf course in order to maintain their patriotic standing, were not playing much during the war. However, the teenage amateurs who were too young for military service had time and opportunity to practice, so they did. And more famous amateurs like Bob Jones and Perry Adair even joined professionals on charity exhibition tours. The result was a large, up-and-coming crop of young golfers whose progress had been invisible because there were no wartime national championships to demonstrate their skill. "The truth of the matter is this," Francis Ouimet wrote, somehow covering the Amateur in a widely syndicated column while playing in it and suffering serious illness at the same time: "Many young stars unheard of before entered this championship. Not having a national reputation[,] they were given but little notice. The fact is that they are good enough to put out anybody."[27]

The other major consequence of the wartime exhibition matches was an increase in spectator interest, especially among working- and middle-class public-links players. The exhibitions had offered a patriotic opportunity to see the sport's best stars in action to Americans who usually did not attend major golf championships because they were held at elite private clubs. However, the downside to this sudden surge of new fans, which included some who had never swung a club, was that the USGA was totally unprepared for dealing with galleries who did not already understand customary golf etiquette.

At Oakmont, the problem of unruly spectators reared its head early. "It should not be necessary to be continually shouting, 'Keep off the green, please.' [Yet] this is the national championship battle cry," E. E. Giles wrote wryly after the second qualifying round. "The matches could best be watched if spectators would take the trouble to move out in front along the line play, in a matter not to interfere with the players they are watching or any others on the course."[28] Pittsburghers had hoped that "during the present tourney, the visitors from the far corners of the country [would] come to know [the city] as it really is—as a virtual hotbed of the golfing bug, as one of the best developed and yet largest growing sections in the whole National Association."[29] Unfortunately, the galleries were making the exact opposite impression. A "legion" of club members armed with "dainty little yellow flags" and approximately thirty "blue-coated police," who were on hand to keep the peace, spent the day herding crowds off of greens and out of fairways.[30]

Much of the gallery's confusion about where to walk or stand stemmed from the USGA and Oakmont's decision not to use ropes. The press roundly condemned this choice as a grievous error for weeks following the event. On the bright side, some suggested, the lack of ropes did allow the many young women in the gallery to get quite close to handsome young college students like Bob Jones (a rising sophomore at Georgia Tech) and Jesse Sweetser (a beginning freshman at Yale). But the spectators' proximity also caused many chaotic delays.

To determine the brackets for the remaining thirty-two competitors, the USGA drew names randomly from a hat instead of using the modern method of seeding, which meant Lady Luck had a chance to create very lopsided matches. "The draw," Walter Hagen wrote, "is a most important detail of match play. In fact, it will very possibly be the decisive factor, especially if several of the strongest contenders like Ouimet, Evans, Gardner, etc. are together in the same half."[31] Grantland Rice made the same observation. He figured a Ouimet-Evans final match was inevitable if they ended up in opposite brackets, though he acknowledged, "It is easily possible that either Evans or Ouimet will find himself face to face with tough competition from the kick-off where the other has a fair sweep of the first two or three days."[32] If both survived, whoever had the easier bracket would have an edge, and in a high-caliber championship, any such advantage mattered. As Angus Perkerson explained in the *Atlanta Journal*, "in a tournament such as the national meet, the winner is the man who has an extra fine edge on his game and who doesn't have the hard luck to meet someone at the outset who is playing better than he knows how."[33]

Unfortunately for the bettors (gambling on golf events was very popular in country club circles), many veterans who, early on, seemed "likely candidates for the championship" lost in the very first round to someone playing hot. "This is surely a tournament of upsets if ever there was one," Walter Wilkes told his Atlanta readers.[34] Evans and Ouimet both survived. But renowned and well-respected players like John Anderson, Louis Jacoby, and legendary Jerry Travers, who despite his struggles all week remained a fan-favorite, fell. In fact, Travers received "the worst beating of his golfing career," losing, 8 and 7, to Detroit's C. G. Waldo, a former Yale golfer and two-time Connecticut State Amateur champion. Meanwhile, New Jersey (later Philadelphia) hot-shot Max Marston lost to Bob Gardner, the golfer who beat Bob Jones at Merion in 1916, despite being 5 up on five separate occasions. Gardner rallied late with "one of those scalp-lifting exhibitions that many golfers dream about, but few ever accomplish" and what Grantland Rice dubbed "the longest putt in the history of the world."[35] It was a sixty- to sixty-five-foot downhill snake to win the seventeenth hole.

Bob Jones defeated Jimmy Manion, who had tied for medal honors the day before. Both were off their games, and the match ended on the thirty-fourth hole. Jones was still hooking his drives and missing short putts but managed to keep the match square through the first eighteen holes. He didn't really start to pull away from Manion until the final nine, when he posted a respectable 38 after carding three consecutive scores of 43. "His game wasn't the best he's shown at Oakmont, but it was enough," Perkerson summarized.[36] Walter Wilkes claimed that Jones's sudden improvement in the afternoon was the result of changing drivers: "He was driving both farther and straighter yesterday afternoon than in the morning due to the fact that he discarded his new driver with which he had been hooking, and went back to his old friend which had stood him in good stead before and could be relied upon to do so again." Whether this was the result of some advice from Stewart Maiden, who was still acting as his coach and trudging alongside Big Bob in every match, is unclear.[37]

Atlanta's other young star, Simpson Dean, lost to co-medalist Paul Tewksbury. New Orleans's Nelson Whitney, however, survived the first round and kept the South's hopes alive. Perkerson noted with optimism, "The south . . . is fortunate in that its two best golfers—Bob and Whitney—aren't in the same brace and won't meet unless the two of them run the gamut of play."[38] Nearly every city (especially New York) had lost one or more of its prominent players, so the South, East, and "West" all stood about the same chance of capturing the title now.

Whether or not Pittsburgh counted as East or West was still a topic of debate, but either way, Oakmont's members continued to represent the club well. In fact, the only Oakmonter eliminated in the first round was Dwight Armstrong, who had qualified with the highest possible score of 172, and he lost to Chick Evans, the clear favorite to win the title. W. C. Fownes Jr. and Grant Peacock, meanwhile, won close matches, as did Dave Herron, who beat "Ham" Gardner of Buffalo, New York, on the seventeenth hole. "It was a great uphill fight for Herron, who stood 2-down at the end of the first 18 holes," the *Pittsburgh Gazette Times* reported. "But the Oakmont youth never let up for a moment and he kept plugging along." In the morning, Gardner shot 79 to Herron's hard-earned 81. (Jones, for comparison, shot 86 in the morning round of his first match.) But Herron rallied dramatically in the afternoon, winning four more holes than his opponent and closing out Gardner on the seventeenth green.[39]

Unlike Evans, who destroyed Armstrong, Francis Ouimet struggled during the first part of his match against a young unknown from Philadelphia, Eddie Cleary. Ouimet claimed his "illness [had] been very much exaggerated," but he was clearly not at full health; he was "pale and drawn with indigo circles under his eyes." And "up to the twelfth hole he did not appear to be himself, lacking strength and playing his shots mechanically." Even after the twelfth, Ouimet was not playing "any remarkable golf." Indeed, he won the fifteenth hole with a double bogey 6. Rather, Cleary appeared to crack under the pressure of playing in front of an enormous gallery and lost his two-hole lead over the last six holes. All Ouimet had to do was hold on. "With an iron will [Ouimet] accomplished what seemed to be a remote possibility," the Pittsburgh press marveled, "and it is doubtful if a player ever staged a pluckier finish than Ouimet did."[40]

Ouimet would have to reach deep and put on a repeat performance because in the second round on Tuesday, the American public would finally get its highly anticipated Evans-Ouimet match. "Their meeting is something for [which] the golfing world has waited with feverish anxiety, and now that the prospect is at the door, it would be a calamity indeed if sickness intervened."[41] But Ouimet was determined to give his absolute all, over the protests of his wife and doctors. "I may be beaten on the golf links, but I'll never be beaten in bed," he said. As long as he could walk, he would play.[42]

The other Round-of-16 match that fans and pundits eagerly anticipated was the rematch between Bob Jones and Bob Gardner. "In fact," Rice commented, "it will be something like looking at a two-ringed circus where the rings are several kilometers apart."[43] Although Gardner was not playing as well as he had at Merion, he could still be difficult. "The trouble with him is he never seems to know when he's beaten," Perkerson remarked. And E. E. Giles, after noting that Gardner "jogged around [Oakmont] in 78" in the first qualifying round, wrote that "[he] is a very long player and a very resourceful one, as well, and with the heart of a lion."[44]

Walter Hagen was still putting his money on Jones though: "I followed Bobby Jones around today and got a good line on his game. He surprised me with his drive, which is quite as good, as far as style is concerned and as far as distance, too, as any golfer's here. He seemed to be a bit timid in his irons and was misjudging the distance, but . . . I am of the opinion that he will play better against Bob Gardner tomorrow, as he will go out after the Chicago crack with all the nerve and skill that he possesses." With all that in mind, however, Hagen admitted that he probably would not watch much of the Gardner-Jones match. "I am so keen about the Ouimet-Evans match that I would not want to miss one hole of it."[45]

The weather for the match was picturesque. "The scene yesterday at times resembled the posters of the prepared paint manufacturing and lawn seed merchants that adorn the street car advertising spaces," Harry Smith remarked in the *Pittsburgh Gazette Times*. "The verdant background of the links, the closely cropped shrubbery, the well-kept paths and the bright gowns . . . of the spectators contributed contrast in tints that would have furnished the designs for a kindergarten picture book."[46] The rain that had plagued Pittsburgh since the championship began stayed away as an estimated gallery of three thousand people, gentlemen and ladies alike, turned out to watch the "two greatest amateurs the country has yet produced . . . these two remarkable exponents of the greatest out of doors game on earth."[47]

The crowd was just as rowdy as it had been the previous few days, perhaps even more so—"it was really the east against the west, and the feeling ran high among the gallery," Hagen reported—although the Pittsburgh press downplayed the gallery's boisterousness as innocent enthusiasm.[48] The gallery, "highly sensitive to the rare golf it was witnessing . . . responded in the fashion of school children to the efforts of the celebrated contestants. Every hole saw an outburst of cheering and the spectators expressed their appreciation of the exhibition unreservedly at every opportunity."[49]

There were many opportunities for cheering, as Evans and Ouimet both played exceptionally well. In fact, Evans won the first hole by sinking a "long putt" for an eagle 3. By the end of the first nine holes, Ouimet had claimed a 1-up lead, but both golfers had carded a 1-under-par 36, the best scores posted so far. Ouimet accomplished this by parring the first eight holes and then birdying the par 5 ninth. Evans's round was less consistent; indeed, he made only one par on the entire front nine. After his opening eagle, he bogeyed the second and third, giving Ouimet a 1-up lead. Evans squared the match with a birdie on the fifth hole. His tee shot had found a bunker, but he recovered spectacularly, leaving himself a five-footer, which he sank. Even better, on the sixth hole, Evans, famous for being a terrible putter, sank a massive forty-foot putt from the very edge of the green for another birdie to go 1 up. Then, he bogeyed the seventh and eighth holes, totally erasing his lead. Then Evans and Ouimet tied the ninth with birdies.

Ouimet's game slipped a little on the back nine of the morning round. He birdied the tenth, and Evans matched Ouimet with his own birdie on the twelfth. But they both bogeyed the two par 3 holes (the thirteenth and sixteenth). Evans found a bunker with his tee shot on both holes, but he still had a chance to square the match on the sixteenth if he had sunk his eight-foot putt. Evans had once complained that the U.S. Open always turned into a "putting championship."[50] The same could usually be said of the Amateur, and this match was no exception. On the seventeenth, Ouimet topped his drive and didn't reach the green with his second shot. Evans, meanwhile, two-putted and laid Ouimet a stymie, taking the hole. They halved the eighteenth with pars, and now, the match was even.

Ouimet posted a 1-over-par 74 for the morning's eighteen, while Evans carded an even-par 73—far and away the two best scores turned in since Jones and Adair scored 73s in the practice rounds. It was a remarkable display of golf on a course where many top amateurs struggled to break 90. "Considered from every angle, the contest will stand out as the greatest match ever played in this country," E. E. Giles declared.[51]

The afternoon's golf was just as exciting.

> Long before the time for the afternoon round and the banner event to start, a huge assemblage surrounded the tee for the first hole in anticipation of obtaining a close view of the start of the famed pair.... The tie after the morning round had whetted [the crowd's] appetite for the fray. Ouimet and Evans started with few preliminaries, amid a throng which had grown to immense proportions. There was a moment of stillness and each swung for his drive and

then bedlam broke loose. Staid business men and dignified leaders of fashion joined in the scramble down the fairway and rough which looked for all the world like the intermission between halves of a football match when the snake dance is over.[52]

Evans and Ouimet rewarded their throng of admirers with opening birdies on the par 5 nineteenth hole. Ouimet then took a 1-up lead on the twentieth when his second shot landed within six inches of the cup and Evans conceded. On the twenty-first, Ouimet extended his lead to two holes by carding his third consecutive birdie. Evans ate into that lead with his own birdie on the twenty-second, but then on the very next hole, Ouimet ripped a drive three hundred yards and followed with a masterful niblick to kick-in range (his fourth birdie in five holes). Evans, who dumped his drive into a bunker, readily conceded.

On the twenty-fourth hole, Ouimet's par was good enough to beat Evans's bogey to extend his lead to three holes. After pars on Nos. 25 and 26, Ouimet had played the first eight holes of the afternoon in a remarkable four strokes under par. Then, alas, on the par 5 ninth, in easy range of setting a new scoring record, Ouimet mishit his brassie second shot into a furrowed bunker, struggled to score a bogey, and lost the hole. Still, Walter Hagen called Ouimet's afternoon front-nine—a score of 34 against a par of 37—"one of the finest exhibitions of pars and birdies I have ever seen. If he had not found the trap at [the twenty-seventh] hole with his second shot, which eventually cost him six, he would have been out in 32, which is golf that has never been approached on this difficult course."[53] Ouimet finished 2 up over Evans heading into the final nine holes.

It was a good thing Ouimet had built up a lead, because, physically, he began to visibly weaken down the stretch. His temperature reportedly climbed back over 100 and he was unable to eat all day.[54] Orange juice was the only thing sustaining him.[55] "It was very apparent that the strain was telling on him. He did not seem to have the pep in his game after the tenth was reached," Hagen claimed.[56] A great deal had been made about Ouimet's illness, but only a few journalists noticed Evans's chronic rheumatism, which had been exacerbated by the persistently damp weather. E. E. Giles noticed that both Ouimet and Evans started to tire around the thirty-third hole.[57] Walter Wilkes claimed that Evans was limping from hole to hole.[58] And two years later, in his own memoirs, Evans admitted that his "old enemy," "neuritis or rheumatism," "disclosed himself with disquieting touches of pain in knee, in heel, and occasionally in my right arm" during much of the summer of 1919.[59]

It is certainly possible that Evans's less-publicized health problems prevented him from capitalizing on Ouimet's many mistakes over the last nine. Instead, the two men matched each other stroke for stroke, posting two bogeys and no birdies, until the thirty-second hole, when Evans sank a tricky par putt from six feet to beat Ouimet's bogey. But it was not the beginning of a streak for Evans; both players double-bogeyed the thirty-third after landing their approach shots in bunkers. On the thirty-fourth, Ouimet found sand again, which led to another double bogey, losing to Evans's par. Now, the match was square with just two holes to play. "It [is] easy to go back over the match and point out wherein one or the other failed to take advantage when opportunity knocked at the door," Giles noted. "But when one considers that the scoring was close to par figures for the double round, shall we require of humans absolute perfection when nerves are tense in battle?"[60]

Both champions were clearly running out of steam as their golf became more erratic, "but how gloriously they both came back on the thirty-fifth hole for a grand halve in [birdie] 3," Giles wrote.[61] Now the stage was properly set: the score after thirty-five holes was dead even between America's two greatest amateurs. The gallery was "delirious with excitement," as everyone "ran and flocked and jammed and swarmed for the home green," all seeking "a place of vantage."[62]

Ouimet and Evans both sailed beautiful tee shots down the eighteenth fairway. Ouimet was away and so hit first, pushing his iron into the bunker guarding the right side of the green. Evans now held the clear advantage. Though he pulled his shot slightly, he successfully skirted several hazards and landed his ball in light rough off the left edge of the green. Thus, despite mediocre second shots by both players, the advantage was still Evans's; a relatively straightforward chip and putt would likely win him the match.

"At the home hole, interest was tense, and you could have heard an even faint whisper when Francis went down into the trap to play out," Walter Hagen recounted.[63] "The gallery sympathized with Ouimet," according to a local reporter.

> Before making the shot [Ouimet] surveyed the lie carefully, he spoke to his caddie and the lad handed him his mashie niblick.... A tense moment followed as Ouimet raised his club to make the shot. There was a shower of sand and the ball soared high in the air, dropped to the green and stopped 10 feet from the cup. It was a remarkable shot. The gallery went wild and the chattering lasted several moments.[64]

And just like that, Evans had lost his advantage. The sudden shift in circumstance seemed to rattle him a little—"Evans faltered as he stepped up to his ball." He chipped clumsily, and the ball broke sharply left, leaving him a putt significantly longer than Ouimet's (E. E. Giles estimated Evans's putt at fifteen feet).[65] The USGA could not have planned it better. The match of the season between Chicago's crack and Boston's favorite son came down to who could sink a makeable putt, albeit on one of Oakmont's most complex greens.

Evans was farther away and therefore putted first. "Chick studied the tricky putt on which his title hinged for a good two minutes, then putted and fell about three inches short," ratcheting the tension even higher.[66] "The gallery gasped as [Ouimet] stepped up and prepared to putt. He took care and then hit his ball. All eyes were focused on the small object plainly visible on the greensward. There was a dramatic moment."[67] Then, after the pause, "Ouimet, with his customary smooth putting stroke . . . rolled the ball sweetly [in]to the cup for the match."[68] The gallery erupted in "pandemonium." "Everybody seemed to want to shake the victor's hand at once, hats were tossed into the air, women screamed, and a few friends clustered around the fallen champion to console him" as "Evans walked to Ouimet and shook the hand of his vanquisher."[69]

Evans's defense of his 1916 U.S. Amateur title was officially over. Ouimet had bested him in "an exhibition of sheer grit and indomitable courage seldom equaled and never surpassed in the annals of sport."[70] As Ralph Davis of the *Pittsburgh Press* put it, "Ouimet will go down into golfing history as one of the gamest men who ever trod the greensward or swung a stick."[71] And the match would go down as one of the best ever played. Ouimet posted a 74-76, and Evans posted a 73-78. (Walter Hagen, America's premier professional, had snuck in a round during the event and scored a 76.[72]) Evans and Ouimet were truly well matched. According to press coverage by the *Pittsburgh Post* and the *Pittsburgh Gazette Times*, Ouimet hit twelve fairways and missed only two during the afternoon round, while Evans hit eleven fairways and missed three.

Walter Wilkes, writing in the *Atlanta Georgian*, claimed Evans "was playing his usual brilliant game from tee to green, but displayed the putting weakness which has been his only golfing fault for many years."[73] Yet, in fact, Evans needed just 62 putts to get around the course twice—the exact same number as Ouimet. And although Evans did miss five short putts, he also sank four putts over eight feet long, including putts of twenty-five and forty feet in the morning. Evans was surely a touch inconsistent on the greens, but on this historic occasion, when it counted, he kept up with one of the best putters in the game. Evans's lack of skill on the greens, at least at Oakmont, seems to have been exaggerated, as had Ouimet's illness.

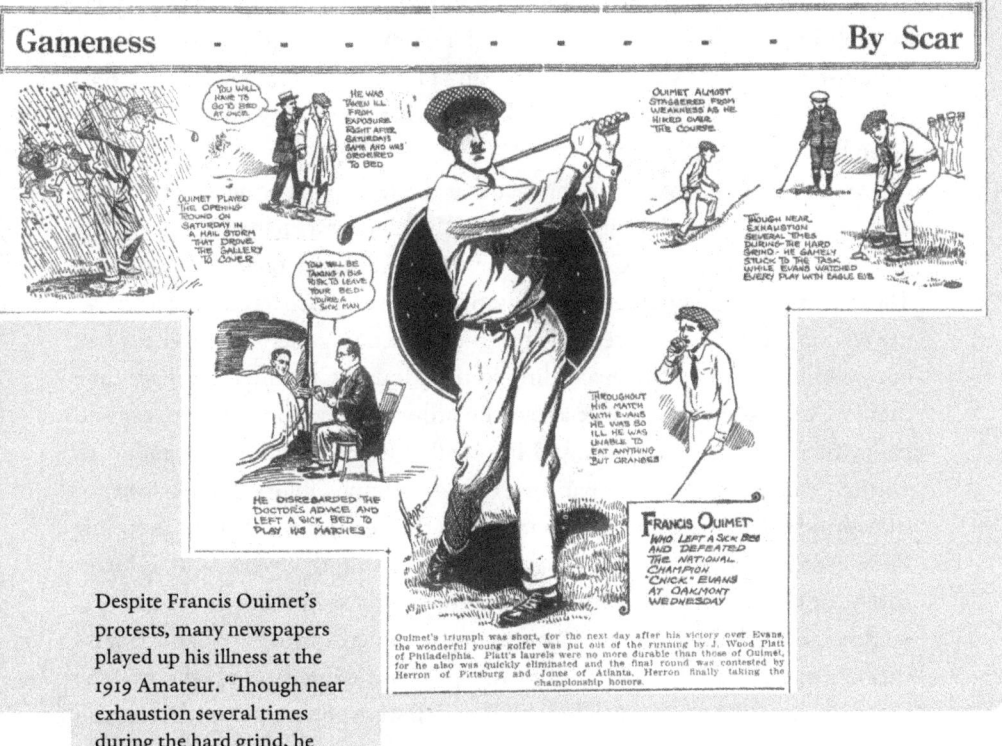

Despite Francis Ouimet's protests, many newspapers played up his illness at the 1919 Amateur. "Though near exhaustion several times during the hard grind, he gamely stuck to the task while Evans watched." Scar, "Gameness," *Anaconda Standard*, 27 August 1919.

To the latter point, Ouimet had said that he was not nearly as sick as his fans worried or as his friends claimed. Evans, rather bitter about the loss, agreed that the press was lionizing Ouimet beyond what he felt was merited. "One of the most remarkable disclosures of the tournament," Evans wrote sarcastically in a syndicated essay a couple of weeks later, "was that Ouimet plays much better golf when slightly ill than when enjoying his usual good health. Of course I had to be the victim of this demonstration, for my record shows that I have a genius for bringing out the best in the other fellow's game."[74]

Continuing his lament, Evans wrote that "the opponent of the interesting invalid is the one to pity. He has no alibi; he is disgraced if he falls and there is no credit if he succeeds."[75] Walter Wilkes concurred: "Evans had rather a raw deal on the whole match today. If he won, he would have said that he beat a sick man and ought to be ashamed of himself for hopping on a cripple, so he could have gotten little if any credit for what would have been a remarkable performance. As it is, Ouimet gets double credit for his victory, which was unquestionably well won and deserved, but which no sick man in the world could have administered to Evans."[76] Even Pittsburgh's Harry Keck had some suspicions: "Hey, old chap, if Ouimet can play like that when he's sick, I'd like to see him when he's well!"[77]

Evans also got a raw deal in the fact that the record-breaking gallery clearly favored his opponent. "Ouimet seemed to [be] almost a unanimous pet of the gallery in his match with 'Chick' Evans," reported the *St. Louis Post-Dispatch*. The newspaper had not sent a representative to the event, so its editor was working off comments made by recently returned St. Louis golfers, all of whom had been eliminated early on. "According to the Mound City men . . . every time that Francis made a shot a little above the ordinary, the 2500 spectators would make the time-worn welkin ring. [Meanwhile,] Evans would have required an 'ostrich' [i.e., scoring 5 under par for a hole—an impossibility at Oakmont] or something better than an 'eagle' to move the throng."[78] It was not the first time Pittsburgh's throngs had been accused of partisanship that week, and unfortunately for the players who had to suffer through it, it would not be the last.

Because of the uncertainty surrounding Ouimet's "tonsillitis" and Evans's rheumatism and the bad behavior of the gallery, the question of who was the superior player, which this head-to-head match was supposed to settle, was still undecided. "In one detail [the match] failed to serve its purpose," Keck wrote. "That was in the matter of proving beyond a question of doubt which man is the better golfer."[79] For most pundits, a 1-up victory was entirely too close to declare one man the nation's true top amateur. They predicted that unsatisfied fans would soon be clamoring for a rematch, too (in their only prior match-play encounter, at Detroit in 1915, Ouimet had also beat Evans 1 up).

For now, though, Ouimet had survived to the third round of match play, despite belonging more in a "hospital ward," as Grantland Rice put it, than on a golf course.[80] And in the quarterfinals he would be facing either J. Wood Platt, who had eliminated one of New York's finest, John Anderson, or Paul Tewksbury, one of the three co-medalists. So when the unknown Platt eliminated the equally unknown Tewksbury, few eyebrows were raised. Regardless, it was still an upset, albeit a small one, and, by now, Platt had demonstrated a knack for them. Ouimet "will have no easy match against the younger golfer," Grantland Rice predicted.[81] Thus, the question Wednesday night on everyone's mind was whether Ouimet could withstand the strain of another thirty-six holes, against a youngster "playing better than he knew how," especially after heroically giving his all to beat Evans.

▶ CHAPTER 14
A YOUTH TAKEOVER

Jimmy Manion had been eliminated in the first round. And Paul Tewksbury had lost in the second. Now they were just waiting for someone to oust Dave Herron so they could play off for U.S. Amateur medalist honors (they'd all tied at 158 in Monday's qualifying rounds) and return home to celebrate their first taste of national glory at their respective clubs in St. Louis and Philadelphia.[1] But Dave Herron persisted. In the Round-of-16 match, he faced veteran Jack Stearns from Nassau Country Club on Long Island, and "few in the gallery conceded a chance to S. Davidson Herron. . . . But their dope was all wrong." After eighteen holes, Dave was only 1 up, but he won the first four holes in the afternoon and scored a decisive 7 and 5 victory.[2]

Of greater interest to the galleries and "overshadowed only by the titanic struggle between the title holder [Chick Evans] and the great Ouimet" was Bob Jones's rematch against his "arch-enemy" Bob Gardner.[3] Many, including Walter Hagen, predicted that Jones would win this match because he had the rare ability to raise his game to whatever level he needed in the moment to win. Plus, Gardner had already beaten him at Merion in 1916, and the lingering memory of that stinging loss was more than enough to spur Jones to victory. Of course, he had also grown up a lot since Merion and gained a great deal of match-play experience. There was also the factor of Gardner's play. Despite Gardner's thrilling victory in an up-and-down match against Max Marston, most writers gave Jones the edge. "Gardner had rather been expected to fail after his unsteadiness Tuesday in the first round against Marston," Harry Smith wrote in the *Pittsburgh Gazette Times*, "but he proved far weaker than forecasted."[4]

By the end of the first five holes, Bob was already 4 up—"Bobby started off like a race horse," Francis Ouimet wrote afterward—but, in fact, he'd only carded one birdie.[5] Both players were missing fairways—switching drivers ultimately did not solve Jones's wildness off the tee—but his recovery shots were much better than Gardner's, which is why he was winning. He was 3 up after eighteen holes, posting nine-hole scores of 39-40 versus Gardner's 41-41.[6]

Remembering Gardner's legendary ability to play from behind, Jones "de-

The press frequently used this photo of Bob Jones in their coverage of the 1919 U.S. Amateur. Bain News Service, ca. 1915–1920, Library of Congress.

cided to beat him to the punch" in the afternoon round.[7] In fact, he put together a performance that, though much sloppier in execution, rivaled Francis Ouimet's remarkable afternoon front nine against Evans. He started with a birdie on the nineteenth hole to go 4 up. Unlike at Merion, Jones was regularly out-driving Gardner, reflecting his greater height and strength. According to Walter Hagen, "Bobby is the longest driver here, and should he be able to keep his shots 'straight down the course he will find it a great help' to scoring, and will be a dangerous rival for any man that he meets."[8]

But that was Jones's main difficulty and what Stewart Maiden had traveled from St. Louis to correct; what Jones had gained in distance, he had lost in accuracy. For instance, on the twenty-first hole he hooked his long drive into the rough. His recovery was spectacular, however, and he nailed an iron that carried him to the green. Gardner, in contrast, found the fairway but was short with his second, and his third "mashie was poor." But he did manage to get up and down, sinking his "long putt for a 4." Jones, however, still couldn't figure out Oakmont's greens, so he "took three putts and lost the hole."[9]

Jones's tee game and putting were erratic for the rest of the match. He hooked again on the twenty-second, sliced on the twenty-third, and found the rough on the twenty-fifth. But each time, he recovered with astonishing skill. His "beautiful" iron shot on the twenty-third "stopped three feet from the pin." And he was still on the green in two strokes on the twenty-fifth, his iron, "as usual," getting "him out of the difficulty."[10] Gardner simply could not keep up and lost hole after hole, unable to take advantage of the many mistakes that Jones continued to make.

On the twenty-seventh hole of the day, Jones found the fairway, for once, while Gardner did not, and took advantage of the error. "Bobby's brassie shot was [t]he best seen during the day. It carried fully 200 yards and stopped four feet from the cup," the reporter for the *Atlanta Constitution* wrote. "Gardner took three to get on and laid Jones a half stymie on his putt" to prevent him from holing out for eagle. It didn't matter, though; Jones was still "down in [birdie] four and won the hole," completing the front nine in 2-under-par 35.[11]

Gardner was now 6 down heading in to the last nine holes of the match. This proved to be an insurmountable lead, which was fortunate for Jones since his game fell to shambles in the last few holes. The trouble started on the twenty-ninth, when he "found all kinds of trouble" and carded a double-bogey 6. On the par 5 thirtieth, he "had a beautiful drive and an equally beautiful brassie shot, but he dubbed his next two shots" and, after Gardner laid his third shot close for an easy birdie, missed his par putt and conceded the hole.[12] On the par 3 thirty-first, both Jones and Gardner drove into bunkers. Jones, once again displaying his superb recovery game, easily got out in one shot whereas Gardner took two. But Gardner's second sand shot was dead to the pin. And Jones's putt, continuing the theme, drifted just a little wide of the cup. They halved the hole with bogey 4s. Jones was now 4 up with five holes to play, having played the last three holes in four strokes over par.

On the thirty-second hole of the day, Jones found yet another bunker off the tee, while Gardner's drive was straight. On his second shot, Jones decided to play safely out of the hazard into the fairway instead of going for the green. Gardner, in contrast, misjudged the distance for his short iron, flew his ball over the green to the left, hit "the side of a trap, [and] buried itself in the soft earth." At the time, there was no rule allowing a one-stroke penalty for an embedded lie. So, Gardner swatted uselessly at his ball three times, only burying it deeper in the mud, before conceding the hole.[13] With that concession Jones was 5 up with four holes left, so the match was over. He and Gardner "shook hands smilingly while the gallery applauded and then wandered off to follow Ouimet and Evans, who had just started on their afternoon round."[14]

"Both were playing spotty golf at the finish," Grantland Rice acknowledged in his coverage of the Round-of-16 match, "but that brilliant outward journey of 35 was more than sufficient to put young Jones beyond want or trouble."[15] Jones's hometown journalists were even more laudatory, despite his meltdown on the final holes of the match. "Bobby played a game that was of the championship brand," Angus Perkerson wrote, while still briefly acknowledging those "few ragged holes toward the last."[16] The sports editor of the *Atlanta Constitution* told readers, "Many bets were placed tonight, because of Jones' remarkable shooting against the veteran crafty Gardner, that the youngster will eliminate all his opponents and get into the finals, with Francis Ouimet, as his opponent."[17] Perkerson believed that a Jones-Ouimet match would be the perfect cap to a championship that had already featured a showdown between America's greatest amateurs.

> There would be something about a match between Jones and Ouimet that would have even more dashing qualities [than Evans-Ouimet]. Both brilliant golfers, both smashing them for great distances from the tee, both match players of the most indomitable kind. What a fight from start to finish it would be! . . . If the Fates want to bring the tournament to its fitting climax, surely they'll arrange to have the finals between these two. . . .They have the best chance of all, they are playing the best golf, they are the best golfers left in the struggle.[18]

Ouimet actually thought that Jones looked "like a splendid bet for the high honor."[19]

Walter Hagen, meanwhile, predicted that Bob Jones would defeat Rudolph Knepper in the quarterfinals in "an easy match."[20] Harry Smith, writing in the *Pittsburgh Gazette Times*, agreed that it would be difficult for anyone to defeat Jones with him "going like a steam roller," though "Knepper had been playing excellent golf and many . . . picked him to down the Georgia comet."[21] W. C. Fownes Jr., "a remarkable putter and on his native heath," was expected to beat George Hoffner easily.[22] And Grantland Rice felt that Dave Herron would be "a strong contender all the way," even though his third-round opponent, the Canadian W. J. Thompson, had defeated Nelson Whitney, 7 and 6, and had "been playing good, sound golf."[23]

For the first time during competition, almost everyone's predictions came true in the quarterfinals, except for one huge upset. "Early in the week it was freely predicted by men who have followed championship golf for years that the national amateur tourney at Oakmont would be productive of more highlights and surprises and upsets than any national tourney ever held," commented Harry Keck. "Verily the tournament is running true to form."[24] Philadelphia's largely unknown twenty-year-old J. "Woody" Platt eliminated Francis Ouimet in a gripping thirty-eight-hole match.

Fans concerned that Ouimet's strength might not hold out in the face of his ongoing illness and the stress of championship play were right to worry. "Anyone who saw the match with Evans Wednesday could hardly realize that this was the same man who had overthrown the champion in one of the most soul-stirring and thrilling matches this country has ever seen," Walter Wilkes wrote. Ouimet "was very weak yesterday and was hardly able to swing a club. The quality of his golf naturally deteriorated. His strength gave out, but his superb nerve and fighting courage didn't, and he made a match of it on pure grit alone." Indeed, Ouimet fought from 3 down with four holes left in regulation to square the match on the last hole.[25]

"The players walked through the seething crowd to the first tee again" to play extra holes in sudden death. The beautiful weather from the day before had disappeared behind roiling black clouds—over a half-inch of rain fell during the day, with sustained heavy bursts in the morning and late afternoon—and rain began to fall especially hard just as Ouimet reached the green in two "beautifully played shots." Platt, according to Walter Wilkes, was twenty to thirty feet short of the green with his second shot on a downhill incline, so "it looked now like Ouimet's hole and match, and praise for his great comeback was heard on all sides." But the rain worsened, immediately drenching the green. With his third shot, Platt somehow laid the ball "a scant 3 inches from the cup, while the crowd went wild." Ouimet, meanwhile, took two putts on the suddenly soggy greens and halved the hole.[26] So Platt and Ouimet had to play on.

On the thirty-eighth hole, Ouimet's "fast-waning strength" proved unequal "to the task of the iron-willing Platt."[27] Ouimet hooked his drive into the rough while Platt found the fairway. Ouimet took two shots to reach the edge of the green, while Platt's 7-iron stopped somewhere between six and twelve feet from the hole. "The situation looked black and the crowd held its collective breath while the great Francis studied the line of his twenty-foot putt, oblivious to the driving rain which was seeping over the course." The loyal gallery was absolutely soaked by this point. Afterward, Wilkes theorized that Ouimet "failed to allow for the wetness of the turf," and that was why his twenty-footer to halve the hole stopped six inches short. With that, Platt played his first putt cautiously before sinking his tap-in to win the hole and the match. "The great crowd cheered and rushed madly for the clubhouse to save what dry spots they had left on them," Wilkes joked. "Many had none to save and accepted the situation philosophically, walking sedately and with measured tread back to the locker room and the hot shower. It was bad to get a drenching, but every[one] agreed that such a match was worthwhile."[28]

Reflecting on the match afterward, Ouimet wrote that he considered Woody Platt "one of the gamest chaps I have ever played against."[29] Walter Hagen was certainly impressed with the young Philadelphian. "He . . . unbottled two of the finest shots I have seen played in the tournament." The first was his approach on the thirty-seventh hole: "With Francis on the green . . . near the pin [Platt] realized that he must chip dead, and pulled off the shot to perfection. The ball looked to be going far over the green, but, with a world of backspin on, it stopped with a sudden jerk a few inches short of the cup. Another turn and he would have holed out." Platt's other marvelous shot was his approach on the thirty-eighth: "It was a long mashie niblick . . . that he shot high in the air, letting it drop ten feet or so from the cup. It showed that he was master of this shot as well, which is a valuable asset." Thus, according to Hagen's observations, Platt's victory was neither a total fluke nor the result of Ouimet's illness alone. "Platt is full of confidence," Hagen pointed out. "He believed he could beat Ouimet and he did."[30]

In the upper right corner, Francis Ouimet shakes J. Wood Platt's hand after conceding the match on the thirty-eighth hole. To the left is Dave Herron, on the right is Bob Jones in his bowtie and flat cap, and on the bottom is a photo of the crowd surrounding the ninth green during the final match. Photographs by Edwin Lerick, Cherry/Herron Family Archives.

But now Platt would have to face Dave Herron, and Herron was regularly turning in the best cards of the competition. In his quarterfinal match, he "started out at a terrific clip," shot 35-38 for a jaw-dropping 73 despite the rain, and had a "commanding" eight-hole lead over W. J. Thompson by the end of the morning. Thompson, one of five superb golfing brothers from Canada, was by no means a weak opponent.[31] He had reached the semifinals of the 1919 Canadian Amateur a few weeks earlier, and had demolished New Orleans's Nelson Whitney in the previous round. But Herron was simply playing better than Thompson, especially in the morning rain. "Rain makes a lot of difference on the Oakmont course," Hagen explained, "as the traps are made out of very heavy sand mixed with clay, and it is a tough job to get the ball out if the lie is a bit bad." Thompson tried to mount a comeback in the afternoon, playing his best golf on the opening nine, but Herron won three consecutive holes and then halved the eleventh to end the match.[32]

"I wrote early in the week about Dave and remarked that he was one of the unknowns that was likely to be found there at the finish," Hagen wrote in his summary of the quarterfinal match. "Herron learned his golf on this very course, and... Dave is not lacking in the old nerve test." As such, Hagen "look[ed] for a great fight" between Herron and Platt in the semifinals, although Hagen didn't reveal who he thought would win.[33] Francis Ouimet was equally ambivalent in his predictions for the semifinals. "I have played against Herron and know Platt's game, since I was forced to defeat by him," Ouimet wrote, "and I think it is a standoff, with both men having a fine chance to win. Herron had the easiest time of the four yesterday, a fact which should favor him."[34]

Joining Herron in the semifinals was fellow Oakmonter W. C. Fownes Jr., who had defeated George Hoffner in a very close match. Hoffner was a young former caddie from Philadelphia and "gave Fownes a bitter tussle." Hoffner led by two holes at the turn but fell apart on the second nine when he started catching hazards on virtually every hole. The rain also complicated matters for both competitors. "Fownes was off his game considerably," his putting was "particularly bad," and he did not "give it the earnestness which usually characterizes his play." Still, Fownes was able to utilize his legendary recovery skills on the course he and his father had designed, and by the end of the morning eighteen had secured a 2-up lead, which he maintained through the thirty-fifth hole.[35] Fownes's semifinal opponent would be Bob Jones, the only non-Pennsylvanian of the four golfers left.[36] (This was also the furthest any Southerner had ever advanced in the U.S. Amateur.)

For the honor of facing Fownes, Bob Jones had defeated Iowa's nineteen-year-old Rudy Knepper in another close match, 3 and 2. Knepper was a solid golfer who in two years would represent the United States at the inaugural Walker Cup. And in contrast to Walter Hagen's prediction, Knepper was not an easy opponent. "Bobby Jones found Knepper, who is the surprise of the tournament, a hard man to shoot along with," the reporter for the *Atlanta Constitution* was forced to admit, "and at the end of the 18th [Jones] was two down." Both men were struggling in the rain—"morning play was sloppy" according to the *Pittsburgh Gazette Times*—and shooting well into the 80s.[37] The weather improved for their afternoon round, but "although the sun was shining, the course was wet and the stances were bad."[38] Bob Jones played much the same in the afternoon as he had in the morning. His irons were still superior, and his tee shots erratic. "The Atlanta star was having a woeful time keeping his tee shots on the course," Grantland Rice explained. "He was hitting too soon and, therefore, hooking badly."[39] But, luckily for Jones, Knepper suddenly "contracted a habit of topping his tee shots," and the match ended on the thirty-fourth green, with Jones 3 up.[40]

Now, Fownes was "surrounded by a flock of youngsters out to prove that golf is far from being a veteran's game."[41] And most people following the matches believed youth and vigor would triumph over age and experience. "The entry who bags the amateur championship at Pittsburgh by Saturday afternoon will have played [approximately] 234 holes," Rice pointed out. "He will have slogged around between 65 and 70 miles under the added stress of a heavy nervous strain. He will have played something approaching 1,200 shots. Taking these vital statistics into consideration, offhand, we should say he will have earned his crown."[42] Certainly, the man who wanted to win would need a great deal of stamina to make it, and under such grueling circumstances, youthful athleticism truly was a boon.

Neither Fownes nor Jones had played their best games in the quarterfinals. Walter Hagen chalked Jones's problems up to the weather: he "is not particularly fond of a wet course, [but] should the sun shine tomorrow he will be his old self again."[43] And Walter Wilkes, rather irreverently, attributed Fownes's difficulties to being "past his best days and never a wonderful player."[44] But all agreed that though Jones was likely to win, he would have his work cut out for him. "Fownes is one of the most resourceful golfers I know of, and a man who has to be beaten, for he will never beat himself," Ouimet wrote. "Jones is playing superbly, but, believe me, he faces a tough customer in Fownes. Bill Fownes has been through the mill before, but I rather think Bobby's brilliancy will pull him through."[45] Angus Perkerson agreed with Ouimet in his own column: "At times

[Jones's] game has been brilliant, for brief moments it has been ragged . . . but always it has been good enough to win. In short, he has proved that he has the championship qualities."[46] In other words, no matter how well Fownes played, Jones would find a way to play better.

Walter Wilkes praised Jones in less modest terms: "Bobby is capable of playing better golf than any of the other three contestants, without doubt, but the question is whether he will do it today and Saturday." And while Wilkes felt Fownes was past his prime, the journalist admitted that Jones would "have to play good golf [to win], as Old Bill Fownes . . . is a steady plugger who never goes far wrong and who knows his home course from A to Z."[47] Unsurprisingly, the Pittsburgh press liked Fownes's chances better than Atlanta's press did. Harry Keck believed that Fownes, "playing over his home course, and with his unusually fine short game to stand him in good stead, would win over the youthful Bobby Jones." Keck acknowledged that Jones had been "ploughing his way through the field," but he figured Fownes's steady play could compensate.[48] Either way, Jones could not afford to be as erratic as he had been in previous matches.

Fownes was not only a skilled golfer but also one of the visionaries behind Oakmont's design, a fact that Wilkes did not hesitate to bring up. "The general impression prevails that Bill played a test round on a course that was all fairway and put traps wherever his ball was not, but of course, this is mere guesswork," he wrote. "When [Fownes] does get in, believe me, he knows how to get out, which is a secret he has kept lo! these many years."[49]

However, this supposed advantage was not in evidence during the Fownes-Jones match. The weather for this round of matches was "fair" (i.e., no rain) and helped dry out the course "fast." Perhaps that was why Fownes struggled all day with green speeds and failed to sink "easy putts."[50] Jones was also much longer off the tee and cleaner with his irons, which gave him a distinct advantage. Still, Jones was not "playing his best game" in the morning—he carded sevens on the par 5 fourth hole and the par 5 twelfth, which was shaping up to be his nemesis hole—but he "steadied as the match progressed."[51]

Importantly, Jones kept his temper in check throughout the match. His only reported emotional outburst came on the 282-yard seventeenth after he drove into a bunker guarding the green. According to the *Atlanta Journal*, "when he failed to get out as well as he wished, he pounded the sand with his club."[52] This behavior was not nearly as volatile as breaking or throwing clubs, but the course was still clearly getting under Jones's skin. He shot an 81 in the morning while Fownes shot 82.

In the afternoon, Jones "gradually crept ahead," "gaining in strength as the grind continued," and eventually Fownes "succumbed" to the teenager "after a gallant fight in which he brought forth every resource born of a ripe experience."[53] And the Pittsburgh galleries loved it. "When Bobby walked across the green ... and grasped Fownes' hand, the big crowd cheered wildly," and Jones requested that someone "send a message to mother."[54] Youth had defeated experience. But E. E. Giles was quick to defend Pittsburgh's native star, writing, "Fownes was obliged to climb the hill because his game was not quite up to his best standard. . . . His game was good enough to get past his first three matches, but yesterday it lacked just enough in finesse to hold the sturdy youth from the land where Sherman marched to the sea."[55] In other words, the Pittsburgh press was not yet ready to concede that seventeen-year-old Bob Jones could beat W. C. Fownes Jr. on a good day. Fownes's best, in their eyes, was still better than Jones's best.

In the other semifinal match, Dave Herron demolished Woody Platt, ending the match on the thirtieth hole. It was supposed to be a much closer affair, but Harry Keck theorized that Platt "in defeating Ouimet in 38 holes on Thursday, did just about what Ouimet did in beating Chick Evans the day before. He played himself out and proved an easy victim for his next opponent."[56] So far, Dave Herron had played eight fewer holes than Bob Jones during his four matches—only a small difference in miles walked and exposure to heavy rain and hot weather. But on a course as demanding as Oakmont, the extra rest, the blowout matches, and the advantage of sleeping in his own bed likely gave Herron a slight edge in a finale that the Pittsburgh and Atlanta presses both agreed would be "a herculean struggle."[57]

No one had predicted that the 1919 U.S. Amateur would come down to a twenty-one-year-old from Pittsburgh and a seventeen-year-old from Atlanta. "Youth is pitted against youth," the *Pittsburgh Press* editorialized the morning of the final match. "Stacking their youthful enthusiasm against the steady nerves of their tournament-broken elders, they have emerged at the top of the heap."[58]

Although most on-site reporters, including the *Atlanta Georgian*'s Walter Wilkes, acknowledged that whoever won would be worthy of the title, seeds were already being planted that Herron's success was due to a healthy dose of luck. "It is through the efforts of Francis Ouimet, the Boston man, that one of the two youths will be the new champion," the sports editor for the *Pittsburgh Press* wrote, "for there was no other player in the tournament who could have defeated Evans."[59] Put another way, if Francis Ouimet hadn't eliminated Chick Evans and exhausted himself in the process, Dave Herron would not be in the finals. Walter Wilkes also insinuated that Herron had had an easier bracket than Jones—"Pittsburghers are backing Davy Herron pretty strongly in the finals today but if I'm not badly mistaken they will have a shock. . . . Anyway, Davie Herron won't have another set-up today like he has had so far through the tournament."[60] Grantland Rice was even blunter: "Herron has had a somewhat easier road to travel in the championship at the final turn."[61] But that was unfair both to Herron's opponents and to Herron, who, unlike Jones, had been shooting regularly in the 70s since the qualifying rounds.

"This has been a peculiar tournament in more ways than one," Walter Wilkes continued. First, Oakmont, he claimed, was an unusually difficult test of championship golf, made all the more challenging by the recurring rains (and even hail). Second, the former champions who were expected to do well fell to the wayside. Byers failed to qualify, Travers lost in the first round, Evans and Gardner in the second, Ouimet in third, and Fownes in the fourth. "It was conceded before the tournament that one of these former champions would come through, while Jones was admitted to be a possibility," Wilkes wrote. "Herron, however, was not thought of at all by the dopesters."[62] Even Pittsburghers who had been paying attention to Herron's outstanding play thought he was a longshot for the finals.

Now, the press split neatly down partisan lines; Pittsburgh's writers were confident in Herron's abilities whereas Atlanta's writers believed their prodigy would walk away with the crown. And they were none too kind to the Pennsylvanian. "Herron is a huge fellow who relies more on the strength he can put behind a drive than on the cut shot for the green or any of the finer points of the game," Wilkes criticized. "He has been practicing at Oakmont for months, they say"—which was untrue, of course, since he did not begin playing regularly until August 1—"and knows the course from top to bottom. Well, he can't know it any better than Old Bill Fownes, and look what happened to Bill."[63] The journalist for the *Atlanta Constitution* pointed out that "Herron, although older . . . has less general golfing experience than Jones, and for that reason many expert golfers" think Jones will win.[64] And the nicest thing the *Atlanta Journal* could say about Herron was that he was "filled with confidence through his victory yesterday over J. Wood Platt" and was therefore "expected to force the equally confident Atlanta youth to the limit." But the implication was clear: Dave Herron would not win.[65]

Grantland Rice was a little more even-handed when comparing the young men's games. "Both are terrific long hitters and both belong to the slashing school which is willing to go after any chance shooting for the pin regardless of any trap or bunker that may wait in surly silence to catch any mistake." Both

Herron and Jones had proved they had the physical power to escape furrowed bunkers laden with wet sand—although in Jones's most recent match against Fownes, he'd had several adverse experiences with embedded lies in bunkers. Still, the two finalists were evenly matched when it came to tee shots and irons. And yet, amid all the compliments, Rice couldn't resist commenting on Herron's weight—"his displacement ranges up around 200 pounds."[66]

Walter Hagen focused on Herron's remarkable string of victories and avoided making any comments on his appearance but still placed his bets on Jones:

> Not much attention has been paid to Herron's game, but I have seen bits of it off and on. His last three matches have been run-away affairs, so far as he outclassed his opponents. [Yet] he has nothing on Young Jones, who will make him hustle to keep up with him on the shots. It is little wonder that these two reached the finals, as this is a course where long driving counts for a great deal. ... Of the two games I fancy Jones' the most, and if he can putt, should beat his Pittsburgh rival.[67]

Ouimet, in contrast, refused to call a winner at all. Instead, he lauded Jones's recent performance against Fownes and declared that it would be a thrilling showdown:

> Jones and Herron are both finished players. Both are capable of performing wonderful stunts on the links. In defeating Fownes yesterday, Jones put out of the running a veteran of many years. This in itself proved the great game that Jones can play. The finals today should bring forth a grand match. Both are aggressive and brilliant. They are long hitters and from the standpoint of the spectators it should be the most interesting final yet played.[68]

Even Harry Keck, the *Pittsburgh Gazette Times*'s sporting editor, didn't come out for Herron—"Who will win the final today? No predictions from us. From where we take in the situation, it looks about a toss-up. Whichever wins will do so by a small margin."[69]

Only E. E. Giles seemed willing to state on the record that he thought Dave Herron would win, and he had several good arguments to support his opinion. One, Herron was scoring better than anyone else, including Bob Jones. "Jones has played just well enough to win his matches," Giles granted, but "Herron to date has played the best golf in the tournament, which is, indeed, a distinction." Two, Herron understood Oakmont's greens in a way Jones hadn't unlocked yet. And three, Herron was imperturbable. He was calm under pressure and not easily rattled. Golf, according to Grantland Rice, was all "a matter of nerve re-

Victor and Vanquished in Recent Golf Tourney

"Victor and Vanquished in Recent Golf Tourney," *Atlanta Constitution*, 26 August 1919.

pression, of constantly holding your nervous system in check" so that you did not become overwhelmed during "the gap of two or three minutes between strokes [when you can] ponder moodily upon all the matters of disaster than can overtake you."[70] And Jones had not yet achieved Herron's level of emotional grace. Furthermore, there were reports that "should [Jones's] opponent at some stage of a match outdrive him by as much as 10 feet, it is said he may become rattled or angry and not put up his best game."[71]

In short, though it remained a minority view, the combination of Dave Herron's personality, comparable power, and greater insight into Oakmont's devilish greens might well give him an edge over Bob Jones during a week when all parts of his game were clicking. But the celebrity attached to Jones's name, his status as a child prodigy, and his reputation as "the Little Golden Tornado" meant that the press would continue to favor him. And even those who—almost begrudgingly—admitted that Herron stood a chance predicted a very close match.

Either way, at the dawn of the Roaring Twenties, youth would triumph at Oakmont.

▶ CHAPTER 15
THE CHAMPIONSHIP MATCH

THE MORNING ROUND

The United States Golf Association did not fully grasp how much golf had grown during the wartime hiatus. Public interest was at an all-time high, but after two years, the organization was rusty at choreographing national championships.[1] As a result, the 1919 U.S. Amateur, despite its star-studded, multi-generational field and first-class venue, was still an administrative mess. USGA officials, whose headquarters were downtown, arrived in Pittsburgh late. They barely got pairing sheets out in time for the qualifying rounds. They didn't expect Pittsburghers to show up in the many thousands and thus didn't set up ropes. Nor did they arrange transportation for players or visiting spectators to get from their hotels to the golf course. Instead, many had to rely on the train, and service was spotty, especially in the evenings.[2]

Despite the hurdles, America's fledgling corps of golf journalists recognized this was their best opportunity yet to reach a national audience and so struggled on to cover the championship. "Press accommodations were wretched," a columnist with the pen-name Gibby wrote in the *Pittsburgh Post*. "Golf scribes gathered from far and near, and found curt treatment and inadequate facilities."[3] For one, because there were no ropes, the press had to compete with spectators to get an eye on the unfolding action. Inevitably, this affected the accuracy and consistency of press coverage, particularly for the final match. Two, the USGA had failed to anticipate how many newspapers would want to cover the event. Thus, even though

> days before the tournament began the telegraph head in that section had been warned that he should arrange for enough men and wires to take on 50,000 words at least[, h]e smiled to himself and prepared to take care of 20,000, with the result that when on the very first day there was thrust at his men 65,000 words they were swamped and the news did not filter through.

According to John Anderson, crowded around the telegraph every day "were fifteen reporters, some duplicating their copy as many as seven times and each one sending from two to four thousand words per day."[4] Among those writers were Walter Wilkes of Atlanta, Joe Davis of Chicago, D. J. McGuiness of Boston, and Perry Lewis and Spick Hall of Philadelphia. Representing New York, in addition to anonymous correspondents for the Associated Press and the *New York Times*, were Innis Brown, William Everett Hicks, William Abbott, P. C. Culver, Harry C. Smith, John Anderson, and by far the most widely syndicated sportswriter of all, Grantland Rice of the *New York Tribune*. Walter Hagen and Francis Ouimet were both trying to send out their syndicated articles every day, too. Hagen and Ouimet were largely nonpartisan (though Hagen clearly leaned toward Bob Jones), but the other writers all came from either the East, the South, or the West. Whether Pittsburgh really counted as "West" was still a matter of debate—Grantland Rice even asked in his "Sportlight" column, "Where is Pittsburgh? Is it East or West?"[5] But the Steel City certainly was not part of the traditional East. That honor belonged to Boston, Philadelphia, and New York.

The rivalry between golf's Eastern and Western factions ran deep. As an example, the Western Amateur still invited Francis Ouimet to compete even after the Eastern-dominated USGA revoked his amateur status in 1916. And in return, Eastern writers trash-talked Western golf, including in an April 1919 column that Hicks wrote in the *Brooklyn Daily Eagle* boasting that the top ten Eastern players would demolish the top ten Western players in a head-to-head competition.[6] Yet, the two finalists of the 1919 Amateur were not Easterners. In fact, none of the Eastern contingent fared well at Oakmont, and New York's writers were livid. It seemed the Big Apple's influence over American golf was fading. "Put one thing in your pipe and smoke it," Harry C. Smith, a nationally syndicated columnist, wrote. "The Metropolitan district has not had the amateur since 1913. . . . There use[d] to be an unwritten law that the contest should go to the New York section every third year, at least, like the National annual meeting, but the game is widening at such a rate new conditions upset traditions."[7]

The behind-the-scenes politics and factional bickering may have influenced newspaper predictions about who would win: Dave Herron or Bob Jones? The Western press was actually fairly neutral in its predictions for the match, though the Pittsburgh papers offered Dave Herron some warm praise. In contrast, the Atlanta papers, which had never been quiet about their full-throated support for Bob Jones, loudly announced that their Wonder Boy would finally put Atlanta on the map as an emerging golf capital. Interestingly, the Eastern press also came out for Jones because a seventeen-year-old winning the first Amateur after a two-year hiatus would make fantastic copy and sell many, many papers—providing, of course, that the writers could actually telegraph their stories in time for the evening editions.

The chaos surrounding press accommodations was reflected in the coverage of the match; even within the same newspaper, accounts of what transpired often varied dramatically by writer. But there were a few basic facts that (almost) everyone agreed on: Jones hit the opening tee shot; the morning round started at 10:37 a.m.; Oakmont played (officially) at 6,707 yards; the day was exceptionally hot and muggy; the match lasted thirty-two holes, with Herron winning 5 and 4; and the gallery doubled, perhaps even trebled in size as the afternoon wore on. At the start, between 2,500 and 4,000 individuals gathered around the first tee and fairway, straining to catch a faint glimpse of the action. By the end of the match, the gallery consisted of somewhere between 6,000 and 8,000 people—probably more than had attended the Evans-Gardner championship match at Merion in 1916.

Adding to the colorful mix, Oakmont's young caddie corps, partisan to a fault and more than ready to jostle for best viewing position, had turned out to see one of their own play for the trophy.[8] Innis Brown, Southern born and bred but now part of New York's sportswriting elite, was amazed. "The real golf enthusiasts, both star and dub alike, in a decided minority mingled with the neophyte and the merely curious but feverish laity," he wrote.

> Staid business and professional men, corpulent, lean and compromises between the two, clad in palm beaches, mohairs and cool clothes, pulled, dragged, hauled and coaxed their helpmates from hill to dale and back again. Small boys, gay youngsters and giddy misses scuttled helter skelter in wild confusion. Plain, ordinary John Does and Richard Does sallied back and forth from mound to flat in the big scramble to watch the excitement.[9]

Brown was especially struck by Pittsburgh's demonstrative working-class spectators: "Gentry who exuded prominence and affluence mingled with the boys who looked on and stared in amazement as though they were taking a first slant at Niagara Falls, the Leaning Tower of Pisa, or some other world wonder, the while their hands betokened the early closing of the steel mills and iron foundries on Saturday afternoons."[10]

Innis Brown's dismissive attitude toward the mill and foundry workers—he referred to the locals as "wild rabble" and "the mob" and bemoaned the USGA's decision not to employ ropes to contain them—was pervasive among the press. Instead of feeling excited that American golf was attracting a new audience, some golf writers took on the mantle of custodians and denigrated the working-class galleries for not knowing where to stand or when to cheer. "Sportsmanship is not a thing to be regulated into a man," O. B. Keeler lamented afterward. "There never was a rule or a law yet that would take the yellow out of a man's system or make a poor sport into a good one."[11] "Doubtless there were many who were not certain whether a niblick was an instrument of play or just merely a condition that a player encountered in the jolly pursuit of the pesky little white ball," Brown mocked.[12]

By 1919, Pittsburgh had already developed a reputation for rowdy crowds at its sporting events. That boisterous partisanship was on full display the previous fall when Pitt demolished Georgia Tech's football team (32–0) along with any claim the Yellow Jackets had to being No. 1 in the nation.[13] Whether it was baseball, football, boxing, or—it turned out—golf, the folk of the Iron City did not hold back. The result was a lot of cheering for Dave Herron's good shots, some nasty applause for Bob Jones's bad ones, and periodic trash talk.[14] The St. Louis contingent reported that, throughout earlier rounds, they heard and saw "many violations of golf etiquette noticeable on the part of the gallery," including "goat-getting prejudiced remarks and actions deliberately intended to disconcert the contestants." Walter Hagen observed that the crowd's jeering visibly upset Bob Jones: "'Bobby' appeared to be worried over the fact that the crowd cheered several times when he got into trouble, as he had never heard any one wish him hard luck before in a golf match." And the *New York Times* correspondent humorously verified Hagen's claim in recounting the crowd's taunting of Bob as the championship match drew to an end: "The crowd was decidedly partisan for the home club player and some of the younger and irrepressible element through [sic] it was 'de rigueur' to give three rousing cheers when young Robbie, 4 down and only 6 to play, pitched from one trap into another at the thirteenth green."[15]

Trying to keep the galleries in check were USGA officials and Oakmont club members armed with little yellow flags and, in a few cases, megaphones. They largely failed in their efforts and managed to annoy both the spectators, who did not care for the constant harassment, and the players, who would have preferred to play with fewer distractions. "The truth is that spectators were woefully handled here during the tourney," Gibby chided in his "Morning Hatchet" column of the *Pittsburgh Post*:

> Much has been said and written of the etiquette of golf. The game has been surrounded with a lot of sacred mummery that the high priests, inmates of the holy of holies, preach upon every occasion. But, so far as our observations

go, and there are hundreds of Pittsburghers honestly interested in the game, but hardly devotees of the game, who also observed that the "etiket" of golf, as practiced and applied at Oakmont last week, particularly in the handling of the gallery, which contained many non-golfers who gathered out of curiosity, drawn by the spectacle of glamor of the National tournament, consists mainly in clothing a number of inconsiderate, ignorami with a little brief authority, arming them with an overwhelming conceit and megaphones, and sending them forth to heckle, annoy, worry and bedevil the spectators.[16]

The battle between the gallery and officials only increased as the tension of the championship match ratcheted up. "It was the noisiest golf final yet seen," claimed the *New York Sun*.[17] And Herron and Jones put on a brilliant show for their fans. "Back and forth, across hill and dale, those two kids fought all day long," Perry Lewis wrote in the *Philadelphia Inquirer*. "One, the 'golden tornado' of the South: the other a son of the City of Iron and Steel—and they battled with a courage that was sublime."[18]

As predicted, the two were very close in length off the tee, although Herron, according to Herron family lore, relied mainly on his brassie, or 2-wood, for driving (see Appendix 2). More importantly, Jones drove the ball straighter than he had all week and hit the fairways as often (more or less) as Herron (see Appendix 3).[19] It was a tremendously exciting and competitive match, and both youths played their hearts out.

On the first hole, Jones sent his ball flying 275 yards straight down the fairway, while Herron, despite skying his opening drive, ended up just twenty-five yards shorter. Oakmont favored golfers who hit a high tee shot with long carry in the air, and punished those—by far the larger number of top amateurs in 1919—who relied on a low, controlled hook to scamper for thirty or forty yards along dry, unirrigated fairways. For Herron and Jones, both long and high hitters, neither the menacing trench on the left or nearby out-of-bounds (Hulton Road) on the right came into play, nor did the endless row of bunkers on either side of the downhill, par 5 opening hole. They both hit their second shots just short of the green, the perfect spot to maximize their chances for birdie. Herron then "mashied" (or chipped) dead, while Jones's ball ran four feet past, and they both sank their putts for birdie 4s and a "half" on No 1. And so they were off, in true championship style.[20]

On No. 2, Herron's sliced drive barely held the wide fairway on the right. In truth, despite his placid demeanor, Herron seemed a little nervous. Meanwhile, Jones launched another beautiful drive on No. 2 but, uncharacteristically for one of the game's best short-iron players, he over-clubbed and found a shallow

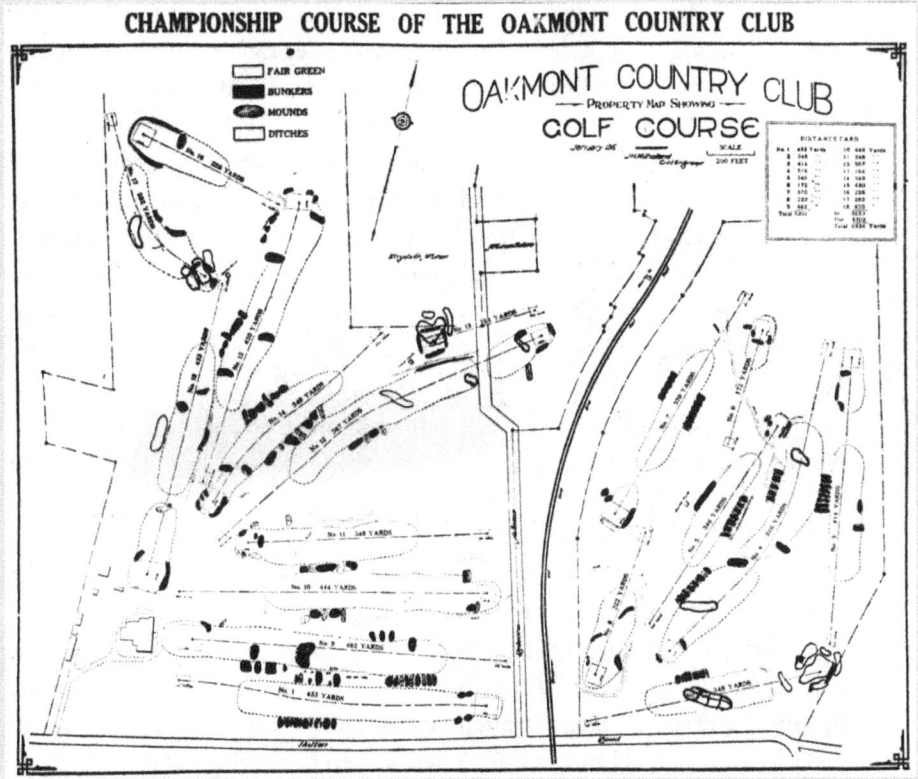

This is the earliest detailed map of Oakmont Country Club (with hole yardages) that we have found. It was published in the *Brooklyn Daily Eagle* on 10 August 1919, six days before the championship officially began. The map was originally drawn in 1915 by J. H. Milholland, a Pittsburgh civil engineer.

bunker over the green with his second. Herron, in contrast, got on the green but was not well-positioned; he was well above the hole on Oakmont's slickest green, and his curling downhill putt might end up fifty yards down the fairway if he hit it too hard. Not surprisingly, his first putt ran as much as ten feet past the hole and he ultimately three-putted, whereas Jones's "chip" from the sand (the sand wedge had yet to be invented) was dead to the pin for a terrific par 4. Jones was now in the lead, 1 up, having one-putted the first two greens and shown how resourceful a scrambler he was.

On No. 3, one of Oakmont's hardest par 4s (later christened "the Church Pews" because of the "pew-like" bunkers on the left, that also protected the left side of the parallel fourth fairway), both young men drove beautifully and equidistant, but neither hit a great second shot, with Jones just short and Herron just off the green's right edge. Both secured pars, however, as Jones chipped dead (his third consecutive 1-putt) and Herron sank a putt of around four to six feet after leaving his chip short. On the par 5, dog-leg right fourth hole, Herron outdrove Jones for the first time and by a considerable distance. He also hit his brassie second closer than Jones to the green and his chip closer to the hole for an easy chance to birdie and even the match. But, whether intentionally or not, Jones's missed birdie putt laid Herron a half-stymie, meaning that Jones's ball was partially blocking Herron's line to the hole. Herron either had to putt around Jones's ball or chip over it, a much riskier gambit that might lead to losing a hole he had played perfectly. Herron chose the safer option; he putted laterally and easily sank his fifth stroke to halve the hole in par 5s. Jones was still 1 up after four holes.

That score changed when Jones—perhaps trying to avoid the new menacing bunker on the left with a huge embankment shaped like a sleeping lion—sliced his tee shot off the fifth tee, nestling either into deep rough or sand (reports varied), while Herron's drive sailed a straight 275 yards. From his bad lie Jones was not confident he could carry the thickly grassed hollow that fronted the green, so he played out onto the fairway instead, less than 100 yards from the green. His patience appeared to pay off when Herron misgauged his short-iron approach and landed squarely in the hollow before the green. Jones seized the opening by hitting an excellent pitch that gave him a real chance to save par and win a hole he looked likely to lose. At worst, he'd halve with a bogey 5.

But Dave Herron had a miraculous shot up his sleeve. He somehow finessed his niblick from the hollow and chipped dead to the pin for a tap-in par 4. It was almost "unfair"—a dubious critique of Herron that the hyper-partisan Atlanta press corps adopted later to diminish his victory. Echoes of Bob Gardner, the man at Merion in 1916 who salvaged par after par from impossible lies to break Bob Jones's spirit, began to emerge. After an initial mistake, Jones had played No. 5 strategically, hoping to be rewarded for using his head, yet Herron—revealing that his finesse indeed matched his power—was now in position to snatch victory from the jaws of defeat. Bob Jones at age seventeen was a highly emotional player. E. E. Giles described him as "a rather demonstrative, peevish youth under adversity" but with "a stout heart for battle," and Innis Brown called him "a fighter every inch, even if he had to fight himself at times."[21] He was probably boiling inside at Herron's wondrous recovery as he lined up his putt to tie. But also, Jones had yet to figure out greens as complex as No. 5 at Oakmont, and had taken a whopping forty putts the day before against Fownes.[22] So, whatever the reason—his emotions or his inexperience—Jones missed his putt to lose the hole and his lead.

But he quickly moved past the upset and hit a brilliant jigger to the narrow, bunker-encased, par 3 sixth green that landed within eight feet of the flagstick, possibly as close as five feet.[23] Herron's jigger, by contrast, considerably overshot the flagstick and rolled to the green's back edge, around thirty feet away. Again, it looked like Jones had a good chance to win and take back the lead by sinking a birdie putt of less than ten feet. But Herron lagged his lengthy putt close and Jones's shorter effort stubbornly lipped out, so the two settled for a half in pars. Certainly, the finalists were well-matched: both bombers off the tee but with exceptionally well-rounded games. Neither could count on a "safe" victory on any hole.

On the 370-yard seventh, Herron drove 275 yards straight down the middle, and Jones hit it slightly farther after bouncing off a fairway bunker. Herron then hit the approach shot of the day: an iron that almost smacked the flagstick and left him a three-footer or less for birdie. Herron's near hole-out surely caught Jones by surprise; though he had a flat lie and clear line to the hole, he hooked his approach and landed in a bunker. But his heart for battle was again in evidence when his sand shot (his third) stopped just outside of Herron's miracle second shot. Jones successfully scrambled his par 4, but Herron easily sank his short putt for a birdie 3 and won the hole to go 1 up for the first time.

On the lengthy par 3 eighth, which usually required at least a brassie for even the longer hitters, it was Dave Herron's turn to scramble from a difficult lie in the sand (whether this lie was complicated by Emil Loeffler Jr.'s patented furrows, we do not know). Like Herron, Jones's tee shot was a bit short of the green, but it lay cleanly in the fairway and left him an unobstructed chip to secure his par.[24] Herron, meanwhile, whaled at the sand but barely managed to extricate his ball, which still lay short of the green. Jones had the advantage; he chipped well but not great, and faced a putt of between four and six feet for par. Herron, playing catch-up, then chipped inside Jones and so gave himself a solid chance to tie the hole in bogey if Jones faltered. Which he did—his short putt hung maddeningly on the rim and would not fall. Dave proceeded to sink his short putt and hold on to his slim 1-up lead—a good bogey (by Herron) matching a bad one (by Jones).

Jones and Herron had only completed eight holes, but it seemed that no matter how well either young man played, his opponent always retained a chance to "steal" the hole. They were both good enough and resilient enough to capitalize on even their opponent's minor mistakes. Not one stroke could be taken for granted, which made for a very exciting match. So far, three holes were won and five holes were tied. Both men were playing great, with Herron at even par and Jones just one over. Not since the already legendary Ouimet-Evans match of three days earlier (where Evans shot par 73 and Ouimet 74 in the morning round) had any pair of top players both scored this well.

Herron extended his lead to 2 up on the dramatic 461-yard par 5 ninth, whose mammoth putting surface served double-duty as Oakmont's practice green—the top half was only a few yards from the clubhouse veranda. Steeply uphill most of the way, No. 9 was the hole at Oakmont that most advantaged long and high drivers like Herron and Jones. The longer they could carry their tee shot to the pitched fairway, the greater their chance to reach the green in two shots (or at least get pretty close) and give themselves a solid birdie or even an eagle opportunity.

Overall, Herron and Jones were bashing their drives like no one else at Oakmont, with each more or less alternating as the longer hitter. Jones's magical swing generated effortless power that belied his modest size. Herron, of course, was older (by three and a half years), taller (by three or four inches), and considerably heavier (by sixty-plus pounds), and he had demonstrated several times during the week that he had a reserve of power to escape deep rough or produce extra distance off the tee when he needed it. So, having escaped No. 8 with his one-hole lead intact, Herron cranked an uphill drive that several observers estimated at 300 yards or longer on No. 9, his longest drive of the week and at least twenty-five yards ahead of Jones's otherwise superb poke. Playing the odd, Jones smashed his brassie as hard as he could but found a deep bunker that guarded the right entry to the green. And though he hit a beautiful sand shot, he still left himself a "difficult" putt of at least ten feet for birdie on one of Oakmont's most terrifyingly undulating greens. Herron, meanwhile, hit a long iron hard and straight (some observers claimed he hit a brassie, but he probably did not need one) that rolled to the front edge of the green; he then ran his approach for eagle to within three or four feet of the cup.[25] Jones missed his longer birdie putt, Herron sank his, and at the end of the first nine holes Herron was suddenly 2 up for the first time in the match.

The brand of golf that both young men produced on the front nine was truly superlative and, historically, almost unthinkable given the pressure in the final rounds of a U.S. Amateur. Dave Herron shot a 1-under-par 36, matching his second-best front-nine performance of the week. Jones shot a 1-over-par 38, which also matched his second-best front-nine performance of the week. Already this was shaping up to be the best golf ever played during the finale of a U.S. Amateur Championship. "The record gallery that followed the players was treated to thrill after thrill," Francis Ouimet commented. "The match was replete with dazzling shots in which neither had the advantage."[26]

But, in fact, Dave Herron did have something of an "advantage" in how well he had been playing the front nine at Oakmont all week. On the front nine (par 37), he had scored 40 or below in eight of his ten prior rounds (a 35 was his best), whereas Bob Jones had scored 40 or below in only six of his eleven prior rounds (a 35 was also his best).[27] Further, Herron had averaged 39 on the front nine, whereas Jones had averaged 40.18, a difference of 1.18 strokes over nine holes. Thus, the two-stroke difference after the morning front nine—36 for Herron versus 38 for Jones—was fairly consistent with the scoring differential between them all week. To be sure, both of their front-nine scores on Saturday morning were notably better than their average front-nine scores during the preceding week: three strokes better for Herron and over two strokes better for Jones, so they were both clearly bringing their best games. But Herron's "A game" all week was just a little bit better than Jones's, and his 2-up lead after the opening nine holes reflected that.

As they made the short walk from the ninth green to the tenth tee, Bob Jones may have sensed an opportunity. He had just gone 2 down for the first time in the match. And as every competitive golfer knows, 2 down feels much further behind than 1 down, and particularly against an opponent who had just broken par on the front nine. If he could jump-start the back nine with a birdie 4 or eagle 3 and shrink Herron's lead without giving him a chance to enjoy it, the match's momentum might shift as they headed into the tougher of the two nines.

Curiously, in contrast to today—when many experts consider No. 10 (now a par 4) among the toughest holes in championship golf—the hole was playing the easiest of all during the 1919 Amateur. On the short, tight, downhill par 5, almost all of the top players were able to reach it in two shots, and they collectively averaged 4.7 strokes, making it one of only two holes where they regularly broke par. Thus, at this championship, No. 10 (playing as a par 5) was actually Oakmont's easiest birdie hole (see Figure 1).

Furthermore, it was Bob Jones's best hole, by far in fact. In his first practice round, he scored an eagle 3. His average score during the week was just 4.36 strokes. And even better, he had birdied No. 10 the last three times he played it. Dave Herron, by contrast, was playing No. 10 at the field average, and he had scored a par 5 on the hole two of the last three times he'd played it (see Figure 2). In other words, Jones owned No. 10, and Herron did not. Despite being 2 down, Jones had reason to feel confident as he began the back nine of the morning round.

And Herron made it pretty easy for Jones. With the honor off the tee, Herron smashed a long drive down the middle, but Jones went perhaps a yard or two farther. Herron, uncharacteristically, then sliced his second shot badly, and it ended up in a narrow trench well to the right of the green. In response, Jones powered his second shot a little offline, but it serendipitously bounced off the edge of a bunker and stopped just in front of the green, leaving a relatively simple up-and-down for a birdie 4. Herron, despite a heroic escape from the trench on his third shot, still faced a challenging pitch over a bunker to a downhill tilted green, which he poorly negotiated, leaving himself a fifteen-footer for par. As expected, Jones chipped dead to the hole and Herron, without hesitation, conceded Jones's tap-in putt for a birdie 4. Jones had returned to even par for the day and was again only 1 down.[28]

In contrast to the surprisingly easy tenth hole, No. 11—though only 363 yards—was deceptively difficult. The top players averaged 4.8 on the hole: third only in difficulty among par 4s to the much longer fifteenth and eighteenth holes (see Figure 1). Herron and Jones, like the others, found No. 11 a tough slog with its sharp uphill, left-to-right slant and massive ditch that crossed in front of the green (with all the rain the past two weeks, the ditch was likely mud at the bottom). Anyone who did not keep his tee shot straight or slightly left would face a very challenging approach shot to the green.

Both players navigated the difficult tee shot beautifully, far enough up the hill and left to have a clear look at the flagstick. Herron's ball was slightly ahead, so Jones had a chance to put immediate pressure on his competitor's slim lead with a mashie niblick, a short iron he hit as well as anyone in the game. But for some reason Jones faltered on this shot, committing an unforced error (one that he would repeat almost exactly in the afternoon round). From a fairly flat lie he pulled his ball sharply left and "hit the top of a trap . . . and fell back into the sand," leaving himself a lengthy bunker shot to the hole.[29] Herron responded with a good approach to the green's edge that left him a conventional 2-putt par. After Jones escaped the bunker, Herron sent his first putt just past the hole and tapped in for a 4. Jones made a great effort to save par from around twenty feet away, rimming the cup but not falling in, and Herron was again 2 up. The Associated Press observed that when good putts did not fall, Jones tended to wear his emotions on his sleeve: "Several times when Bobby had a putt for win," or, in this case, par, "he would look over the ground carefully and then stroke the ball. But often they would not drop. When they would roll off, or stop at the lip, Bobby looked as if he was ready to cry, but he kept plugging along, playing and hoping that the tide would turn."[30]

The twelfth hole, a 601-yard par 5, was not just the longest but, in most experts' opinion, the single most troublesome hole at Oakmont. It was certainly

FIGURE 1
Rank Order of Individual Holes at Oakmont Country Club—Most to Least Difficult—by Average Strokes Over/Under Par, for Top Eight Players through Quarterfinals and Semifinals

Figure 1 shows which holes played toughest, and which were easiest relative to par, for the top eight players during the 1919 U.S. Amateur. We only include data through the quarter- and semifinal rounds.

ORDER OF DIFFICULTY	HOLE #	PAR	AVERAGE SCORE	AVERAGE STROKES +/- PAR	HARDEST/EASIEST PAR
1	18	4	4.89	+0.89	Hardest Par 4
1	16	3	3.89	+0.89	Hardest Par 3
3	15	4	4.85	+0.85	
4	11	4	4.79	+0.79	
5	8	3	3.68	+0.68	
6	12	5	5.64	+0.64	Hardest Par 5
7	7	4	4.56	+0.56	
7	14	4	4.56	+0.56	
9	2	4	4.53	+0.53	
10	3	4	4.46	+0.46	
10	13	3	3.46	+0.46	
12	4	5	5.4	+0.40	
13	6	3	3.35	+0.35	Easiest Par 3
14	5	4	4.13	+0.13	
15	9	5	5.12	+0.12	
16	17	4	4	Equal	Easiest Par 4
17	1	5	4.83	-0.17	
18	10	5	4.69	-0.31	Easiest Par 5

the hardest of Oakmont's par 5s, and it may well have been the most difficult hole overall for the players that initially teed off the previous Saturday. But for the top players, No. 12 actually proved to be only the sixth most difficult hole. On average, the top players scored two-thirds of a shot over par there (see Figure 1).

Not Bob Jones though. In fact, despite his exceptional power off the tee, Jones had played No. 12 worse than any of the other top players, averaging just under a bogey 6 for his previous eleven rounds. Dave Herron, by contrast, was in the middle of the pack, averaging a half-stroke over par on No. 12. And unlike Jones, Herron had only once played No. 12 disastrously, scoring a 7, whereas

FIGURE 2
Herron v. Jones: Hole-by-Hole Scores for Front and Back Nine through the Semifinal Rounds

This table (parts a and b) shows hole-by-hole scoring by Herron and Jones for their three qualifying rounds, plus their four prior victories in one-on-one matches (i.e., through the semifinals).

PART A

FRONT NINE

PLAYER	DAY	ROUND #	OPPONENT	1	2	3	4	5	6	7	8	9	# HOLES SCORED
HERRON	8-16-1919	QUALIFIER 1		4	5	6	5	5	2	4	3	6	9
	8-18-1919	QUALIFIER 2		4	5	3	5	3	3	5	3	7	9
		QUALIFIER 3		5	4	5	5	4	4	4	3	6	9
	8-19-1919	MATCH 1 morning	W. H. Gardner	5	4	4	6	4	3	4	3	5	9
		afternoon		*	*	*	*	*	*	*	*	*	*
	8-20-1919	MATCH 2 morning	J. N. Stearns	6	4	4	6	4	3	5	4	4	9
		afternoon		4	5	4	7	3	4	5	5	4	9
	8-21-1919	MATCH 3 morning	W. J. Thomson	4	4	3	6	4	2	5	3	4	9
		afternoon		4	5	4	6	5	4	4	4	4	9
	8-22-1919	MATCH 4 morning	J. Wood Platt	6	4	4	5	4	4	5	4	5	9
		afternoon		5	4	4	4	5	3	4	2	6	9
HERRON		Average Strokes/Hole		4.7	4.4	4.1	5.5	4.1	3.2	4.5	3.4	5.1	

*The data for Herron's afternoon round in match 1 (against William Gardner of Buffalo) are unavailable.

PART B

BACK NINE

PLAYER	DAY	ROUND #	OPPONENT	10	11	12	13	14	15	16	17	18	# HOLES SCORED
HERRON	8-16-1919	QUALIFIER 1		6	5	6	4	5	5	4	4	5	9
	8-18-1919	QUALIFIER 2		5	5	5	3	4	4	4	5	4	9
		QUALIFIER 3		5	5	6	4	4	5	3	4	5	9
	8-19-1919	MATCH 1 morning	W. H. Gardner	4	6	5	4	6	5	5	4	4	9
		afternoon		*	*	*	*	*	*	*	*	*	*
	8-20-1919	MATCH 2 morning	J. N. Stearns	4	4	7	2	5	4	4	3	5	9
		afternoon		4	5	6	2	x	x	x	x	x	4
	8-21-1919	MATCH 3 morning	W. J. Thomson	5	4	6	4	4	4	3	4	4	9
		afternoon		5	4	x	x	x	x	x	x	x	2
	8-22-1919	MATCH 4 morning	J. Wood Platt	4	5	5	3	3	5	3	5	4	9
		afternoon		5	4	5	x	x	x	x	x	x	3
HERRON		Average Strokes/Hole		4.7	4.7	5.7	3.3	4.4	4.6	3.7	4.1	4.4	

The table also shows, in the column "Number of Holes Scored," how many holes each player completed en route to the championship match.

FRONT NINE

PLAYER	DAY	ROUND #	OPPONENT	HOLE # 1	2	3	4	5	6	7	8	9	# HOLES SCORED
JONES	8-16-1919	QUALIFIER 1		6	5	6	4	5	3	5	3	6	9
	8-18-1919	QUALIFIER 2		5	4	4	6	3	3	5	4	4	9
		QUALIFIER 3		6	4	4	6	4	5	5	4	4	9
	8-19-1919	MATCH 1 morning	J. B. Manion	6	5	5	5	5	2	5	4	5	9
		afternoon		6	5	5	5	4	2	4	4	7	9
	8-20-1919	MATCH 2 morning	Robert Gardner	5	3	4	5	4	3	5	5	5	9
		afternoon		4	4	5	5	3	3	4	3	4	9
	8-21-1919	MATCH 3 morning	Rudy Knepper	5	4	5	4	3	3	5	5	5	9
		afternoon		4	5	5	5	4	3	4	4	6	9
	8-22-1919	MATCH 4 morning	W. C. Fownes Jr.	5	5	4	7	4	4	4	4	5	9
		afternoon		6	5	5	5	3	3	4	4	5	9
JONES		Average Strokes/Hole		5.3	4.5	4.7	5.2	3.8	3.1	4.5	4.0	5.1	

BACK NINE

PLAYER	DAY	ROUND #	OPPONENT	HOLE # 10	11	12	13	14	15	16	17	18	# HOLES SCORED
JONES	8-16-1919	QUALIFIER 1		4	4	6	4	5	5	3	3	5	9
	8-18-1919	QUALIFIER 2		4	6	8	3	5	5	3	4	5	9
		QUALIFIER 3		5	3	5	3	4	4	4	4	4	9
	8-19-1919	MATCH 1 morning	J. B. Manion	4	4	6	4	5	5	4	4	5	9
		afternoon		4	5	5	5	3	4	4	X	X	7
	8-20-1919	MATCH 2 morning	Robert Gardner	4	4	5	4	5	6	4	4	4	9
		afternoon		5	6	6	4	5	X	X	X	X	5
	8-21-1919	MATCH 3 morning	Rudy Knepper	6	7	8	4	4	4	3	5	5	9
		afternoon		4	3	5	4	5	5	4	X	X	7
	8-22-1919	MATCH 4 morning	W. C. Fownes Jr.	4	4	7	3	4	5	3	4	5	9
		afternoon		4	6	4	4	4	X	X	X	X	6
JONES		Average Strokes/Hole		4.4	4.7	5.9	3.8	4.5	4.7	3.6	4.0	4.7	

Jones had experienced regular disasters, twice scoring 8s and once a 7. In retrospect, it is hard to explain why longer holes at Oakmont where power was a huge asset—like Nos. 12 and 8, the longest par 5 and par 3—were Jones's two worst holes throughout the week (see Figure 2).

Herron hit a long drive on No. 12 but into the right rough, which necessitated an iron to escape. Relying on brute strength, he smashed his shot far down the fairway, with lots of topspin so that he only needed a short iron to the green. He placed his third shot safely and easily two-putted for par—only his fifth par there all week. No doubt he was happy to move on to No. 13.

Jones's play on No. 12, in comparison, was much more adventurous and a lot less successful. His drive was long (though shorter than Herron's) and straight, helped by a favorable bounce off the side of a bunker that kept his ball in the fairway. He was not able to take advantage of this good luck, though, and sliced his brassie into deep rough on the right. With Herron already on the green in three strokes, Jones was unable to do likewise; for all the remarkable clubhead speed he could generate for a teenager of his size, he could not cut through the thick, damp grass, and his pitch fell short. Undismayed, he mashied superbly to within two or three feet of the cup and seemed certain to tie Herron in par 5s. But he missed the short one, and No. 12 continued to be his worst hole at Oakmont. Now, he was 3 down and in serious trouble against an opponent for only the second time all week.

Given Herron's steady play, there was every reason to think he would continue scoring near par for the remainder of the morning round. Shockingly, that didn't happen. For some reason, Herron's brilliant tee-to-green game suddenly collapsed, and he bogeyed or double-bogeyed the next five holes.[31] It was inexplicable and changed the momentum of the match completely.

On the short par 3 thirteenth, which he had already birdied twice (see Figure 2), Herron bunkered his tee shot, escaped to less than ten feet, and then missed his "difficult" downhill putt for par (Jones barely missed a ten- to fifteen-footer for birdie but won the hole anyway). On the fourteenth, after Jones hit a long and straight drive, Herron scurried the gallery on his left with a sharply hooked tee shot and ended up in a deep "sand pocket" not far from the twelfth fairway. This time Herron did not recover nicely (and ultimately conceded the hole). "The big Pittsburger [sic] took a mighty swipe with his niblick and snapped the shaft off at the head of the club," Innis Brown reported.[32] Yesteryear's niblick was the equivalent of a 9-iron (more or less; niblicks came in a great variety of sizes and shapes too) and, for almost all players, was their heaviest and highest lofted club. Because sand wedges did not exist yet, the niblick was essential for escaping hazards and deep rough. In fact, other than the driver and putter, the niblick was arguably the most important club in a 1919 bag, and Dave Herron had just shattered his.[33] Most likely a friend or family member—perhaps one of his brothers—ran the broken club to the pro shop so Charlie Rowe could fix it. In the meantime, Herron would have to struggle on. And after losing Nos. 13 and 14, he was just 1 up, playing without a niblick, and losing ground to Jones fast.

Bob Jones was looking to apply pressure to his flagging opponent, but the fifteenth was the most difficult par 4 on the course (tied with the eighteenth), with a scoring average just under 5 (see Figure 1). The fairway was narrow with a dramatic left-to-right tilt and several difficult bunkers jutting in from both sides—all to punish golfers who did not perfectly control the direction, distance, or even the spin of their tee shots. It is unclear which one Jones landed in, but he found the back of a bunker on the left, and his recovery shot stopped far short of the green (some reporters claimed it landed in another bunker). He did reach the green in three shots, however, but still faced a lengthy par putt from the far edge.

Herron, in contrast, managed to thread the needle with a long and straight drive. But, from the sharply slanted fairway, he double-crossed his iron and hooked it so badly that it landed on the sixteenth tee, with a grass trench between him and the fifteenth green.[34] A player less familiar with Oakmont might have panicked in this odd situation, especially if they were down a niblick. But Herron, surely to the delight of spectators, chose to putt as if there were no trench between him and the green. He applied just the right amount of force to propel his ball along the ground and through the trench—the Associated Press said that somehow the ball "just kept going and climbed over onto the green"— to within five or six feet of the flagstick. It was a dangerous but fabulous shot. Jones then tried to sink his long putt for the win, but his ball came to rest just inside Herron's. Now, Herron only had to sink his putt for an incredible par save to return his lead to 2 up. Except he missed, Jones sank his own short putt, and after many miscues both players halved Oakmont's toughest par 4 with bogey 5s. Dave remained 1 up in the match despite three consecutive bogeys.

Both young men struggled again on the 226-yard, par 3 sixteenth, which, as noted earlier, was tied with No. 18 as Oakmont's most difficult hole during the 1919 Amateur. In fact, the top players averaged approximately nine-tenths of a stroke over par on this hole (see Figure 1). No. 16, it must be emphasized, was a very different hole in 1919 from what it is today, even though its overall distance is around the same.[35] The hole ran slightly downhill for the first 200 yards or so and then ascended slightly uphill, with a sharp fairway slant to the right, for the last twenty-five yards. A "punishing trench" of enormous proportion surrounded a small crowned green that repelled balls in three directions toward the trench, while a deep sandy bunker, short and right of greenside, ran halfway across the fairway to capture balls with insufficient carry. As best we can reconstruct, the green on this "lost hole of Oakmont" was blind or at least partially blind from the tee. Perfect shots that took the fairway's rightward tilt into account enjoyed a direct path to the green, but judging by the average scores on No. 16 these were few and far between. That said, all week Jones and Herron had been beating the average score on No. 16 (see Figure 2), perhaps because they could carry their fairway woods longer and higher than most players.

But not in the championship match. From the sixteenth tee it was impossible to see exactly where Herron's and Jones's tee shots ultimately ended up, and reporters' accounts varied widely. According to the *Brooklyn Daily Eagle*'s William Everett Hicks—known as "the analyst" for his detailed statistical portraits of each match—Jones hooked his tee shot into deep rough left of the trench, while Herron hooked into the trench itself. Jones slashed out, and though he went well past the hole, he still held the green. Herron's pitch from the trench, even without his niblick to elevate the ball quickly, settled on the green in two. In the end, Jones managed to get down in two putts for a bogey 4 while Herron three-putted for a double-bogey 5 when he missed a two-footer. This was his second three-putt of the morning round (the other came on No. 2). It was also Herron's second missed short putt in a row. Contrary to the impression given by most observers at the time—and by golf historians ever since—Herron was not lighting up Oakmont with brilliant putting (see Figure 3).

Herron and Jones both bogeyed the seventeenth hole, too: Oakmont's most talked-about par 4 (and not always favorably) in the course's early years. No. 17 was a short dog leg left (282 yards), sharply uphill all the way to the green, that offered bold players an alternative beeline to the flagstick over numerous hazards while side-stepping the steeply slanted, right-to-left fairway. Even from a well-positioned drive to the fairway's crest, the entry to the green was quite shallow, making it difficult to hold and bringing the rear bunkers directly into play. For the strongest of the strong, it was possible to putt for eagle by hitting straight from tee to green without touching more than a sliver of the troublesome fairway. But for those who miscalculated, Oakmont's biggest bunker of them all, a yawning, deep, sand-filled "pit" located front and right, known today as "Big Mouth," awaited.

Neither Herron nor Jones had been playing No. 17 particularly well com-

An aerial photograph of the entire course was printed in the USGA program for the 1925 U.S. Amateur championship. No. 17, as pictured here, looks today much as it did in 1919, but No. 16 was radically transformed before the 1927 U.S. Open at Oakmont.

pared to the other top players. Canada's William Thompson (whom Herron thrashed in the quarterfinals) averaged just 3.5 strokes for the hole. But both Herron and Jones were averaging around par (see Figure 2). With the match now tied, neither had a distinct advantage going into the seventeenth.

From his first round in Pittsburgh onward, Jones had usually chosen the risky beeline path to the green, even if it meant (because of his great power) risking placing his tee shot in "Big Mouth." There was no way he was going to play safe into the fairway in the championship match—not this seventeen-year-old with something to prove to an unfriendly Pittsburgh gallery. It was time for Jones to shut up Herron's increasingly vocal fans.

Whatever either player intended to do at this critical juncture, neither executed his tee shot well. Herron landed far short of the green in deep rough left of the fairway, and Jones, despite an enormous drive, dumped his ball into "Big Mouth" for the third time that week. Jones then lost a stroke when he failed to escape the bunker on his first try. In the meantime, without his niblick, Herron could not do much to control the direction or spin on his second shot, and his ball scampered across the front of the green and also fell into "Big Mouth." Jones got out of the bunker on his second attempt (that is, his third shot on the hole); Herron somehow escaped onto the green on his first. They then two-putted to halve this supposed "birdie hole" with bogey 5s.

There was one hole left in the morning round. What had started out as a brilliantly played match with sparkling golf on the front nine had become a grind. Bob Jones had successfully mounted a comeback and chiseled Dave Herron's 3-up lead to nothing, but—contrary to what most reporters later claimed—Jones was not beating Herron with great golf. Depending on how one counts conceded putts, Herron and Jones were both 5-over-par coming into the eighteenth despite their superb play earlier in the day on the front nine. A fourth straight bogey for Jones and a sixth consecutive hole-over-par for Herron would be a demoralizing way to end the round and break for lunch.

Perhaps trying too hard to grab the lead, Jones hooked his drive into deep rough. Meanwhile, Herron, in a sudden return to form, hit long and straight and reached the green easily with his second shot. Jones did, too, and in a very impressive fashion. From a terrible lie that would have forced most players to chip out weakly to the fairway, he muscled a "beautiful" iron onto the green, uphill all the way. His ball settled around the same distance from the hole as Herron's. The end of the hole was just as thrilling. Herron missed his birdie putt by mere inches, and Jones rimmed the cup, but both were doubtless quite happy to halve with pars on Oakmont's toughest par 4. That said, Jones had failed to seize the lead, even while Herron was down a niblick. "To be able to smash one's trusty niblick and still go through to victory was deemed by some the supreme test," William Everett Hicks commented, highlighting Herron's imperturbability.[36]

The morning round had produced not just good golf, with both players scoring 78, but an incredibly exciting, topsy-turvy match. Five of the first eight holes were tied, but in the next eight holes, Nos. 9 to 16, zero holes were tied. Herron's lead went from 1 up at No. 8 to 2 up at No. 9, down to 1 up at No. 10, back to 2 up at No. 11 and 3 up at No. 12, only to decline from 3 up to all-even over the next four holes. And though Nos. 17 and 18 were tied, the players' performance on both was riveting: Jones squandered a clear advantage after nearly driving the green on No. 17, then somehow slashed through thick rough to reach the sharply uphill eighteenth green in two before his birdie putt rimmed out. Time and again the two most powerful players in the field proved themselves brilliant scramblers and never conceded a hole just because of an errant shot. The makings of Herron and Jones's lifelong friendship were already sealed by lunchtime, as each acknowledged the other's grit.

Their morning eighteen was, in terms of scoring, the second best-played match of the entire championship. No other contestants combined raw power with accuracy as Herron and Jones did. Unquestionably, too, this was Jones's

FIGURE 3
Herron v. Jones: Hole-by-Hole Scores in Championship Match Compared to Prior Scoring Averages

This graph, created by George Cann, shows how Herron and Jones scored on each hole in the championship match compared to the average of his prior scores on that hole in all previous rounds. The data capture just how well both players rose to the occasion and exceeded their prior performance levels. For more detailed discussion, see Appendix 4.

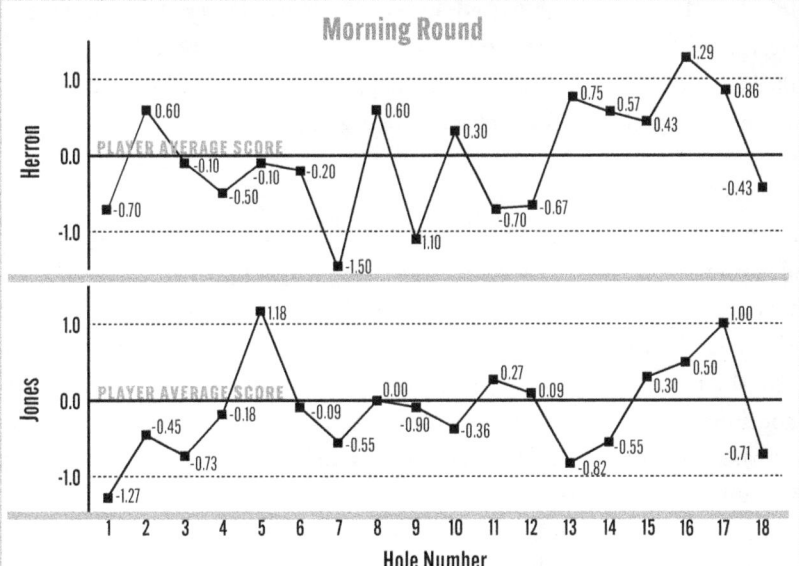

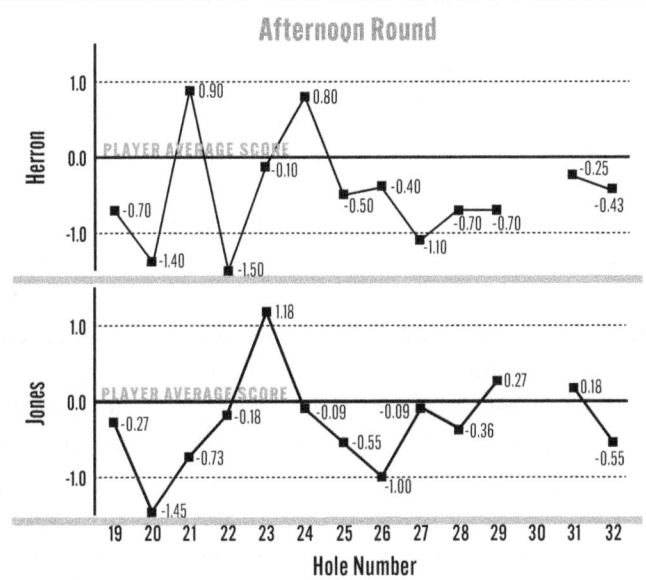

best eighteen holes since the qualifying rounds, and by far his straightest hitting off the tee as well. He also demonstrated his competitive fire, his "stout heart," in coming back to tie Herron from 3 down. In all ways, he was rising to the occasion with extraordinary maturity for a famously "peevish," cursing, club-throwing, club-smashing seventeen-year-old.

Yet as the lunch break passed, Jones must have pondered whether the Dave Herron of the front nine or the back nine would show up for the eighteen-hole afternoon match. Whichever Herron appeared, Jones could not be confident that his best golf could beat Herron's best golf at Oakmont.

THE AFTERNOON ROUND

Herron and Jones had played their morning round at an exceedingly fast pace, finishing in well under three hours, giving spectators plenty of time to get their bets in before the second round started. "By drawing level on the first round," Harry Keck, The *Pittsburgh Gazette Times* sports editor, wrote, "the finalists gave the book-binders a busy time during the luncheon respite and hundreds 'got down' one or more."[37] Gambling at Oakmont had been prevalent throughout the week. In fact, a pool had started well before the championship began, and anyone could buy as many players as they liked to win. W. G. Costin, president of the Pittsburgh Screw and Bolt Co., a member of Allegheny Country Club, and a good enough player to advance the previous Saturday to Monday's thirty-six-hole qualifying rounds, was serving as the day's chief marshal. Costin had purchased two players, one from the top bracket and one from the bottom, for $1,600 each (the equivalent of over $50,000 today). The players he chose? Dave Herron and Bob Jones. Whichever way the match went, Costin was guaranteed to win a very considerable sum.[38]

As Jones and Herron ate their lunches and Charlie Rowe continued working on Herron's niblick—he would finish replacing the shaft of the club with just fifteen minutes to spare—more and more spectators began arriving at Oakmont. Most factories, as had become their custom, closed for Saturday afternoon, so many workers came out to see their local boy take on the volatile teen star from Georgia. Herron and Jones would continue their quick pace, which meant that several thousand people trying to walk with them would have to hustle to keep up. Inevitably, the result was chaos. E. E. Giles called the gallery "barking maniacs."[39] And the reporter for the *New York Times* was quick to point out that the gallery was there in spite of the oppressive weather. "It was particularly hot at the links today, and the 218 pound winner [Dave Herron] was bathed with perspiration from start to finish as was the entire gallery that galloped wildly over fair green and rough to witness every shot of Pittsburgh's favorite for the title."[40]

By the time lunch was finished, an estimated five thousand people were massed along the first tee and fairway. "Both boys went out in the afternoon to face perhaps the greatest crowd in the history of the championships," Giles wrote.

> Again, as in the morning, they started on even terms. Nothing more could have been desired from the gallery viewpoint. There was an air of expectancy that could be felt as the impatient crowd watched the first tee for a glimpse of the two young heroes. There is a compelling force in buoyant youth, and every man and woman present caught the inspiration of the moment, as the boys teed for the final decision.[41]

Jones, once again, had the honor on the downhill par 5 opening hole. Though both players in the morning round had birdied No. 1 from just off the green, in earlier rounds Jones had actually played No. 1 quite poorly, with the worst average score among the top eight players. Indeed, he bogeyed the hole five of the eleven times he'd previously played it (see Figure 2). Perhaps, then, it is unsurprising that in front of the largest, loudest, and most irreverent gallery he had ever played before, Jones sliced his drive into a deep bunker that guarded the fairway on the right, not too far from the out-of-bounds marker that fronted Hulton Road. Herron, in contrast—likely comforted by the knowledge that his niblick was back in his bag and that his last two trips around the front nine were extraordinarily successful (37, 36)—hit a splendid opening tee shot, long and straight.

Some unrehearsed gamesmanship on the part of the gallery and marshals may have figured into Jones's poor opening drive. Walter Wilkes, The *Atlanta Georgian*'s tennis reporter who accompanied Jones to Oakmont instead of the *Georgian*'s star golf scribe, O. B. Keeler, wrote a few days after the match:

> Little things were happening all the way around. I noticed that when Bobby played first from the tee, the officials permitted the crowd to mass back of him. No effort was made to hold the gallery with ropes, as is usually done, the sole bars to interference being the stentorian bellows of the committeemen, which were themselves a thousand times more harmful than a closely pressing gallery could have been. When Herron came up to play, however, the people were scrupulously cleared away from behind him that his eye might not be distracted by the forms and gaily colored gowns of the women who thronged the course.[42]

Wilkes may have been exaggerating to provide Jones an alibi for missed shots, but the *New York Times* reported similar anecdotes. "According to the magic yellow flag which was the symbol of office at the Oakmont links, the large and picturesque gallery consisted of approximately four thousand officials and seven spectators," quipped the *Times* correspondent. "After meeting an impenetrable human wall around one of the greens, Bob Jones had to call out 'excuse me, please, I'd like to do a little putting on that green.'" On another hole, an "excited" official "roared" through a megaphone, "'Get back there; get back there. . . . Davie's in the rough, and we want to give him every chance for the hole.' The retort courteous came from a Jones supporter, who answered: 'While you're about it, give Jones a chance, too.'"[43]

Only Bob Jones could say whether the gallery's partisanship impacted his game, but from the very start of the afternoon round the spectators were overwhelmingly cheering for Dave Herron, who had just gotten his round off to a much better start than his opponent did. What happened next was disputed. The *Atlanta Georgian* and the *Pittsburgh Gazette Times* claimed Herron's second shot on No. 1 was just as good as his drive, but the *New York Times*, the *New York Sun*, and the Associated Press reported that he hit into a greenside bunker. Either way, Herron hit a fine third shot and left himself a makeable birdie putt. Jones, playing catch-up already, had no choice on his second but to loft a conservative 100-yard sand shot over an embankment that left him a difficult pitch to the green from the crest of the sharply downhill fairway. His third barely rolled onto the green's edge, and his fourth shot, whether a chip or a putt (reports varied), was also weak. Herron, meanwhile, picked the right time to hole the first "long" putt (i.e., at least six feet, in our golf lexicon) that either player had made all day, variously estimated at six to twelve feet, for a birdie and a win. Also, for the first time, Herron had the pleasure of conceding a sizeable par putt to Jones as Herron retook the lead, 1 up.[44]

In contrast, there was no disagreement about the shot-making on the twentieth hole because both youngsters played it superbly. Herron hit a great drive followed by a fantastic approach shot that put him about five to seven feet from the flagstick. Jones matched him stroke for stroke (although his second may not have been as close to the hole as Herron's[45]), and they halved No. 2 with birdie 3s, both sinking medium-length putts. This was Jones's first holed putt of the day over six feet, and Herron's second in a row (see Appendix 5). The gallery, which was now large enough to ring the green several people deep, roared their approval. "With the sun streaming down in the afternoon in a way to wilt any one who went faster than a slow doze, 'Davie' went on like a whirlwind."[46]

On the twenty-first hole, Herron hit another "fine" drive, while Jones hooked badly into one of the half-dozen or so "Snake Mound" bunkers that were aligned to the left of the fairway (as noted earlier, these "snake mounds" were later rebuilt to form the famous "Church Pew" bunkers).[47] A par 4 hole, No. 3 at Oakmont went downhill at first before climbing severely uphill the rest of the way, leading to a large blind green that required a middle iron for the second shot. With the "Snake Mounds" on the left, the drive presented a mental challenge for long hitters like Jones who were fighting a hook. It was thus no surprise that prior to the final match he had scored worse on No. 3 (along with No. 11) than on any other par 4 at Oakmont. Meanwhile, for Herron, curiously, No. 3 had been his very best par 4 hole all week. So, it seemed likely that Herron would win No. 3 and surge to a two-hole lead.

But things actually turned out quite differently; indeed, one might say that Bob Jones "stole" the hole. Herron's iron approach stopped just off the green's edge; he then chipped crisply to four or five feet of the cup, perhaps closer (William Everett Hicks of the *Brooklyn Daily Eagle* said he was only two feet away). Jones, in the meantime, made a good escape from one of the "Snake Mounds" fairway bunkers but barely advanced his ball past Herron's drive; he still faced a largely blind 100-yard shot to the green. But for the second hole in a row, Jones hit a terrific short-iron approach that stopped within six to ten feet of the cup. With Herron likely to make par, Jones doubtless felt intense pressure to sink this putt and avoid going 2 down. He studied the line, stroked his ball, and sank his second consecutive medium-length putt of six feet or longer—while Herron rimmed his shorter one to lose the hole.[48] It was a shocking turnaround. Jones had shown his "stout heart" and returned the match to all-even, as Herron learned yet again that Jones was good enough to take advantage of any small mistakes he made. Herron had more than earned his reputation for imperturbability, but the closeness of this match would rattle anyone.

Jones, with some of his confidence back, hit a clean, straight drive on the par 5 twenty-second hole, while Herron landed on the fairway's right edge, slightly shorter than Jones. They both hit fine brassies past the large bunker that crossed the fairway from the right (420 yards from the tee). But Jones's excellent brassie was particularly noteworthy. As he was addressing the ball, his play was interrupted by movement and noise in the gallery. In response, Jones stepped away and waited for the fans to settle down (many of them, no doubt, scurrying into good position by cutting into the diagonal fairway to watch Herron's third shot close-up).[49]

Throughout the afternoon, just as it had been all week, keeping spectators out of the fairways was a persistent problem. "The crowd was everywhere, and the players often had to suffer delays on the tee while the men in charge rushed down the course and cleared the path for the players to drive," reported the *Atlanta Constitution*.[50] Neophyte Pittsburgh fans were happily running hither and yon across fairways as players prepared to hit their second shots toward the greens.

Dave Herron was first to play to the green on No. 4, and his short game, like Bob Jones's, had been sharp all day. Not this time, though. Inexplicably, Herron "hooked" his short pitch shot, and it stopped rolling outside easy birdie range. As on No. 3, Jones now had an unexpected opportunity to win a hole outright where it looked a few seconds earlier he might only earn a half. Jones's chip with his jigger was good, stopping around five feet from the hole. If he sank his putt and Herron missed his longer try, Jones would return to all-even and potentially swing all of the match's momentum to his side. Herron had to be careful. He and Jones were both playing well, and though Herron had been setting a pace that his opponent had to make "a gritty effort to maintain," there was always a chance he would crack like he had on the back nine of the morning round.[51]

But how long was the putt Herron needed for birdie? Alas, next-day newspaper accounts of the length of his putt on No. 4 varied to a much greater degree than estimates of putts on any hole the entire week. Even journalists whose writing style was less prone to hyperbole offered substantially different "facts" as to how long a putt Herron faced. The *Pittsburgh Gazette Times* and *New York Sun* reported the putt as twenty feet, but the *New York Times* claimed it was only twelve feet, and the Associated Press said it was only ten feet.

Does it matter, for interpretive purposes, who was "right"? Yes, because, whereas sinking a ten-footer is always in the realm of possibility for a top-notch golfer, no one really expects his opponent to steal a hole by sinking a twenty-footer—especially at Oakmont, where even great putters struggled on the greens. Indeed, only a handful of players throughout the entire week of competition had sunk anything over twenty feet on Oakmont's terrifying greens, and neither Herron nor Jones had come close to making a putt of that length. If Herron's putt was actually only ten to twelve feet long, sinking it would be admirable but certainly not astonishing; but if it was twenty feet long, that would be substantially more noteworthy. And if indeed the putt was between twenty-five and thirty-five feet long, as Grantland Rice, Innis Brown, Walter Wilkes, and a few other writers claimed, then Herron's sinking it—especially after missing a four- or five-footer on the hole before—would seem fantastical and might ignite Jones's inner boil and throw him off his game.

So, when Herron's "long" putt disappeared into the cup for a birdie 4, many in the press were gobsmacked. And the diverse (both in class and ethnicity) crowd of thousands erupted in a long, loud, and unnerving series of hurrahs. As Charles Doyle of the *Pittsburgh Gazette Times* observed, "Herron's putt was sufficient to unnerve any player if a star can be affected by a spectacular shot. The crowd shouted and clapped as the ball trickled in the hole after the long runup."[52]

Herron's fine putt on the twenty-second hole didn't surprise just the gallery; it visibly upset Jones. And when, moments later, Jones blew his own short putt to lose the hole to Herron, the crowd cheered even more. It was a decisive moment in the psychology of the match; Herron had "stolen" No. 4 from Jones immediately after Jones had "stolen" No. 3 from him. It was also the origin of three related narratives: (1) this match was won and lost on the putting greens; (2) Dave Herron only won because his putter got hot; and (3) Bob Jones lost because, despite his superior ball-striking, he couldn't sink any short putts. With regard to the first and second points, the *New York Times* correspondent wrote, "[Herron's] putting as evidenced by his battle with Jones is a thing to wither the heart of the stoutest opponent."[53] The Associated Press characterized Herron's putting as "deadly."[54] And Grantland Rice, America's most widely syndicated sports columnist, described it as almost supernatural. "Wielding his Schenectady putter with all the magic wizardry of a Travis, when the veteran was at his best," Herron, according to Rice, "could make a golf ball do a jazz, a shimmy and a Pittsburgh glide, when it was necessary to find the bottom of the waiting expectant hole."[55] As for Herron's opponent, "Time and again [Jones] missed short ones that would have given him the hole, or, at least, a half."[56]

Even journalists who acknowledged that Herron's ball-striking was at least as good as, perhaps even superior to, Jones's still emphasized Herron's putting as the key factor. "It may be said that Herron's victory was due to his getting to more greens in fewer strokes than Bobby," wrote William Everett Hicks, "and when the latter beat him to the greens to halve with a long putt to kill the boy's superior work to the green."[57] In other words, Hicks recognized that Herron's long game was fully comparable to Jones's, often better, yet he complained that even when Jones did outplay Herron to the green, the latter just had to pull out his magic putter to negate all the Wonder Boy's hard work. Rice had a more succinct way of putting it that even more subtly downplayed Herron's overall skill: "Herron played exceptionally sound golf today from the tee to the green. But it was upon the velvet surface of the green itself that Dashing Dave held young Jones at bay."[58]

The problem with this narrative is that, empirically, neither player putted particularly well during the championship match (a total of thirty-two holes).

As Figure 4 shows, the *New York Times* reported 51 putts for Herron and 52 putts for Jones, whereas the *Pittsburgh Gazette Times* reported 52 putts for Herron and 51 for Jones. As America's best amateur golfers had been learning all week, Oakmont's greens were among the fastest in the world, mystifyingly difficult to read, and unusually large. Not in 1919 (and hardly ever since) has anyone putted "lights out" at Oakmont during a major championship. Herron's birdie putt on No. 4 was the only putt over thirteen feet (if indeed it was that long) that either player sank in the entire match. Beyond that, both players also missed several short clutch putts of six feet or less. Indeed, Jones had just "stolen" the twenty-first hole only because Herron missed a short putt. And, as noted earlier, Jones had yet to three-putt whereas Herron had done so twice (losing both holes).

In truth, the available empirical data suggest that Herron's main edge on Jones was not putting but ball-striking from tee to green. Although Jones's ball-striking in the championship match was significantly better than it previously had been, Herron was at least as accurate and long off the tee as Jones, and was decisively better at hitting greens in regulation and avoiding greenside and fairway bunkers. But these prosaic truths apparently did not make as compelling copy as Bob Jones, the Southern prodigy, being "denied" a rightful victory by Dave Herron the Putting Magician. Even Joe Davis in the *Chicago Tribune*, arguably a more neutral observer than several writers of the East and South, embraced this narrative. Despite the undisputed fact that Herron was leading for most of the match, Davis wrote, "Jones was really the attacking force and most of the time Herron was on the defensive. It was only by consummate nerve shown on the greens that he was able to keep ahead of the Georgia boy."[59] That conclusion, in our judgment, is simply not supported by empirical evidence. Herron won the title because he outplayed Jones in all phases of the game—just as he'd been doing all week.

Following his missed short birdie putt on No. 4, Jones was again 1 down to Herron. His return to all-even on No. 3 had lasted only one hole, and he would never draw even in the match again. Visibly red-faced and distraught, while the crowd backing Herron was loud and euphoric, he nonetheless refrained from yelling, cursing, or throwing his ball or clubs. He walked hurriedly to the next tee, "plainly upset by the turn of things."[60]

Herron had the honor and smashed his drive 275 yards down the middle; he was easily on the green in two, about fifteen feet from the flagstick, with a virtually guaranteed par. Jones, in contrast—playing in anger even more quickly than usual—cold-topped his drive. He ended up 170 yards behind Herron's

FIGURE 4
Herron v. Jones: Putting Comparisons (Number of Putts Made/Missed by Distance)

This table displays four types of data to compare Herron's and Jones's putting prowess during the championship match, as reported in the *New York Times* and the *Pittsburgh Gazette Times*: total putts, "short" missed putts of 6 feet or less, putts sunk of 7–12 feet, and "long" putts (13-plus feet). For more detailed discussion, see Appendix 5.

ROUND	HOLES SCORED	NEWSPAPER	HERRON MISSED <6 ft	JONES MISSED <6 ft	HERRON MADE 7–12 ft	JONES MADE 7–12 ft	HERRON MADE 13+ ft	JONES MADE 13+ ft
Morning	18	New York Times	3	3	0	0	0	0
		Pittsburgh Gazette Times	3	4	0	0	0	0
Afternoon	13	New York Times	1	1	3	1	0	0
		Pittsburgh Gazette Times	1	1	3	1	1	0
Total	31	New York Times	4	4	3	1	0	0
		Pittsburgh Gazette Times	4	5	3	1	1	0

tee shot and more than 250 yards from the green. This was Jones's second miserable drive on No. 5 that day—a real surprise because No. 5 had been his best par 4 hole at Oakmont. Indeed, he had birdied No. 5 three of the last six times he had played it.

Still furious as he walked to his ball—a mere 105 yards off the tee—Jones chose to go for broke and hit a brassie from a difficult lie.[61] He managed to make solid contact but sliced the shot horridly, so far to the right that it came to rest in No. 4's adjacent fairway. As Jones tried to locate his ball, he "knew that Herron had put [his] shot home, for he could hear the hand clapping by those who were standing about the green."[62]

As he had learned to do during his youth because of his volatile on-course temper, Jones gathered his emotions in time to carefully plan his third shot. His anger was always inwardly, not outwardly directed, as Francis Ouimet would emphasize to readers of his regular newspaper column a few weeks later.[63] His resilience and capacity to refocus after a temper tantrum were as much defining features of his "lean years" as his more publicized blow-ups. He remained confident he could still make par on No. 5 with a wild scramble, as he'd done on No. 3. That, in fact, is exactly what Jones did: with a poise defying his age, he hoisted a niblick over a deep bunker to hold the quick green just inside of Herron's ball. Eventually, Herron two-putted, giving Jones a reasonable chance to halve the hole. But Jones's par putt rimmed the cup, and Herron was now 2 up after the twenty-third hole.

For all his short-term anger, Jones must have known that he was playing his best golf of the week. He was unquestionably rising to the occasion. Even with the bogey on No. 5, he was even par in the afternoon, and he surely felt that Herron's remarkable pace of three birdies on the first five holes was unsustainable. There were thirteen holes left, and just a few hours earlier he had come back from 3 down in only four holes; he could surely do it again.

Herron finally gave Jones an opening on the short par 3 twenty-fourth hole. In the morning round, Herron's approach shot had scooted to the back edge of the green, but a fine lag putt had yielded a conventional par. In the afternoon, he was not so fortunate: he pulled his tee shot to the narrow green, and his ball snagged in soft, deep rough on a sharp downslope, forcing him to make a pitch from an unstable stance. Jones's tee shot on No. 6 was not his best either, but it stopped on a flat lie just off the far edge of the green. Herron managed to hit out to about twenty feet of the flagstick, while Jones chipped dead, his ball jumping over the hole and stopping two feet away. Herron's par putt was six inches short, and Jones reduced Herron's lead to just 1 up. It was still anyone's match, much to the crowd's excitement, with both competitors playing par or better golf.

Herron and Jones halved the next two challenging holes, the seventh and eighth. Jones remained at even par and Dave at 1 under—a level of golfing excellence that continued to equal the Ouimet-Evans match. But the Associated Press writer nonetheless detected early signs of fatigue in both young men and wondered if they could keep up the pace in the rising heat and humidity: "It was stiflingly hot and both players were soaked with perspiration. They took unusually long to size up the putts."[64]

Herron and Jones briskly walked the bridge over the ravine (today the Pennsylvania Turnpike) to play the uphill par 5 ninth, whose immense green fronted the clubhouse veranda from which members and guests could observe in the shade with a suitable drink in hand. (Prohibition would begin a few months later.) Prior to the championship match, the two young men had played the ninth hole exactly even, with average scores just over par (see Figure 2). Interestingly, neither had previously birdied all three front-nine par 5s in a single round. Herron now had a chance to do just that. He unleashed another massive drive, almost as long as his morning tee shot on No. 9. This time, though, Jones was not far behind.

With his best brassie Jones could reach the green in two—he had done so at least once in a previous match—but he hooked his second shot left and ended up in deep rough. The way was now clearly open for Herron to expand his lead by again smashing his second shot onto the green. And that is precisely what he did—onto the green itself rather than on its edge, as in the morning, and significantly closer to the flagstick (twelve to twenty feet, by most estimates). Jones was obviously in danger of losing the hole, but he dug hard and struck his ball cleanly from the rough, stopping it closer to the cup than Herron's brilliant second shot. Fatefully, however, Jones's birdie putt was on nearly the same line as Herron's putt for eagle.

In this era of the stymie it is hard to know exactly how Herron sized up his situation on the ninth green. An eagle would win the hole, of course, but if the eagle putt missed and ran past the cup, Jones would still have a makeable birdie chance that would tie Herron for the hole. An alternative tactic would be for Herron to strike his putt just firmly enough to theoretically fall into the cup, but to stop just short of the hole in case it did not. If executed perfectly, that would leave him a tap-in birdie and, more importantly, would block Jones's direct access to the cup. That way, Herron would ensure his own birdie but prevent Jones from making his.

Whatever Herron's actual intent, he did in fact hit an excellent putt that stopped just short of the hole and served as a "half-stymie," partially obstructing Jones's ability to sink his own birdie putt. Jones tried nonetheless to do so but simply could not; No. 9 went to Herron, who had played it as perfectly as humanly possible. For the first time in the championship, Herron had now birdied all three front-nine par 5s, and he won all three of them. In other words, he was 2 up after the front nine precisely because he was playing the par 5 holes much better than Jones. That is not to say Jones was playing badly; Herron had simply unlocked a new level of all-around excellence in the championship match. "It would take superhuman courage not to be disheartened when you play the first nine holes in even par and you are still two down," Walter Wilkes commented in the *Atlanta Georgian*.[65]

Bob Jones was not throwing clubs, but that did not mean he was any less combustible as he made the turn 2 down. Yet he put his emotions to good use on the downhill par 5 twenty-eighth—his best par 5 hole by far at Oakmont—when he threaded a 300-yard drive down the middle, in between numerous bunkers, leaving himself only a middle iron to the green. Herron, by contrast, sliced into the rough off the tee but drew a good lie and hit a beautiful iron that rolled and rolled down the fairway's steep decline to just a few yards short of the green. Jones's second shot was also a good one, safely onto the left edge of the green in two shots, hole-high with a sharply breaking, right-to-left putt for eagle on a green that would in later years be recognized as one of the most difficult in the world.

Lucky for Jones, Herron faltered slightly just then; his chip onto the very quick green ran past the hole, leaving him an uphill birdie putt variously estimated at eight to twelve feet long. Jones now had a clear opening to win back a hole—until, that is, a horde of grasshoppers suddenly descended onto the green forcing a delay of several minutes as he and Herron, the consummate gentlemen, worked in tandem to swat the intruders away. Once the line was clear, Jones stroked his approach putt dead and Herron conceded his tap-in birdie. Now, it was Herron's turn to putt. "When Herron's approach overran the cup 8 or 10 feet, while Bobby was dead for his 4," William Everett Hicks surmised,

> The boy's admirers felt that if Herron lost the tenth again [Jones had won the tenth in the morning round], as he seemed pretty sure to do, he would recall what happened in the morning and become correspondingly depressed. But all these calculations and hopes were knocked away when Herron's long putt went plunk against the back of the cup and dropped in for the half. Who knows but that this unexpected half caused Bobby's fatal approach on the eleventh?[66]

That "fatal approach" to No. 11 of which Hicks wrote—the twenty-ninth hole of the match—came after both men had hit their drives on the short but severely uphill hole, which played in 1919 as the third-hardest par 4. The layout of Oakmont is such that Nos. 1, 9, 10, and 11 run parallel to each other along the same hillside, and thus No. 11's fairway slants left to right (the slant is especially severe right of the fairway). The best way to play the hole is to hit a tee shot (usually with a fairway wood) of about 230 yards up the hill to the left, where the lie is relatively flat. Dave Herron, however, for the second hole in a row, sliced his tee shot. He had virtually no view of the green for his approach shot, and he had to perch one foot well above the other on the hillside and hit the ball cleanly in order to clear the huge ditch and the deep bunker just beyond it that crossed the fairway and safeguarded the green.

Bob Jones's drive was longer and, more important, safely to the left of Herron's, with a flatter lie and a clear view of the diagonally placed green. The question for him, though, was less the actual shot he was facing, which was fairly simple, but rather his mindset in light of how unevenly he had been playing No. 11 the past few days. In his last six rounds, he had scored everything from a triple bogey to a birdie on No. 11, and there was no predicting how his luck would pan out this time. Meanwhile, Herron was on track to set a new course record (having just recorded his fifth birdie of the afternoon on No. 10), and that had to be frustrating to watch for Atlanta's Boy Wonder.

Standing awkwardly, Herron used every ounce of his great power to successfully hit his approach over both the ditch and the huge bunker right and front of the green, only for his ball to roll into a smaller and shallower bunker just behind. Jones, meanwhile, despite his good lie in the fairway and perfect angle to the flagstick, pull-hooked his iron so that his ball bounced "plump" in the left-middle of the green and then careened into a deep bunker—the same bunker he'd hit into in the morning round. Herron had the much shorter and easier play. Jones hit a fine explosion shot from the sand, while Herron chipped so accurately from the shallow bunker that his ball smacked the flagstick before running, by most reporters' estimates, a yard or two by. "Every golf match of consequence has a turning point, which can be discerned by one player or the other, or by the onlooker," E. E. Giles mused.[67] And "when all is said and done the turning point of the match was on the eleventh hole." The *New York Times* observed:

> [Jones] had an easy mashie pitch to the green that should have won the hole for him. If he had won, he would have been only 1 down, coming strong, with seven holes yet to play; instead of winning, he pulled his mashie shot off to the left into a trap and came out short on the green. Heartened by the change in the tide, Herron pitched out well and holed a good putt to win in 4, putting himself 3 up. Thus was the golden opportunity lost, and from that moment Jones was almost doomed.[68]

This turn of events "broke the Southern youngster's great heart," the *Philadelphia Inquirer*'s Perry Lewis claimed, "and the handwriting was on the wall."[69] He was 3 down with only seven holes to play, and his opponent remained 3 under par for the afternoon round. It was shaping up to be easily the finest golf ever played in the final round of a U.S. Amateur, and on the hardest golf course that had ever hosted an Amateur championship. Dave Herron was making golf history, in part because the most precocious American youth ever to play the game was forcing him to play the best golf of his life by scoring par or better on every hole.

Outwardly, Jones remained calm. He certainly was not finished, as Herron's game had fallen apart on Nos. 13 to 17 in the morning round for no apparent reason. Furthermore, Jones had overcome Herron's 3-up lead in the morning in just four holes, and now he had seven holes left to make up the same deficit. Yes, a comeback was certainly possible—but, realistically, only if Jones could win or at least tie No. 12 and stall Herron's growing momentum after Herron had won two of the last three holes.

Unfortunately for Jones, as noted earlier, his record on No. 12 was even worse than on No. 11. His average score on the 601-yard monster was a shade under six strokes, the worst of any top player that week (see Figure 2). He had fallen apart in all sorts of ways, including missing a tiny putt in the morning round for a bogey 6, and he seemed never to know what to expect on No. 12. In other words, Bob Jones absolutely had to win a hole that had been giving him fits all week.

He started off well enough on the thirtieth hole of the match. Both players hit far down the fairway, but Herron sliced slightly to the edge of the rough while Jones drove straight and true. Herron was playing the odd and struck his long iron cleanly, but it leaned slightly right, may have run along a lengthy trench parallel to the fairway, and finally stopped in a small, shallow bunker at the fairway's right edge, around 135 yards from the center of the green. As Herron would later tell E. E. Giles of the *Pittsburgh Gazette Times*, he had a good lie in the sand (the bunker was apparently not furrowed) and was confident he could score a par 5 on the hole.[70]

That Dave Herron had a decent lie in the sand was not apparent to everyone present, however, including many journalists.[71] Thousands of dedicated fans, trying to see every shot, struggled in the heat and humidity to keep pace with Herron and Jones and get good viewing positions. Many onlookers herded down the left side of the fairway, where they could get a better angle on the players' second and third shots and still have just a short walk to observe tee shots afterward on the par 3 thirteenth green. But these "witnesses" would have been poorly positioned to observe Herron's second shot and determine exactly where it ended up. That limitation applied to journalists as well, especially this late in the afternoon, when some of them probably chose to stick as closely as possible to the clubhouse (a short jaunt from the twelfth fairway) so that as soon as the match ended, they could jog back, write up their stories, and get them to the telegraph office. At the end of the day, journalists claimed to have seen a bewildering variety of contradictory things on the thirtieth hole. Determining what actually happened at this iconic (and chaotic) moment in American golf history is much more problematic than writers at the time and historians since have acknowledged.

From Jones's clear view, Herron now lay close enough to the green, even though in a shallow bunker, to have a very good chance of scrambling a par 5. Three down in the match, Jones had no choice but to go for broke, swing as hard as he could, and hit his brassie as close to the green as possible to maximize his birdie chance—and this, on the very hole he had played the worst during the entire competition. Perry Lewis of the *Philadelphia Inquirer* put the point bluntly: Jones "needed the hole no more than he does his right arm. The time had come when Jones must make a grandstand finish or admit defeat, and it was patent that he was nerving himself up to a dying effort."[72]

Interestingly, during the week, Jones had often hit good drives on No. 12, but the downhill lie where long drives ended up made a solid strike with a low-lofted brassie (2-wood) difficult to execute. Yet he had only one play: with "the gallery as still as death and as silent as night," he had to smack his brassie far enough to leave a pitch of perhaps 75–100 yards to optimize his birdie chances. For a player with Jones's preternatural short-iron skills, success was quite possible—but only if he could crunch a perfect brassie shot from a tricky downhill lie.

Stoking every ounce of his considerable power for the strike, Jones "drew back his brassie to paste the ball" when a sharp, loud noise suddenly echoed across the course. Oakmont's chief marshal, W. G. Costin—the millionaire certain to win the $1,600 betting pool, "playing the role of major domo" and "doing no end of stentorian shouting"—called out through his megaphone.[73] John Anderson heard, "Hush!" William Everett Hicks heard, "Get back there!" Everyone else heard, "Fore!"[74]

Whatever exactly Costin shouted, his amplified voice had an immediate and devastating effect on Jones, who cold-topped his brassie into a huge, deep cross-bunker just ahead of him, in the right center of the fairway. "The noise was so loud and so unexpected that Bobby actually started and came very near missing the ball altogether," Walter Wilkes wrote in the *Atlanta Georgian*. "Bob says that he recollect[ed] nothing between the time of hearing the cry and seeing the ball pop into the bunker some fifty yards ahead of him [actually, the bunker was much closer]. The impression produced on his mind was so vivid as to efface everything else and leave his mind for several seconds a complete blank."[75]

Some writers claimed that Costin shouted just as Jones was taking back his club; Grantland Rice and Francis Ouimet, for example, wrote that Jones was at the top of his swing. But others implied that he had already started downward when he heard the shout. According to Charles Doyle, a Pittsburgh sportswriter, "Fans who were close to the kid claim that he shook as the loud shout was emitted. Others say he tried to hold the club, but it had gone too far."[76] Perry Lewis, contradicting his peers, reported that Jones "stopped, looked up, relaxed, nervously took his stance once more and then promptly smashed that ball right in a trap."[77]

But most accounts agreed with the spirit of the *New York Times*'s reporting:

> Jones was well down the fairway on his drive, and looked to have the hole won. He pulled out his brassie and was just at the top of his swing as a horn-rimmed be-spectacled official, with his yellow standard in one hand and a megaphone

in the other, saw a boy four hundred yards down the course move two inches to the right. "Fore," he shouted in a voice to wake the dead, and young Bob Jones came down atop his ball like a ton of brick, spilling it into a yawning bunker, just ahead.[78]

Costin later explained in a heartfelt apology that he had not meant to intercede in the match. In fact, he was trying to prevent the gallery from interfering, but he had instantly realized his mistake. "I'd give a million dollars to recall that shout. I made the boy miss his ball," he told the press with disarming honesty.[79] Charles Doyle reflected the next day, "Silence is supposed to be golden in the matter of golf success, that is at the point of where the shot is being played, but a little buzzing along the lines would not have as much bad effect as a misplaced fast ball from a megaphone."[80]

Nevertheless, the damage was done. But where exactly—physically—did Bob Jones's topped shot end up? This is more of a puzzle than golf historians have realized. As best we can determine from multiple, often conflicting accounts, his ball, after he had taken two or three hard swings, came to be "embedded" either under the lip of the bunker's sharp bank or in the soft, soaking grass of the embankment, rather than in the heart of the bunker itself.[81] The ball may even have been physically irretrievable, a possibility that would help explain why Jones was quick to concede the hole to Herron even though Herron was in a bunker himself. Jones had personally witnessed this "embedding" phenomenon at least twice during the week—first to his opponent Bob Gardner in the grass of a bunker to the left of the fourteenth green ending their match on Tuesday, and then to himself in his semifinal match against Fownes after he had hooked his tee shot on No. 1 into a fairway bunker and, after several tries, buried the ball so deeply into the bunker's soft embankment that no one could locate it. This odd outcome—a concession forced by an irretrievable ball—happened to several other players during the week and was a result of (1) persistent rainstorms and (2) Emil Loeffler Jr.'s last-minute efforts to toughen Oakmont by sodding new embankments guarding the bunkers.

In the end, we are still uncertain about what actually transpired on No. 12. Likely, no one besides Bob Jones and his caddie ever really knew, because it would have been difficult for anyone else to get close enough to look down into the deep bunker to see precisely where Jones's ball had landed. Furthermore, we suspect the marshals compelled the gallery to remain quietly in place and did not let them (journalists included) follow Jones and his caddie the relatively short distance to the bunker. Thus, we cannot be confident that any journalist actually witnessed what they claimed to have seen firsthand, close up, regarding Jones's travails in the fairway bunker on No. 12.[82]

What is certain is that Bob Jones had struggled on this hole all week, he was 3 down, and his composure had just been shattered by a man with a megaphone. Now, he had to hit his ball far enough out of this deep bunker (which may have been furrowed) to have a chance of tying Dave Herron for the hole and not falling 4 down with only six holes to play. Walter Hagen claimed that Jones's "goat was gone so completely" after the incident that he took one solitary swat before "pick[ing] up the ball in disgust."[83] Francis Ouimet and the Associated Press writer reported that Jones tried three times—"plung[ing] his club into the heavy grass"—before giving up.[84] And Grantland Rice was alone in claiming that Jones took four swings. But most of the press corps agreed that he swung only twice before conceding the hole to Herron.[85]

Jones's rather quick decision to concede only makes sense—given how badly he needed to win or at least tie this hole—if the ball was indeed physically irretrievable. That is, if with every swing, the ball was only sinking more and more into the spongy grass embankment. "It was an unfortunate incident, as what chances [Jones] had to come back were ruined," Hagen commented. "He would surely have won this hole and would have been only two down, which would have changed the complexion of the match completely."[86]

Rice agreed with Hagen that Jones would have won the hole if not for the unfortunate incident. "In place of an easy chance to win this hole back and thereby stand [two] down," he wrote, "Jones was four down with only six holes to go through the extreme carelessness of one man who through his failure to guard against any such mistake broke up the match then and there. Rendering the conclusion as sure and certain as death itself."[87] Innis Brown, John Anderson, and the anonymous reporter for the *New York Times* concurred, as did Walter Wilkes—who characterized the incident as "their 'piece de resistance' of discourtesy."[88] "They," as Wilkes phrased it, clearly referred not only to the megaphone blast but also to the rowdy Pittsburgh fans who had loudly cheered for Herron throughout the afternoon. Thus, Wilkes implied that, on some level, Costin's actions were intentional.

R. P. Jones, Bob's father, did not imply intentionality but was equally outraged:

> [Bob] had a good lie and a straight road to the green. Herron was in a trap with his second. I did not mind the hostility of the crowd, shown so plainly in the applause which frequently came when Bobby made a poor shot. That did not

bother him at all. Bob could fight that. But to have some fool shout "fore" just as he was swinging at this ball was mighty unfair.[89]

Only E. E. Giles, writing in the *Pittsburgh Gazette Times*, stood up for Dave Herron:

> The call of "fore" which undoubtedly affected Bobby Jones' swing was most unfortunate in the circumstances... but its relative influence on the final result, not only of the match itself, but on the hole in question, have [sic] been magnified and exaggerated beyond all reason by men of otherwise sound judgment and analytical minds. Practically all writers and most men who are accustomed to having their opinions formulated by the press, have taken it for granted that Jones already had won the hole, the moment Herron played his second shot, forgetting that Jones was nearly 300 yards away with plenty of trouble ahead.

Giles went so far as to condemn "Jones, Sr.'s rushing into print" as "bad taste if not poor sportsmanship," and something that neither Dave Herron nor his father Andrew Sr. would ever do.[90] Since Jones conceded, Herron did not have to play out of the shallow bunker where his second shot had landed, so we will never know if he really would have reached the green and won the hole from there. Costin may or may not have robbed Jones, but he did rob Herron of the chance to prove himself.

Bob Jones walked the long trek, some 300 yards, from the bunker in the middle of the fairway where he had conceded the hole to the thirty-first tee, visibly angry and in "no mood to shoot golf."[91] "Jones appeared as though this uncalled for loud talk at the latter hole," D. J. McGuiness of the *Boston Globe* wrote, referring to the megaphone incident, "got on his nerves, for he promptly hooked his tee shot to the 31st hole into a trap."[92] His dismay only grew as he hit out of one bunker only to land in another on the other side of the green. He finally calmed down enough to hit a brilliant third shot from the sand within easy one-putt range. Still, Herron, following a fine middle iron that stopped just beyond the flagstick, two-putted for a conventional par and the win, so Jones's post-meltdown efforts came to naught.

The match was now dormie, with Jones five holes down and only five holes left to play. This was the make-or-break moment. Jones had to win No. 14 to extend the match; anything less and his chance to become the youngest player ever to win a U.S. Amateur championship was over. By now, his equanimity had returned, and he matched Herron's beautiful drive on the short par 4 hole with one of his own. They were both on the green in two and had good birdie chances, with Jones's ball closer to the flagstick. Herron's approach putt was dead, and Jones conceded his par. "This gave Jones an opportunity to stave off defeat by dropping his comparatively easy putt for a win," Perry Lewis described in the *Philadelphia Inquirer*.

> There was absolute silence as he cleared away the turf to the hole and then took his stand. The putter fell and sent the tiny globe on its journey—a journey that meant defeat for the South and weeping, wailing and gnashing of teenth [sic] in Georgia, for the ball came to rest three inches short of the objective. A great cheer fairly rocked the clubhouse, echoed and reechoed from the hills of Pittsburgh.
>
> Eager hands hoisted the victor in the air and it took some hoist to get that 218 pounds up. In triumph they bore him toward the club he had so honored, a screaming, cheering, victory-mad multitude. But as they neared the lawn in front of the building, Herron saw someone in the crowd whose embrace meant more to him than the congratulations of the world. With a heave he shook himself loose, knocking two of his bearers flat on their faces—and in a second Herron, the 21-year-old golf champion of America, was in the arms of his mother and her hearty kiss had been implanted on his dut-incrusted [sic] and perspiring forehead—did she care, and she did not.[93]

"Dave, I'm proud of you," she said. "I am the happiest woman in the world." According to Ralph Davis of the *Pittsburgh Chronicle-Telegraph*, Herron replied, "Mother, I'm glad for your sake that I won. . . . I tried hard to win."[94]

Of course, Bob Jones had been the first to congratulate Dave Herron, offering his hand as soon as it was clear that his putt would not drop. Despite the many frustrations of this match, Jones at least had not audibly cursed, kicked any balls, smashed a single club, or thrown any equipment—something the partisan crowd would have loved to see. "The manner in which Jones controlled that tempestuous personality, which is the heritage of the South," Perry Lewis commented, "was one of the remarkable phases of the match."[95]

After Herron and his fans finished their quick celebration, everyone went back outside to watch the trophy presentation. For the entire match the skies had remained clear, William Everett Hicks wrote, "but old J. Pluvius would not let the tournament go without another wetting and as the crowd gathered under the trees for the presentation of the cup and medal to the winner . . . a light shower sprinkled the assemblage."[96] With that done and the new Amateur champion officially crowned, journalists polished their stories for Sunday's morning edition and shared the news with the rest of the country.

"Hail to hefty Davie Herron of Pittsburgh," the *New York Times* proclaimed.[97] In fact, nearly every major newspaper made note of Herron's 218

Dave Herron with the USGA committee and the original Havemeyer Trophy after besting Bob Jones, 5 and 4. Cherry/Herron Family Archives.

pounds. Grantland Rice described him as "sturdily and stockily built, a young 200-pounder with a massive frame and a full swing."[98] The writer for the *Atlanta Journal* pointed out, "Dave is just as big as Bobby is little."[99] Walter Wilkes compared Herron to New England's "Siege Gun" Jesse Guilford.[100] And New York sportswriter Harry Smith ("The Runner-Up") joked,

> One would be almost tempted to say that Herron yesterday won the United States heavyweight [boxing] championship, but for the fact that the National Association hasn't got so far yet as to establish medium and featherweight competitions. Some railroad men who looked over both finalists began to talk about excess baggage, which a lot of the players here this week would be glad to carry long enough to win the premier American honor.

Smith even made a pun on Herron's name, simultaneously celebrating him as "a bird of a golfer" while pointing out that he would not "measure up to what the dictionary says under the name of a long-legged, slender-bodied wading member of the bittern family"—also known as a heron.[101]

Innis Brown wrote that Herron was "a powerful, strong limbed chap, who carries just a bit too much fat to meet the full approval of the appraising eye of a football coach for varsity material. But . . . that heft he carries is doubtless solid from the bone out."[102] The *New York Times* reporter agreed, writing, "From the way in which 'Davie' moves around and plays his shots one would judge that of his total weight of 218 pounds there should be about three-quarters of an ounce of fat. The rest seems to be pure muscle, with a good strong heart and a genial soul."[103] The comments of Smith, Brown, and the *Times* sound like backhanded compliments, but Perry Lewis's description of Herron's skill was perhaps the most extreme blend of classicism, weight-related criticism, and *faux* admiration published in the immediate days following the match:

> Herron, the victor, played with a will that was as hard as the iron he worked with those powerful paws of his every day. Not once during the terrific grind did he falter, and he handles his clubs with [the] same ease, grace, and power as he does Every Satur[d]ay afternoon in friendly matches with fellow clubmen. Big and brawny, with the shoulders of a Hercules, he made a striking contrast with the rosy-cheeked stripling from the South.[104]

The Eastern writers could not stop themselves from pointing out that Dave Herron did not look like a typical athletic champion. Certainly, the Eastern (as well as Southern) writers were terribly

Supposedly, Dave Herron's "only rival in size in the amateur ranks [was] WM H Taft." Scar, "Champ of Champs," *Anaconda Standard*, 1 September 1919.

disappointed that Bob Jones did not win. Grantland Rice basically admitted as much when he wrote, "Jones made a gallant bid to smash all records by winning a championship at 17, but his showing in traveling this far was wonderful considering the men he had to beat before he found Herron's putter barring the road. He has a greater variety of shots than his conqueror but he had nothing to stop the spectacular putting which broke up the match."[105] If Bob Jones, Atlanta's famous Boy Wonder, had won a national championship at age seventeen, smashing all records for pure precocity, the papers would have sold themselves. A local golfer who worked in a foundry making wrought-iron pipes, winning because he played well on his own home course in the City of Soot, just wasn't good copy. Even worse, Herron was calm, collected, and overall wholesome. At least recent champions like Chick Evans and Walter Hagen were loud and eccentric, and poor John McDermott, who won two consecutive U.S. Opens in 1911 and 1912, may have just been mentally ill.[106]

From a newspaperman's point of view, Dave Herron was boring. And he had no name recognition. "I'm awfully sorry Bob didn't win," wrote O. B. Keeler from Atlanta. "After putting away men like Gardner and Fownes it is a bit tough to lose to somebody named Herron, who happens to be getting all his putts in the tin on that particular round."[107] The only way to make this story interesting enough was to suggest that perhaps Herron did not deserve to win. Jones, after all, had the better shots and the harder bracket, and the mean-spirited Pittsburgh crowd against him. Herron's victory was just a lucky upset. "Far be it from us to take even one iota of credit away from Herron for the fact remains that he played the most consistent golf of a big and representative field," the *New York Sun*'s featured columnist Daniel granted, "but we doubt if any neutral follower of the ancient and honorable game will declare that the laurels really went to the best golfer in the land."[108]

Over the course of a hard-fought week, Herron had played the best golf of the entire field from start to finish—he tied as low medalist, tied for the *American Golfer* Trophy (he and Grant Peacock would win that on Sunday), and decisively defeated Bob Jones, 5 and 4, for the match-play championship. It was impossible to deny that the crown rightfully rested on his "broad brow." Yet, in fact, that was all now hotly contested. The championship was over, but the battle over what exactly Dave Herron's victory signified and what his legacy would be was just beginning.

PART IV
AFTERMATH

▶ CHAPTER 16
THE BOY WONDERS GO HOME

Bob Jones and his childhood golf coach, Stewart Maiden, parted ways and left Pittsburgh the day after the championship match. Jones returned to Atlanta and Maiden to St. Louis, where he had taken a new head pro job six months earlier. Instructor and pupil had enjoyed more than two weeks of nonstop togetherness, first in St. Louis and then in Pittsburgh, in their effort to make Jones the youngest major champion in American golf history.

Over this long stretch Jones demonstrated just how dependent on Maiden he had always been to fix flaws that emerged in his seemingly perfect swing.[1] The common claim that Jones was self-taught in golf, as promulgated most zealously by his publicist and confidante O. B. Keeler, is overstated. As sports commentator Morgan Blake of the *Atlanta Journal* observed in 1919:

> Bobby seems to have struck his stride after playing in an[d] out golf all the season. With Stewart Maiden, his old instructor on the ground to give him valuable advice Bobby is going to make trouble for the big boys in the tournament. Bob has implicit confidence in Maiden, who started him out in the golf game when Bob was but a baby. He always plays his best when Stewart is present. The mental part of golf is a factor in it, and Atlanta golfers who know that Bob looks up to Stewart as a sort of golf father, feel renewed confidence that the former East Lake pro is with his youngsters at the big show.

While together in St. Louis, Maiden tutored Jones individually for several days and then, just before leaving for Pittsburgh, partnered with him in a best-ball match where Jones showed the two sides of his seventeen-year-old game and personality. On the one hand, he broke the course record; on the other hand, he sullied his achievement with several temper tantrums where he hurled clubs long distances and angrily kicked golf balls off greens after chipping or putting poorly.

Coach and pupil drove together to Pittsburgh, picking up Perry Adair and Richard Hickey in Cincinnati along the way, before arriving at their hotel late on the evening of Tuesday, August 12. During Jones's golf-packed two weeks at Oakmont (he would play nearly three hundred holes by the end) there was not one day that Maiden did not either play with him in an informal match or instruct him on the practice range or putting green. Nonetheless, Jones's ball-striking at Oakmont, despite many stretches of brilliance, remained erratic. Jones was still mystified (as was Maiden) by his tendency to hook or pull both tee shots and irons at inopportune moments for no apparent reason. As for his putting, it remained mediocre, although his chipping was superb. In truth, Jones never felt comfortable on Oakmont's slick and undulating greens—not in 1919 and not in his later two major championship appearances there (the 1925 Amateur, which he won in a runaway, and the 1927 U.S. Open, his worst U.S. Open performance ever).

In the end, Maiden probably assisted Jones most at Oakmont not by correcting his swing flaws but by containing his temper, or at least reducing it to a low boil. During his entire stay at Oakmont, and to the pleasant surprise of both friends and USGA officials, Jones did not kick balls or hurl his clubs through the air. And it was a good thing he did not: both the Pittsburgh press and the neophyte working-class golf fans who lacked "etiket" had heard many stories about his volatile temper, and any overt displays would have egged them on.

Bob Jones's temper was one thing; his father's, another. By the time the teenager arrived home on Monday, August 25, Big Bob's temper had already lit a fuse and ignited Atlantans' furor regarding how his son had (allegedly) been mistreated in Pittsburgh by both the fans and USGA-appointed officials. Big Bob let loose to the press even before he left Pittsburgh, and he continued his diatribe after he returned to Georgia. The local press delightedly reported every word that was fit to print: "'I would not have cared if he had been given a fair chance and had lost the match,' he said, 'but it surely was bitter to have him robbed of his chance for victory. It was nothing short of robbery.'"[2]

Young Bob did his best to tamp down the outrage his father stoked. He showered praise on Dave Herron for both his humility and the extraordinary golf he had played. "Bobby said that Herron is a great sportsman, and that he was not in any way liable for Bob's defeat through unfair or unsportsmanlike tactics. . . . [He] said that Herron deserves all the credit in the world for his victory, as he played wonderful golf at all times, particularly as to the putting game." And he was quick to remind Atlantans, too, that Herron had immediately offered Jones "the privilege" of a do-over after the megaphone incident on No. 12—an offer, of course, that Jones had refused and that the USGA, in any case, would not have allowed.

At the same time, he did admit, despite Big Bob's denial, that the gallery's unruly behavior had upset him, especially the loud cheering of his topped or misdirected shots and his missed short putts. Prior to the final match, most fans in Pittsburgh had embraced Jones for the precocious golfing wonder he clearly was. That included most local reporters, who would have loved to celebrate a seventeen-year-old winning a national championship.

But deference to golf etiquette or even-handedness went out the window in the finale between Jones and Herron, where the gallery—younger, louder, more socially heterogeneous—grew in the afternoon to three times larger than the Ouimet-Evans gallery. Thus, Bob Jones was candid enough to admit that hostile fans at Oakmont did unnerve him, despite the fact—and this was a point Big Bob was also trying to make—that he had risen to the occasion and played splendidly in the championship match. Indeed, however unfortunate the distractions or lopsided his 5 and 4 loss, he actually played his best golf of the entire week in the championship match against Herron.[3]

Perhaps the best way for Jones to avoid the swirling controversies about what happened at Oakmont was to hang out full-time at East Lake. This is, in fact, what he did, except to visit Georgia Tech in preparation for his sophomore year. Practicing golf all day, every day was also the best way for him to shine at the biggest golf championship ever held in the South: the inaugural Southern Open, scheduled to begin two weeks later at East Lake.[4]

The idea for the Southern Open had emerged only two months earlier in New Orleans, at the Southern Amateur when Nelson Whitney, the South's greatest player for over a decade, had thumped Jones in the semifinals, garnering them both national press coverage. Discussions to hold a high-prestige "open" championship in the South had continued throughout the summer. Big Bob and other Atlanta Athletic Club honchos, notably Scott Hudson and John Bothamley, energetically advocated for Atlanta as the "New South's" most dynamic city and for East Lake as the South's best golf course. Indeed, in the eyes of many top golfers in the South, not just those from Atlanta, East Lake was actually a harder test than the courses in Cleveland and Hamilton, Ontario, where, respectively, the 1919 Western Open and Canadian Open championships had recently been held.

Despite enthusiastic initial interest, plans for a Southern Open did not gain formal approval from the Southern Golf Association (SGA) until early August. And that decision came only after Atlanta pro J. Douglas Edgar's PGA record–shattering sixteen-shot victory over Jones and Jim Barnes in the Canadian Open had stirred up intrigue throughout the golfing world. East Lake's Bothamley had accompanied Jones, Edgar, and Willie Ogg to Canada, and

Bothamley made sure that everyone back home understood the miracle of Edgar's performance.

> He played much better golf than I had ever seen before. We haven't realized here in Atlanta what a wonderful golfer he is but the truth is he is one of the best in the world.... Edgar hasn't been at his best in any of the matches he has played in Atlanta, for the simple reason that he hasn't been able to accustom himself to our [Bermuda-grass] greens.... His game in the Canadian open wasn't a flash in the pan, there was nothing in the nature of a fluke about it.[5]

Even though Edgar had only arrived in Atlanta a few months earlier, his extraordinary achievement in Canada stirred regional Southern pride. And with Edgar, Bob Jones, Perry Adair, and Willie Ogg guaranteed to participate, the top prize for professionals pegged at $500, and second prize at $350 (comparable to the PGA championship), Horace Smith, president of the Southern Golf Association, formally sanctioned the event. Thus, with only a month's notice, the SGA sent invitations to all top professionals in the United States urging them to compete and help make the first Southern Open a success.

Initially, hope ran high that some of the nation's top amateurs who had appeared at Oakmont might also come to Atlanta—if not Ouimet and Evans then surely stars of the South like Nelson Whitney and Reuben Bush of New Orleans. Among the professionals, Atlantans were confident that Jim Barnes would participate because, they believed, he would want revenge after losing by sixteen shots to Edgar in Canada. Tournament sponsors were also optimistic that Oakmont professionals Charlie Rowe and Emil Loeffler Jr. (classified as a professional though, technically, a greenkeeper) would play to reciprocate Atlanta for sending its five finest amateurs to compete at Oakmont. In addition, based on both in-person and telephone conversations, some boosters felt that professional luminaries like Jock Hutchison, Fred McLeod, and Emmet French—perhaps even the recent finalists in the U.S. Open at Brae Burn, Walter Hagen and Mike Brady—might play as well.

All in all, as many as 150 professionals and amateurs were predicted for the inaugural Southern Open. The tournament was expected to validate East Lake and Atlanta as belonging to the upper crust of American championship golf—just like the U.S. Amateur had done for Pittsburgh and Oakmont. "It can't be said too many times," hyped Atlanta's premier golf writer at the time, Angus Perkerson, of the *Atlanta Journal*, "that the Southern Open is going to be the biggest golfing event in the history of the south, because that's exactly the proportions it will take."[6]

Bob Jones, of course, was thrilled that the Southern Open would be played at his home course. That would give him the same putative advantage—at least in the eyes of some commentators—that Dave Herron had enjoyed at Oakmont and that (sometimes forgotten) Francis Ouimet had enjoyed in winning the U.S. Open at Brookline in 1913. Like Herron, moreover, Jones could count on tremendous local fan support (and pressure too) because the Jones family's ties to East Lake were at least as strong as the Herron family's ties to Oakmont. Event boosters in Atlanta were not shy about alerting Jones to hometown expectations following his near-miss in Pittsburgh.

> Perhaps enough has been said about the tournament at Oakmont. It's done and over with. . . . One of the most interesting things about [the Southern Open] is . . . whether any player in the country can beat Bob Jones over Bob's own course. Until now Bob has always been playing someone over that someone's home links. . . . But in the Southern Open, Bob will be playing over a course as familiar to him as his own backyard, the course where he holds the record score of 69. And it's going to take everything Walter Hagen, Jim Barnes and Jock Hutchison have to stay with him.[7]

In the run-up to the Southern Open, Jones was fortunate (like Herron at Oakmont) to have exceptionally strong local competition to sharpen his game—peers like Perry Adair and Richard Hickey, but especially the two recent additions to Atlanta's professional ranks: Willie Ogg, at East Lake, and the now world-famous professional J. Douglas Edgar, at Druid Hills. Though Jones was surely sorry to lose Stewart Maiden as his regular teacher, Ogg and Edgar carried reputations comparable to Maiden's in both the United Kingdom and United States. Not surprisingly, soon after their arrival, Jones began to compete regularly against them, and some felt that his second-place finishes at both Canada and Oakmont reflected how rapidly he was learning from them.

After Jones returned to Atlanta, Edgar and Ogg played with him several times at East Lake to prepare for the Southern Open and for exhibition matches against other visiting professionals that might attract a paying gallery.[8] Jones was always quite generous in assisting professionals by participating with them in exhibitions (though, as an amateur, he did not share in any of the gate receipts). The professionals truly appreciated his readiness to play against them because Jones's national celebrity burnished their own reputations and raised the fees they could charge for lessons and exhibitions. No doubt, too, Jones learned to perform at his very best against professionals, who all desperately wanted to beat him.

Unfortunately, the grand expectations of Atlanta's boosters for the Southern Open did not materialize. For one, it was naïve to expect many professional

At the top left is Willie Ogg. Jim Barnes is on the right, and Perry Adair, then twenty years old, is shown at bottom right. "Stars in Action at East Lake Monday," *Atlanta Constitution*, 9 September 1919.

golfers from the Northeast and Midwest to drop everything on short notice and make the long trek to Atlanta, especially with the PGA championship scheduled a week later at Engineers Country Club on Long Island. For another, why would the nation's leading amateurs who played at Oakmont want to travel all the way to Atlanta to compete against lesser amateurs (excluding Bob Jones) and an unpredictable bevy of professionals—particularly on slow-as-molasses Bermuda greens that many of them were unfamiliar with?

In the end—though precise numbers are hard to tally from newspaper accounts—less than half the expected field showed up to play at the inaugural Southern Open. Further, the number of professionals who stayed to play the entire tournament plummeted each day. The no-shows made a mockery of the plan to utilize the first two eighteen-hole rounds to select a "championship flight" of sixty-four for the thirty-six-hole finale on Wednesday. In actuality, perhaps fifty players were still around to advance to the "championship flight," and these included a local amateur whose qualifying score for two rounds was 204 (tournament sponsor John Bothamly got into the "championship flight" with 198). Nearly all of the amateurs in attendance were from Atlanta; no one from the Northeast or Midwest showed up, and, most discouragingly, neither did the Big Easy's Nelson Whitney or Reuben Bush. Though Hagen and Brady remained in communication with tournament sponsors until the last minute, the two high-profile pros ended up hustling a nearby exhibition match that paid the victor around the same as if he'd won the Southern Open. Embarrassingly, by the tournament's end on Wednesday, only twenty-four competitors turned in scorecards.

If the inaugural Southern Open attracted fewer top players than hoped for (though no one would know that from the hype of the local press), the quality of the golf played by the leaders was fabulous. East Lake lived up to expectations as a championship venue and played very hard, with only four competitors able to post scores of 300 or lower on the par 73 course. Thankfully, too, Atlantans came out to watch in large numbers, the press covered the event in great detail, and, perhaps most satisfyingly for the organizers, the entire event provided another large feather in the cap of Bob Jones. He was featured, before the tournament, in match-play exhibitions with Jim Barnes, Leo Diegel (the twenty-year-old pro sensation from Detroit), and J. Douglas Edgar. And, most impressively during the tournament itself, he lost by only one shot to Barnes (293 to 294), with the two superstars paired together for the final thirty-six holes. Barnes was the reigning Western Open champion and, in most experts' eyes, the world's best golfer of 1919 (he would win his second PGA championship a week later). Jones beat Edgar by three shots and Diegel by six shots. Not surprisingly, he putted much better at East Lake than at Oakmont, and his ball-striking remained as solid as during his championship match against Dave Herron a few weeks earlier.

Though the Atlanta press were as reluctant as ever to report Jones's temper tantrums, his performance was also impressive in terms of his own maturity. Tied with Barnes after the opening two days, he held his emotional composure in the thirty-six-hole finale even after Barnes went on a miraculous run of 4 under par in six holes to take a commanding 5-shot lead after fifty-four holes. The spurt included back-to-back scores of eagle-birdie, and though Jones started the last nine holes five shots behind Barnes, he never gave up, and managed to erase all but one stroke of that deficit with a 1-under-par 35. As he had demonstrated during the wartime Red Cross matches and in the more recent Canadian Open, Bob Jones had never been intimidated playing head-to-head against the best professionals in North America. That self-confidence, bordering on hubris, was a life-long gift of his tutelage by Maiden, Ogg, and Edgar.

As Jones began his sophomore year at Georgia Tech, he could reflect with great satisfaction on the most extraordinary success any seventeen-year-old American golfer had ever achieved: nothing less than three second-place finishes in a row in the Canadian Open, the U.S. Amateur, and the Southern Open. In head-to-head, medal-play battles against the best professional golfer of 1919, Jim Barnes, he had tied Barnes in Canada and finished just one stroke behind him in Atlanta. And against Dave Herron in the U.S. Amateur, he had kept up with Herron's record-setting pace until the last few holes and turned in one of the best performances ever in America's most prestigious golf championship. He also reinforced his dual reputation as one of the best short-iron players in the game, professional or amateur, and one of the longest hitters in golf.

Jones, of course, had first achieved national celebrity at Merion in 1916, at the tender age of fourteen. But no less remarkable was how, by age seventeen, he had continued to improve his game and expand his celebrity in each successive year, despite—one might better say, because of—the profound disruptions of World War I. By 1919, wherever he played, he was nearly as much an object of public and expert adoration as Ouimet, Evans, Barnes, and Hagen. With his beautiful golf swing and exceptional distance, he exuded certainty that he could defeat any adult in the game. No longer could he be viewed as a future superstar. At age seventeen, he was already the most celebrated teen there had ever been in all of American sport. And J. Douglas Edgar knew why all too well: for all their matches together at East Lake or Druid Hills, Edgar had yet to beat

Jones once. Indeed, Jones was still alleged to be spotting Edgar one stroke each nine.[9]

Jones spent the fall semester playing golf, studying, cheering the football team, and overseeing Georgia Tech's golf team, which was the first Southern team accepted into the Intercollegiate Golf Association. Playing less frequently than during the summer did not mean that his game deteriorated, however. His golf remained at the peak level it had reached at both the Amateur and Southern Open, including a team win by Jones and Adair against Chick Evans and a local professional in Nashville, with Jones turning in the lowest score of 70.[10] As 1919 wound to a close, Jones had nothing more to prove to himself or others. Winless or not, he remained golf's brightest star in postwar America.

"DAVE HERRON CAN PLAY ANY COURSE, AND THIS IS THE ANSWER TO THE QUESTION: IS HE A CLASS PLAYER?"[11]

It was already late afternoon when Herron and Jones shook hands after both missing makeable putts on Oakmont's fourteenth green. Pittsburgh's boisterous fans—including caddies Herron had known since childhood and work colleagues from the ironworks—went ballistic. "'It was the finest finals ever played in any amateur championship in this country,' Frederick S. Wheeler, president of the United States Golf Association remarked after the match was completed. 'I never saw finer golf than that played by Davidson Herron.'"[12]

Herron, however, had only a moment to savor his "dark horse" triumph.[13] That was because he had to return to Oakmont early Sunday morning to compete in the delayed playoff for the team-based *American Golfer* Trophy. Though club members, fully cognizant that Prohibition was just months away, celebrated raucously through the night ("until the milkmen were getting ready to make their morning calls"), Herron politely snuck out early and went to bed. He was indeed quiet and reserved by nature and uncomfortable with "hero stuff," as a local reporter observed.[14] But he also had a lot at stake on Sunday morning that reflected his dual identity as both a Princeton and Oakmont man.

A week earlier—on Sunday, August 17—Herron and his Oakmont/Princeton former teammate Grant Peacock had tied for first place in the best-ball *American Golfer* Trophy event sponsored by the journal's esteemed editor, Walter Travis. This tie necessitated a playoff that could finally take place now that Herron was available. Walter Travis had initiated the event just a few years earlier and persuaded the USGA to incorporate it into the National Amateur protocol. The rationale for the competition built on elite country club traditions where winning and prominently displaying team medals and trophies was

Some cartoonists, rather than emphasizing Dave Herron's size, focused on his work ethic and quiet dignity. He "was a caddy just to be around golfers," "always admired Bill Fownes," "gets up at daybreak to start to work in a steel foundry [sic]," and "when presented with medal was least interested of all." H. B. Martin, "The New Golf Champion," *Globe and Commercial Advertiser*, 29 August 1919.

integral to club honor and boosting interclub rivalries.

Dave Herron had grown up with these elite traditions, as did his entire family. The Herrons were founding Oakmont members and close personal associates of the Fownes family—W. C.'s son Henry II was Dave's best friend. Throughout his childhood and youth, even as a caddie, Dave Herron had loved representing Oakmont in fierce team and individual matches against nearby clubs, and so had his brothers and father. Furthermore, this particular playoff for the *American Golfer* Trophy raised the ante because all four competitors were former or current members of Princeton's golf team. By 1919 Princeton had supplanted Yale as the nation's dominant college golf team, and this playoff attested to their supremacy. No wonder, then, that Herron and Peacock arrived early Sunday morning to prepare for the playoff against Princeton stars Richard Haight and Simpson Dean.

In deciding to compete for the *American Golfer* Trophy, Dave Herron did not please everyone because he had also decided not to compete in a Sunday playoff for the low-score medal—a prestigious award the USGA presented in a formal ceremony at all of its major championships. The previous Monday, he had tied Paul Tewksbury of Philadelphia and Jimmy Manion of St. Louis for medalist honors at 158 strokes in the Amateur qualifying rounds. USGA officials would have preferred that Herron compete in the low-scorer playoff because of the special historic opportunity he alone had earned: no American had ever been both low medalist and winner of the U.S. Amateur. Winning the low-scorer medal was, potentially, "a distinction quite unparalleled" and would be an extraordinary feather in Herron's cap if he could do it.[15]

But Herron was an ardent Princetonian, a true scholar-athlete who had not only captained the golf team but earned special academic distinction. He made his priorities clear to USGA president Frederick S. Wheeler at the clubhouse festivities on Saturday evening. Herron's "excuse" was not that Princeton mattered more but that Manion (a public course player with limited financial resources) had chosen to return to St. Louis several days earlier and not wait around to see when Herron might be free to compete against him and Tewksbury. Because there could be no three-way playoff, Herron felt the honorable move was to cede the low-qualifier medal to Tewksbury and focus all his energies on winning the *American Golfer* Trophy with his college buddies.

Still, the decision did not sit right with some traditionalists who viewed the low-scorer medal as second only to the prizes the USGA presented to finalists and semifinalists at major championships. Critics of Herron's decision included one of his most fervent local supporters, Pittsburgh's leading golf journalist, E. E. Giles of the *Pittsburgh Gazette Times*.

Giles—in his mid-50s and still one of Pittsburgh's better golfers—had closely followed Dave Herron's game since childhood. He was awed by Herron's combination of power, touch on the greens, and serene temperament as well as his unaffected humility and intellect. Given his admiration for Herron, Giles was disappointed by his decision to turn down a chance to make golf history—an achievement that, in fact, might never be duplicated. "As a matter of record, would it not have been much better to have gone forward with the play to determine the actual low score man? The fact that a medal is awarded at all signifies its important relation to the qualifying test." Further, Giles argued, the honor simply was not "transferable" and would be "empty" of meaning if Herron merely ceded it to Tewksbury, without a formal competition.[16]

But Herron disagreed, stuck to his decision, and personally congratulated Tewksbury at the clubhouse celebrations on Saturday evening. On Sunday, he and his Princeton buddies played a noticeably relaxed, low-stakes round of best-ball golf. "Herron did not seem to exert himself to the limit, but seemed more in the spirit of pleasant competition."[17] He and Grant Peacock won by four strokes against Haight and Dean, who could do no better than a 6-over-par 79.[18]

At long last, the nine days of the 1919 Amateur were over. Herron had spent every single one of the first twenty-four days of August—his "vacation" from the A. M. Byers ironworks—playing golf at Oakmont. He might reasonably have chosen at this point to rest a week before returning to work at the beginning of September, as per the agreement between him and his boss. But it turned out that Herron, or perhaps his father, had made other plans several weeks earlier that required the entire family to travel the very next day to Sharon, Pennsylvania, seventy miles to the northwest. That personal commitment was apparently too important to break, even for the new national champion.

The Herron men had agreed to compete in a small-scale regional golf tournament at Sharon Country Club, a course that local steel magnate Franklin Buhl had built a few years earlier. Buhl had died in 1918, and playing in this event was probably viewed by the Herrons as a way to honor Buhl's memory. (J. F. Byers, who ran the ironworks where Dave Herron worked, also played in the Sharon tournament, as did other notable Pittsburgh golfers including E. E. Giles, George Ormiston, Dwight Armstrong, and R. L. James.)

On Tuesday morning, in cold, windy conditions, Dave Herron, his father, and his eldest brother arrived for the best-ball competition that launched the tournament.[19] Dave and his father shot the low gross score of 71 (par was 69), even though neither had played the course before. Dave played exceptionally well but was initially confounded by the slow greens. Indeed, the Sharon course was so fundamentally different from Oakmont—short in length, slow greens, few bunkers—that many of his friends felt he was taking an unwise chance with his newfound celebrity by competing on a mediocre venue that simply did not suit his game, where he could easily lose to a lesser golfer.[20]

Herron, however, was unconcerned. After all, over the years, he had played often and successfully at nearby Stanton Heights Golf Club, which was considerably shorter, hillier, and had much smaller and slower greens than Oakmont. Furthermore, he had practiced regularly on the very short public track with tiny greens in Pittsburgh's Schenley Park, which was just a long walk from his Shady Side home. Nonetheless, his friends were probably right to raise the issue with him: anything less than a truly decisive win would sully his national reputation as "king of the amateur golfers."[21]

As he quickly learned upon arrival in Sharon, his fame as U.S. Amateur champion had already spread throughout Western Pennsylvania and beyond. The members of Sharon Country Club surprised him with an elaborate banquet and a gift of diamond-studded cuff links to honor his victory at Oakmont (their generosity probably complicated Oakmont's own celebration plans, which did not take place until nearly three weeks later).²² Dozens of enthusiastic golfers within several hours' drive of Sharon submitted last-minute entries to the tournament so they could get a close-up glimpse of the new champion, or at least tell friends they had competed at the same venue. Tournament organizers suddenly found themselves hosting nearly 150 participants—the largest tournament held anywhere in Western Pennsylvania for the past several years (larger even than the Amateur at Oakmont). Organizers fretted that some players would not have time the next day to complete their qualifying rounds before darkness.²³ Organizers assembled dozens of cars to shine lights on the final greens just in case, but, ultimately, the preparation was unnecessary.

Dave Herron decimated the competition, setting a new thirty-six-hole scoring record of 140 and winning the low-scorer medal by nine shots (despite penalties for two stray tee shots). His putting remained a frustration on the slow greens, but he was starting to adapt, and his scoring was good because his niblick was sharp. True to recent form, his tee shots were long and straight, "many of his wallops off the tee startling the on-lookers."²⁴ Not surprisingly, finishing immediately behind Herron in the standings were several Pittsburghers, including Ormiston, James, Giles, and Andrew Herron Jr., with scores in the 150s (Herron's father shot 172). Unless he tired, he seemed likely to romp to victory.

Which he did: playing around par figures in the Round of 16 (all eighteen-hole matches), Dave won, 5 and 4, against the previous year's winner (another Pittsburgher), H. H. Pearce of Sewickley Country Club. In the afternoon quarterfinals, he demolished one of the best local golfers, S. H. Hadley, which set up a semifinal match against the one player still in the field who just might, on his best day, beat Dave: R. L. James, the reigning Pennsylvania State Amateur champion, who was having the best season of his career.²⁵ Both men played well, but Herron again won decisively. And then, in the final match, he rolled over Dr. R. H. Darragh of nearby Beaver, Pennsylvania, 6 and 4, with another 1-over-par performance of 70.

Obviously, the competition at Sharon Country Club was far below the level of the U.S. Amateur. Equally apparent, the combined public and private courses in Sharon bore almost no similarity to Oakmont. That said, all aspects of Herron's tee-to-green game remained at the same high level he had demonstrated the previous week—his mashie and niblick play especially but also his bomber reputation. In the championship match, for instance, Herron was flagstick high with his tee shot on the slightly uphill, 286-yard, par 4 thirteenth hole. His putting stroke remained pure, several commentators noted, and several of his

Dave Herron with Sharon Country Club president John Murchie, "the grandaddy of Western Pennsylvania golf." "Two Champions," *Pittsburgh Gazette Times*, 31 August 1919.

rounds would have dropped deep into the 60s had he adjusted quicker to the slow greens. Whether at Oakmont or Sharon, Herron "played every shot as if the match . . . depended upon it," proving himself "the type of champion who does not believe in fooling in any kind of a golf match," Giles wrote in the *Pittsburgh Gazette Times*. "Dave Herron can play any course, and this is the answer to the question: Is he a class player?"

For all his humility, Dave Herron must have been extraordinarily proud of these two consecutive weeks of stellar golf, played in front of his family. It was the pinnacle of his golfing career, and all centered in his beloved Western Pennsylvania. He had finally erased the gnawing memory of not winning at Oakmont in the 1916 Intercollegiate. Indeed—though no one called attention to it at the time—he had now won the last three events he competed in, including the Allegheny Invitation in Sewickley in 1918, shortly before he entered military service. Allegheny Country Club, the oldest golf course in the Pittsburgh region (1895), was yet another venue that was radically different from Oakmont. So much for claims that he could only win on his home course.

Herron and his family returned to Pittsburgh on Friday evening, August 29, where he made it widely known that he was done with tournament golf until the 1920 season. Much to the dismay of Pennsylvania golf fans, he chose not to compete in the upcoming State Championship in Philadelphia (mid-September) or the more prestigious Lesley Cup matches in Long Island and Boston (early October). Perhaps to reinforce the point, neither Dave nor any of the Herrons played in their customary intraclub matches at Oakmont over the weekend.

Dave Herron was certainly planning to defend his U.S. Amateur title in 1920, but he had already proven that he could put down his clubs for long stretches without ruining his game. That model of intermittent play, after all, was the amateur ideal that the USGA espoused, and the basis of his mentor W. C. Fownes Jr.'s dual careers as champion golfer and business tycoon. If Herron, with two weeks of intense practice, could spend virtually all of the past year in the combined vocations of naval aviator and manual laborer and still win the U.S. Amateur, why couldn't he do something like that again in 1920, after his apprenticeship was over and he transitioned to the more flexible work schedule of an iron salesman?

For the moment, then, it was Mission Accomplished: time for all the Herrons to take a short break from golf and for Dave—now more than a year after his Princeton graduation—to resume serious preparation for his adult career. Not for a moment did he think of living off his father's or grandfather's wealth to find out just how great a golfer he might become. He aspired to be a championship contender for many years, at both the state and national levels, but one grounded in his own vocational identity. He would not be a "professional amateur" whose social and business life centered mainly on golf.

Thus, after spending five glorious days in Sharon, including a tournament victory and a banquet in Dave's honor, one can only imagine the Herron family's dismay when they opened their Pittsburgh Sunday newspaper on August 31 to learn how controversial Dave's ascension to the Amateur crown had become. Spearheaded by New York's and Atlanta's press corps, the denigration of Dave Herron's victory over Bob Jones had spread countrywide, and the century-long smearing of his brilliant victory in the 1919 U.S. Amateur had begun.

▶ CHAPTER 17
DAVE HERRON VERSUS THE PRESS

"Golf matches have been won before with drivers, brassies, mashies, niblicks and putters, but this is the first time one was officially and finally decided with a megaphone." Grantland Rice first published his damning summary of the 1919 U.S. Amateur on August 25 in the *New York Tribune*.[1] Rice's claim that Herron was merely a megaphone champion spread quickly across the nation. Reprinted again and again, his clever put-down kicked off several weeks of debate in the press over the validity of Herron's victory. Did he win fairly and squarely? Was he really a good enough golfer to wear the mantle of national champion?

Atlanta's journalists were predictably outraged that a USGA marshal had interfered with the final match and that the galleries had dared to applaud their Boy Wonder's bad shots. "It is typical of the Pittsburg gallery that the newspapers of that city either failed to mention the incident or passed it over lightly and as inconsequential," complained the *Atlanta Constitution*'s sports editor.[2] The *Constitution*, *Atlanta Georgian*, and *Atlanta Journal* all demanded an apology on behalf of the city of Atlanta, but the closest they got was W. G. Costin's public admission of guilt, though even that seemed to fall short. "The first word from any Pittsburg source relative to the unsportsmanlike treatment afforded Bobby Jones while playing for American golf honors several weeks ago, at last has reached the city," the *Atlanta Constitution* reported angrily on September 8.

> It is a direct statement from W. C. [G.] Costin, millionaire and golf enthusiast who was chief marshal of the gallery guards during the Jones-Herron match. "I'd give one million dollars to recall that shout," wails the millionaire, but in his lengthy article [he] describes in detail his personal feelings over the affair but he does not attempt to defend the conduct of the gallery which yelled and yelled every time Jones would make a play.[3]

When no further apology from either Oakmont or the USGA was forthcoming, the Atlanta press moved on. Bob Jones had other events to play, and there was not much use rehashing his runner-up performance at the Amateur. In fact, Walter Wilkes claimed that he had only revisited the megaphone incident in the August 27 issue of the *Atlanta Georgian* because "Grantland Rice, Innis Brown, and William Everett Hicks ... [had] come out with their opinions so boldly." Consequently, he decided "to join my feeble voice in the chorus which is going up from the South against the disgraceful conduct of which the Pittsburg people in general were guilty."[4]

Grantland Rice, Innis Brown, and William Everett Hicks were all New York journalists, writing for the *New York Tribune, New York Sun*, and *Brooklyn Daily Eagle*, respectively, but Rice and Brown had deep connections to the South and, interestingly, to each other. They had both attended and played for Vanderbilt University in Nashville in several different sports, although they did not play together.[5] Brown also served as editor of Vanderbilt's campus newspaper, *The Hustler*, and in 1906 he started writing for the *Nashville American*, a newspaper that Rice also briefly worked for. A few years after that, Brown moved to Atlanta and became the successful manager of an automobile parts and accessories store. In his spare time, he contributed to the *Atlanta Constitution*'s sports page. He also did some work as a talent scout and football referee. In late 1913, the *Atlanta Journal* hired Brown to take the place of its outgoing sports editor—Grantland Rice. A few years later, Brown followed Rice to New York and joined the *New York Sun*'s staff.

Clearly then, Grantland Rice's Southern connections ran just as deep as Brown's. Born in Murfreesboro, Tennessee, Rice attended Vanderbilt, wrote the sports page for the *Nashville Daily News*, and eventually landed a job with the *Atlanta Journal*. It was while living in Atlanta that Rice reconnected with his old friend Bob Jones Sr. and met his three-year-old son. Rice and Jones first became acquainted while playing for their respective college's baseball teams (Vanderbilt and Mercer), and Rice made sure to look up Big Bob as soon as he got into town.[6] Rice was also close with the Adairs, and when Perry Adair and Bob Jones went north during the war to play in the Red Cross exhibitions, they stayed with Rice (who had since begun writing for the *New York Tribune*) and his wife in their spacious Upper West Side apartment.[7]

It was during this visit that Young Bob and Rice became especially close. Bob's performance at Merion in 1916 had duly impressed the sportswriter, and Rice believed that once Bob got his temper under control, journalists would have to toss the old record books. Rice's fondness and high expectations for Bob Jones explain his detailed coverage of Jones's play throughout the 1919 Amateur, including his match against Bob Gardner, which was predictably overshadowed by the iconic Ouimet and Evans battle that started an hour afterward. In fact, Rice devoted several lines of his column to Jones's play and committed several noticeable errors in his summary of the Ouimet-Evans match—suggesting, perhaps, that he walked mainly with Jones and Big Bob and delegated coverage of the Ouimet-Evans match to a runner. It is no wonder then that Rice so harshly criticized Dave Herron's victory in the immediate aftermath of the megaphone incident. He had wanted Jones to win, not only because it would have sold newspapers and increased American interest in golf, but because he adored the boy and his family as if they were kin.

Unfortunately for Dave Herron, Grantland Rice's opinion carried enormous weight. In 1920, the *Pittsburgh Post* described Rice as the "greatest sport writer and most famous golf critic in America whose articles on golf are recognized as the most authoritative that appear in the American press."[8] Rice's "Sportlight" column was the most widely syndicated sports column in the country. When Rice declared that Herron had won only because of the megaphone, he damaged Herron's reputation in a way that Rice could never fully take back.

And he did try to take it back. On August 31, less than a week after his first remarks on the megaphone incident were published, Rice clarified that Dave Herron really was a remarkable golfer: "Any man who can play thirteen holes in a final round in 2 better than 4s and 3 better than par over the hardest test ever offered in any title affray will bear considerable inspection when the next test comes along."[9] In a September column, he acknowledged Herron's exceptional length off the tee and admitted that the champion "earned at least a portion of his triumph by his ability to get fine distance over a water-soaked course and by the tremendous power he displayed in ripping his way out of bunkers."[10]

And on September 12, Rice declared that Herron's competitive bona fides were authentic, "beyond the faint glimmer of a doubt." He explained:

> Herron's exhibition of nerve control in his final match was a masterpiece of cool and unruffled serenity—of quiet and determined confidence. His ability to finish a week of fine golf with the finest round played by anyone in the field on the edge of championship honors lifts him high in the list.... And he is the only amateur champion we have ever known who would also have landed the title if the result had been determined by medal play in place of match. This should about wind up the argument in his case.[11]

The case, however, was far from settled, especially in the Big Apple. New York's golfing elite had been humiliated at Oakmont: none of their star players reached the quarterfinals, and few even qualified for match play. So the New York press corps was on the hunt for an alibi. If they could convince the wider public that the USGA had flubbed the U.S. Amateur and crowned an underserving champion, their hometown players would be off the hook for their poor performances. Perhaps this is why a New York daily paper described the final championship round as "a battle of youth versus youth, with quite an absence of skill thrown in to complicate the problem of the ultimate winner"—a statement that ran contrary to all available evidence and belittled the performances of both Herron and Jones.[12]

Most writers conceded that Dave Herron and Bob Jones were brilliant golfers. After all, Jones was a well-known prodigy, and it was hard to deny that "Herron got away with about everything in sight" at Oakmont, that is, posted the lowest qualifying score, won the *American Golfer* Trophy, and won all of his matches, most by substantial margins.[13] Some writers decided to fixate on the fact that Herron did not face either Francis Ouimet or Chick Evans even though they were both in his bracket. "With one accord the pack is yelping 'Whom did he ever lick?'—and truth to tell Herron did have rather an easy march toward the title," the *Brooklyn Daily Eagle* claimed. "His last match was his hardest but it must be admitted that he was there with the goods in the pinch."[14]

It was hardly Herron's fault, though, that the USGA was still using a random draw instead of a ranking system. Lopsided brackets were a matter of course, and many prior champions had benefited from a lucky draw without being accused of being a fluke. "It would undoubtedly be a complete test for any man in winning the title to meet and defeat in turn Evans, Ouimet, Gardner, Jones, Travers, Marston, Fownes, etc.," E. E. Giles argued, "but nobody has ever been called upon to perform such a task, and nobody ever will under our present method of play."[15] Furthermore, even if Herron's bracket was easier than Jones's, Herron still trounced his opponents, including Jones. Herron did "something more than win," Grantland Rice wrote. "He played the best golf from Monday to Saturday—turned in more par holes—upset the old theory that no man can win on his home course—cracked the old tradition that no low qualifier can ever come through at match play—and otherwise took almost complete possession of the entire works."[16] Herron's domination of all phases of the national championship from start to finish refuted the idea that the "luck of draw" was responsible for his victory.

Occasional references to Herron's magic putter still appeared throughout September, but admitting that Herron played better than the rest of the field on the greens as well as off the tee did not make him seem like an accidental champion. Soon, New York sportswriters were arguing instead that he played so well, especially on the greens, only because he knew the course better than anyone else. Playing a championship on one's home course had never been considered an advantage before, but for Herron at Oakmont it suddenly was. "For some reason golfers are not inclined to lay much stress on this home course stuff," Innis Brown complained. "They point out that few golfers ever come through a big tournament on their home courses. It being especially notable that professional players rarely win on their home courses. Wherefore the prophecy that Herron would prove a formidable entry at Oakmont wasn't taken over seriously by the visitors."[17]

The *New York Times* argued that home-course advantage mattered specifically at Oakmont because of the course's harsh sanction for the slightest misplay on each and every hole. "Oakmont is regarded as one of the toughest propositions of eighteen holes in the United States. This favored Herron and acted as a handicap for every other competitor."[18] Even Ralph Davis of the *Pittsburgh Press* conceded that "the instances of a golfer winning an important title at his own club are rare, yet every reason in the world exists why he should have a distinct advantage over the remainder of the field provided all other things are equal."[19] So now the question for the sporting press became: could Dave Herron win on an unfamiliar course?

Every event Herron played for the rest of 1919 would be portrayed as a test of whether he deserved to win the U.S. Amateur. His supporters wanted to see him prove his critics wrong. "A host of admirers of Herron, among whom are many who never have seen the modest young athlete, would like to see Herron go across the state [to Philadelphia] and annex the [Pennsylvania State Amateur] title," E. E. Giles opined. "A success of this sort following the more important Oakmont win would prove the final word for the season."[20] But Herron chose not to play in the Pennsylvania State Amateur. In fact, he seemed wholly uninterested in trying to prove himself to a state or national audience. He had decisively won what he came to win. It was time to go back to his regular life and his job.

But pressure from the press, mentors in Pittsburgh, and perhaps even the USGA continued to mount. "Viewed from any angle Herron ought to get out and get busy," the *Brooklyn Daily Eagle* remarked.[21] Many fans in Pittsburgh felt the same way. Exactly who convinced Herron to take off from work again in early October to participate in the 1919 Lesley Cup matches, we cannot say. Undeniably, the USGA, the Fowneses, and Herron's friends and family all had a vested interest in seeing him compete. The USGA needed to convince the golfing public that the first Amateur championship after the wartime hiatus had not produced a false champion. And Oakmont wanted to be known as a tough, but ultimately fair, test of all-around golfing prowess. For whatever reason, whether it was personal pride, as a favor to W. C. Fownes Jr. (his mentor) and J. F. Byers (his boss), or a result of pressure from the USGA, Herron changed his mind and agreed to represent Pennsylvania in the Lesley Cup matches at the National Golf Links on Long Island. Metropolitan-area writers would finally get to see Herron in action, up close, on an unfamiliar course. "There is still a rather pronounced disposition to have Davy's performance verified before giving him the full mead of a champion," the *New York Sun* commented, "and the approaching matches will offer the first opportunity for such."[22] But certainly not the last opportunity either, for Herron now seemed determined to show the hypercritical New York press just how confident he was in his game.

In addition to the Lesley Cup, which started October 3, he agreed to play a best-ball charity exhibition at Scarsdale Golf and Country Club on October 5 with his long-time friend and Oakmont buddy, Grant Peacock. Interestingly, their opponents at Scarsdale would be the same two professionals that Bob Jones and Chick Evans had competed against a year earlier as part of the Red Cross exhibitions: Jack Dowling (of the home club) and Tom McNamara. Finally, Herron accepted an invitation to compete in a multiday tournament, starting on October 9, against a few big-name Eastern amateurs at the Piping Rock Invitation Championship at Locust Valley, Long Island. C. B. McDonald had designed the course along Northern Nassau County's "Gold Coast," and while its style was very different from Oakmont's, it was considered among the sternest tests in Eastern golf.

Theoretically, Herron had the month of September to prepare for his two-week stint in New York, but he also had to work and could not practice nearly as much as he had in August. Weekend competition at Oakmont, supplemented by early evening chipping and putting at Schenley Park, was probably the best he could manage. He would have to play off any rust in competition and find his A game on the road.

The first test was the two-day Lesley Cup, at (arguably) America's second-toughest golf course, the National Golf Links of America at Southampton, Long Island. The best amateur golfers from Massachusetts, metropolitan New York, and Pennsylvania faced off in singles and foursomes matches to capture the trophy. Since Massachusetts had won the 1916 match (the last played prior to the war), New York and Pennsylvania would be playing for the right to face the Bay Staters. Dave Herron would play one foursomes match in the morning and one singles match in the afternoon both days, or a total of four matches. On the first day, he and his playing partner, E. M. Byers, had a quick and easy match against Frank Dyer and Willie Reekie, winning, 5 and 4. The Pennsylvania team almost swept the foursomes matches entirely, losing just one out of the five played. The afternoon singles matches were much harder.

The New York team played their best player against Herron, the three-time Metropolitan Open champion Oswald Kirkby. "By a queer kink of fate," Kirkby had not qualified for match play at Oakmont, but he knew the National Links "like a book," and dopesters expected an even contest between the two wallopers.[23] What no one expected was Kirkby to dominate the match from start to finish.[24] According to the *New York Times*, Kirkby made noticeable mistakes on just two holes—on the seventh, he half-topped his second shot and slashed his third into a trap, and on the eleventh, he had to scramble for a bogey. Otherwise, he played at even par or better.[25]

It was obvious to all onlookers that Herron was out of practice. "Herron was plainly off on his iron play, a disastrous fault at the National, and never had a chance to fight back hard," *Golf Illustrated*'s Jean Portland commented.[26] The *New York Times* writer noted, "Herron was playing far below the form that enabled him to romp through to a winning finish in the national championship quest. Herron's game today was something else again from that which bowled over Bobby Jones at Oakmont."[27] And Innis Brown reported, "He certainly played a game far different from what he developed in wading through the national championship tournament on his home course some six weeks ago."[28]

But every writer also acknowledged that even the Dave Herron who won the U.S. Amateur would have struggled to beat the Oswald Kirkby who showed up for the Lesley Cup. "Herron at his best would have had a man-sized job at stopping Kirkby today," the *Times* wrote.[29] Innis Brown mused, "Losing to Kirkby to-day was a poor idea of something to sit nights and brood over. Herron might well have made the final outcome closer. But there is only a small handful of talent so to speak who could have taken Kirkby's measure, going as he did throughout the round."[30] Still, Brown remained unimpressed by Herron's golf and continued to insist that his knowledge of Oakmont was crucial to his Amateur victory. "Either the champion has dropped off somewhat in his playing or else that home course business meant a considerable advantage for Herron."[31]

Despite Herron's loss, Pennsylvania still came out on top with nine points to New York's six, and the Pennsylvania team advanced to play Massachusetts on day two of the Lesley Cup. This time Herron and Byers came up against a pair they couldn't beat: Arthur "Buck" Whittemore and "Bunny" Estabrook, who won the match, 5 and 4. Jean Portland posited that Byers may have lacked the power to match well with Herron in foursomes, but that claim was problematic since they had paired successfully numerous times at Oakmont and had obliterated their opponents the day before by the same score of 5 and 4.³²

Whatever the reason for the loss, Herron took his revenge in the afternoon, beating Whittemore, 3 and 1. Still, he did not win his singles match with awe-inspiring golf. Rather, Whittemore kept missing makeable putts. Herron answered Whittemore's uneven short game with his own steady putting. "Herron became two up at the twelfth, was one up going to the fifteenth which he halved by a grand curling putt of a dozen feet, and then brought the match to a finish with wins on the next two due mainly to a bit of putting weakness on the Boston man's part."³³ In other words, Whittemore was erratic whereas Herron played consistently enough to secure the win. After a month without practice Herron was still struggling to find his championship game from tee to green, but at the end of the day, he was 2–2 and Pennsylvania was the new Lesley Cup titleholder, beating Massachusetts ten points to seven. Herron had done his share.

Nevertheless, the Eastern press came down hard on him. The *Philadelphia Public Ledger* published a scathing opinion piece by "Sandy McNiblick":

> The champion shied from the Keystone state championship, his own state battle, when he had a chance to prove his worth and settle the argument on a different course than his own and a good test. Other Pittsburghers came to battle with the class.
>
> Herron did not.
>
> After the hurling of the den he could not well cease to listen and came on for the Lesley Cup with a team of stars to back him up. He met the veteran Oswald Kirby [sic], metropolitan champion, who has been playing golf for years, and many say his best golf has been buried in the cards of other years.
>
> Did the champion of the new era rise to the heights and swamp this veteran?
>
> He did not.
>
> Herron was beaten 5 and 4 over eighteen holes.³⁴

McNiblick incorrectly reported that Dave Herron "was twice beaten in foursomes in the same tourney—three defeats in two days." In fact, he had won one foursomes and one singles match, for a respectable 2–2 record. Still, McNiblick challenged, "Does Chick Evans think he can beat Herron? Or Francis Ouimet? Or Bobby Jones at the next tournament? Ask them. . . . In some circles they whisper of him as the cheese champion."³⁵

There was obvious venom in McNiblick's piece that Herron did not deserve. In many ways, the Philadelphia press had the same axe to grind as their fellow Eastern writers. The City of Brotherly Love (showing little) had rejoiced when Philadelphia native Woody Platt defeated Francis Ouimet in the quarter-finals of the U.S. Amateur, but then Herron trimmed Platt, 7 and 6, in the very next round. It seemed that, just by playing well, he had run afoul of two cities' wounded pride.

With the Lesley Cup concluded on Saturday, Herron turned to the exhibition match he was playing at two o'clock against pros Jack Dowling and Tom McNamara at Scarsdale Golf and Country Club, nearly a hundred miles away. His tight schedule left no time for practice. On the one hand, Scarsdale was a much easier course than the National Golf Links, so maybe he did not need his A game to score well. On the other hand, he would lose his biggest advantage over his competitors. "Scarsdale is rather short and compact," Innis Brown told his readers. "No such walloping proclivities are needed to negotiate the Scarsdale course in low figures.... It will be interesting indeed to watch Herron perform."[36]

Remarkably, about a thousand people turned out in Westchester to see the new Amateur champion for themselves, and they got a show. Dave and his fellow Princetonian Grant Peacock kept pace with Dowling and McNamara throughout the match and even took the lead at one point with a birdie on the thirteenth hole. After exchanging a few more holes, Dowling and McNamara finally won on the eighteenth, 1 up, when Dowling sank a lengthy putt for a birdie 3 (variously estimated by newspapers in New York and Pittsburgh at ten, fifteen, twenty, and thirty feet!).[37]

Dave Herron had lost again, against two of America's top professional golfers, but he impressed almost everyone with his tremendous drives. The *New York Times* described the match as a "gala day." "After the final putt had been tapped down, there was little wondering why Bobby Jones went down in defeat at Oakmont in August for the national title," the unnamed reporter gushed. "Herron, a heavy-set man with broad shoulders and a powerful build, smacked out the longest ball of the four on nearly every hole, and many of his second shots with the brassie were almost as far-carrying."[38] The *New York Evening World* was equally generous in its praise: "Herron played his usual steady game, hitting one long drive after another and running down his putts with little difficulty."[39] Several newspapers highlighted as particularly impressive the sixteenth hole, which measured 232 yards and where Herron, using only a spoon (3-wood), over-hit the green by some fifty yards (resulting in a bogey 4). The writer for the *New York Times* also thought Herron's approaches to the green were "brilliant, but, if anything, his putting was weak at times."[40] The excuse that Herron had beaten Bob Jones because he had a magic putter did not hold up. His game was obviously solid from tee to green.

Only Herron's harshest critic, the *New York Sun*'s Innis Brown, disagreed. In an article titled "Herron's Showing Is Not Impressive," Brown claimed that Herron's appearances at the Lesley Cup and Scarsdale had done nothing "to provoke any wild enthusiasm." "He wasn't putting with the deadly accuracy that he displayed, especially in his match with Bobby Jones. . . . His placement of long iron shots was only fair and his short game wasn't of championship calibre." Brown further complained that

> Scarsdale isn't a tough test of golf by any means. As a matter of fact, it ought to prove a very easy course indeed for the new champion. With his long walloping he can get home on every two shot hole of the course with a driver and mashie, save in possibly two or three cases. Given a day on which he is putting well, he should have no trouble in keeping in even fours without much difficulty.[41]

In reality, Brown mischaracterized Herron's card at Scarsdale. There were small discrepancies in scoring between newspapers. For example, the *New York Times* claimed Herron posted a 71, while everyone else including Brown's paper the *Sun* reported his score as 72. Nevertheless, by all accounts, Herron matched Jack Dowling's low medal score, either with an even-par 71 or a 1-over-par 72. In other words, Herron did "keep in even fours" without much difficulty, just as Brown said he should, and he played Scarsdale as well as the home pro did even though he had never played there before.

Furthermore, Herron was the only player to break par on the back nine, where he made four consecutive birdies. It is hard to know what more he could have done at Scarsdale to raise Brown's estimation of his game. The only concession Brown made in his column was that "it seems fairer to assume, however, that [Herron] was a bit out of kilter in these matches, rather than to jump at conclusions to say that his showing here tends to prove his victory at Oakmont a fluke."[42] Brown would not write off Herron's U.S. Amateur performance as just luck, but he still did not believe Herron was the best amateur in the country. Fortunately for Herron, he had one more chance to impress Innis Brown and any other New York skeptics.

The Piping Rock Invitation was a noteworthy event in the eyes of the *New York Times* that featured 119 entrants including "the best congregation of Metropolitan golfers it [was] possible to assemble."[43] Herron had three days to prepare before the medal-qualifying round on Thursday, October 9, and he secured the help of a veteran caddie named Jimmy West.[44] It turned out that two events and three days of practice (one of which he may have spent at nearby Engineers Country Club in anticipation of the 1920 U.S. Amateur) were enough to return him to peak fighting form.

On the opening hole of the qualifying round, Herron "laid his mashie shot dead to the pin and ran down a single putt" for a birdie 3.[45] It was a great start that became a great round. He played the first nine holes in even par and had only one bad hole.[46] On the long and difficult par 5 eighteenth, he reached the green in two shots but needed three putts and could only secure his par. Still, William Abbott of the *New York Evening World* described those first two shots on the last hole as "monster wood shots."[47]

Everyone was again awed by Herron's power. His "phenomenally long drives" were working to perfection. "Next to his whippy wooden driver, Herron likes best a mashie-niblick, and on such holes as the long 400-yard first and the 300-yard thirteenth his drives actually brought him into pitching distance of the greens," the *New York Times* reported.[48] William Abbott was more colorful: "They may tell you anyone can play this game of golf, but nobody can clout a ball as far as Herron unless his arms and shoulder pack the driving strength of a blacksmith."[49] The most remarkable thing about Herron's drives were that they looked easy, almost effortless, as they sailed 300 yards down the fairway. "The national champ . . . just stepped out and hit 'em a mile," gushed Abbott.[50]

Herron's 74 for the round also dropped jaws. "Davie Herron didn't quite set a new Piping Rock record," the *Times* commented, "but what he did was sufficient to cause the old marks to shiver and shake under the strain." His 74 was good enough for medal honors by three shots. Plus, it was only one stroke off Piping Rock's official best medal-play score: 73, held by Archie Reid.[51] All in all, Herron had played a fantastic round of golf, "a display of form," Abbott believed, "that ought to come near silencing the doubting Thomas-es."[52] Even Innis Brown had to admit Herron's performance was champion-caliber. He wrote, "This three score ten and four stood out as boldly as the three gilt balls before the shop of a pawnbroker."[53] In other words, even to an unrepentant critic like Brown, Herron's opening round at Piping Rock was eye-catching.

All eyes were certainly on Herron the next morning as he faced off against Archie Reid, the course record holder. Like Herron, Reid was a World War I veteran, but unlike Herron, he had seen actual service—three years of it—and was therefore even more out of practice than Herron was. As a result, "the robust Pittsburg golfer, did a steam roller act on the opposition thrust into his pathway," Innis Brown wrote.[54] Herron shot a solid 78, while Reid managed just "enough of his old skill" to extend the match to the seventeenth hole. "The boss walloper of the amateurs was quite on his game from tee to green," Brown marveled, "and once on the putting surface wielded his club with considerable effect, not to say brilliance and éclat."[55]

In the afternoon, Herron played against his friend Grant Peacock. Together, they made a formidable pair in match play, but, on his own, Peacock could not keep up with Herron's distance. "With the best he had in stock Peacock could rarely hope to keep within less than twenty or thirty yards of his opponent," Brown reported, "and it was a battle for him to splice up his efforts so as to reach the green on even terms, even when he found no traps, bunkers or other hindrances."[56] Herron won the first, third, fourth, seventh, and ninth holes, while only losing the fifth, where the writer for the *New York Times* posited that "Herron's arm muscles and huge wrists brought him into trouble."[57] He easily beat his friend, 5 and 4.

Once again, it was Herron's raw power that both won him the match and earned applause from the press corps. He was a "good approach shot maker and a good man with a putter in his hands, but others equal him," the *Times* reporter explained. "When it comes to swinging a driver, however, if S. Davidson Herron hasn't cracked his ball a good thirty or forty yards down the course further than his opponent, then something is going wrong."[58] Indeed, the *Times* reporter was deeply impressed by Herron's tee shots. After the final round, he wrote, "It is no wonder that a rumbling of 'ahs' and 'ohs' from the gallery followed each of Herron's drives. If a golf ball ever were hit further than he smashes his with a wooden driver, then a high-powered rifle must have been the propelling force."[59]

Like William Abbott, writing for the *New York Evening World*, the *Times* reporter believed Herron's performance at Piping Rock would silence critics. "Even if he had only one stick in his caddy bag, those who marveled at his driving would feel convinced of his just deserts [sic] in winning at Oakmont last August from Bobby Jones."[60] All the same, the *Times* writer could not resist taking a jab at Herron's weight. "Davie Herron is a heavy, chunky, good-natured, and happy champion, weighing some 218 pounds, and he needs plenty of exercise."[61] Alas, even journalists who accepted that Herron played like a champion still could not move past the fact that he did not look like one.

The columnist "Gibby," writing for the *Pittsburgh Post*, satirized this Eastern habit when he ironically referred to Dave Herron as "the 215-pound Oakmont midget."

> Ever since young Davy Herron, the 215-pound Oakmont midget, won the National tourney here in August, the East has been skeptical about the Pittsburgh product. They thought that something must have been wrong, or that it was all a mistake, even though it did extend clear over the playing of the tournament, or that it was a case of playing quite above himself and never could happen

again. For, they argued, "can anything good come out of Pittsburgh?" But Herron, apparently, has convinced the Eastern critics that they were wrong, demonstrating his class right in their own territory.... After making a rather indifferent showing in the Lesley matches, Herron ran off with the honors in the Piping Rock tourney, which ended Saturday, in rather easy style. That convinced them.[62]

Indeed, Herron "won the Piping Rock invitation tournament without the semblance of a hard struggle."[63] He demolished his semifinal opponent, G. C. Greenway, winning, 6 and 5. In fact, the match was so one-sided, that is all the press really had to say about it. In the afternoon, Greenwich's Sam J. Graham, a finalist (against Travers) at the 1907 U.S. Amateur and at the top of his game throughout the tournament, "made the issue just a bit closer," Innis Brown noted wryly, "losing in the final match 5 and 4."[64]

Herron stood 3 up at the turn against Graham. On nearly every hole, he pulled off a spectacular shot that elicited "gasps of surprise and admiration" from the "fair-sized" gallery.[65] On the second, for instance, he found himself in deep rough after his tee shot, but he made escaping look easy. Gibby quoted "one hard-to-convince expert" who wrote, "With his trusty 'scoop' the pride of Oakmont tore out something that resembled a young doormat, and as the wind swept the vegetation from the air the ball could be seen rainbowing gracefully within easy two-shot putting distance of the cup."[66]

But two other holes really stood out for The *Brooklyn Daily Eagle*'s William Everett Hicks: the ninth and twelfth.[67] On the ninth, Herron landed his ball behind a large groundskeeping shed that completely blocked his path to the green. He had no choice but to go over and hope his ball held the green, instead of rolling into the giant bunker at the back. Hicks reported that the gallery had little faith he could pull off the shot. "'He can't hold the green as the grass won't let him put cut on the ball,' said some in the gallery. But Herron's powerful stroke cut through the grass as if it didn't exist."[68] Gibby's anonymous expert dramatically recounted, "There was a rattle of gravel and turf on the top of the house, then a little white sphere dropped from on high, and there was Herron just as well off as his opponent."[69] His ball landed within eight feet of the flagstick, four feet closer than Graham's, and he halved the hole, all in spite of being stymied by a building.[70]

Herron pulled off a similar feat on the twelfth. He was once again in deep rough "that reached half way to the knee" with a "huge sand bunker" between him and the hole. A less-gifted player would have to pitch out to the fairway and then hit over the trap to the green. Herron, however, was an extraordi-

This cropped photograph shows the building at Piping Rock that Dave Herron miraculously hit his ball over. Times Wide World Photos, Cherry/Herron Family Archives.

nary player. "Taking up a quantity of grass as if his club was a scythe, [he] dug the ball out and deposited it on the green, only 6 feet from the cup, holing the putt for a bird 3."[71] The match ended two holes later on the fourteenth. Graham had won just two holes, and, according to Hicks, Herron had never been farther away from the green after his tee shot (i.e., had never "played the odd," in early twentieth-century golf lingo). On the greens, Herron and Graham showed equal skill. In fact, Herron needed twenty-five putts to Graham's twenty-four.[72] Graham had been thoroughly outclassed by Herron's driver and niblick, not by his putter.

The verdict of the New York press was that Dave Herron had more than proved his mettle; the high quality of his overall skills and the unmatched power behind his every shot showed that he had won the Amateur fair and square. One of the writers that Gibby quoted, who presumably hailed from the New York area, remarked that every "enthusiast who had run out to see him play against Graham after making a bet with his brother that Herron was sailing under false colors, went home ready to pay up and admit that his estimate of Davy was all wrong, all wrong."[73]

One particular unexpected observer at Piping Rock stood out in the gallery: Walter J. Travis, founder of the *American Golfer*, former British Amateur champion, and three-time U.S. Amateur champion. Travis watched Dave Herron with obvious delight, laughing each time he hit a miraculous shot out of thick, deep rough.[74] "What appeared to delight Davy's distinguished predecessor even more keenly was the deftness with which he wields that big niblick of his," Brown commented. "Rough means but little to the champion. . . . Whenever [Herron] dumped one of the high shots to the green from the rough, Travis chuckled audibly."[75]

After ten days of playing golf that ranged from competent to sparkling, Herron had finally convinced Eastern pundits that he was worth taking seriously. Unfortunately, this also meant that New York had to reckon with the fact that the East had been eclipsed by both South and West. "Unhappily, the presence of Herron hereabouts last week simply emphasizes and accentuates the knowledge that a New Yorker's chances for the 1920 amateur title are not what may be truthfully called rosy," the *New York Times* acknowledged. "Perhaps New York is going through the transitory stage, bidding adieu to its former champions, and waiting for the youngsters to get their full growth. . . .Yet the shadow cast by Davie Herron, with his driving, his approaching, and his putting, fails to brighten these same sombre prospects for next season."[76]

Herron could not stick around for any more competitions—he had to get back to work!—nor did he feel he needed to. So he turned down Graham's invitation to compete the following weekend at Graham's home course, Greenwich Country Club, and returned to Pittsburgh instead, confident he had demonstrated his championship credentials, and confident too that East Coast golf pundits would no longer dare deride him as a "cheese champion."[77]

Whether Dave Herron was truly the best American golfer was immaterial because Bob Jones was not America's best golfer either—yet. They were both young, with great games and phenomenal long drives, and they seemed destined to run into each other again. As the game of golf surged in popularity immediately after the war, the stage seemed set for an era-defining 1920s rivalry between America's two most promising youth stars: Dave Herron versus Bob Jones.

▶ EPILOGUE
HERRON AND JONES
"TEN-TENTHS" THE HEROES OF PITTSBURGH AND ATLANTA[1]

Place played a critical role in the development of both Bob Jones and Dave Herron, as golfers, as competitors, and as men. Donald Ross's 1913 redesign of Thomas Bendelow's original East Lake course did not have the same tight fairways, treacherous hazards, and ultrafast and confounding greens as Oakmont, but East Lake did attract a high-quality caliber of Southern players. Jones's early exposure to champion amateur and professional golfers, as well as his regular competition against other child prodigies like Perry Adair and Alexa Stirling, sharpened his skills and pushed him to improve his game. Stewart Maiden, the professional at East Lake, helped him fine-tune the mechanics of his swing, including curbing a persistent hook that bedeviled him for much of the 1919 summer. Maiden, who walked every hole with his protégé at Oakmont, also tried to help Jones tamp down his temper. Jones did make it through the entire competition without throwing any clubs, but it would be a few years still before he truly gave up the practice. Without Maiden in his life, though, or the Adairs, or J. Douglas Edgar, or his own father—Big Bob—who carefully guided and publicized his son's golfing career from a young age, Jones probably would not have reached the heights of fame that he did. Regular access to a premier course like East Lake also helped, as did Jones's opportunities to play wartime exhibitions when most high-profile amateurs were forced to put away their clubs.

In a similar way, the cocoon of Oakmont produced Dave Herron. Oakmont was a severe test of golf, but Herron from age seven onward got to spend much of his childhood playing on the course against some of the best golfers in the United States. Just like Jones, Herron's proximity to champions such as W. C. Fownes Jr. and Eben Byers, and his friendly rivalries with Emil Loeffler Jr. and his fellow caddies, shaped him into a champion. He did not have the same branding opportunities (or a publicity-seeking dad) as Bob Jones, so as a youth Dave Herron was nowhere near as famous outside of Pittsburgh as Jones was outside of Atlanta. Thus, Herron's success at the national level was a surprise to many.

However, by the end of 1919 most pundits had accepted that Dave Herron was a worthy U.S. Amateur champion. The *New York Times* put him at the top of its end-of-year list of the nation's best golfers. The sports editor reasoned that even though Herron might not be a repeat champion in 1920—a healthy Ouimet or Evans might be able to outplay him at his best—he would "go down in history as one of the longest drivers of all time and one of the greatest handlers of a mashie niblick," so he deserved the top spot. In second place was Bob Jones, who played "sensational golf and nothing else," even without the "benefit of long years of experience and training in important matches."[2]

Herron and Jones would have made exciting rivals. In some ways, they were perfect foils—one large and one small; one from the North, the other from the South; one shy and reserved, the other boisterous and intemperate; one whose parents remained in the background and let their (third) son find his own way, the other whose parents pampered their once-sickly child well into adulthood and, for all their nurturance of his golf, never gave a thought to having him caddie.

Still, in other ways, Dave Herron and Bob Jones grew up quite similarly. They were both wealthy, well-bred, and conservative white Christians; each inherited a secure place in his city's social and economic elite. They were both studious at school and of cosmopolitan intellectual bent. Neither was especially religious (to the chagrin of Jones's evangelical grandfather), but both were enthusiastically Calvinist in their dedication to hard work and strong family orientation.

And, of course, they shared most of all an exceptional athletic talent. Though their bodies and golf swings were radically different, each was somehow able to smash a golf ball 275-plus yards—farther than any of their peers. Yet, no matter how much Herron and Jones loved the game, both deferred to the gentlemanly amateur ideal. Neither was prepared to forsake a prestigious career to find out just how good he might become by full-time commitment to golf. E. E. Giles accurately predicted Herron's future when he wrote three days before year's end in 1919, "Herron's game from August to the season's close was of championship caliber, and is bound to remain there if he plays."[3]

"If he plays. . . ." Herron had proven at Oakmont, Piping Rock, Scarsdale, and the National Golf Links how quickly he could shake the rust off his clubs and revive his championship game. But following graduation from Princeton in 1918, short-term service in the U.S. Navy, and a tough, yearlong apprenticeship in an ironworks, he was anxious to move onto the next phases of adult life: establishing a distinguished career, earning an income consistent with his social class and educational attainments, and starting an independent life apart from

The growing Herron clan, including Dave and Louise and their two children, Nancy and Dave. Cherry/Herron Family Archives.

his parents, wherever that might take him.

The result was that Dave Herron did not play much golf in 1920. He still played club events on weekends at Oakmont. He even won the Pennsylvania State Amateur Championship played at Oakmont in 1920, setting a new low-scoring record for the course in the process. He could still reliably find his A game with very little practice—at least on his home course.

But he also had other priorities. He got engaged to Louise Johnston of Philadelphia, and they were married in January 1921. He soon became a full-time sales manager for Byers Ironworks and moved to Chicago, where he won the club championship at Exmoor Country Club in Highland Park in 1921 and 1922 (he would also represent the United States in the 1923 Walker Cup in Great Britain). Also in 1922, he and Louise welcomed their daughter Nancy to the world. Several more career-related moves followed, including one that took him and Louise back to her hometown of Philadelphia. There he would become a member at Merion and—sure enough, again showing that his A game never entirely left him—he won the Pennsylvania State Amateur a second time in 1929 on his new home course at Merion.

Meanwhile, of course, Bob Jones won a major championship every year after 1923, with his streak culminating in the first-ever Grand Slam in 1930. He was indisputably the most famous and perhaps the greatest golfer that had ever played.

The divergent golfing careers of Dave Herron and Bob Jones in the 1920s reflected not just growing differences in talent—Jones's putting improved dramatically from 1922 onward, whereas Herron's ability to revive his A game on short notice predictably declined—but also fundamental differences in personality that transcended their shared love of the game. Put at its simplest, and evident from a very early age, Jones's high-strung intensity and aspirations to golfing perfection were much higher priorities in his mind than they ever were in Herron's. Jones achieved not just personal satisfaction but also emotional ecstasy (and pain) through golf, which was a psychological response entirely alien to Herron's placid demeanor.

Dave Herron had the game to be one of golf's best just as the sport was surging to nationwide popularity in the 1920s. His superlative play at Oakmont should be remembered not as a "tainted victory" but as one of the greatest displays of power and skill in early twentieth-century American golf. But ultimately, he did not have the desire or temperament for fame. In truth, he always seemed uncomfortable in the spotlight. Nor did he seem to have Bob Jones's passion for endlessly raising the bar for his own success. Herron adored the game, to be sure, but it was wrapped in the nostalgia of boyhood summers spent at Oakmont with his family, the Fownses, and the Loefflers. The pastime never consumed him the way it possessed Jones. And unlike Jones, Herron never sought self-validation in the game. He never became angry with himself for making a poor shot, just a bit disappointed if he let his parents or playing partners down. For Dave Herron (as well as his family), golf remained a tremendously fulfilling social activity and hobby, but never a vocation or path to fame and fortune.

Perhaps then, it is not so surprising that Dave Herron's and Bob Jones's paths

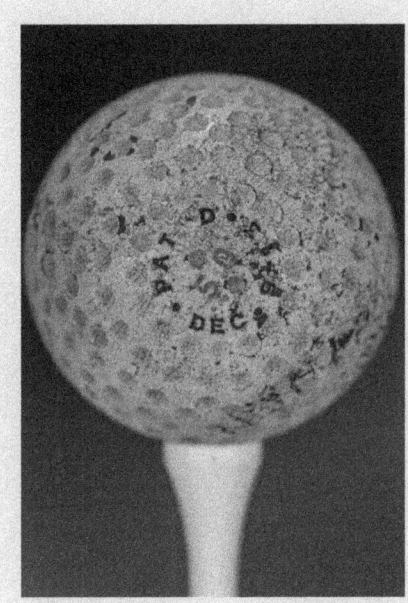

The winning ball that Dave Herron used at Oakmont in 1919. It was a Spalding 50 rubber-core ball that had debuted on the market that very same year. Cherry/Herron Family Archives.

diverged so widely after 1919. They simply wanted different things. That Herron chose a quieter lifestyle away from the pressures of championship golf and the scrutiny of the press undoubtedly contributed to his unfair erasure from American golfing lore. If seventeen-year-old "Bobby" Jones had won the final match of the 1919 U.S. Amateur over Dave Herron, that truly would have been an upset because "Bobby" Jones was not yet Bob Jones. The amazing player and person he would be were still emerging, and his time would come. But 1919 belonged to another truly exceptional young golfer of postwar America, twenty-one-year-old Dave Herron of Pittsburgh.

PART V
APPENDICES

APPENDIX 1

William Abbott, Hole-by-Hole Overview of Each Hole at Oakmont Country Club on the Eve of the 1919 U.S. Amateur Championship (August 16–23, 1919)

William Abbott's hole-by-hole descriptions of Oakmont Country Club, published on the eve of the U.S. Amateur in the *New York Evening World* (August 15, 1919), are the most complete we have found—not only in 1919 but any time since the formal opening of Oakmont for play in 1904.

William Abbott, "Gleaned by the Golf Gallery. Description of Famous Oakmont Course, Where National Championship Will Be Fought," the *Evening World* (New York), August 15, 1919.

> Oakmont, scene of the national amateur championship starting to-morrow, is one of the finest golf courses in America. Great wealth, effort and long experimenting have made the beautiful links just outside Pittsburgh the equal of England's famous courses, Sandwich, Hoylake and Prestwick.
>
> Oakmont is now a true golf test every inch of its 6,700 yards. Par is 73. Severe rough, cunningly placed traps and undulating greens demand, first of all, unerring direction. Undeserved scores are hardly possible on the celebrated Pennsylvania course.
>
> Rains this week have put the course in grand condition for the amateur classic. Playing from the regular tees, Oakmont's distance is nearly 6,700 yards. This can be increased to 7,000 yards by employing the back tees. Francis Ouimet, Jerry Travers, Bobby Jones and other contenders for the national title have been practicing at Oakmont since early in the week.
>
> They found Oakmont's characteristics as follows:
>
> ### Oakmont's Front Nine (August 1919)
>
> | HOLE | LENGTH | PAR | CHARACTERISTICS |
> |---|---|---|---|
> | 1 | 482 yards | 5 | Water hazard ditch and cross traps on left. Rough entire length of fairway on right. Out of bounds on extreme left. Green guarded by traps in foreground on right and left. Rolling green. |
> | 2 | 363 yards | 4 | Cop bunker runs diagonally nearly across course, necessitating a carry of at nearest point of 150 yards. Widest point 200 yards. Traps to left for a pull. Rough and bunkers on right. Green closely trapped on all sides, with narrow entry from the right. Fine hole. |
> | 3 | 428 yards | 4 | Rough in front of tee. Trap at right to catch slices. Traps line the way on left for a pull. Second shot uphill, with well-placed traps to catch indifferent shot. Tableland green. |

HOLE	LENGTH	PAR	CHARACTERISTICS
4	516 yards	5	Elevated tee. Traps each side fairway. Pit on left to catch topped second. Large cop bunker extending fairway from right, 420 yards from the tee, forcing timid player to left, whence approach to green must be made over an oyster shell trap. Green tilted forward to meet the ball is small and closely trapped, with deep pit in back. Fine three shot hole.
5	371 yards	4	Rough in front and side traps for tee shot. New cop bunker resembling sleeping lion cuts half way across fairway from the left 200 yards from tee. Wide water hazard front of green. Insert trap in left foreground of green, with trouble on all sides. Very interesting hole of this length.
6	172 yards	3	Rough, uneven ground from tee to green. Closely trapped on three sides. Deep pit close up in front. Open at back of green. Length of hole altered by change of tees.
7	370 yards	4	Tee shot slightly uphill. Water hazard immediately in front of tee. Yawning pit and cop bunker on left 170 yards away, extending across course to dovetail similar hazard and which enters 20 yards from the right. Very exacting tee shot. Green nearly surrounded by pits, with narrow entrance on left centre.
8	233 yards	3	Level ground. Traps en route and at right and left of green. Open in front and back.
9	462 yards	5	Uphill all way. Traps to right and left for tee shot. Parallel water hazard ditch, to left of fairway. Wide trap 300 yards from tee in left centre of course. Bunker 400 yards from tee, also on left—forcing safety play to right—whence approach is made over pit inserted in right corner of green. Large green connects with practice green in front of club house.

Oakmont's Back Nine (August 1919)

HOLE	LENGTH	PAR	CHARACTERISTICS
10	461 yards	5	Slightly down hill. Parallels No. 9. Parallel hazard ditch on right side of fairway for tee shots. Narrow water hazard diagonally across course. Mounds in foreground of green on either side. Bush fence 15 yards behind green.
11	365 yards	4	Ground rises sharply 180 yards from tee. Deep water hazard crosses fairway 300 yards away at longest point on left, 250 yards from the tee on the right. Mounds and traps on left for hook. Green nearly surrounded by traps. Deep pit out into right corner of green.
12	601 yards	5	Longest and most difficult hole on course. Ground falls away from right to tee for 400 yards. Line of play severely trapped on both sides all the way. Entering the narrow fairway from the left and extending into the course 400 yards from the tee a new cop bunker has been placed, forcing a carry to insure best line to the hole. Green is well trapped on three sides, with open front door. Fine testing hole.
13	164 yards	3	This very excellent one-shot hole may be lengthened or shortened by use of the different teeing grounds. The green is pear-shaped in formation, with undulating surface and entirely surrounded by deep pits.
14	349 yards	4	High mounds and pits line the fairway. Cross bunker extending into course on right near green. Deep pit cuts into left front of green. Traps surround green on three far sides.
15	420 yards	4	Carry of 160 yards for tee shot. Traps and bunker for slice or pull. Second to green must carry wide trap 360 yards from tee. Lines of traps on lower right corner of green. Mounds on left and trap in rear.

HOLE	LENGTH	PAR	CHARACTERISTICS
16	226 yards	3	Slightly down hill for 200 yards, then gradual ascent to green's centre. Punishing trench on left and trap half across course on right 30 yards from green. Open door to hole when correct line is taken from tee.
17	282 yards	4	Uphill from tee to green. Hole planned as dogleg or bee line to the pin. Yardage materially shortened by taking direct line. Play on dogleg in from right to left with bounding fence on right and in front. Green open on left corner for bold slugger. Severe penalty for failure in straight line play to the pin. Deep pit in right front of green. Pits behind the green. A hole neither short nor long but with much character.
18	442 yards	4	Carry of 180 yards from the tee. Ditch and mounds on left for pull. Large mound 60 yards in front of green. Pits on right and left of green. Green recently made smaller.

APPENDIX 2

Driving Distance Comparisons, Herron v. Jones in Championship Match

Appendix 2 provides a brief overview of the number of holes on which Herron or Jones hit the longer drive (or their drives were deemed equal in length) in the championship match, as reported in the *New York Times* and the *Pittsburgh Gazette Times*.

ROUND	DRIVES	NEWSPAPER	LONGER DRIVE
Morning	14	*Pittsburgh Gazette Times*	6 Herron, 6 Jones, 2 Equal-length
	14	*New York Times*	8 Herron, 4 Jones, 2 Equal-length
Afternoon	11	*Pittsburgh Gazette Times*	4 Herron, 5 Jones, 2 Equal-length
	11	*New York Times*	5 Herron, 6 Jones
Total	25	*Pittsburgh Gazette Times*	10 Herron, 11 Jones, 4 Equal-length
	25	*New York Times*	13 Herron, 10 Jones, 2 Equal-length

APPENDIX 3

Ball-Striking Comparisons, Herron v. Jones in Championship Match

Appendix 3 provides a brief overview of the ball-striking prowess of Herron and Jones in the championship match, as reported in the *New York Times* (NYT) and the *Pittsburgh Gazette Times* (PGT).

HOLES		NEWSPAPER	PLAYER	FAIRWAYS HIT		GREENS HIT		BUNKER STROKES
MORNING ROUND	Front Nine	NYT	Herron	7 yes	0 no	6 yes	3 no	1
			Jones	6 yes	1 no	4 yes	5 no	4
		PGT	Herron	7 yes	0 no	6 yes	3 no	1
			Jones	6 yes	1 no	4 yes	5 no	4
	Back Nine	NYT	Herron	4 yes	3 no	3 yes	6 no	5
			Jones	5 yes	2 no	4 yes	5 no	4
		PGT	Herron	4 yes	3 no	3 yes	6 no	5
			Jones	4 yes	3 no	4 yes	5 no	5
	Morning Round Totals	NYT	**Herron**	**11 yes**	**3 no**	**9 yes**	**9 no**	**6**
			Jones	**11 yes**	**3 no**	**8 yes**	**10 no**	**8**
		PGT	**Herron**	**11 yes**	**3 no**	**9 yes**	**9 no**	**6**
			Jones	**10 yes**	**4 no**	**8 yes**	**10 no**	**9**
AFTERNOON ROUND	Front Nine	NYT	Herron	7 yes	0 no	6 yes	3 no	1
			Jones	4 yes	3 no	4 yes	5 no	2
		PGT	Herron	7 yes	0 no	6 yes	3 no	0
			Jones	4 yes	3 no	4 yes	5 no	2
	Back Nine	NYT	Herron	1 yes	3 no	3 yes	1 no	1
			Jones	3 yes	1 no	2 yes	2 no	5
		PGT	Herron	1 yes	3 no	3 yes	1 no	1
			Jones	3 yes	1 no	2 yes	2 no	5
	Afternoon Round Totals	NYT	**Herron**	**8 yes**	**3 no**	**9 yes**	**4 no**	**2**
			Jones	**7 yes**	**4 no**	**6 yes**	**7 no**	**7**
		PGT	**Herron**	**8 yes**	**3 no**	**9 yes**	**4 no**	**1**
			Jones	**7 yes**	**4 no**	**6 yes**	**7 no**	**7**

Grand Totals (Morning and Afternoon Rounds)

NEWSPAPER	PLAYER	FAIRWAYS (out of 25) HIT		GREENS (out of 31) HIT		BUNKER STROKES
New York Times	Herron	19 yes	6 no	18 yes	13 no	8
	Jones	18 yes	7 no	14 yes	17 no	15
Pittsburgh Gazette Times	Herron	19 yes	6 no	19 yes	12 no	7
	Jones	17 yes	8 no	14 yes	17 no	16

The fairways hit data suggest that Herron played with equal, perhaps greater accuracy off the tee than Jones at Oakmont, although Jones brought his "A" driving game when it counted most and drove with greater accuracy in the final match than he had all week.

The data on greens in regulation (GIR) suggest that neither player truly excelled, although Herron was clearly superior to Jones, hitting four more greens in regulation according to the *New York Times* and five more according to the *Pittsburgh Gazette Times*.

An especially notable gap in ball-striking between the two players was how many bunker shots (fairway and greenside) each was forced to play in the championship match: Jones had to hit nearly twice as many bunker shots (14 or 15) as did Herron (8). That Jones had to play nearly twice as many bunker shots as Herron was surely key in explaining his loss to an equally powerful but more accurate player.

APPENDIX 4

Herron v. Jones—Hole-by-Hole Scores in Championship Match Compared to Prior Scoring Averages

Morning Round

FRONT NINE

HOLE	PAR	PLAYER	AVERAGE SCORE THROUGH SEMI-FINALS	STROKES/HOLE
1	5	Herron	4.7	4
		Jones	5.3	4
2	4	Herron	4.4	5
		Jones	4.5	4
3	4	Herron	4.1	4
		Jones	4.7	4
4	5	Herron	5.5	5
		Jones	5.2	5
5	4	Herron	4.1	4
		Jones	3.8	5
6	3	Herron	3.2	3
		Jones	3.1	3
7	4	Herron	4.5	3
		Jones	4.6	4
8	3	Herron	3.4	4
		Jones	4.0	4
9	5	Herron	5.1	4
		Jones	5.1	5

BACK NINE

HOLE	PAR	PLAYER	AVERAGE SCORE THROUGH SEMI-FINALS	STROKES/HOLE
10	5	Herron	4.7	5 (conceded)
		Jones	4.4	4
11	4	Herron	4.7	4
		Jones	4.7	5
12	5	Herron	5.7	5
		Jones	5.9	6
13	3	Herron	3.3	4
		Jones	3.8	3
14	4	Herron	4.4	5 (conceded)
		Jones	4.5	4
15	4	Herron	4.6	5
		Jones	4.7	5
16	3	Herron	3.7	5
		Jones	3.6	4
17	4	Herron	4.1	5
		Jones	4.1	5
18	4	Herron	4.4	4
		Jones	4.6	4

Afternoon Round

FRONT NINE					BACK NINE				
HOLE	PAR	PLAYER	AVERAGE SCORE THROUGH SEMI-FINALS	STROKES/ HOLE	HOLE	PAR	PLAYER	AVERAGE SCORE THROUGH SEMI-FINALS	STROKES/ HOLE
1	5	Herron	4.7	4	10	5	Herron	4.7	4
		Jones	5.3	5 (conceded)			Jones	4.4	4
2	4	Herron	4.4	3	11	4	Herron	4.7	4
		Jones	4.5	3			Jones	4.7	5
3	4	Herron	4.1	5	12	5	Herron	5.7	5 (imputed)
		Jones	4.7	4			Jones	5.9	7 (imputed)
4	5	Herron	5.5	4	13	3	Herron	3.3	3
		Jones	5.2	5			Jones	3.8	4
5	4	Herron	4.1	4	14	4	Herron	4.4	4
		Jones	3.8	5			Jones	4.5	4
6	3	Herron	3.2	4					
		Jones	3.1	3					
7	4	Herron	4.5	4					
		Jones	4.6	4					
8	3	Herron	3.4	3					
		Jones	4.0	3					
9	5	Herron	5.1	4					
		Jones	5.1	5					

Appendix 4 offers a different visualization of the data previously displayed as a graph in Figure 3 in the text. It records Herron's and Jones's hole-by-hole scores in the championship match, for both the morning and afternoon rounds, and compares those scores to each player's prior scoring averages on each hole.

Overall, the data show that Bob Jones unquestionably rose to the occasion and raised the level of his game in the final match. Despite his youth, there was no "choke" in Bob Jones—not at Oakmont, not ever. That said, Jones faltered in three major ways in the afternoon round of the final match that enabled Herron to win more holes (of the fourteen holes played, Herron won seven, Jones won two, and five holes were tied).

First, and most decisively, Herron dominated the five par 5 holes in the afternoon round. For the first time all week, Herron birdied four of the five par 5s, whereas Jones birdied only one and double-bogeyed another. Second, in the afternoon round, Jones faltered dramatically in how he played No. 5—his best hole during the week, where his scoring average of 3.8 was under par. In the final match, however, he bogeyed No. 5 in both the morning and afternoon rounds, and thereby lost the hole twice to Herron in the final match.

And third, Jones in the final match, unlike Herron, was unable to improve his scoring on a hole that had bedeviled both players all week: No. 11. Each had averaged substantially over par at 4.7, but in the final match, Herron scored par 4s in both the morning and afternoon rounds. In contrast, Jones scored bogey-5s on No. 11 both times by pulling his iron shots from clean fairway lies into a difficult left-side bunker.

These three major scoring differences on the par 5 holes and on Nos. 5 and 11 (both par 4s) go far to explain why Jones lost to Herron by the substantial margin of 5 and 4 even though the two were tied after the morning round. We use here the scoring of the *Pittsburgh Gazette Times*, which recorded Herron as shooting a 78 (with a score of 5 on No. 10) in the morning round. As explained earlier, this was the score for Herron on No. 10 that most newspapers (though not the *New York Times*) used. This practice was consistent with amateur golf customs at the time of adding only one additional stroke to a recorded score when a player conceded the hole to his opponent.

APPENDIX 5

Putting Comparisons, Herron v. Jones

PART A

MORNING ROUND

		NEW YORK TIMES						PITTSBURGH GAZETTE TIMES			
HOLE	PLAYER	PUTTS/HOLE	MISSED PUTT ≤6FT	MADE PUTT 7-12FT	MADE PUTT 13FT+	HOLE	PLAYER	PUTTS/HOLE	MISSED PUTT ≤6FT	MADE PUTT 7-12FT	MADE PUTT 13FT+
1	Herron	1				1	Herron	1			
1	Jones	1				1	Jones	1			
2	Herron	3				2	Herron	3			
2	Jones	1				2	Jones	1			
3	Herron	1				3	Herron	2			
3	Jones	1				3	Jones	1			
4	Herron	2	YES			4	Herron	2	YES		
4	Jones	2	YES			4	Jones	2	YES		
5	Herron	1				5	Herron	1			
5	Jones	2				5	Jones	2			
6	Herron	2				6	Herron	2			
6	Jones	2				6	Jones	2		YES	
7	Herron	1				7	Herron	1			
7	Jones	1				7	Jones	1			
8	Herron	1				8	Herron	1			
8	Jones	2	YES			8	Jones	2	YES		
9	Herron	1				9	Herron	2			
9	Jones	2				9	Jones	2			
10	Herron	2*				10	Herron	1			
10	Jones	1				10	Jones	1			
11	Herron	2				11	Herron	2			
11	Jones	2				11	Jones	2			
12	Herron	2				12	Herron	2			
12	Jones	2	YES			12	Jones	2	YES		
13	Herron	2				13	Herron	2			
13	Jones	2				13	Jones	2			
14	Herron	1				14	Herron	1			
14	Jones	2				14	Jones	2			

APPENDIX FIVE | 291

		NEW YORK TIMES						PITTSBURGH GAZETTE TIMES			
HOLE	PLAYER	PUTTS/HOLE	MISSED PUTT ≤6FT	MADE PUTT 7-12FT	MADE PUTT 13FT+	HOLE	PLAYER	PUTTS/HOLE	MISSED PUTT ≤6FT	MADE PUTT 7-12FT	MADE PUTT 13FT+
15	Herron	2	YES			15	Herron	2	YES		
	Jones	2					Jones	2			
16	Herron	3	YES			16	Herron	3	YES		
	Jones	2					Jones	1			
17	Herron	2				17	Herron	2			
	Jones	2					Jones	2			
18	Herron	2				18	Herron	2			
	Jones	2					Jones	2			
Total	Herron	31	3	0	0	Total	Herron	32	3	0	0
	Jones	31	3	0	0		Jones	30	4	0	0

* The *New York Times* scored 6 for Herron with two putts and a final score of 79, whereas the *Pittsburgh Gazette Times* scored 5 for Herron with one putt and a final score of 78. See comments in Appendix 4 on this difference in our two data sources.

PART B

AFTERNOON ROUND

		NEW YORK TIMES						PITTSBURGH GAZETTE TIMES			
HOLE	PLAYER	PUTTS/HOLE	MISSED PUTT ≤6FT	MADE PUTT 7-12FT	MADE PUTT 13FT+	HOLE	PLAYER	PUTTS/HOLE	MISSED PUTT ≤6FT	MADE PUTT 7-12FT	MADE PUTT 13FT+
1	Herron	1		YES		1	Herron	1		YES	
	Jones	2*					Jones	1***			
2	Herron	1				2	Herron	1		YES	
	Jones	1					Jones	1		YES	
3	Herron	2	YES			3	Herron	2	YES		
	Jones	1		YES			Jones	1			
4	Herron	1		YES		4	Herron	1			YES
	Jones	2	YES				Jones	2	YES		
5	Herron	2				5	Herron	2			
	Jones	2					Jones	2			
6	Herron	2				6	Herron	2			
	Jones	1					Jones	2			
7	Herron	2				7	Herron	2			
	Jones	2					Jones	2			

NEW YORK TIMES

HOLE	PLAYER	PUTTS/HOLE	MISSED PUTT ≤6FT	MADE PUTT 7-12FT	MADE PUTT 13FT+
8	Herron	1			
8	Jones	1			
9	Herron	2			
9	Jones	2			
10	Herron	1		YES	
10	Jones	2			
11	Herron	1			
11	Jones	2			
12	Herron	**	**	**	**
12	Jones	**	**	**	**
13	Herron	2			
13	Jones	1			
14	Herron	2			
14	Jones	2			
Total	Herron	20	1	3	0
Total	Jones	21	1	1	0

PITTSBURGH GAZETTE TIMES

HOLE	PLAYER	PUTTS/HOLE	MISSED PUTT ≤6FT	MADE PUTT 7-12FT	MADE PUTT 13FT+
8	Herron	1			
8	Jones	1			
9	Herron	2			
9	Jones	2			
10	Herron	1		YES	
10	Jones	2			
11	Herron	1			
11	Jones	2			
12	Herron	**	**	**	**
12	Jones	**	**	**	**
13	Herron	2			
13	Jones	1			
14	Herron	2			
14	Jones	2			
Total	Herron	20	1	3	1
Total	Jones	21	1	1	0

* Jones conceded after his first putt; *New York Times* scored him a 5 with two putts.
** No putts recorded, as Jones conceded the hole before either player reached the green.
*** Jones conceded after his first putt; *Pittsburgh Gazette Times* scored him a 5 with one putt.

NYT and PGT Grand Total of Putts for Morning and Afternoon Rounds

NEWSPAPER	PLAYER	PUTTS/HOLE	MISSED PUTT ≤6FT	MADE PUTT 7-12FT	MADE PUTT 13FT+
New York Times	Herron	51	4	3	0
New York Times	Jones	52	4	1	0
Pittsburgh Gazette Times	Herron	52	4	3	1
Pittsburgh Gazette Times	Jones	51	5	1	0

We earlier presented data of several kinds to dispute the claim that Jones's ball-striking was superior to Herron's. The data on putting, as displayed in Appendix 5-a and 5-b, support a similar challenge to Atlanta sportswriters who complained that Jones only lost because Herron sank one lengthy putt after another to off-set Jones's superior ball-striking.

Our data indicate that both players missed about the same number of "short" putts—six feet and under, by our definition: four by Herron and four by Jones according to the *New York Times*, and four by Herron and five by Jones according to the *Pittsburgh Gazette Times*. Both Herron and Jones missed putts of three feet or less to lose key holes (in the morning round, Jones did so on No. 12, and Herron did so on No. 16). And, as noted in our narrative, it was Herron, not Jones, who tallied two three-putt greens during the match (losing both holes).

The Atlanta press, however, was loathe to report anything that might suggest Herron was greatly superior to Jones in all aspects of putting and, thus, simply ignored a key empirical reality. Herron and Jones tallied around the same number of putts in their championship match: 51 putts for Herron versus 52 for Jones according to the *New York Times*, and 52 putts for Herron versus 51 for Jones according to the *Pittsburgh Gazette Times*.

Our data also speak to the claim that Jones lost because Herron continuously sank "lengthy" putts that only a player enjoying home-course advantage could have done. However, our data indicate that Herron sank only one "lengthy" putt (thirteen feet or over, by our criteria) during the entire match. This was his birdie putt on No. 4 in the afternoon round.

To be sure, as Appendix 5-b shows, Herron did sink a small number of critical medium-length putts in the afternoon round (though none in the morning round). These putts did indeed enable Herron to move ahead or tie holes against Jones; that's what winners usually do, after all. And in that sense Herron was indeed the better putter; he won by the large margin of 5 and 4 because he was.

NOTES

FOREWORD AND ACKNOWLEDGMENTS

1. The pioneer in using newspapers effectively to revivify early twentieth-century U.S. golf is Stephen R. Lowe, *Sir Walter and Mr. Jones: Walter Hagen, Bobby Jones, and the Rise of American Golf* (Chelsea, Mich.: Sleeping Bear Press, 2000).

INTRODUCTION. THE MEGAPHONE DIDN'T DO IT

1. For discussion on how Oakmont's founders, H. C. and W. C. Fownes Jr., did *not* view their creation as a finished miracle—an "immaculate conception"—see the following articles by Steven Schlossman: "America's Toughest Golf Course: Oakmont Country Club, 1903–1922," *Western Pennsylvania History* 93, 2 (Summer 2010): 44–60; "Moment in the Sun: When a Pittsburgh Lad Beat Golf's Wonder Boy at Oakmont," *Pittsburgh Quarterly* (Fall 2019): 136–142; "The Lost Hole of Oakmont," *Pittsburgh Quarterly* (Summer 2021): 60–63, 125.

2. Joe Davis, "Herron Crowned Golf Champion; Beats Jones, 5–4," *Chicago Tribune*, 24 August 1919.

3. Herbert Warren Wind, *The Story of American Golf: 1888–1941* (New York: Callaway Editions, 2000), 140.

4. Wind, *The Story of American Golf*, 178.

CHAPTER 1. DAVE HERRON: GENTLEMAN CADDIE AND PITTSBURGH PRODIGY (1897–1914)

1. Western Pennsylvania Interscholastic Athletic League, *History of the WPIAL*, https://www.wpial.org/about-us/history-of-the-wpial/. See also Jonathan L. Silver, *Approaching the Pinnacle of Privilege: The History of Shady Side Academy, 1883–Present*, PhD diss., Carnegie Mellon University, 2004.

2. Pittsburgh's first golf courses were part of the extraordinary boom in golf course creation in the United States (mainly in the Northeast and Midwest) that took off in the mid-1890s. By 1900, there were an estimated one thousand courses nationwide, with at least one in every state. New York had the most courses, followed by Massachusetts, Pennsylvania, New Jersey, Connecticut, and Illinois. Very few of these initial courses included eighteen holes—the standard in Scotland and Great Britain—and quite a few had less than nine. When it was built in 1903, Oakmont Country Club was one of the few Western Pennsylvanian courses that had a full eighteen holes. See H. B. Martin, *Fifty Years of American Golf* (New York: Argosy-Antiquarian, 1936, 1966); and Robert L. A. Adams and John F. Rooney, "Evolution of American Golf Facilities," *Geographical Review* 75 (October 1985): 419–438.

3. College golf in "the Ivies" (including the construction of university golf courses) was thriving by the turn of the twentieth century, and expanded to other universities in the years before American entry into World War I. Yale won the first collegiate championship in 1897. See Martin, *Fifty Years of American Golf*, 187–191.

4. E. Ellsworth Giles, "Herron Third National Champion Accredited to Oakmont Golf Club," *Pittsburgh Gazette Times*, 25 August 1919. Andrew Sr. almost definitely started playing golf with a gutta percha ball. But by the time Dave Herron started to learn the game in 1905, the rubber-core Haskell ball—which enabled stronger golfers to hit their drives 20–25 yards longer—had become the new standard. H. C. and W. C. Fownes Jr. likely designed Oakmont to be one of the longest courses in America based on the assumption in 1903 that the rubber-core ball would displace "the gutty" entirely. On the introduction of the Haskell ball see Herbert Warren Wind, *The Story of American Golf: 1888–1941* (New York: Callaway Editions, 2000), 41–42; and George B. Kirsch, *Golf in America* (Urbana: University of Illinois Press, 2009), 35–36.

5. Steven Schlossman, interview with Gene Sarazen, 29 September 1995. Many thanks to Bob Ford, then head golf professional at Oakmont Country Club, for helping to arrange this interview.

6. Harry C. Smith, "Jones-Herron Finalists, Both Kid Wonders," *Pittsburgh Gazette Times*, 23 August 1919. During his caddying years, Dave Herron, as the son of a club member, often stayed overnight on the upper floors of Oakmont's clubhouse. E. Ellsworth Giles, "S. Davidson Herron. Personal Observations on the Golf Champion," *Pittsburgh Gazette Times*, 11 April 1920.

7. See Richard J. Moss, *Golf and the American Country Club*, passim, and *The Kingdom of Golf in America* (Lincoln: University of Nebraska Press, 2013), chap. 3.

8. The journalist who reported on the day's events singled out Dave Herron: "The feature today was the remarkable playing of S. D. Herron, the 14-year-old . . . who survived both elimination rounds." "S. D. Herron, 14-Year-Old Golfer, Wins Butler Tournament: Surprise in Butler Tourney," *Pittsburgh Post*, 4 August 1912; "Butler Tournament Delayed by the Rain: Heavy Downpour Comes during Afternoon Play—Herron Shows Class," *Pittsburgh Post*, 3 August 1912.

9. James was a strong opponent indeed; he was good enough to win the West Penn Amateur years later in 1919 and, at Butler, was playing on his home course.

10. "S. D. Herron, 14-Year-Old Golfer, Wins Butler Tournament," *Pittsburgh Post*, 4 August 1912.

11. "Good Scores Returned at New Castle Tourney: Herron and Crawford Likely to Fight It Out in the Finals Today," *Pittsburgh Post*, 17 August 1912.

12. "Fordyce Wins Tourney: New Castle Golf Events Prove Exciting on Final Day," *Pittsburgh Post*, 18 August 1912.

13. "J. B. Crookston Is Star in Altoona Golf Match: Pittsburgher Wins Gold Medal and Will Likely Triumph in Tourney," *Pittsburgh Post*, 29 August 1912.

14. "George A. Ormiston of Oakmont Club Returns Lowest Score," *Pittsburgh Post*, 27 June 1913.

15. Ibid.

16. "Byers Defeats Fownes in Second Round of Big Golf Tourney," *Pittsburgh Post*, 28 June 1913.

17. "Byers Wins 6 and 5: Earlier, Byers Beat R. L. James, 3 and 2," *Pittsburgh Post*, 29 June 1913.

18. "Low Scores Returned by Golfers," *Pittsburgh Post*, 5 July 1913.

19. "Golfers Enter Local Tourney: Three-Day Event Will Attract Throngs to Stanton

Heights, Links," *Pittsburgh Post*, 13 July 1913; "Stanton Tourney Ready for Start: Golfers Will Tee Off in Annual Invitation Affair This Morning," *Pittsburgh Post*, 15 July 1913; "Youngster Plays Great Golf and Veterans Are Surprised," *Pittsburgh Post*, 19 July 1913.

20. "Herron Plays Brilliant Golf: 15-Year-Old Lad Wins Stanton Heights Invitation Tournament," *Pittsburgh Sunday Post*, 20 July 1913.

21. "Ohio Golfer Leads Large Field in New Castle Qualifying Play," *Pittsburgh Post*, 22 August 1913; "Herron Beaten on New Castle Links," *Pittsburgh Post*, 23 August 1913.

22. "Golf Tourney at Altoona: Pittsburgh Entrants Well Up in List on First Day," *Pittsburgh Post*, 27 August 1913; "Davidson Herron Leads Field at Altoona Golf Tournament," *Pittsburgh Post*, 28 August 1913.

23. "Pittsburgh Golfer Reach [sic] Finals in Altoona Tourney," *Pittsburgh Post*, 29 August 1913; "Pittsburghers Capture Cups in Golf and Tennis Tourneys," *Pittsburgh Post*, 30 August 1913.

24. "Golf Match Is Arranged," *Pittsburgh Post*, 13 August 1913.

25. "Youth Returns Low Score in Golf Tourney," *Pittsburgh Gazette Times*, 26 June 1914.

26. "Herron Plays a Remarkable Game of Golf," *Pittsburgh Gazette Times*, 27 June 1914.

27. See "Andrew W. Herron," *Pittsburgh and Allegheny County Blue Books*, early 1910s.

28. "Davidson Herron Is Sensation in the Local Golf Circles," *Pittsburgh Gazette Times*, 12 July 1914.

29. "George Ormiston First in Qualifying Round," *Pittsburgh Gazette Times*, 15 July 1914; "Four Players Survive in Elimination Round," *Pittsburgh Gazette Times*, 16 July 1914.

30. "Local Golfers in Altoona Tourney," *Pittsburgh Gazette Times*, 26 August 1914; "Four Survive in Altoona Tourney," *Pittsburgh Gazette Times*, 28 August 1914.

CHAPTER 2. THE KID WONDERS OF ATLANTA: "LITTLE BOB" JONES AND PERRY ADAIR (1902–1915)

1. There are numerous books that discuss the early life of Bob Jones, although none that systematically track his progress as a precocious child athlete in Atlanta and the wider South. For some very good discussions of Jones's childhood see Sidney L. Matthew, *The Life and Times of Bobby Jones* (Chelsea, Mich.: Sleeping Bear Press, 1995); Stephen R. Lowe, *Sir Walter and Mr. Jones: Walter Hagen, Bobby Jones, and the Rise of American Golf* (Chelsea, Mich.: Sleeping Bear Press, 2000); Mark Frost, *The Grand Slam* (New York: Hyperion, 2004); and Ron Rapoport, *The Immortal Bobby* (Hoboken, N.J.: John Wiley, 2005). We chart Jones's emergence as a golf prodigy using local newspapers from across the South, including Atlanta's three main outlets—the *Constitution*, the *Georgian*, and the *Journal*.

2. Robert T. Jones Jr. and O. B. Keeler, *Down the Fairway* (London: A & C Black, 1990), 38.

3. The 1914 Southern Amateur was, in fact, the thirteenth annual Southern Championship. The name of the tournament changed in 1920 when it became necessary to distinguish the Amateur from the Southern Open, which the Southern Golf Association launched in September 1919. For simplicity, we refer to the amateur tournament prior to 1920 as the Southern Amateur.

4. "Munger of Dallas Turns in a '73,'" *Atlanta Constitution*, 3 June 1914.

5. The Colonel, "From the South," *American Golfer* 11, 9 (July 1914): 837. The Colonel became the Southern correspondent and writer of the "From the South" section in 1911. When he began writing in March, The Colonel revealed that Grantland Rice was the former writer

of "From the South" and had been writing under the pseudonym "The Judge." We suspect that The Colonel, in these early years, was none other than Robert Purmedus "The Colonel" Jones—that is, Bob Jones's father ("Big Bob").

6. Ibid., 837–838.
7. "Perry Adair Wins, Bill Rowan Also," *Atlanta Constitution*, 4 June 1914.
8. The Colonel, "From the South," *American Golfer* 11, 9 (July 1914): 838.
9. Ibid., 837.
10. "Perry Adair Meets Present Champion," *Atlanta Constitution*, 5 June 1914.
11. "Youthful Adair Meets Champion Whitney Today," *Atlanta Constitution*, 6 June 1914.
12. "Perry Adair Meets Present Champion," *Atlanta Constitution*, 5 June 1914.
13. Ibid.
14. Perry's month of birth is unclear; newspapers, even in the same town, would claim he was somehow both fourteen and fifteen.
15. "Southern Golf Champion Swamps Atlanta Youngster Who Cracks under Fire," *Atlanta Constitution*, 7 June 1914.
16. The Colonel, "From the South," *American Golfer* 11, 9 (July 1914): 839.
17. "Won Runner-Up Trophy," *Atlanta Constitution*, 7 June 1914.
18. "Perry Adair Shows Form at Montgomery," *Atlanta Constitution*, 3 July 1914.
19. The Colonel, "From the South," *American Golfer* 11, 12 (October 1914): 1143.
20. Jones and Keeler, *Down the Fairway*, 48.
21. Ibid., 48.
22. "Qualifying Round in Golf Meet to Begin Here Today," *Montgomery Advertiser*, 3 June 1915.
23. "Qualifying Scores of 26 under 90; Texan Takes Lead: Showing on First Day of Golf Meet Rather Disappointing: Conditions Are Ideal," *Montgomery Advertiser*, 4 June 1915.
24. Jones and Keeler, *Down the Fairway*, 48.
25. "Father and Son Meeing [Meeting] for Golf Championship Today," *Montgomery Daily Times*, 5 June 1915.
26. "Adair Eliminates Heard, but Extra Hole Is Required," *Montgomery Advertiser*, 5 June 1915.
27. "Good Golf Played at Montgomery," *Atlanta Constitution*, 5 June 1915.
28. "Adair Eliminates Heard, but Extra Hole Is Required," *Montgomery Advertiser*, 5 June 1915.
29. "Elder Adair Wins over Skillful Son at Sixteenth Hole: Enthusiastic Gallery Witnesses Absorbing Match between Atlanta Players Here: Montgomerians Beaten," *Montgomery Advertiser*, 6 June 1915.
30. Jones and Keeler, *Down the Fairway*, 48.
31. "Elder Adair Wins over Skillful Son at Sixteenth Hole," *Montgomery Advertiser*, 6 June 1915.
32. Jones and Keeler, *Down the Fairway*, 48.
33. The Colonel, "From the South," *American Golfer* 14, 2 (June 1915): 171.
34. Jones and Keeler, *Down the Fairway*, 49.
35. Ibid., 49.
36. "East Lake Closed Two Days to High Handicap Golfers," *Atlanta Constitution*, 8 June 1915.

37. "Over Three Hundred Golfers Will Compete Here in the Fourteenth Annual Southern Golf Championship," *Atlanta Constitution*, 13 June 1915.

38. The Colonel, "From the South," *American Golfer* 14, 2 (June 1915): 171–172.

39. Dick Jemison, "Four Hundred of South's Leading Golfers Qualify for the Championship Today," *Atlanta Constitution*, 15 June 1915; Jones and Keeler, *Down the Fairway*, 49.

40. Jones and Keeler, *Down the Fairway*, 49.

41. Dick Jemison, "Whitney and Dexter Are Tied for the Low Qualifying Score; Atlanta Wins the Team Trophy," *Atlanta Constitution*, 16 June 1915.

42. Ibid.; Jones and Keeler, *Down the Fairway*, 51.

43. Jones and Keeler, *Down the Fairway*, 51.

44. The Colonel, "From the South," *American Golfer* 14, 3, (July 1915): 273.

45. Ibid., 274.

46. Dick Jemison, "Whitney v. Bush, Adair v. Dexter Pairings in Semi-Finals Friday," *Atlanta Constitution*, 18 June 1915.

47. Jones and Keeler, *Down the Fairway*, 54.

48. Ibid., 52.

49. Francis E. Price, "They Captured the Team Golf Trophy," *Atlanta Constitution*, 20 June 1915.

50. The Colonel, "From the South," *American Golfer* 14, 3 (July 1915): 274.

51. "Nelson Whitney Plays Charlie Dexter for Southern Golf Title on Saturday," *Atlanta Constitution*, 19 June 1915.

52. Dick Jemison, "Nelson Whitney's Crown Lifted by Charlie Dexter: Dexter Wins Southern Championship and Medal Play-Off from Whitney; Frank Clark Sets a Course Record," *Atlanta Constitution*, 20 June 1915.

53. Jones and Keeler, *Down the Fairway*, 53.

54. Dick Jemison, "Southern Golf Aftermath," *Atlanta Constitution*, 21 June 1915.

55. "Alexa Stirling Fraser, Golfer, 79," *New York Times*, 17 April 1977.

56. "Birmingham Will Raise 1914 Pennant Today; Four Atlantans Win Tourney at Rome," *Atlanta Constitution*, 3 July 1915.

57. "'Little Bob' Jones Turns in '77' Card," *Atlanta Constitution*, 8 July 1915.

58. Dick Jemison, "Little Bob Jones Makes New Record at Druid Hills," *Atlanta Constitution*, 18 July 1915.

59. "Several Stars Are Eliminated in Western Golf," *Atlanta Constitution*, 21 July 1915.

60. "Golfers of South Here for Tourney at Roebuck Club," *Birmingham News*, 21 July 1915; "Atlanta Golfers Enter Tourney," *Atlanta Constitution*, 22 July 1915.

61. "Birmingham Pins Hopes on William Badham Today in the Roebuck Semi-Finals," *Birmingham Age-Herald*, 24 July 1915.

62. "Roebuck Springs Golf Tournament Begins Today with Large Entry List," *Birmingham Age-Herald*, 22 July 1915.

63. Ibid.

64. Jones and Keeler, *Down the Fairway*, 54.

65. Richard F. Lussier, "J. H. Doughty Is Winner of the Qualifying Rounds: Birmingham Golfers Take All the Honors in the First Day of the Roebuck Tournament—There Will Be Six Flights of 18 Hole Match Play This Morning—Begin Second Round This Afternoon," *Birmingham Age-Herald*, 23 July 1915.

66. "Little Bob Wins over Perry Adair," *Atlanta Constitution*, 24 July 1915; "Birmingham Pins Hopes on William Badham," *Birmingham Age-Herald*, 24 July 1915.

67. "Little Bob Jones Wins Birmingham Invitation Meet," *Atlanta Constitution*, 25 July 1915.

68. Ibid.

69. "Badham Is Defeated by Atlanta Phenom," *Birmingham Age-Herald*, 25 July 1915.

70. Ibid.

71. "Little Bob Jones Wins Birmingham Invitation Meet," *Atlanta Constitution*, 25 July 1915.

72. "'Little Bob' Ties for Low Medal," *Atlanta Constitution*, 12 September 1915.

73. "East Lake Golfers Start Match Play: Begin Play in Five Flights for Club Championship on Monday," *Atlanta Constitution*, 13 September 1915.

74. "Ten Flights Fill for the City Title," *Atlanta Constitution*, 26 September 1915.

75. "Some Second Round Matches Completed," *Atlanta Constitution*, 30 September 1915.

76. "Father and Son for City Title," *Atlanta Constitution*, 3 October 1915.

77. Ibid.

78. "George Adair Again Wins City Golf Championship, Defeating his Son, 6–5," *Atlanta Constitution*, 4 October 1915.

CHAPTER 3. GRINDING TOWARD STARDOM: DAVE HERRON AT OAKMONT AND PRINCETON (1915–1916)

1. "On The Local Links," *Pittsburgh Gazette Times*, 1 November 1914; "Herron Golf Champion: Defeats Washburn on 20th Hole in Final Match for Title," *Daily Princetonian*, 27 October 1914.

2. "Golf," *Pittsburgh Gazette Times*, 25 April 1915. In *Fifty Years of American Golf*, H. B. Martin observes, in a chapter on "Golf and the Press," that "golf had taken a great leap forward in 1910 and many papers added golf writers to their staffs." However, before American entry into World War I, most golf writers had other writing obligations. Greater specialization finally came after. "So many newspaper men turned to golf writing at the close of the War that it is impossible to enumerate them all. The press-tent became an important part of the game." H. B. Martin, *Fifty Years of American Golf* (New York: Argosy-Antiquarian, 1936, 1966). 349, 351.

3. "Herron Loses Out in Golf Tourney," *Pittsburgh Gazette Times*, 12 May 1915.

4. "Golf Team Loses but Two Veterans by Graduation: Three Victories and Two Defeats in Past Season—Excellent New Material for Intercollegiates," *Daily Princetonian*, 29 May 1915.

5. "Four Golfers Remaining: Final Contests in Tournament on Today," *Pittsburgh Gazette Times*, 26 June 1915.

6. "Golf Rivalry Keen during Past Week," *Pittsburgh Gazette Times*, 1 August 1915.

7. Ibid.

8. "Herron and Sawyer Tied for Low in First Qualifying Round. Oakmont Lad Startles Oldest Followers of Game by His Remarkable Demonstration in First U.S. Championship in Which He Ever Played," *Pittsburgh Gazette Times*, 29 August 1915.

9. John G. Anderson, "Herron's Play Championship Caliber. After Seeing Pittsburgher's Work Expert Hesitates to Pick Amateur Titleholder," *Pittsburgh Gazette Times*, 29 August 1915.

10. "Herron and Sawyer Tied for Low in First Qualifying Round," *Pittsburgh Gazette Times*, 29 August 1915.

11. "Shermans Win American Golfer Trophy: Utica Cracks Take Match with a 72," *Pittsburgh Gazette Times*, 30 August 1915.
12. John G. Anderson, "Pennsylvania Golfers Are Defeated," *Pittsburgh Gazette Times*, 3 October 1915.
13. "Oakmont Awarded Big College Golf Event," *Pittsburgh Gazette Times*, 12 December 1915.
14. "'Dave' Herron Wins Medal at Allegheny: Oakmont Golfer Turns in Remarkable 73 for Round of Rain-Soaked Course," *Pittsburgh Post*, 16 June 1916.
15. "Rain Mars Local Tourneys: Herron Beaten in Allegheny Club Tourney," *Pittsburgh Post*, 17 June 1916.
16. "Fownes Wins Tourney," *Pittsburgh Post*, 19 June 1916.
17. "Golfers Win in Rain: West Penn Team Matches Test Endurance of Golfers; Oakmont's Easy Win," *Pittsburgh Post*, 22 June 1916.
18. "Oakmont Country Club," *Pittsburgh Sunday Post*, 23 July 1916.
19. "Chick Evans Plays Four-Ball Match Here: Open Champ and W. Fownes Lose to Pros," *Pittsburgh Post*, 10 July 1916. See also "Davidson Herron Wins From W. C. Fownes, Jr.: Oakmont Youth Defeats Western Pennsylvania Amateur Golf Champion in Play-off of Tie, 2 Up and 1," *Pittsburgh Post*, 26 July 1916.
20. "Semi-Finals Reached in W. Pa. Amateur Golf: Byers, Fownes, Ormiston and Herron Remain," *Pittsburgh Post*, 15 July 1916.
21. "Heat Hampers Local Golfers in 4-Ball Play: Miller and Ralston, Bellevue, Win Opening Event of West Penn Tourney," *Pittsburgh Post*, 14 July 1916.
22. "Fownes Medalist in West Penn Golf Play; Long the Runner-Up," *Pittsburgh Post*, 14 July 1916.
23. "Semi-Finals Reached in W. Pa. Amateur: Byers, Fownes, Ormiston and Herron Remain," *Pittsburgh Post*, 15 July 1916.
24. "W. C. Fownes, Jr., Wins W. Pa. Amateur Golf Title: Oakmont Star Beasts [sic] Byers in Final, 2 Up," *Pittsburgh Sunday Post*, 16 July 1916.
25. "Fred Brand Wins the W. Pa. Open Golf Title: Bellevue Pro Leads Field in 36-Hole Play," *Pittsburgh Post*, 20 July 1916.
26. "Star Golfers in Tourney. All District Leaders Except Fownes and Byers Enter Stanton Heights Play," *Pittsburgh Post*, 29 July 1916.
27. "P. H. Preston Wins Stanton Heights Golf: Home Player Defeats Ellen in the Final," *Pittsburgh Post*, 5 August 1916.

CHAPTER 4. "GEORGIA HAS GOLF MARVEL": JONES OVERTAKES ADAIR (1916)

1. "South's Best Golfers Here for Tourney: 200 Experts from All Parts of South Come to Play on Perfect Golf Course," *Montgomery Advertiser*, 8 June 1916.
2. "Play Qualifying Round Thursday; All in Readiness," *Montgomery Advertiser*, 7 June 1916.
3. "South's Best Golfers Here for Tourney: 200 Experts from All Parts of South Come to Play on Perfect Golf Course," *Montgomery Advertiser*, 8 June 1916; "Qualifying Scores of 26 under 90; Texan Takes Lead," *Montgomery Advertiser*, 4 June 1915.
4. "South's Best Golfers Here for Tourney: 200 Experts from All Parts of South Come to Play on Perfect Golf Course," *Montgomery Advertiser*, 8 June 1916.
5. "Play Qualifying Round Thursday; All in Readiness: Sixth Annual Invitation Tourna-

ment of Montgomery Country Club to Be Largely Attended," *Montgomery Advertiser*, 7 June 1916.

6. "South's Best Golfers Here for Tourney: 200 Experts from All Parts of South Come to Play on Perfect Golf Course," *Montgomery Advertiser*, 8 June 1916.

7. "Perry Adair Turns in Low Score of Day: Youngster from Atlanta Makes Course in 76; Roebuck Golf Club Wins Team Match," *Montgomery Advertiser*, 9 June 1916.

8. "Birmingham, Atlanta, and Macon Are Represented in Championship Flight: Perry Adair Meets R. T. Jones and R. H. Baugh: Plays Ches Jones This Morning," *Montgomery Advertiser*, 10 June 1916.

9. Ibid.

10. Ibid.

11. Jones and Keeler, *Down the Fairway*, 56.

12. O. B. Keeler, *The Boys' Life of Bobby Jones* (Canada: Sleeping Bear Press, 2002), 61.

13. L. S. Betty, "Qualifying Round of Golf Tourney Today at the Country Club," *Birmingham Age-Herald*, 22 June 1916.

14. Ibid.

15. "Birmingham Divides Honors with Atlanta in Qualifying Round at the Country Club," *Birmingham Age-Herald*, 23 June 1916; "How They Qualified," *Birmingham News*, 23 June 1916.

16. L. S. Betty, "Atlanta Youth Scores Close Victory over Jack Allison for Championship Cup at Country Club," *Birmingham Age-Herald*, 25 June 1916.

17. "Four Flights Fill at Druid Hills Club: G. W. Adair Turns in Low Qualifying Score for President's Cup," *Atlanta Constitution*, 28 June 1916.

18. "G. W. Adair Wins Qualifying Round; A. A. C. Team Match in Invitation Golf Event," *Atlanta Constitution*, 7 July 1916.

19. "Semi-Finals Are Reached In Invitation Tournament," *Atlanta Constitution*, 8 July 1916.

20. "Little Bob Jones Wins Invitation Golf Tournament," *Atlanta Constitution*, 9 July 1916.

21. "Meredith Will Not Join New York A.C.," *New York Times*, 6 July 1916.

22. "Advance Guard of Golf Devotees Reach the City for Invitation Tourney," *Knoxville Sentinel*, 26 July 1916.

23. "John Fox, Jr., Perry Adair, Bob Jones, Other Well Known Golfers Entered in Invitation Tourney Here This Week," *Knoxville Sentinel*, 25 July 1916.

24. Ibid.; "Everything Now Ready for Invitation Golf Tourney Here This Week," *Knoxville Sentinel*, 24 July 1916.

25. "Perry Adair Most Unassuming Young Man Imaginable," *Knoxville Sentinel*, 26 July 1916.

26. "Advance Guard of Golf Devotees Reach the City for Invitation Tourney," *Knoxville Sentinel*, 26 July 1916.

27. "Qualifying Round of Invitation Tourney Is Played at Cherokee," *Knoxville Sentinel*, 27 July 1916.

28. Grantland Rice quoted in Larry Schwartz, "Bobby Jones Was golf's Fast Study," ESPN, 2019, https://www.espn.com/sportscentury/features/00014123.html.

29. "Advance Guard of Golf Devotees Reach the City for Invitation Tourney," *Knoxville Sentinel*, 26 July 1916; "George and Perry Adair Eliminated in Knoxville Meet," *Atlanta Con-*

stitution, 29 July 1916; "R. Van Gilder Loses to Simpson Deane [*sic*] in Tourney Semi-Finals," *Knoxville Sentinel*, 29 July 1916.

30. "Little Bob Wins Knoxville Golf," *Atlanta Constitution*, 30 July 1916.

31. Ibid.

32. "Jones Easily Defeats Dean in Championship Match of Invitation Golf Tournament," *Sunday Journal and Tribune*, Knoxville, 30 July 1916.

33. "Club Championship Meet Next Event at Cherokee," *Knoxville Sentinel*, 1 August 1916.

34. Stephen R. Lowe, *Sir Walter and Mr. Jones: Walter Hagen, Bobby Jones, and the Rise of American Golf* (Chelsea, Mich.: Sleeping Bear Press, 2000), 46.

35. Harold H. Martin, *Atlanta and Environs: A Chronicle of Its People and Events, 1940s–1970s* (Athens: University of Georgia Press, 1987), 362.

36. "1st Round Matches on Today," *Atlanta Georgian*, 3 August 1916.

37. "Youngsters Starring in Golf Play," *Atlanta Georgian*, 4 August 1916.

38. Westward Ho, "Western Department," *American Golfer* 2, 1 (July 1909): 45; The Judge, "From the South," *American Golfer* 5, 2 (December 1910): 152; "Perry Adair and Jones in Finals," *Atlanta Georgian*, 5 August 1916.

39. "Bob Jones Beats Dean in Finals," *Atlanta Georgian*, 30 July 1916.

40. "Perry Adair and Jones in Finals," *Atlanta Georgian*, 5 August 1916.

41. Robert T. Jones Jr. and O. B. Keeler, *Down the Fairway* (London: A & C Black, 1990), 58.

42. "Perry Adair 3 Up on 'Little Bob' Jones," *Atlanta Georgian*, 5 August 1916.

43. Jones and Keeler, *Down the Fairway*, 58.

44. O. B. Keeler, "'Little Bob' Jones Wins State Golf Title. Defeats Perry Adair in Hard Uphill Fight," *Atlanta Georgian*, 6 August 1916. After a stint at the *Kansas City Star*, Keeler returned to the *Atlanta Georgian* in 1913. He didn't cover a golf tournament as a reporter, however, until 1915, when he saw Jones in action for the first time at the Southern Amateur.

45. Jones and Keeler, *Down the Fairway*, 58.

46. "Stroke-by-Stroke Story of Great Golf Game," *Atlanta Georgian*, 6 August 1916.

47. Ward Greene, "Bob Jones Wins State Golf Title," *Atlanta Journal*, 6 August 1916, as reprinted in Sidney L. Matthew, *The Life and Times of Bobby Jones* (Chelsea, Mich.: Sleeping Bear Press, 1995), 16.

48. Interestingly, Keeler mistakenly referred to Bob as age fifteen (rather than fourteen), although he correctly identified Perry as age seventeen. O. B. Keeler, "'Little Bob' Jones Wins State Golf Title. Defeats Perry Adair in Hard Uphill Fight," *Atlanta Georgian*, 6 August 1916.

49. Ibid.

50. Keeler, *The Boys' Life of Bobby Jones*, 67.

51. Catherine Lewis, *Bobby Jones and the Quest for the Grand Slam* (Chicago: Triumph, 2005), 7.

52. Keeler, *The Boys' Life of Bobby Jones*, 67.

53. "Boy Cracks Enter U.S. Golf Meet," *Atlanta Georgian*, 17 August 1916.

54. The Colonel, "From the South," *American Golfer* 15, 3 (January 1916): 221.

55. O. B. Keeler, "Keeler Tells How Kids Are Able to Play Golf," *Atlanta Georgian*, 20 August 1916.

56. O. B. Keeler, "Whitney, Bush, Aldredge, Rotan, Dexter, Adairs and Bob Jones Off for Tourney," *Atlanta Georgian*, 27 August 1916.

57. William H. Evans, "Can You Pick the Next Amateur Golf Champion? Eleven Names

Submitted and What They Have Done in Previous National Tournaments—Merion to Be Scene of Luring Game," *Philadelphia Public Ledger*, 6 August 1916.

58. Ibid.

59. Travers ultimately withdrew due to illness; his and Ouimet's absence (because the USGA had ruled he was a professional) inevitably made the 1916 field less competitive. Nevertheless, attendance at the final match was quite good, with an estimated six thousand fans.

60. The Colonel, "From the South," *American Golfer* 14, 6 (October 1915): 566. As noted earlier, we suspect that "The Colonel" was R. P. Jones, i.e., Bob Jones's father, who was colloquially known in Atlanta as both "Big Bob" and "The Colonel."

61. The Colonel, "From the South," *American Golfer* 14, 6 (October 1915): 566–567.

62. O. B. Keeler, "Keeler Tells How Kids Are Able to Play Golf," *Atlanta Georgian*, 20 August 1916.

CHAPTER 5. THE 1916 U.S. AMATEUR AT MERION: HERRON AND JONES CROSS PATHS

1. "Fourteen Pittsburgh Golfers in National Play: Fownes and Byers in Hunt for the Title," *Pittsburgh Sunday Post*, 3 September 1916.

2. Later in October, the *American Golfer* would compare the scores of the East and West courses, revealing "an average of 79–21/32 strokes for the West course as against 82–5/32 for the East course." *Philadelphia Public Ledger*, 27 August 1916; "Around the 19th Hole," *American Golfer* 16, 6 (October 1916): 463–444.

3. Jeff Silverman, *Merion: The Championship Story* (West Chester, Pa.: Merion Golf Club, 2013), 104.

4. Robert T. Jones Jr. and O. B. Keeler, *Down the Fairway* (London: A & C Black, 1990), 62.

5. Ibid., 61.

6. "Around the 19th Hole," *American Golfer* 16, 6 (October 1916): 464.

7. Jones and Keeler, *Down the Fairway*, 62.

8. Harry C. Smith, "Bobby Jones' Career; Other Tourney Tidbits," *Pittsburgh Post*, 8 September 1916.

9. Jones and Keeler, *Down the Fairway*, 61.

10. "Age and Youth Tee Off Together," *Philadelphia Inquirer*, 5 September 1916.

11. "Pittsburgh Golfer Now Wears Crown. W. C. Fownes Wins National Championship over Merion Cricket Club Course," *Philadelphia Inquirer*, 5 September 1916.

12. After qualifying, Perry beat a Homestead/Pittsburgh golfer, L. B. Patton, in the first round only to fall to Dave's friend D. C. Corkran in the second. "Souteern [sic] Golf Cracks Hold Own in Tourney," *Atlanta Georgian*, 5 September 1916.

13. "Fownes Medalist in Title Tourney: Oakmont Golfer Leads Star Field in Qualifying Round at Haverford—Beyers [sic] Third, Ormiston Fourth," *Pittsburgh Post*, 5 September 1916; Harry C. Smith, "Ormiston Is Last Hope of Pittsburgh Golfers," *Pittsburgh Post*, 6 September 1916.

14. The Runner-Up, "National Golf Play Gets Warmer. Annual Contests Wax Closer—Weather Conditions Important—Davidson Herron, Local Star, Is Lauded by Dr. Nelson of Altoona," *Pittsburgh Gazette Times*, 10 September 1916.

15. Jones and Keeler, *Down the Fairway*, 63.
16. Ibid., 67. Jones's comments were clearly meant as a joke (recall that O. B. Keeler coauthored *Down the Fairway*), although some readers seemed to take the joke literally.
17. John Anderson, "The Amateur Championship," *Golf Illustrated*, September 1916, 22–23.
18. Ibid., 23.
19. "Champion Defeats Young Bob Jones: Gardner Eliminates Southern Marvel from National Golf Tourney 4 and 3," *Philadelphia Inquirer*, 8 September 1916.
20. George C. Mason, "Atlanta's Boy Golf Prodigy Playing Crucial Match Today," *Atlanta Georgian*, Afternoon Edition, 7 September 1916.
21. "'Little Bob' Jones Wins; Adair Loses: GA. Champion Is Going Strong," *Atlanta Georgian*, Night Edition, 6 September 1916.
22. "South's Hopes Now Rest with 'Little Bob' Jones," *Atlanta Constitution*, 7 September 1916.
23. "Georgia Golf Prodigy Blasts Hopes of Dyer: 14-Year-Old Southern Star Eliminates Pennsylvania Champion," *Philadelphia Public Ledger*, 7 September 1916.
24. "'Lost Ten Pounds Playing Gardner,' Says Boy Golfer: Fourteen-Year-Old Southern Wonder Started to Play Because His Health Was Poor—Now State Champion and Growing Big," *Philadelphia Public Ledger*, 9 September 1916.
25. "Largest Gallery Watches Struggle by Boy and Man," *Philadelphia Inquirer*, 8 September 1916.
26. "Boy Golfer Falls before Champion," *New York Times*, 8 September 1916.
27. "Champion Plays Par Golf to Beat Young Southerner," *Louisville Courier-Journal*, 8 September 1916.
28. "Boy Golfer Falls before Champion," *New York Times*, 8 September 1916.
29. Ibid.
30. "15-Year-Old Boy Golf Star," *Los Angeles Morning Tribune*, 7 September 1916. Located in Sidney L. Matthew, *Bobby Jones Collection and Research Files, 1862–2015,* Manuscript Collection No. 1250, OP 16, Stuart A. Rose Manuscript, Archives, and Rare Book Library, Emory University.
31. James R. Crowell, "Youth in the Old Man's Game," *The Spur* 18, 7, 7 1 October 1916, 14.
32. Jones and Keeler, *Down the Fairway*, 61.
33. Ibid., 71.
34. "Champion Plays Par Golf to Beat Young Southerner," *Louisville Courier-Journal*, 8 September 1916.
35. "'Lost Ten Pounds Playing Gardner,'" *Philadelphia Public Ledger*, 9 September 1916.
36. "Champion Plays Par Golf to Beat Young Southerner," *Louisville Courier-Journal*, 8 September 1916.
37. "Boy Golfer Falls before Champion," *New York Times*, 8 September 1916.
38. Ibid.
39. "Largest Gallery Watches Struggle by Boy and Man," *Philadelphia Inquirer*, 8 September 1916.
40. Ibid.
41. "Young Atlanta Abroad," *Atlanta Constitution*, 8 September 1916.
42. "'Lost Ten Pounds Playing Gardner,'" *Philadelphia Public Ledger*, 9 September 1916.

43. "Tom Morris and 'Bob' Jones: The Young and the Old, the Ancient and the Modern," *Golf* 39 (September 1916): 142.
44. "'Little Bob,' U.S.A., Drops Clubs and Is a Schoolboy Again," *Atlanta Georgian*, 11 September 1916.
45. H. B. Martin, "Side-Lights on the Amateur Championship," *Golf* 39 (September 1916): 149.
46. "'Little Bob,' U.S.A., Drops Clubs and Is a Schoolboy Again," *Atlanta Georgian*, 11 September 1916.
47. Ibid.
48. "The Old Sport's Musings," *Philadelphia Inquirer*, 11 September 1916.
49. John G. Anderson, "Few Extra-Hole Matches," *Sporting Life* 68, 4 (1916): 15.
50. "Tom Morris and 'Bob' Jones," *Golf* 39 (September 1916): 142.
51. As Jeff Silverman further observes: "With the victory, Evans joined Englishman John Ball, who won Britain's Open and Amateur titles in 1890, as the only men then to hold their nation's two most prestigious trophies at the same time." Jeff Silverman, *Merion: The Championship Story* (Ardmore, Pa.: Merion Golf Club, 2013), 123.

CHAPTER 6. STILL GRINDING: DAVE HERRON AND DISAPPOINTMENT AT OAKMONT (1916–1917)

1. "Intercollegiate Golf Tourney Opens at Oakmont: Yale, Harvard and Cornell Win Matches: Penn, Williams and Illinois Are Respective Victims in Team Contests: Surprise by Ithacans," *Pittsburgh Post*, 15 September 1916.
2. The *New York Times* seemed to consider Yale the team to beat. "East and West to Clash on Links: Oakmont Course Chosen as the Half-Way Meeting Place for College Golfers," *New York Times*, 15 December 1915; "Three Teams Out of College Golf," *New York Times*, 15 September 1916.
3. "Tigers Win College Golf Championship. Princeton Makes Clean Sweep of Nine Matches in Team Play Final Round. Harvard Is Outclassed," *Pittsburgh Sunday Post*, 17 September 1916.
4. "Harvard and Princeton Golf Teams in Finals: Tigers Beat Out Yale in Hard Match," *Pittsburgh Post*, 16 September 1916; "Tigers Win College Golf Championship: Princeton Makes Clean Sweep of Nine Matches in Team Play Final Round," *Pittsburgh Sunday Post*, 17 September 1916.
5. "Yale Eliminated in College Golf Tourney: Blossom, 1915 Champ, Loses; Other Upsets," *Pittsburgh Post*, 19 September 1916.
6. "Herron Beaten in Intercollegiate Tourney: Corkran Plays Hubbell Today in Final Round," *Pittsburgh Post*, 20 September 1916.
7. Ibid.
8. "Harvard Golfer Captures Intercollegiate Title: Hubbell Wins Uphill Battle from Corkran," *Pittsburgh Post*, 21 September 1916.
9. "Golf Booming; Season of 1917 Looms Best Yet," *Pittsburgh Post*, 10 December 1916.
10. "Pittsburghers Play Good Golf at Brookline," *Pittsburgh Post*, 30 September 1916.
11. Ibid.
12. "Close Match in Golf League to Allegheny . . . Oakmont Wins Easily," *Pittsburgh Post*,

5 October 1916; "State Title Golf Coming... Oakmont Country Club," *Pittsburgh Post*, 8 October 1916.

13. "State Championship Next on Local Golf Card: Pennsylvania Title Tourneys at Allegheny," *Pittsburgh Post*, 1 October 1916.

14. Harry C. Smith, "Eben Byers Not Rated in Met Handicap List," *Pittsburgh Sunday Post*, 1 April 1917.

15. "Golf Status during the War Is to Be Settled Soon: Title Play at Oakmont in Balance," *Pittsburgh Sunday Post*, 22 April 1917.

16. Ibid.

17. Ibid.

18. Harry C. Smith (The "Runner-Up"), "Western Pennsylvania Golf District Is in a Class 'Peculiar' to Itself," *Pittsburgh Sunday Post*, 20 May 1917.

19. Ibid.

20. "Home Club Men Win Allegheny Golf Prelim," *Pittsburgh Post*, 14 June 1917.

21. "Allegheny Golf Tourney Prelim Carded Today," *Pittsburgh Post*, 13 June 1917; "Home Club Men in Allegheny Golf Prelim," *Pittsburgh Post*, 14 June 1917.

22. "Amateurs and Pros Pointing for Western Pen Golf Play: Beaver Valley Pro Tourney Tuesday Is Fine Introductory," *Pittsburgh Post*, 6 July 1917.

23. "Next District Golf Fixture at Bedford Springs: Many Local Men to Be in Big Tourney," *Pittsburgh Sunday Post*, 29 July 1917.

24. Ibid.

25. Ibid.

26. "Not Yet Certain Whether Ouimet Can Play Here: Chick Evans Writes He'll Play, Though," *Pittsburgh Sunday Post*, 23 September 1917.

27. "S. D. Herron 1918 Sets New Course Record with a 72," *Daily Princetonian*, 8 October 1917; "S. D. Herron 1918 Captures Title in Golf Tournament: Defeats T. J. E. Puling 1920 Five and Four in Final Round—B. S. Horne Wins Second Sixteen," *Daily Princetonian*, 22 October 1917; "Herron Wins Atlantic City Golf Tournament," *Daily Princetonian*, 29 October 1917.

28. The Field Club in 1917 moved from Regent Square to its current location in O'Hara Township, a suburb just north of Pittsburgh, across the Allegheny River.

29. "Red Cross Golf Match Scheduled over Local Course; 'Chick' Evans and Sawyer to Appear Here," *Pittsburgh Sunday Post*, 7 October 1917.

30. "Evans and Sawyer to Appear at the Field Club," *Pittsburgh Sunday Post*, 21 October 1917.

31. "Ouimet May Play Here for Red Cross Next Month," *Pittsburgh Sunday Post*, 16 September 1917.

32. "Evans and Sawyer to Appear at the Field Club," *Pittsburgh Sunday Post*, 21 October 1917.

33. "Local Golfers Think of Spring: What Is Next?" *Pittsburgh Sunday Post*, 4 November 1917.

CHAPTER 7. BECOMING A CELEBRITY: BOB JONES AND THE RED CROSS CIRCUIT

1. Robert T. Jones Jr. and O. B. Keeler, *Down the Fairway* (London: A & C Black, 1990), 74.

2. Joe Davis, "Edwards Boys Lead Golfers in Title Meet," *Chicago Tribune*, 10 July 1917; Joe Davis, "Medal Honors to D. Edwards in Golf Play," *Chicago Tribune*, 11 July 1917.

3. "Play for Dixie Golf Title Will Begin Tuesday," *Birmingham News*, 3 June 1917.

4. Henry Vance, "On the Level," *Birmingham News*, 4 June 1917.

5. Fred Bodeker, "Dixie's Greatest Golfers to Compete for Honors in Annual Southern Meet," *Birmingham Age-Herald*, 3 June 1917.

6. "Nelson Whitney Primed for Play in Southern Tourney," *Birmingham Age-Herald*, 3 June 1917.

7. "Play for Dixie Golf Title Will Begin Tuesday," *Birmingham News*, 3 June 1917.

8. "Final Practice Done by Golfers for Big Tourney," *Birmingham News*, 4 June 1917.

9. Fred Bodeker, "Dixie's Greatest Golfers to Compete for Honors in Annual Southern Meet," *Birmingham Age-Herald*, 3 June 1917.

10. "Atlanta's Kids after Dixie Cup," *Atlanta Georgian*, 5 June 1917.

11. Fred Bodeker, "Visiting Golfers Make Fine Showing in Initial Practice," *Birmingham Age-Herald*, 4 June 1917.

12. "Final Practice Done by Golfers for Big Tourney," *Birmingham News*, 4 June 1917.

13. Fred Bodeker, "Qualifying Round of Southern Golf Tournament at Roebuck," *Birmingham Age-Herald*, 5 June 1917.

14. "Jones and Adair Win Practice Foursome," *Atlanta Journal*, 5 June 1917.

15. Fred Bodeker, "Qualifying Round of Southern Golf Tournament at Roebuck," *Birmingham Age-Herald*, 5 June 1917.

16. Ibid.

17. Henry Vance, "On the Level," *Birmingham News*, 5 June 1917.

18. "The Youngest and Oldest Men in Golf Tourney Are Meeting Today," *Birmingham News*, 5 June 1917.

19. "Perry Adair Wins Match from Mays," *Atlanta Journal*, 6 June 1917; "Adair and Little Bob Favorites," *Atlanta Georgian*, 7 June 1917.

20. "Adair and Little Bob Favorites," *Atlanta Georgian*, 7 June 1917.

21. "Little Bob' Jones Winner over Southern Champion; Other Atlantans Beaten," *Atlanta Constitution*, 8 June 1917.

22. Fred Bodeker, "Perry Adair and Champion Bush Suffer Defeat in the Southern Golf Tournament," *Birmingham Age-Herald*, 8 June 1917.

23. "Bob Seen as Sure Champion," *Atlanta Georgian*, 8 June 1917.

24. Fred Bodeker, "Perry Adair and Champion Bush Suffer Defeat in the Southern Golf Tournament," *Birmingham Age-Herald*, 8 June 1917.

25. Fred Bodeker, "Bob Jones and Louis Jacoby Clash in Finals for Dixie's Golf Crown," *Birmingham Age-Herald*, 9 June 1917.

26. "'Little Bob' Jones Plays Louis Jacoby in Finals for Southern Golf Title," *Atlanta Constitution*, 9 June 1917.

27. Fuzzy Woodruff, "'Little Bob' Certain to Be Winner," *Atlanta Georgian*, 9 June 1917.

28. John G. Anderson, "The Month at a Glance," *Golf Illustrated*, July 1917, 16–17.

29. Special to the *New York Times*, "Adair Medalist on Druid Hills Links," *New York Times*, 28 March 1917. See also The Colonel, "From the South," *American Golfer* 14, 2 (June 1915): 171.

30. "Young Bob Jones Wins South's Golf Title by Easily Downing Jacoby," *Birmingham Age-Herald*, 10 June 1917; "Local Boy Maintains His Lead Easily," *Atlanta Georgian*, 9 June 1917.

31. Henry Vance, "On the Level," *Birmingham News*, 7 June 1917.

32. Jones and Keeler, *Down the Fairway*, 75.
33. Frank P. Glass Jr., "Dazzling Skill of Georgia Star Bewilders Texan," *Birmingham News*, 10 June 1917.
34. "Young Bob Jones Wins South's Golf Title by Easily Downing Jacoby," *Birmingham Age-Herald*, 10 June 1917.
35. Frank P. Glass Jr., "Dazzling Skill of Georgia Star Bewilders Texan," *Birmingham News*, 10 June 1917."
36. "'Little Bob' Jones Broke Title Trust of New Orleans," *Atlanta Constitution*, 11 June 1917.
37. "Atlanta's Kid Wonder Downs Veteran Jacoby," *Atlanta Georgian*, 10 June 1917.
38. Jones and Keeler, *Down the Fairway*, 76.
39. "Boy Wonders in Golf Benefit," *Chicago Daily Tribune*, 10 June 1917.
40. "Some Kid!" *Chicago Daily Tribune*, 14 June 1917.
41. Joe Davis, "Shots on the Links," *Chicago Daily Tribune*, 15 June 1917.
42. "Golf," *Chicago Daily Tribune*, 17 June 1917; "Georgia Stars to Play Today," *Chicago Daily Tribune*, 17 June 1917; "Golf Stars in Foursome," *New York Times*, 18 June 1917; Martin, *Fifty Years of American Golf*, 348–349.
43. Charles (Chick) Evans, *Chick Evans' Golf Book: The Story of the Sporting Battles of the Greatest of All Amateur Golfers* (Chicago: Thos. E. Wilson, 1921), 241.
44. Joe Davis, "Stars of Golf Brave Throng for Red Cross," *Chicago Daily Tribune*, 18 June 1917.
45. Ibid.
46. "Golf Architects under U.S.G.A. Ban," *New York Times*, 12 January 1917.
47. "Official Cognizance: Of Amateur Rule Will Not Be Taken by Western Golf Association," *Cincinnati Enquirer*, 20 January 1917.
48. Special to the *New York Times*, "U.S.G.A. Will Not Reinstate Ouimet," *New York Times*, 6 July 1917.
49. "Ouimet Will Play for Western Title," *New York Times*, 8 July 1917.
50. "Western Amateur Golf Title Will Be the Prize," *Detroit Free Press*, 9 July 1917.
51. Stephen R. Lowe, *Sir Walter and Mr. Jones: Walter Hagen, Bobby Jones, and the Rise of American Golf* (Chelsea, Mich.: Sleeping Bear Press, 2000), 59–60.
52. Stephen Lowe, "Golf, the Flag, and the 1917 Western Amateur," 2002, Faculty Scholarship—History, Paper 2, http://digitalcommons.olivet.edu/hist_facp/2.
53. "Western Amateur Golf Title Will Be the Prize," *Detroit Free Press*, 9 July 1917.
54. W. H. F., "This Month at a Glance," *Golf Illustrated* 7, 5 (August 1917): 19; Lowe, "Golf, the Flag, and the 1917 Western Amateur," 2002, Faculty Scholarship—History, Paper 2, http://digitalcommons.olivet.edu/hist_facp/2.
55. "Western Amateur Golf Title Will Be the Prize," *Detroit Free Press*, 9 July 1917.
56. "Western Golfers Abolish Stymies," *New York Times*, 21 May 1917. The *Times* article details differences between the old and new stymie rule created by the WGA, for both match and medal play.
57. "Ouimet Will Play for Western Title," *New York Times*, 8 July 1917.
58. Ibid.
59. Evans, *Chick Evans' Golf Book*, 240. Gardner did indeed enlist as an officer and served in a field artillery unit in France. Gardner and Evans were the same age; we are uncertain why Evans did not serve in the military.

60. A. Behrendt, "Five Atlanta Golfrs Equalify" [sic], *Atlanta Constitution*, 10 July 1917.

61. Joe Davis, "Medal Honors to D. Edwards in Golf Play," *Chicago Daily Tribune*, 11 July 1917; "Game Fight by Southerners," *Atlanta Constitution*, 11 July 1917.

62. "Bobbie Jones Is Eliminated," *Los Angeles Times*, 11 July 1917.

63. Francis Ouimet, "The Western Amateur Championship," *Golf Illustrated*, August 1917, 14–18.

64. "Group Top Golfers for Open Struggle," *New York Times*, 22 July 1917.

65. "Scotch Foursomes Contest at Englewood Won by Miss Bishop and Hobens," *New York Times*, 24 July 1917.

66. Ibid.

67. "Nicholls Victim of Travers's Fine Golf," *New York Times*, 26 July 1917.

68. "Home Bred Golfers Trim Scotch Team; English Side Wins," *Chicago Daily Tribune*, 26 July 1917.

69. "Nicholls Victim of Travers's Fine Golf," *New York Times*, 26 July 1917.

70. Ibid.

71. Jones and Keeler, *Down the Fairway*, 80.

72. "'Little Bob' Wins, But Perry Loses," *Atlanta Constitution*, 26 July 1917.

73. "Put Hopes in Maxwell," *New York Times*, 5 May 1917.

74. "Hutchinson Wrests Golf Victory from Travers in a Thrilling Finish," *New York Times*, 27 July 1917.

75. "Jones and Adair Save Amateurs from Golf Rout," *Chicago Daily Tribune*, 27 June 1917.

76. "Hutchinson Wrests Golf Victory from Travers in a Thrilling Finish," *New York Times*, 27 July 1917.

77. "Atlanta Youngsters Win in Fine Style," *Atlanta Constitution*, 27 July 1917.

78. "Homebred Golfers Score a Triumph," *New York Times*, 29 July 1917.

79. O. B. Keeler, *The Boys' Life of Bobby Jones* (Canada: Sleeping Bear Press, 2002), p. 92.

80. The *Atlanta Constitution* reported Jones's score as one stroke lower. "Home Breds and Scots Win Golf Matches," *Atlanta Constitution*, 29 July 1917.

81. "Homebred Golfers Score a Triumph," *New York Times*, 29 July 1917.

82. Jones and Keeler, *Down the Fairway*, 79.

83. "Consider Formation of Golf Team This Spring," *Daily Princetonian*, 2 February 1918.

84. We have tracked Herron's campus activities through Princeton's student newspaper, the *Daily Princetonian*, https://theprince.princeton.edu/. We have also benefited from other student documents retrieved for us by archivists at Princeton's Seeley G. Mudd Manuscript Library regarding Herron's time at Princeton and shortly afterward (including his military record, family formation, and other personal data).

85. E. Ellsworth Giles, "Herron Third National Champion Accredited to Oakmont Golf Club," *Pittsburgh Gazette Times*, 25 August 1919.

86. "Announce the Results of Senior Statistics," *Daily Princetonian*, 20 April 1918.

87. "Byers-Herron Deadlocked in Medal Round: Both Turn in Cards of 162 for Qualifying Round of Red Cross Tourney at Allegheny Country Club: Scores Are Rather High," *Pittsburgh Post*, 21 June 1918.

88. Ibid.

89. "Great Golf in Red = X Tourney: Graham, Oliver, Herron and Crookston Left in Title Flight at Allegheny," *Pittsburgh Post*, 22 June 1918.

90. "Shooting Great Golf, S. Davidson Herron Wins Allegheny Tourney," *Pittsburgh Sunday Post*, 23 June 1918.

91. Ibid.

92. "Boches" was a derisive French word used to refer to German soldiers in World Wars I and II. "Bedford Springs Golf Tourney Next on the Schedule: Usual Large Entry Certain for Fixture," *Pittsburgh Sunday Post*, 4 August 1918.

CHAPTER 8. "AN OPPORTUNITY TO WITNESS THE GAME": THE NEW SPECTATORS OF WARTIME GOLF

1. Stephen R. Lowe, *Sir Walter and Mr. Jones: Walter Hagen, Bobby Jones, and the Rise of American Golf* (Chelsea, Mich.: Sleeping Bear Press, 2000), 63.

2. Joe Davis, "Golf Stars Break Sabbath Rule to Play for Red Cross," *Chicago Daily Tribune*, 18 May 1918.

3. "'Little Bob' Jones Defeats Champion," *Atlanta Constitution*, 23 May 1918.

4. Joe Davis, "Red Cross Golf Today Enlists Stars of Game," *Chicago Daily Tribune*, 16 June 1918. In actuality, Jones grew notably in both height and strength but not necessarily in weight in the three years following his appearance at Merion at age fourteen.

5. Joe Davis, "Indian Hill Women Win First Contest of Series for Cup," *Chicago Daily Tribune*, 15 June 1918.

6. Joe Davis, "Miss Stirling and Adair Win Red Cross Golf Match," *Chicago Daily Tribune*, 17 June 1918; Lochinvar, "Western Department," *American Golfer* 20, 3 (July 1918): 813–814.

7. Robert T. Jones Jr. and O. B. Keeler, *Down the Fairway* (London: A & C Black, 1990), p. 78.

8. Joe Davis, "Fore, Fore, Fore! Golfing 'Tips' By Hutchinson," *Chicago Daily Tribune*, 2 July 1918.

9. "Everything Set for Big Golf Meet Here on July 4th," *Atlanta Constitution*, 1 July 1918.

10. "Bob and Perry to Play Chicago Stars for the Red Cross," *Atlanta Constitution*, 9 June 1918; "Golf Match Details Arranged," *Atlanta Constitution*, 15 June 1918.

11. "Every Atlantan Invited to See Golf Stars Play," *Atlanta Constitution*, 16 June 1917.

12. "Big Gallery Sees Local Golfers Down Westerners," *Atlanta Constitution*, 5 July 1918.

13. O. B. Keeler, *The Boys' Life of Bobby Jones* (Canada: Sleeping Bear Press, 2002), 89.

14. Jones and Keeler, *Down the Fairway*, 76.

15. "Alexa Stirling, Golf Champion, to Play for the Red Cross," *Atlanta Constitution*, 20 February 1918.

16. Joe Davis, "Shots on the Links," *Chicago Daily Tribune*, 5 June 1918.

17. Jones and Keeler, *Down the Fairway*, 76.

18. "Miss Rosenthal on Winning Side Again," *New York Times*, 21 July 1918.

19. "Stirling-Adair Lost to Rosenthal-Jones," *Atlanta Constitution*, 25 July 1918.

20. "Miss Rosenthal Gets Card of 84," *Chicago Daily Tribune*, 28 July 1918.

21. Bunker Hill, "New England Department," *American Golfer* 20, 5 (September 1918): 30.

22. Alexa Stirling Fraser, "The Most Unforgettable Character I've Met," *Reader's Digest*, April 1960, 57.

23. Bunker Hill, "New England Department," *American Golfer* 20, 5 (September 1918): 31.

24. Special to the *New York Times*, "Golf Stars at Ekwanok," *New York Times*, 1 August 1918.

25. "Jones Lowers Golf Mark," *New York Times*, 3 August 1918. Perry Adair celebrated his

nineteenth birthday at Ekwanok, and Bob Jones humorously recounted the "celebration" years later. "I remember Perry had a birthday at Ekwanok and got a pipe for a birthday present and smoked it; the first time he ever had smoked. Gosh—he was sick! And when I say sick, I mean sick as our British cousins mean sick, if you get what I mean." Jones and Keeler, *Down the Fairway*, 77.

26. "Around the 19th Hole," *American Golfer* 20, 5 (September 1918): 66; "Youngsters Take Part in Red Cross Match," *Louisville Courier-Journal*, 12 August 1918.

27. "Social Items," *Atlanta Constitution*, 18 August 1918.

28. "Jones and Adair Defeat Evans and Edwards," *Atlanta Constitution*, 23 August 1918.

29. Lochinvar, "Western Department," *American Golfer* 20, 5 (September 1918): 49–50.

30. "Around the 19th Hole: What Golf Is Doing in the War," *American Golfer* 20, 4 (August 1918): 908.

31. Jones and Keeler, *Down the Fairway*, 78.

32. "Evans and Jones Take Golf Match," *New York Times*, 15 September 1918.

33. "Chick Evans and Bobbie Jones Beaten by Two Pros on Scarsdale Links," *New York Times*, 16 September 1918.

34. "Evans and Jones Beaten," *New York Times*, 18 September 1918.

35. "Evans-Jones Beaten by Pros," *Chicago Daily Tribune*, 18 September 1918.

36. Evans shot 73, Marston 77, and Anderson 78. The match raised $3,000 for the Red Cross. Special to the *New York Times*, "Jones Sets Record in Red Cross Golf," *New York Times*, 20 September 1918.

37. Joe Davis, "Tellier and McNamara Beat Evans and Jones," *Chicago Daily Tribune*, 21 September 1918.

38. "Evans and Jones Beaten," *New York Times*, 22 September 1918.

39. Hazard, "Eastern Department," *American Golfer* 20, 6 (October 1918): 101.

40. Ibid.

41. Jones and Keeler, *Down the Fairway*, 82.

CHAPTER 9. A GENTLEMAN LABORER: DAVE HERRON FINDS HIS GAME (1919)

1. "Pittsburgh Golfers Lay Plans for Great Tourney: Oakmont Links to Be Improved for Big Event," *Pittsburgh Sunday Post*, 26 January 1919.

2. Ibid.; "Officials Arrive to Complete Golf Tourney Details," *Pittsburgh Post*, 12 August 1919; "Oakmont Course Ready for Tourney," *New York Times*, 6 July 1919.

3. "Comments on Current Events in Sport," *New York Times*, 11 August 1919; "Western Pennsylvania Golf Association Meets Thursday: To Shape Plans for Banner Year in Local History," *Pittsburgh Sunday Post*, 20 April 1919.

4. "Pittsburgh Golfers Lay Plans for Great Tourney: Oakmont Links to Be Improved for Big Event," *Pittsburgh Sunday Post*, 26 January 1919.

5. Ibid.

6. "Officials Arrive to Complete Golf Tourney Details," *Pittsburgh Post*, 12 August 1919.

7. "Golfing Talent of the Country Meets at Oakmont in Trial Matches Preparatory to Tournament Play," *Pittsburgh Post*, 15 August 1919.

8. "Oakmont Course Ready for Tourney," *New York Times*, 6 July 1919. Interestingly, the

columnist also revealed that in 1917 the USGA was not entirely satisfied with the course's level of difficulty when it awarded the Amateur to Oakmont. "Two years ago, the United States Golf Association awarded the title event to the Oakmont Country Club in Pittsburgh. The course at that time was not all that the officials desired, and it was the intention to do as much work as possible before the tournament was held.... Since that time, however, the club has made many improvements.... To the new bunkers that were installed a few years ago many more have been added."

9. "Oakmont Course Hardest Test That Title Field Has Ever Faced. Only Finest Golf Will Win Out Here in National Event," *Pittsburgh Post*, 15 August 1919.

10. "Comments on Current Events in Sport," *New York Times*, 11 August 1919.

11. "Officials Arrive to Complete Golf Tourney Details," *Pittsburgh Post*, 12 August 1919; "Star Golfers Arrive Today for Tourney," *Pittsburgh Gazette Times*, 12 August 1919.

12. "Top-Notch Field for Oakmont Golf," *New York Times*, 13 August 1919.

13. "Comments on Current Events in Sport," *New York Times*, 11 August 1919.

14. "Golf Stars Will Meet at Siwanoy," *New York Times*, 3 August 1919.

15. "Plan More Team Matches on Links," *New York Times*, 24 March 1918; "Promotion for Ouimet," *New York Times*, 6 July 1918; "Golf Stars Will Meet at Siwanoy," *New York Times*, 3 August 1919.

16. "Golfing World Looking Forward to National Tourney: National Tourney Adds Interest on Many Local Links," *Pittsburgh Sunday Post*, 3 August 1919; "Golf Stars Will Meet at Siwanoy," *New York Times*, 3 August 1919.

17. "Officials Arrive to Complete Golf Tourney Details," *Pittsburgh Post*, 11 August 1919. The *New York Times* also flagged Bob Jones for special consideration. "Golf Stars Will Meet at Siwanoy," *New York Times*, 3 August 1919.

18. "Oakmont Awaits Big Meet: All of Nation's Amateur Stars Will Take Part," *Pittsburgh Gazette Times*, 10 August 1919; "What Chances Do PA Pitt's Golfers Have?," *Pittsburgh Gazette Times*, 9 August 1919.

19. Walter C. Hagen, "Big Golf Week Stage Now Set," *Atlanta Constitution*, 18 August 1919.

20. "What Chances Do PA Pitt's Golfers Have?," *Pittsburgh Gazette Times*, 9 August 1919.

21. "Golfers Look Forward to West Penn Title Tournaments. Open and Amateur Events Carded for Field Club Course. Record Breaking Field Will Compete in First Local Tournaments Played since War. Event Preliminary to National Title Play Here Next August," *Pittsburgh Post*, 29 June 1919.

22. "Oakmont Links Excellent for Golf Tourney," *Pittsburgh Gazette Times*, 7 August 1919. E. Ellsworth Giles, "Giles Reviews Chances of Golfers, by Districts in Tourney at Oakmont," *Pittsburgh Gazette Times*, 9 August 1919; E. Ellsworth Giles, "Fownes, Byers, Herron, Pittsburgh's Hopes in Title Play, Says Giles," *Pittsburgh Gazette Times*, 10 August 1919.

23. "Pittsburgh Golfers Lay Plans for Great Tourney," *Pittsburgh Sunday Post*, 26 January 1919.

24. "Western Pennsylvania Golf Association Meets Thursday: To Shape Plans for Banner Year in Local History," *Pittsburgh Post*, 20 April 1919.

25. "Golfing World Looking Forward to National Tourney: National Tourney Adds Interest on Many Local Links," *Pittsburgh Post*, 3 August 1919.

CHAPTER 10. THE "GOLDEN TORNADO" AND THE SUMMER OF 1919

1. Nationally, prohibition had not fully begun yet, but the sale of hard liquor was prohibited in New Orleans starting July 1, 1919. Robert T. Jones Jr. and O. B. Keeler, *Down the Fairway* (London: A & C Black, 1990), 82.
2. "2 Young Atlantans Center of Interest at New Orleans Club," *Atlanta Constitution*, 22 June 1919.
3. Ibid.
4. "Dixie Golf Classic Open This Morning; Sets Course Record," *New Orleans Times-Picayune*, 24 June 1919.
5. Ibid.
6. "Bush-Whitney Defeat Jones-Adair 2 and 1 in Four Ball Match." *New Orleans Times-Picayune*, 23 June 1919.
7. Leslie Rawlings, "Sports: Bobby Jones Third—Adair Fifth: Whitney and Knowles Tie for Low Score in Qualifying Round," *Atlanta Constitution*, 25 June 1919.
8. "Whitney Is Tied with Pensacolan in Golf Tourney," *New Orleans Times-Picayune* 25 June 1919.
9. "Atlanta Boy Golfers Get Back on Stride; Bobby Pulls Sensation," *Atlanta Constitution*, 26 June 1919. One might suspect this story as apocryphal, but Stephen Lowe has done the requisite research to confirm its authenticity. According to Lowe: "George Turpee, who refereed the event, looked at the lie and decided that under the existing rules, Jones was not entitled to relief. Jones hacked the shoe and ball out of the wheelbarrow, both landed on the green, and the ball rolled free. . . . Jones later said that the wheelbarrow episode inspired him to learn all the rules of golf, so that he would never again be caught ignorant about them." Lowe, *Sir Walter and Mr. Jones*, 79, 346 nn 42–43.
10. "Choices Run True in Golf Tourney; Good Card Today," *New Orleans Times-Picayune*, 26 June 1919; Leslie Rawlings, "Sports: Perry Adair Eliminated: 'Bobby' Jones Fights to Sight of Victory but Team Mate Loses," *Atlanta Constitution*, 27 June 1919.
11. Leslie Rawlings, "Sports: Perry Adair Eliminated," *Atlanta Constitution*, 27 June 1919.
12. Ibid.
13. Ibid.; "Two New Orleanians Reach Semi-Finals in Link Contest," *New Orleans Times-Picayune*, 27 June 1919.
14. Leslie Rawlings, "Sports: Nelson Whitney Beats Bobby Jones: Championship Title Lost by Youngster; Jacoby Beats Bouden," *Atlanta Constitution*, 28 June 1919; "Two New Orleanians Reach Semi-Finals in Link Contest," *New Orleans Times-Picayune*, 27 June 1919.
15. Rawlings, "Sports: Nelson Whitney Beats Bobby Jones," *Atlanta Constitution*, 28 June 1919; "Whitney and Jacoby Reach Finals in Big Golf Classic," *New Orleans Times-Picayune*, 28 June 1919.
16. Ibid.
17. *United States Golf Association: Year Book*, August 1920, https://books.google.com/books?id=H10QAAAAYAAJ&printsec=frontcover&source=gbs_ge_summary_r&cad=0#v=onepage&q&f=false.
18. Special to the *New York Times*, "Americans Win at Golf," *New York Times*, 26 July 1919.
19. "American Golf Team Outplays Canada's Best," *Chicago Daily Tribune*, 26 July 1919.

20. Special to the *New York Times,* "Americans Win at Golf," *New York Times*, 26 July 1919.

21. "Bob Jones Wins Twice in Canada," *Atlanta Georgian,* 26 July 1919; Special to the *New York Times,* "Americans Win at Golf," *New York Times,* 26 July 1919.

22. Special to the *New York Times,* "Americans Win at Golf," *New York Times,* 26 July 1919.

23. Coastwise, "Eastern Department," *American Golfer* 21, 11 (September 1919): 900.

24. *United States Golf Association: Year Book,* August 1920.

25. Armour was also famous for strangling a German tank commander to death with his bare hands during the war.

26. Steve Eubanks, *To Win and Die in Dixie: The Birth of the Modern Golf Swing and the Mysterious Death of Its Creator* (New York: Ballantine Books, 2010), 120–121.

27. Willie Ogg, the professional at East Lake, shot 80–78 for 158. And H. C. Fownes II, Dave Herron's closest friend, shot 84–81 for a 165. "Atlanta Player by Great Golf Leads for Canuck Title," *Chicago Daily Tribune,* 30 July 1919.

28. "Atlantans Set Pace in Canada," *Atlanta Georgian,* 30 July 1919.

29. "J. Douglas Edgar Wins Canadian Golf Championship," *Atlanta Georgian,* 31 July 1919.

30. Tiger Woods fell one stroke short of tying this record in the 2000 U.S. Open at Pebble Beach. See Steve Schlossman and Kari Thomas, "'Bullet Proof': Tiger Woods' 2000 U.S. Open," *The Golf* (Spring 2020): 28–31 and *The Golf* (Summer 2020): 24–27. See also Steven Schlossman and Emma Slayton, "By the Numbers," *Through the Green* (March 2022): 2–7.

31. O. B. Keeler, "Here's New Canadian Golf Champ," *Atlanta Georgian,* 31 July 1919.

32. Ibid.

PART III. THE 1919 U.S. AMATEUR CHAMPIONSHIP AT OAKMONT

1. Led by the American Federation of Labor (AFL), steelworkers in Colorado, Illinois, West Virginia, Ohio, and New York walked off their jobs, forcing almost half of the nation's mills to shut down production. The United Mine Workers' national strike just a few months later would be even bigger in size. For more on the Great Steel Strike, see Ryan C. Brown, *Pittsburgh and the Great Steel Strike of 1919* (Charleston, S.C.: History Press, 2019); David Brody, *Labor in Crisis: The Steel Strike of 1919* (Philadelphia: Lippincott, 1965); Leon Fink, *The Long Gilded Age: American Capitalism and the Lessons of a New World Order* (Philadelphia: University of Pennsylvania Press, 2014).

2. Assaults perpetrated by whites against Blacks were covered by the press but were often inaccurately dismissed as "race riots." In reality, these attacks were almost always targeted and premeditated. Armed vigilantes, in both the North and South, urban and rural, sometimes aligned with the KKK and other times not, attacked, maimed, and murdered innocent Black men and teens, including those who had served in the military. See Ann Hagedorn, *Savage Peace: Hope and Fear in America, 1919* (New York: Simon & Schuster, 2007).

3. William Elliott Hazelgrove, *Madam President: The Secret Presidency of Edith Wilson* (Washington, D.C.: Regnery, 2016).

4. Nancy Bristow, *American Pandemic: The Lost Worlds of the 1918 Influenza Epidemic* (Oxford: Oxford University Press, 2017).

5. University of Michigan Center for the History of Medicine and Michigan Publishing, University of Michigan Library, https://www.influenzaarchive.org/cities/city-pittsburgh.html#.

CHAPTER 11. "TRUE TO THE ULTIMATE WIGGLE": DISCOVERING OAKMONT

1. "Evans Is Due Today. Champion Coming Early for Practice on Oakmont Course before Title Tournament Opens Saturday," *Pittsburgh Press*, 12 August 1919.

2. E. Ellsworth Giles, "U.S.G.A., Not Oakmont Club, Responsible for Any Tourney Shortcomings, Writes Giles," *Pittsburgh Gazette Times*, 7 September 1919; "Banquet at Oakmont for Herron, New King of Links: Local Golfer Will Be Feted for Conquest: Club, Whose Course Was Scene of Victory Last Month, Plans Social Affair in Champion's Honor—Reforms in National Body," *Pittsburgh Gazette Times*, 7 September 1919.

3. "Star Golfers Arrive Today for Tourney," *Pittsburgh Gazette Times*, 11 August 1919.

4. Fownes, Byers, Herron, and Ormiston, in that order, topped locals' predictions about the most likely qualifiers from Western Pennsylvania, and they were all Oakmont members. "Officials Arrive to Complete Golf Tourney Details," *Pittsburgh Post*, 12 August 1919; "Star Golfers Arrive Today for Tourney," *Pittsburgh Gazette Times*, 11 August 1919; E. Ellsworth Giles, "Oakmont Course Not Yet Tested by Out-of-Town Tourney Entrants," *Pittsburgh Gazette Times*, 11 August 1919.

5. "Golfing World Looking Forward to National Tourney: National Tourney Adds Interest on Many Local Links," *Pittsburgh Sunday Post*, 3 August 1919.

6. See John Barry, *The Great Influenza: The Story of the Deadliest Pandemic in History* (New York: Penguin, 2005).

7. "Officials Arrive to Complete Golf Tourney Details," *Pittsburgh Post*, 12 August 1919.

8. E. Ellsworth Giles, "Chick Evans, Proverbial Late Arrival, Always 'on Time' at Finish," *Pittsburgh Gazette Times*, 15 August 1919.

9. "Ouimet Arrives for National Tourney: Praises Oakmont Course After a Practice Round," *Pittsburgh Gazette Times*, 15 August 1919; "Golf Title Play Today," *New York Times*, 16 August 1919.

10. E. Ellsworth Giles, "Chick Evans, Proverbial Late Arrival, Always 'on Time' at Finish," *Pittsburgh Gazette Times*, 15 August 1919.

11. Harry C. Smith, "Golfers Pronounce Oakmont Club Course Best in Land: Links Afford Real Test, Stars Tell 'Runner-Up,'" *Pittsburgh Gazette Times*, 17 August 1919.

12. "Chick Evans Will Start Qualifying Round for Today without Practice; Great Field Assembled for National Play," *Pittsburgh Post*, 16 August 1919.

13. Harry Keck, "Sporting Chit-Chat," *Pittsburgh Gazette Times*, 16 August 1919.

14. "Chick Evans Will Start Qualifying Round for Today without Practice," *Pittsburgh Post*, 16 August 1919.

15. Angus Perkerson, "Cups and Tees," *Atlanta Journal*, 8 August 1919.

16. *Atlanta Constitution*, 9 August 1919; Morgan Blake, "Sport Barrage," *Atlanta Journal*, 14 August 1919.

17. "George Adair Must Be Getting Well, According to This," *Atlanta Georgian*, 25 July 1919.

18. As best we can determine, O. B. Keeler was not at Oakmont in August 1919. Rather, Walter Wilkes, the *Atlanta Georgian*'s tennis writer, substituted for him as the newspaper's on-site journalist in Pittsburgh. It should be noted that Mark Frost, in *The Grand Slam* (New York: Good Comma Ink, 2005), 100–109, claims not only that Keeler was present but that

he was Bob Jones's roommate at the Schenley Hotel, where they drank together and reflected on golf's mysteries. We know of no empirical evidence to support this claim. In fact, our research indicates that Keeler did not accompany Jones to Pittsburgh in August 1919, nor did he assume his central role as Jones's confidante and raconteur until 1920, after he left (or was pushed out of) his job at the *Atlanta Georgian* and joined the *Atlanta Journal*. Although Keeler's name remained on the *Atlanta Georgian*'s sports section masthead until near the end of 1919, he played only a minimal role in its sports reporting during those last several months. When he did write for the *Atlanta Georgian* it was more likely to be about college football than golf. By his own account, Keeler spent most of 1919 learning to fly airplanes (and writing about the experience) in addition to working for several months in Los Angeles as a publicity director for Hollywood movies. See O. B. Keeler, *The Autobiography of a Golfer* (New York: Greenwood, 1925), 208–210.

19. Walter P. Wilkes, "Bob Goes Great at Oakmont," *Atlanta Georgian*, 14 August 1919; "Southern Golfer Leads at Oakmont," *New York Times*, 17 August 1919; Harry C. Smith, "Golfers Pronounce Oakmont Club Course Best in Land,'" *Pittsburgh Gazette Times*, 17 August 1919.

20. "Ouimet Qualifies Despite Sickness. Former Champion Gives Fine Example of Pluck in Play for Amateur Golf Honors. Triple Tie for Medal. Manion, Herron, and Tewkesbury Turn in Cards of 158. Byers and Kirkby Fall," *New York Times*, 19 August 1919.

21. Walter P. Wilkes, "Bob Goes Great at Oakmont," *Atlanta Georgian*, 14 August 1919. In a letter shortly before his death, Jones wrote to historian Herbert Warren Wind: "Without a doubt, the fastest greens I ever putted were those at Oakmont." Quoted in Stephen R. Lowe, *Sir Walter and Mr. Jones: Walter Hagen, Bobby Jones, and the Rise of American Golf* (Chelsea, Mich.: Sleeping Bear Press, 2000), 80.

22. "Bobby Jones Shoots 4 Strokes below Par and Breaks Record," *Atlanta Constitution*, 14 August 1919.

23. Ibid. See Adam Lazarus and Steve Schlossman, *Chasing Greatness: Johnny Miller, Arnold Palmer, and the Miracle at Oakmont* (New York: Penguin, 2010), 260–272.

24. "Golfing Talent of the Country Meets at Oakmont in Trial Matches Preparatory to Tournament Play," *Pittsburgh Post*, 15 August 1919.

25. "Atlanta Boy to Show Oakmont Crowds Class," *Atlanta Constitution*, 15 August 1919; Walter Wilkes, "Large Crowd Watches Atlantans in Match," *Atlanta Georgian*, 15 August 1919.

26. "Golfing Talent of the Country Meets at Oakmont in Trial Matches Preparatory to Tournament Play," *Pittsburgh Post*, 15 August 1919.

27. Ibid.

28. "Chick Evans Will Start Qualifying Round for Today without Practice; Great Field Assembled for National Play," *Pittsburgh Post*, 16 August 1919.

29. Walter Hagen, "Monday's Rounds Will Show Real Positions in Amateur Tourney, *Atlanta Constitution*, 17 August 1919; Walter Hagen, "Ouimet and Evans to Furnish Big Feature of Tournament Today," *Atlanta Constitution*, 20 August 1919.

30. Beyond Jones and Adair, Jesse Sweetser, one month Jones's junior, was the other young player considered to have the most potential to upset the Big Four, based largely on his defeat of Ned Sawyer the week before in New York. Sweetser arrived late for the championship, but

an 84 on his first round at Oakmont on Friday stoked confidence that he would still be able to compete on equal terms with his Atlanta age peers.

31. E. Ellsworth Giles, "Good Scoring Features in Trophy Match," *Pittsburgh Gazette Times*, 18 August 1919.

32. Grantland Rice, "Long Grind for National Golf Title Begins at Nine This Morning: 87 Round Enough to Place Golfer among Survivors," *Pittsburgh Post*, 16 August 1919.

33. Special to the *New York Times*, "Real Test on Tomorrow," *New York Times*, 17 August 1919.

34. Harry Keck, "Sporting Chit-Chat," *Pittsburgh Gazette Times*, 16 August 1919.

35. "141 Star Amateurs on Edge for Championship Contest; Evans to Arrive This Morning," *Pittsburgh Gazette Times*, 16 August 1919.

36. "Chick Evans Will Start Qualifying Round Today Without Practice; Great Field Assembled for National Play," *Pittsburgh Post*, 16 August 1919.

37. Special to the *New York Times*, "Real Test on Tomorrow," *New York Times*, 17 August 1919.

38. "Southern Golfer Leads at Oakmont," *New York Times*, 17 August 1919.

39. E. Ellsworth Giles, "Fownes, Byers, Herron, Pittsburgh's Hopes in Title Play, Says Giles," *Pittsburgh Gazette Times*, 10 August 1919.

CHAPTER 12. THE TERROR OF OAKMONT

1. "Chick Evans Will Start Qualifying Round for Today without Practice," *Pittsburgh Post*, 16 August 1919.

2. Grantland Rice, "Tales of a Wayside Tee," *Atlanta Journal*, 10 August 1919.

3. "Golfer Who Started," *Pittsburgh Sunday Post*, 17 August 1919.

4. Special to the *New York Times*, "Real Test on Tomorrow," *New York Times*, 17 August 1919.

5. "Louis Jacoby Leader in First Elimination Round of National Amateur Golf Tourney," *Pittsburgh Gazette Times*, 17 August 1919; "Golfer Who Started," *Pittsburgh Sunday Post*, 17 August 1919.

6. Grantland Rice, "Louis Jacoby, Southerner, Makes Low Score Saturday," *Atlanta Journal*, 17 August 1919.

7. Charles (Chick) Evans Jr., *Chick Evans' Golf Book: The Story of the Sporting Battles of the Greatest of All Amateur Golfers* (New York: Thomas E. Wilson,1921), 276.

8. "Golfer Who Started," *Pittsburgh Sunday Post*, 17 August 1919.

9. Grantland Rice, "Tales of a Wayside Tee," *Atlanta Journal*, 17 August 1919.

10. "Golfer Who Started," *Pittsburgh Sunday Post*, 17 August 1919.

11. Ibid.

12. Special to the *New York Times*, "Real Test on Tomorrow," *New York Times*, 17 August 1919.

13. "Saturday on the Links," *Pittsburgh Sunday Post*, 17 August 1919.

14. Angus Perkerson, "Cups and Tees," *Atlanta Journal*, 18 August 1919.

15. "Louis Jacoby Leader in First Elimination Round of National Amateur Golf Tourney: Eighty-Nine Top Score," *Pittsburgh Gazette Times*, 17 August 1919.

16. E. Ellsworth Giles, "Bold Golfers Play Despite Dripping Skies," *Pittsburgh Gazette Times*, 17 August 1919.

17. "Elimination of P. Adair Big Shock," *Atlanta Journal*, 17 August 1919.

18. Angus Perkerson, "Cups and Tees," *Atlanta Journal*, 18 August 1919; Walter P. Wilkes, "Reviews Golf Play Saturday," *Atlanta Georgian*, 18 August 1919.

19. "Third Member Shows Worth of Atlanta's Young Golfing Trio: Jones Starred Wednesday, Hickey Thursday and Adair Captured Honors for Friday's Practice Play—Bobby Given Wrist Watch," *Atlanta Constitution*, 16 August 1919; Gene Hinton, "Atlanta's Chance Good for Big Title in National Event: Alexa Stirling Is Only One to Hold National Crown—Up to the Male Element to Come through with Victory Now," *Atlanta Constitution*, 16 August 1919.

20. "Today's Grind Feared by Contestants—171 Will Qualify, Evans Believes—Sweetser and Tewkesbury Turn in 73s in Practice, Best for the Day," *Pittsburgh Post*, 18 August 1919.

21. "Comment on Current Events in Sports," *New York Times*, 18 August 1919.

22. "Today's Grind Feared by Contestants—171 Will Qualify, Evans Believes—Sweetser and Tewkesbury Turn in 73s in Practice, Best for the Day," *Pittsburgh Post*, 18 August 1919.

23. Walter C. Hagen, "Big Golf Week Stage Now Set," *Atlanta Constitution*, 18 August 1919; Walter C. Hagen, "Hagen Picks Evans to Win Tourney: Open Champion Dopes 'Chick' as Winner of Oakmont Tournament," *Atlanta Constitution*, 19 August 1919.

24. Special to the *New York Times*, "Princeton and Oakmont Pairs Tie for American Golfer Trophy: American Golfer Play Ends in Tie," *New York Times*, 18 August 1919.

25. E. Ellsworth Giles, "Top Qualifying Score Highest in a Decade: 171 Strokes Six Worse Than at Merion in 1916," *Pittsburgh Gazette Times*, 19 August 1919.

26. Special to the *New York Times*, "Princeton and Oakmont Pairs Tie for American Golfer Trophy: American Golfer Play Ends in Tie," *New York Times*, 18 August 1919; "Two More Georgians Spring into Golf Fame at Oakmont Club Links," *Atlanta Constitution*, 18 August 1919.

27. "Stage Is Set for Tourney: Record Gallery Expected at Oakmont Tomorrow for First Qualifying Amateur Golf Round," *Pittsburgh Press*, 15 August 1919; "Richard Hickey Next Atlanta Boy to Show Oakmont Crowds Class: Large Galleries Followed Boy Golfers and Were Given Exhibition by 'Bobby's' Teammate," *Atlanta Constitution*, 15 August 1919.

CHAPTER 13. SURPRISES, UPSETS, AND JUST HOW SICK IS FRANCIS OUIMET?

1. "Many Golfers Fall by Way in Champion Tournament at Oakmont," *Pittsburgh Press*, 17 August 1919.

2. Walter Hagen, "Big Golf Week Stage Now Set: No Lucky Golfer Can Get Away with Anything Like Poor Golf on Oakmont Course," *Atlanta Constitution*, 18 August 1919.

3. Eight men tied at 172 and had to play off for the last two spots in the field for match play. Walter P. Wilkes, "Jones Meets Manion in Match Play Today: Three Tied for First Honors in Qualifying Round Monday—Bobby Follows Trio by Turning in Card of 159," *Atlanta Georgian*, 19 August 1919; Walter Hagen, "Open Champion Dopes 'Chick' as Winner of Oakmont Tournament: Youthful Atlantan's Stock Rose Many Points by His Brilliant Play in Monday's Qualifying Rounds—Bobby Is Fighting," *Atlanta Constitution*, 19 August 1919.

4. Hagen, "Open Champion Dopes 'Chick' as Winner of Oakmont Tournament," *Atlanta Constitution*, 19 August 1919.

5. Grantland Rice, "R. Jones, Whitney and Jacoby, Three Dixie Aces, Qualify: Match Play Begins Today at Oakmont," *Atlanta Journal*, 19 August 1919.

6. Walter P. Wilkes, "Jones Meets Manion in Match Play Today: Three Tied for First Honors in Qualifying Round Monday—Bobby Follows Trio by Turning in Card of 159," *Atlanta Georgian*, 19 August 1919.

7. Walter Hagen, "Big Golf Week Stage Now Set: No Lucky Golfer Can Get Away with Anything Like Poor Golf on Oakmont Course," *Atlanta Constitution*, 18 August 1919.

8. E. E. Giles calculated the average scores by hole for the first qualifying round. The field needed an average of 7.25 strokes to complete No. 12. E. Ellsworth Giles, "Good Scoring Features in Trophy Match: Many Players Participating in American Golfer Contest," *Pittsburgh Gazette Times*, 18 August 1919.

9. "Bobby Jones Fourth in Qualifying Round of National Tourney: Manion, Herron and Tewkesbury in Triple Tie for Low Medal—Jones Paired with Manion Today," *Atlanta Constitution*, 19 August 1919; Angus Perkerson, "Cups and Tees," *Atlanta Journal*, 19 August 1919.

10. Perkerson, "Cups and Tees," *Atlanta Journal*, 19 August 1919.

11. Angus Perkerson, "Cups and Tees," *Atlanta Journal*, 11 August 1919.

12. Angus Perkerson, "Cups and Tees," *Atlanta Journal*, 18 August 1919.

13. "Third Member Shows Worth of Atlanta's Young Golfing Trio: Jones Starred Wednesday, Hickey Thursday and Adair Captured Honors for Friday's Practice Play—Bobby Given Wrist Watch," *Atlanta Constitution*, 16 August 1919; "Perry Adair Eliminated at Oakmont: Four Atlantans Will Start in Tournament for Big Title Monday," *Atlanta Constitution*, 17 August 1919; Perkerson, "Cups and Tees," *Atlanta Journal*, 18 August 1919.

14. Walter Hagen, "Open Champion Dopes 'Chick' as Winner of Oakmont Tournament. Youthful Atlantan's Stock Rose Many Points by His Brilliant Play in Monday's Qualifying Rounds—Bobby Is Fighting," *Atlanta Constitution*, 19 August 1919.

15. Ibid.

16. Grantland Rice speculated that if Ouimet, despite his health, and Evans both qualified, they would meet in match play because only a few at Oakmont could "cudgel either out of the tournament before they meet." Grantland Rice, "Tales of a Wayside Tee," *Atlanta Journal*, 17 August 1919.

17. Grantland Rice, "R. Jones, Whitney and Jacoby, Three Dixie Aces, Qualify: Match Play Begins Today at Oakmont," *Atlanta Journal*, 19 August 1919; "'Chick' Evans Is Picked to Win at Oakmont," *Atlanta Georgian*, 19 August 1919.

18. E. Ellsworth Giles, "Top Qualifying Score Highest in a Decade: 172 Six Strokes Worse Than at Merion in 1916," *Pittsburgh Gazette Times*, 19 August 1919.

19. Walter Hagen, "Open Champion Dopes 'Chick' as Winner of Oakmont Tournament," *Atlanta Constitution*, 19 August 1919.

20. "Play Resumed in Big Event after Two Years' Lay Off Due to War, Stars Entered," *Atlanta Georgian*, 17 August 1919.

21. Walter Hagen, "Open Champion Dopes 'Chick' as Winner of Oakmont Tournament," *Atlanta Constitution*, 19 August 1919.

22. "Six Local Players Still in Running for National Title," *Pittsburgh Gazette Times*, 19 August 1919; *Pittsburgh Press*, 19 August 1919. "With four Pittsburghers still in the tournament, hope for bringing the championship to this city is bright.... Much is also expected from Davidson Herron."

NOTES TO CHAPTER THIRTEEN | 321

23. Walter Hagen, "Open Champion Dopes 'Chick' as Winner of Oakmont Tournament," *Atlanta Constitution*, 19 August 1919.

24. Walter Hagen, "Ouimet and Evans to Furnish Big Feature of Tournament Today: Excellent Golf, under Favorable Conditions, Was Played on Oakmont Course during Tuesday's Matches," *Atlanta Constitution*, 20 August 1919.

25. John G. Anderson, "Nerve Strain Responsible for Upsets in Oakmont Golf Tournament: New York Expert Tells Why Untried Youngsters Stood Fire and Experienced Veterans Cracked under Stress of Championship Play," *Pittsburgh Gazette Times*, 26 August 1919.

26. Michael Trostel, "100 Years Ago: The U.S. Open Stops for World War I," *USGA*, 25 April 2017, https://www.usopen.com/2017/articles/100-years-ago-the-u-s--open-stops-for-world-war-i.html.

27. Francis Ouimet, "Bob Gardner Is Praised by Star Golfer," *Atlanta Georgian*, 20 August 1919.

28. E. Ellsworth Giles, "Top Qualifying Score Highest in a Decade: 172 Six Strokes Worse Than at Merion in 1916," *Pittsburgh Gazette Times*, 19 August 1919.

29. Harry Keck, "Sporting Chit-Chat: The National Golf Tourney," *Pittsburgh Gazette Times*, 16 August 1919.

30. Angus Perkerson, "Cups and Tees," *Atlanta Journal*, 26 August 1919; "Big Golf Match on at Oakmont Country Club," *Pittsburgh Press*, 16 August 1919.

31. Walter Hagen, "Monday's Rounds Will Show Real Positions in Amateur Tourney: National Open Champion," *Atlanta Constitution*, 17 August 1919.

32. Grantland Rice, "Tales of a Wayside Tee," *Atlanta Journal*, 17 August 1919.

33. Angus Perkerson, "Cups and Tees," *Atlanta Journal*, 10 August 1919.

34. Walter P. Wilkes, "Jones Meets Gardiner [*sic*]; Ouimet Plays Evans: Crack Golfers Clash over Oakmont Course Today—'Little Bob' Defeated J. S. Manion Tuesday," *Atlanta Georgian*, 20 August 1919.

35. Grantland Rice, "Bob Jones Faces Gardner, and Evans Faces Ouimet Today: Bob Drops Mannion [*sic*] after a Hot Match," *Atlanta Journal*, 20 August 1919.

36. Angus Perkerson, "Cups and Tees," *Atlanta Journal*, 20 August 1919.

37. Walter P. Wilkes, "Jones Meets Gardiner [*sic*]; Ouimet Plays Evans: Crack Golfers Clash over Oakmont Course Today—'Little Bob' Defeated J. S. Manion Tuesday," *Atlanta Georgian*, 20 August 1919.

38. Angus Perkerson, "Cups and Tees," *Atlanta Journal*, 19 August 1919.

39. "Evans and Ouimet Victors in First Round Matches: Favorites Will Clash Today; Bob Gardner Makes Brilliant Finish in Beating Max Marston," *Pittsburgh Gazette Times*, 20 August 1919.

40. "Evans and Ouimet Victors in First Round Matches: Favorites Will Clash Today; Bob Gardner Makes Brilliant Finish in Beating Max Marston," *Pittsburgh Gazette Times*, 20 August 1919; "Ouimet and Evans in Great Golf Match . . . Jones Three Up at 18th; Champion Behind: 'Chick' Playing Marvelous Game at Start—Francis Driving Hard," *Atlanta Georgian*, 20 August 1919; Walter P. Wilkes, "Jones Meets Gardiner [*sic*]; Ouimet Plays Evans: Crack Golfers Clash over Oakmont Course Today—'Little Bob' Defeated J. S. Manion Tuesday," *Atlanta Georgian*, 20 August 1919; Grantland Rice, "Bob Jones Faces Gardner, and Evans Faces Ouimet Today: Bob Drops Mannion [*sic*] after a Hot Match," *Atlanta Journal*, 20 August 1919.

41. E. Ellsworth Giles, "Top Qualifying Score Highest in a Decade: 172 Six Strokes Worse Than at Merion in 1916," *Pittsburgh Gazette Times*, 19 August 1919.

42. "Bobby Jones Fourth in Qualifying Round of National Tourney: Manion, Herron, and Tewksbury in Triple Tie for Low Medal—Jones Paired with Manion Today," *Atlanta Constitution*, 19 August 1919.

43. Grantland Rice, "Bob Jones Faces Gardner, and Evans Faces Ouimet Today: Bob Drops Mannion [sic] after a Hot Match," *Atlanta Journal*, 20 August 1919.

44. E. Ellsworth Giles, "Good Scoring Features in Trophy Match: Many Players Participating in American Golfer Contest at Oakmont Finish in Par," *Pittsburgh Gazette Times*, 18 August 1919.

45. Walter Hagen, "Ouimet and Evans to Furnish Big Feature of Tournament Today: Excellent Golf, under Favorable Conditions, Was Played on Oakmont Course during Tuesday's Matches: Great Battle Scheduled for Galleries Wednesday," *Atlanta Constitution*, 20 August 1919.

46. Harry C. Smith (The Runner-Up), "Ouimet-Evans Take Place of Travers-Travis," *Pittsburgh Gazette Times*, 21 August 1919.

47. E. Ellsworth Giles, "Ouimet-Evans Match Greatest Ever Played in U.S., Says Giles," *Pittsburgh Gazette Times*, 21 August 1919.

48. Walter Hagen, "Hagen Says Contest Was Finest Amateur of Any Tournament: Expert Dopes 'Bobby' to Reach Finals and Praises Game Put Up by Youthful Georgian against Old Enemy," *Atlanta Constitution*, 21 August 1919.

49. "Jubilant Fans in Golf Gallery of Champions: Crowd of 3,000 Follows Thrilling Competition of Ouimet and Evans: Hard to Control," *Pittsburgh Gazette Times*, 21 August 1919.

50. Harry C. Smith (The Runner-Up), "Ouimet-Evans Takes Place of Travers-Travis," *Pittsburgh Gazette Times*, 21 August 1919.

51. E. Ellsworth Giles, "Ouimet-Evans Match Greatest Ever Played in U.S., Says Giles," *Pittsburgh Gazette Times*, 21 August 1919.

52. "Jubilant Fans in Golf Gallery of Champions: Crowd of 3,000 Follows Thrilling Competition of Ouimet and Evans: Hard to Control," *Pittsburgh Gazette Times*, 21 August 1919.

53. Walter Hagen, "Hagen Says Contest Was Finest Amateur of Any Tournament: Expert Dopes 'Bobby' to Reach Finals and Praises Game Put Up by Youthful Georgian Against Old Enemy," *Atlanta Constitution*, 21 August 1919.

54. Ralph Davis, "Ralph Davis Column: Ouimet, Game and Gritty," *Pittsburgh Press*, 21 August 1919.

55. "In Sensational Match National Champion Is Defeated at Oakmont: Francis Ouimet, Playing under Physical Difficulties Wrests Greatest Match of Year from Adversary—Bobby Jones Wins in Match with Robert Gardner, 5 Up and 4 to Play," *Atlanta Constitution*, 21 August 1919.

56. Walter Hagen, "Hagen Says Contest Was Finest Amateur of Any Tournament," *Atlanta Constitution*, 21 August 1919.

57. E. Ellsworth Giles, "Ouimet-Evans Match Greatest Ever Played in U.S., Says Giles," *Pittsburgh Gazette Times*, 21 August 1919.

58. Walter P. Wilkes, "Jones, in Good Form, Plays Knepper Today," *Atlanta Georgian*, 21 August 1919.

59. Charles (Chick) Evans Jr., *Chick Evans' Golf Book: The Story of the Sporting Battles of the Greatest of All Amateur Golfers* (New York: Thomas E. Wilson, 1921), 275.

60. E. Ellsworth Giles, "Ouimet-Evans Match Greatest Ever Played in U.S., Says Giles," *Pittsburgh Gazette Times*, 21 August 1919.

61. Ibid.

62. Walter P. Wilkes, "Jones, in Good Form, Plays Knepper Today," *Atlanta Georgian*, 21 August 1919; Harry Keck, "Sporting Chit-Chat: When Chick Met Francis," *Pittsburgh Gazette Times*, 21 August 1919.

63. Walter Hagen, "Hagen Says Contest Was Finest Amateur of Any Tournament," *Atlanta Constitution*, 21 August 1919.

64. "Ouimet Beats Evans in Remarkable Golf Match: Champion Loses Title, 1-Up, on 36th Hole; Winner Sinks 10-foot Putt to Win," *Pittsburgh Gazette Times*, 21 August 1919. Estimates of Ouimet's putt varied considerably; some claimed it was as close as six feet or less.

65. Ibid.

66. Walter P. Wilkes, "Jones, in Good Form, Plays Knepper Today," *Atlanta Georgian*, 21 August 1919.

67. "Ouimet Beats Evans in Remarkable Golf Match: Champion Loses Title, 1-Up, on 36th Hole; Winner Sinks 10-foot Putt to Win," *Pittsburgh Gazette Times*, 21 August 1919.

68. E. Ellsworth Giles, "Ouimet-Evans Match Greatest Ever Played in U.S., Says Giles," *Pittsburgh Gazette Times*, 21 August 1919.

69. Walter P. Wilkes, "Jones, in Good Form, Plays Knepper Today," *Atlanta Georgian*, 21 August 1919; "Ouimet Beats Evans in Remarkable Golf Match: Champion Loses Title, 1-Up, on 36th Hole; Winner Sinks 10-foot Putt to Win," *Pittsburgh Gazette Times*, 21 August 1919.

70. Ralph Davis, "Ralph Davis Column: Ouimet, Game and Gritty," *Pittsburgh Press*, 21 August 1919.

71. Ibid.

72. "Hagen Makes a 76," *Pittsburgh Gazette Times*, 21 August 1919; Walter Hagen, "Hagen Says Contest Was Finest Amateur of Any Tournament," *Atlanta Constitution*, 21 August 1919.

73. Walter P. Wilkes, "Jones, in Good Form, Plays Knepper Today," *Atlanta Georgian*, 21 August 1919.

74. E. Ellsworth Giles, "Chick Evans Resents Attitude of Gallery in Match with Ouimet," *Pittsburgh Gazette Times*, 8 September 1919.

75. Ibid.

76. Walter P. Wilkes, "Jones, in Good Form, Plays Knepper Today," *Atlanta Georgian*, 21 August 1919.

77. Harry Keck, "Sporting Chit-Chat: When Chick Met Francis," *Pittsburgh Gazette Times*, 21 August 1919.

78. "Goat-Getting and Nagging by 'Galleries' at Oakmont Surprise St. Louis Players," *St. Louis Post-Dispatch*, 25 August 1919.

79. Harry Keck, "Sporting Chit-Chat: When Chick Met Francis," *Pittsburgh Gazette Times*, 21 August 1919.

80. Grantland Rice, "Atlanta's Brilliant Youngster in Sight of the Promised Land," *Atlanta Journal*, 22 August 1919.

81. Grantland Rice, "Jones Is Two Down at End of 18 Holes," *Atlanta Journal*, 21 August 1919.

CHAPTER 14. A YOUTH TAKEOVER

1. "Manion Here, Will Not Play Off Tie for Medal Honors at Pittsburgh," *St. Louis Post-Dispatch*, 24 August 1919.

2. "Ouimet Beats Evans in Remarkable Golf Match: Champion Loses Title, 1-Up, on 36th Hole: Winner Sinks 10-Foot Putt to Win," *Pittsburgh Gazette Times*, 21 August 1919.

3. "Played to Standstill, Former Title Holder Goes Down in Defeat: Gardner Eliminated Young Atlantan at Merion Three Years Ago, But Revenge Was Found in Wednesday's Victory," *Atlanta Constitution*, 21 August 1919.

4. "Ouimet Beats Evans in Remarkable Golf Match: Champion Loses Title, 1-Up, on 36th Hole: Winner Sinks 10-Foot Putt to Win," *Pittsburgh Gazette Times*, 21 August 1919; Harry C. Smith (The Runner-Up), "Ouimet-Evans Take Place of Travers-Travis," *Pittsburgh Gazette Times*, 21 August 1919.

5. Francis Ouimet, "Bob Jones Good Bet—Ouimet," *Atlanta Georgian*, 21 August 1919.

6. "Played to Standstill, Former Title Holder Goes Down in Defeat: Gardner Eliminated Young Atlantan at Merion Three Years Ago, But Revenge Was Found in Wednesday's Victory," *Atlanta Constitution* 21 August 1919.

7. Grantland Rice, "Francis Ouimet and Bob Jones Are Favorites for Final," *Atlanta Journal*, 21 August 1919; Walter P. Wilkes, "Jones, in Good Form, Plays Knepper Today," *Atlanta Georgian*, 21 August 1919.

8. Walter Hagen, "Big Golf Week Stage Now Set," *Atlanta Constitution*, 18 August 1919.

9. "Played to Standstill, Former Title Holder Goes Down in Defeat: Gardner Eliminated Young Atlantan at Merion Three Years Ago, But Revenge Was Found in Wednesday's Victory," *Atlanta Constitution*, 21 August 1919.

10. Ibid.

11. Ibid.

12. "Ouimet Is Victor over Evans in Great Golf Match by 10-Foot Putt on Last Green," *New York Times*, 21 August 1919; "Played to Standstill, Former Title Holder Goes Down in Defeat," *Atlanta Constitution*, 21 August 1919.

13. "Played to Standstill, Former Title Holder Goes Down in Defeat," *Atlanta Constitution*, 21 August 1919. As John Kieran elaborated in the *New York Times*, 21 August 1919: "The caddie carefully searched the side of the bank for the lost ball. It was practically buried and the Chicago player had to get on his hands and knees into the trap even to see it and to play it he had to stand on the bank above and hit in the general direction of the ball. He took one terrific swing that dislocated several cubic feet of mud and grass with no other result. He peered down again to make sure the ball was still there, resumed his trapeze-swinging position and again smashed into the bank. Still no ball. One final despairing crash hurled the sod and mud clear across the green, but the ball was buried still deeper than ever. Digging in with his hands, Gardner lifted it out and hurried over to offer smiling congratulations to the youngest winner in the tournament."

14. Walter Wilkes, "Jones, in Good Form, Plays Knepper Today," *Atlanta Georgian*, 21 August 1919.

15. Grantland Rice, "Francis Ouimet and Bob Jones Are Favorites for Final," *Atlanta Journal*, 21 August 1919.

16. Angus Perkerson, "Cups and Tees," *Atlanta Journal*, 21 August 1919.

17. "Played to Standstill, Former Title Holder Goes Down in Defeat: Gardner Eliminated Young Atlantan at Merion Three Years Ago, But Revenge Was Found in Wednesday's Victory," *Atlanta Constitution*, 21 August 1919.

18. Angus Perkerson, "Cups and Tees," *Atlanta Journal*, 21 August 1919.

19. Francis Ouimet, "Bob Jones Good Bet—Ouimet," *Atlanta Georgian*, 21 August 1919.

20. Walter Hagen, "Hagen Says Contest Was Finest Amateur of Any Tournament: Expert Dopes 'Bobby' to Reach Finals and Praises Game Put Up by Youthful Georgian Against Old Enemy," *Atlanta Constitution*, 21 August 1919.

21. Harry C. Smith, "Ouimet-Evans Take Place of Travers-Travis," *Pittsburgh Gazette Times*, 21 August 1919; "Bobby Jones Overcomes Young Knepper's Lead," *Pittsburgh Gazette Times*, 22 August 1919.

22. Smith, "Ouimet-Evans Take Place of Travers-Travis," *Pittsburgh Gazette Times*, 21 August 1919.

23. Grantland Rice, "Francis Ouimet and Bob Jones Are Favorites for Final," *Atlanta Journal*, 21 August 1919.

24. Harry Keck, "Sporting Chit-Chat: Tourney Running True to Expectations," *Pittsburgh Gazette Times*, 22 August 1919.

25. Walter P. Wilkes, "Jones Plays Fownes in Semi-Finals Todays [sic]: Davy Herron and J. Woods [sic] Platt Are Other Survivors—Ouimet Weakened at Close of Brilliant Match," *Atlanta Georgian*, 22 August 1919.

26. Wilkes, "Jones Plays Fownes in Semi-Finals Todays [sic]," *Atlanta Georgian*, 22 August 1919.

27. "Herron, Local Boy, Leading Platt in Semi-Finals: Ouimet Lost Fighting," *Pittsburgh Press*, 22 August 1919.

28. Walter P. Wilkes, "Jones Plays Fownes in Semi-Finals Todays [sic]: Davy Herron and J. Woods [sic] Platt Are Other Survivors—Ouimet Weakened at Close of Brilliant Match," *Atlanta Georgian*, 22 August 1919.

29. Francis Ouimet, "Ouimet Likes Jones in Match against Fownes," *Atlanta Georgian*, 22 August 1919.

30. Walter Hagen, " After Match with Evans Wednesday: Walter Hagen Says Former Champion Put Everything He Had in the Battle against 'Chick' and Went Bad Thursday," *Atlanta Constitution*, 22 August 1919.

31. See "The Amazing Thompsons," *Golf Canada*, 26 June 2017, https://www.golfcanada.ca/articles/the-amazing-thompsons/.

32. "Herron and Fownes Steady in 3rd Round," *Pittsburgh Gazette Times*, 22 August 1919; Walter Hagen, " After Match with Evans Wednesday: Walter Hagen Says Former Champion Put Everything He had in the Battle Against 'Chick' and Went Bad Thursday," *Atlanta Constitution*, 22 August 1919; "Jones Is Two Down at End of 18 Holes," *Atlanta Journal*, 21 August 1919.

33. Hagen, " After Match with Evans Wednesday," *Atlanta Constitution*, 22 August 1919.

34. Francis Ouimet, "Ouimet Likes Jones in Match against Fownes," *Atlanta Georgian*, 22 August 1919.

35. "Herron and Fownes Steady in 3rd Round," *Pittsburgh Gazette Times*, 22 August 1919.

36. Walter P. Wilkes, "Jones Plays Fownes in Semi-Finals Todays [sic]," *Atlanta Georgian*, 22 August 1919.

37. "In Great Comeback, Atlantan Is Victor: Sioux City Player Led Bobby at Eighteenth, but Georgia Boy, in Great Exhibition, Fought Way Out," *Atlanta Constitution*, 22 August 1919; "Bobby Jones Overcomes Young Knepper's Lead," *Pittsburgh Gazette Times*, 22 August 1919.

38. Walter Hagen, "After Match with Evans Wednesday," *Atlanta Constitution*, 22 August 1919.

39. Grantland Rice, "Atlanta's Brilliant Youngster in Sight of the Promised Land," *Atlanta Journal*, 22 August 1919.

40. "Bobby Jones Overcomes Young Knepper's Lead," *Pittsburgh Gazette Times*, 22 August 1919.

41. Grantland Rice, "Atlanta's Brilliant Youngster in Sight of the Promised Land," *Atlanta Journal*, 22 August 1919.

42. Grantland Rice, "The Sportlight," *Atlanta Journal*, 21 August 1919.

43. Walter Hagen, " After Match with Evans Wednesday," *Atlanta Constitution*, 22 August 1919.

44. Walter P. Wilkes, "Jones Plays Fownes in Semi-Finals Today," *Atlanta Georgian*, 22 August 1919.

45. Francis Ouimet, "Ouimet Likes Jones in Match against Fownes," *Atlanta Georgian*, 22 August 1919.

46. Angus Perkerson, "Cups and Tees," *Atlanta Journal*, 22 August 1919.

47. Walter P. Wilkes, "Jones Plays Fownes in Semi-Finals Today," *Atlanta Georgian*, 22 August 1919.

48. Harry Keck, "Sporting Chit-Chat: Final Likely to Be Close," *Pittsburgh Gazette Times*, 23 August 1919.

49. Walter P. Wilkes, "Jones Plays Fownes in Semi-Finals Today," *Atlanta Georgian*, 22 August 1919.

50. "Bobby Jones 1 Up on Fownes at End of Morning Round," *Atlanta Journal*, 22 August 1919; International News Service, "Bobby Jones to Play Herron for Golf Title: Atlanta Boy Defeats Fownes, 5 and 3," *Atlanta Georgian*, 22 August 1919.

51. "Herron, Local Boy, Leading Platt in Semi-Finals; Ouimet Lost Fighting," *Pittsburgh Press*, 22 August 1919.

52. "Bobby Jones 1 Up on Fownes at End of Morning Round," *Atlanta Journal*, 22 August 1919.

53. E. Ellsworth Giles, "Fownes' Game Not at Best in Match with Jones: Giles Looks for Hard-Fought Final," *Pittsburgh Gazette Times*, 23 August 1919; "Dave Herron and Bobby Jones in Title Clash: Native Son Eliminates Platt while Youthful Prodigy from Atlanta Defeats Bill Fownes," *Pittsburgh Gazette Times*, 23 August 1919; "'Bobby' Fights for Title Today: Veteran Goes Down before Atlanta Boy," *Atlanta Constitution*, 23 August 1919.

54. "'Bobby' Fights for Title Today," *Atlanta Constitution*, 23 August 1919; "'Send Mother Word' Is First Command," *Atlanta Constitution*, 23 August 1919.

55. E. Ellsworth Giles, "Fownes' Game Not at Best in Match with Jones: Giles Looks for Hard-Fought Final," *Pittsburgh Gazette Times*, 23 August 1919.

56. Harry Keck, "Sporting Chit-Chat: Final Likely to Be Close," *Pittsburgh Gazette Times*, 23 August 1919.

57. E. Ellsworth Giles, "Fownes' Game Not at Best in Match with Jones: Giles Looks for Hard-Fought Final," *Pittsburgh Gazette Times*, 23 August 1919.

58. "Jones-Herron Match at Oakmont Today Will Produce New Champion," *Pittsburgh Press*, 23 August 1919.

59. Walter P. Wilkes, "Jones Tackles Herron for Golf Title Today: Atlanta Youth Has Fine Chance to Get Revenge for Tech's Defeat—Bob Outplayed Veteran Yesterday," *Atlanta Georgian*, 23 August 1919; "Jones-Herron Match at Oakmont Today Will Produce New Champion," *Pittsburgh Press*, 23 August 1919.

60. Wilkes, "Jones Tackles Herron for Golf Title Today," *Atlanta Georgian*, 23 August 1919.

61. Grantland Rice, "Bobby Jones, the Pride of Dixie, Battling for National Title," *Atlanta Journal*, 23 August 1919.

62. Walter P. Wilkes, "Jones Tackles Herron for Golf Title Today," *Atlanta Georgian*, 23 August 1919.

63. Ibid.

64. "'Bobby Fights for Title Today: Veteran Goes Down before Atlanta Boy," *Atlanta Constitution*, 23 August 1919.

65. "Jones All Square in First Eighteen Holes," *Atlanta Journal*, 23 August 1919.

66. Grantland Rice, "Bobby Jones, the Pride of Dixie, Battling for National Title," *Atlanta Journal*, 23 August 1919.

67. Walter Hagen, "Herron and Jones Reach Golf Final," *Buffalo Evening News*, 23 August 1919.

68. Francis Ouimet, "Ouimet Predicts Great Match," *Atlanta Georgian*, 23 August 1919.

69. Harry Keck, "Sporting Chit-Chat: Final Likely to Be Close," *Pittsburgh Gazette Times*, 23 August 1919.

70. Grantland Rice, "The Sportlight," *Atlanta Journal*, 21 August 1919.

71. E. Ellsworth Giles, "What Chances Do PA Pitt's Golfers Have? Local Players Are Conceded Equal Rating with Other Contestants in Oakmont Tournament—Ouimet Is Picked by Many to Win," *Pittsburgh Gazette Times*, 9 August 1919.

CHAPTER 15. THE CHAMPIONSHIP MATCH

1. Daniel, "High Lights and Shadow in All Spheres of Sport," *New York Sun*, 25 August 1919.

2. John G. Anderson, "Oakmont Proves Need of Big Tournament Changes," *New York Sun*, 31 August 1919.

3. Gibby, "The Morning Hatchet: Herron's Happy Win," *Pittsburgh Post*, 25 August 1919.

4. John G. Anderson, "Oakmont Proves Need of Big Tournament Changes," *New York Sun*, 31 August 1919.

5. Grantland Rice, "The Sportlight: Where, Indeed?" *Indianapolis Star*, 28 August 1919.

6. William Everett Hicks, "Says Western Golfers Can Beat Eastern—Is It So?" *Brooklyn Daily Eagle*, 26 April 1919.

7. The Runner-Up, "Oakmont Best Trapped Course over Which a National Ever Was Played," *Pittsburgh Gazette Times*, 24 August 1919.

8. Harry C. Smith ("The Runner-Up"), "Herron Made Real Clean-up in Tourney," *Pittsburgh Gazette Times*, 24 August 1919.

9. Innis Brown, "Herron Takes Golf Title by Beating Jones," *New York Sun*, 24 August 1919.

10. Ibid.

11. O. B. Keeler, "Pittsburg Is Our Nemesis: No Sportsmanship in That City: Bob's Bad Shots Applauded," *Atlanta Georgian*, 26 August 1919.

12. Innis Brown, "Herron Takes Golf Title by Beating Jones," *New York Sun*, 24 August 1919.

13. On this short-term rivalry see Kartik Gupta, *Pitt vs. Georgia Tech: The Rivalry That Catapulted College Football beyond the Ivy League, 1916–1920*, seminar paper, 79-420, Department of History, Carnegie Mellon University, Fall 2023.

14. Walter P. Wilkes, "Herron Played His First Golf 7 Years Ago," *Atlanta Georgian*, 24 August 1919. On Sundays, the *Georgian* was published as the *Sunday American*, part of the Hearst newspaper chain.

15. "Goat-Getting and Nagging by 'Galleries' at Oakmont Surprise St. Louis Players," *St. Louis Post-Dispatch*, 25 August 1919; Walter Hagen, "Losing Tournament Will Not Hurt Bob, Says Hagen," *Atlanta Constitution*, 24 August 1919; Special to the *New York Times*, "Herron Takes National Golf Title, Defeating Jones in Final at Oakmont By 5 and 4," *New York Times*, 24 August 1919; Innis Brown, "Herron Takes Golf Title by Beating Jones," *New York Sun*, 24 August 1919.

16. Gibby, "The Morning Hatchet: Herron's Happy Win," *Pittsburgh Post*, 25 August 1919.

17. "Gallery Swells to Record Size as Golfers Start on Afternoon Round," *New York Sun*, 24 August 1919.

18. Perry Lewis, "Pittsburgh Player Captures Amateur Golf Title of Country: S. Davidson Herron Wins Open Golf Title on 32 Green: Oakmont Youngster Crowned National Amateur Champion after Sensational Struggle with Bobby Jones in Final Round—Both Show Brilliant Form," *Philadelphia Inquirer*, 24 August 1919.

19. We derived our ball-striking and putting statistics for the 1919 U.S. Amateur mainly from two eyewitness journalists who, we believe, reported the most complete, consistent, and nonpartisan data: E. Ellsworth Giles of the *Pittsburgh Gazette Times* and the unnamed principal correspondent for the *New York Times* who, we believe, was the young John Kieran, arguably the best sportswriter of his generation. Kieran had begun working for the *Times* in 1915 and, like all of its sportswriters then, wrote anonymously. See John Kieran, *Not Under Oath* (Boston: Mifflin, 1964), 17–20, 25, 31–32, 38–39, 46, 157; H. B. Martin, *Fifty Years of American Golf* (New York: Argosy-Antiquarian, 1936, 1966), 349, 351; and Jerome Holtzman, *No Cheering in the Press Box* (New York: Henry Holt, 1995), 34–45. Giles, by contrast, was near the end of both his journalistic and competitive golf career (in earlier years he was good enough to be selected several times to Pennsylvania's elite Lesley Cup team). Giles had long been the most knowledgeable chronicler of Western Pennsylvania golf.

20. The only contemporary description of Oakmont's course layout we have for the 1919 U.S. Amateur was part of William Abbott's article "Gleaned by the Golf Gallery: Description of Famous Oakmont Course, Where National Championship Will Be Fought," *New York Evening World*, 15 August 1919. See Appendix 1. The same description was printed the following day, without attribution, in the *Pittsburgh Daily Post*, 16 August 1919, under the title "Oakmont Course."

21. Innis Brown, "Herron Takes Golf Title by Beating Jones," *New York Sun*, 24 August 1919.

22. Grantland Rice, "Herron and Jones in Golf Final Today," *New York Tribune*, 23 August 1919.

23. A single or precise definition of a "jigger" in early twentieth-century golf is hard to pin down, as variants of the club were used for both short approach shots around the green and, as both Jones and Herron used the club in the morning round, for medium-length iron shots. As defined in 1937 by the English golf professional Abe Mitchell in his book *Essentials of Golf*, "The jigger resembles a cleek in appearance, but is shorter in the shaft and has the weight of a No. 4." See Peter Davies, *The Historical Dictionary of Golfing Terms* (London: Robson Books, 1993), 98.

24. In 1919 the green on No. 8 was around ten yards closer than it is today to the huge ravine that separates Nos. 2 through 8 from the remainder of the course. No. 8's green had to be moved in order to accommodate construction of the Pennsylvania Turnpike (opened on October 1, 1940), which cuts directly through Oakmont Country Club.

25. Special to the *New York Times*, "Herron Takes National Golf Title, Defeating Jones in Final at Oakmont by 5 and 4," *New York Times*, 24 August 1919.

26. Francis Ouimet, "Jones Showed His Gameness Even in Defeat," *Atlanta Georgian*, 24 August 1919.

27. Herron and his opponent, William Gardner, did not turn in official scorecards for the afternoon round of the match they played on Tuesday, August 19. We cannot know the reason why, but they were not the only competitors to fail to turn in a scorecard, especially for afternoon matches. Our hole-by-hole statistics, therefore, include one less round for Herron than for Jones.

28. By amateur conventions of the time, most reporters scored Herron 5 for the hole, even though he still lay around fifteen feet away when he conceded the hole to Jones. However, some reporters did not do so, including the *New York Times* correspondent, who added two imaginary putts and scored Herron a 6 on No. 10. We have chosen to honor the majority convention of the time and score Herron a par 5 on No. 10, but in truth there is no definitive "right answer"—in 1919 or today—on how to score the losing player when he is conceded a putt on a hole he has irretrievably lost. As a result, we compute Herron's score in the morning round as 78 (as did most golf writers) and not a 79, as the *New York Times* reported.

29. Special to the *New York Times*, "Herron Takes National Golf Title, Defeating Jones in Final at Oakmont by 5 and 4," *New York Times*, 24 August 1919.

30. Associated Press, "Herron of Oakmont Club Is New Amateur Golf Champ: Pittsburg Man Defeats Youthful Bobby Jones of Atlanta in a Hard-Fought Match on Oakmont Course for the Championship," *Montgomery Advertiser*, 24 August 1919. This syndicated article, under different titles, was reprinted in many newspapers across the country, e.g., "Herron Vanquishes Jones in Match for Golf Title: Oakmont Player's Putting Beats Young Atlantan, 5 Up and 4," *Washington Post*, 24 August 1919; and "Sports: Atlanta Boy Is 1919 Runner Up: Strain Is Too Great and Bob Jones Loses with Goal in Sight," *Atlanta Constitution*, 24 August 1919.

31. William Everett Hicks, "Davidson Herron Wins National Golf Title at 22: Oakland Player Beats Bobby Jones of Atlanta, 5 Up and 4 to Play, in Finals, after Match Is Squared at End of Morning Round—New Champion Outdrives and Out-putts His Boy Rival," *Brooklyn Daily Eagle*, 24 August 1919.

32. Special to the *New York Times*, "Herron Takes National Golf Title, Defeating Jones in Final at Oakmont By 5 and 4," *New York Times*, 24 August 1919; Innis Brown, "Herron Takes Golf Title by Beating Jones," *New York Sun*, 24 August 1919.

33. Grantland Rice incorrectly reported that Herron broke his niblick in a bunker on the fifteenth rather than the fourteenth hole. Grantland Rice, "Herron Smothers Jones in Final Round for National Amateur," *New York Tribune*, 24 August 1919.

34. This location is today the women's tee on No. 16.

35. The radical transformation of the original No. 16, as described in Steve Schlossman, "The Lost Hole of Oakmont, *Pittsburgh Quarterly* (Summer 2021): https://pittsburghquarterly.com/articles/the-lost-hole-of-oakmont/, was the largest change ever made to H. C. Fownes's 1903 course design.

36. William Everett Hicks, "Davidson Herron Wins National Golf Title at 22," *Brooklyn Daily Eagle*, 24 August 1919.

37. Harry C. Smith, "Herron Made Real Clean-up in Tourney," *Pittsburgh Gazette Times*, 24 August 1919.

38. "Million-Dollar Shout Regretted by Costin; What about Gallery?" *Atlanta Constitution*, 8 September 1919.

39. E. Ellsworth Giles, "Herron Third National Champion Accredited to Oakmont Golf Club," *Pittsburgh Gazette Times*, 25 August 1919.

40. Special to the *New York Times*, "Herron Takes National Golf Title, Defeating Jones in Final at Oakmont by 5 and 4," *New York Times*, 24 August 1919.

41. E. Ellsworth Giles, "Herron Third National Champion Accredited to Oakmont Golf Club," *Pittsburgh Gazette Times*, 25 August 1919.

42. Walter P. Wilkes, "Pittsburg Fans Acted Like Poor Sportsmen," *Atlanta Georgian*, 27 August 1919.

43. Special to the *New York Times*, "Herron Takes National Golf Title, Defeating Jones in Final at Oakmont by 5 and 4," *New York Times*, 24 August 1919.

44. D. J. McGuiness, "Herron New Golf King. Former Caddy Beats Bobby Jones in Final by 5 and 4," *Boston Globe*, 24 August 1919.

45. Estimates of the length of both players' putts on the second green varied widely, and a few reporters, including Charles Doyle of the *Pittsburgh Gazette Times*, thought that Jones's ball was closer to the flagstick than Herron's. Charles J. Doyle, "Herron Wins Amateur Golf Title, Beating Jones, 5–4." *Pittsburgh Gazette Times*, 24 August 1919.

46. Special to the *New York Times*, "Herron Takes National Golf Title, Defeating Jones in Final at Oakmont by 5 and 4," *New York Times*, 24 August 1919; Joe Davis, "Herron Crowned Golf Champion; Beats Jones, 5–4," *Chicago Tribune*, 24 August 1919.

47. Today's giant "Church Pews" on No. 3 evolved from these wiggly-shaped mounds, originally six in number, which separated individual "sand traps" (as opposed to grass bunkers) that were adjacent to one another and not particularly deep. We are not certain how many mounds existed in 1919, but by 1925 an aerial photograph of all eighteen holes shows that there were seven.

48. D. J. McGuiness, "Herron New Golf King," *Boston Globe*, 24 August 1919; Charles Doyle, "Herron Takes National Golf Title," *Pittsburgh Gazette Times*, 24 August 1919; Joe Davis, "Herron Crowned Golf Champion; Beats Jones, 5–4," *Chicago Tribune*, 24 August 1919.

NOTES TO CHAPTER FIFTEEN | 331

49. "Herron Beats Jones at Golf Title Play," *Washington Post*, 24 August 1919.

50. Special, "Jones Defeated in Game Battle for Golf Crown," *Atlanta Constitution*, 24 August 1919.

51. Perry Lewis, "Pittsburgh Player Captures Amateur Golf Title of Country: S. Davidson Herron Wins Open Golf Title on 32 Green: Oakmont Youngster Crowned National Amateur Champion after Sensational Struggle with Bobby Jones in Final Round—Both Show Brilliant Form," *Philadelphia Inquirer*, 24 August 1919.

52. Charles Doyle, "Herron Takes National Golf Title, Defeating Jones in Final at Oakmont by 5 and 4," *Pittsburgh Gazette Times*, 24 August 1919.

53. Special to the *New York Times*, "Herron Takes National Golf Title, Defeating Jones in Final at Oakmont by 5 and 4," *New York Times*, 24 August 1919.

54. Associated Press, "Herron of Oakmont Club Is New Amateur Golf Champ," *Montgomery Advertiser*, 24 August 1919.

55. Grantland Rice, "Little 'Bob' Jones Is Defeated in Big Match. Magic Use of His Putter Enables Dave Herron to Win Natl. Championship," *Atlanta Journal*, 24 August 1919.

56. Special, "Jones Defeated in Game Battle for Golf Crown," *Atlanta Constitution*, 24 August 1919.

57. William Everett Hicks, "Bad Brassies Fatal to Bobby in the Oakmont Golf Final," *Brooklyn Daily Eagle*, 25 August 1919.

58. Grantland Rice, "Little 'Bob' Jones Is Defeated in Big Match," *Atlanta Journal*, 24 August 1919.

59. Joe Davis, "Herron Crowned Golf Champion," *Chicago Tribune*, 24 August 1919.

60. Innis Brown, "Herron Takes Golf Title by Beating Jones," *New York Sun*, 24 August 1919; Walter P. Wilkes, "Herron Played His First Golf 7 Years Ago," *Atlanta Georgian*, 24 August 1919.

61. Amusingly, a reporter for the *Atlanta Georgian* decided not to tell hometown readers that Jones had topped his tee shot, writing with considerable understatement, "Jones' smash was somewhat shorter." "Herron Defeats Jones for Golf Championship," *Atlanta Georgian*, 24 August 1919; Wilkes, "Herron Played His First Golf 7 Years Ago," *Atlanta Georgian*, 24 August 1919.

62. Associated Press, "Herron of Oakmont Club Is New Amateur Golf Champ," *Montgomery Advertiser*, 24 August 1919.

63. Francis Ouimet, "Youth Upsets Golf Dope," *Philadelphia Inquirer*, 22 September 1919.

64. "Herron Vanquishes Jones in Match for Golf Title," *Washington Post*, 24 August 1919.

65. Walter P. Wilkes, "Herron Played His First Golf 7 Years Ago," *Atlanta Georgian*, 24 August 1919.

66. William Everett Hicks, "Bad Brassies Fatal to Bobby in the Oakmont Golf Final," *Brooklyn Daily Eagle*, 25 August 1919.

67. E. Ellsworth Giles, "Herron Third National Champion Accredited to Oakmont Golf Club," *Pittsburgh Gazette Times*, 25 August 1919.

68. Special to the *New York Times*, "Herron Takes National Golf Title, Defeating Jones in Final at Oakmont by 5 and 4," *New York Times*, 24 August 1919.

69. Perry Lewis, "Pittsburgh Player Captures Amateur Golf Title of Country," *Philadelphia Inquirer*, 24 August 1919.

70. E. Ellsworth Giles, "U.S.G.A., Not Oakmont Club, Responsible for Any Tourney Shortcomings, Writes Giles," *Pittsburgh Gazette Times*, 7 September 1919.

71. Walter Hagen did not even realize that Herron's second shot had ended up in the sand rather than the rough. Grantland Rice reported that Herron's drive landed in "heavy rough, leaving him a wicked second," instead of on the edge of the fairway. Rice also claimed that the bunker that caught Herron's second shot was 200 yards from the green. If true, Dave would have indeed struggled to reach the green in three shots. But the bunker was, in fact, only 135 yards from the green. And in 1919, unlike today, the bunker was quite shallow and without an embankment. Walter Hagen, "Losing Tournament Will Not Hurt Bob, Says Hagen," *Atlanta Constitution*, 24 August 1919; Grantland Rice, "Herron Captures National Amateur: Bobby Jones Bows before Brilliant Playing of Older Opponent in Title Round," *Indianapolis Sunday Star*, 24 August 1919.

72. Perry Lewis, "Analysis of Play in 1919 National Golf Championship Pictures Herron Assisted to Throne by Fickle Goddess," *Philadelphia Inquirer*, 31 August 1919.

73. Walter Hagen, "Losing Tournament Will Not Hurt Bob, Says Walter Hagen," *Atlanta Constitution*, 24 August 1919.

74. John G. Anderson, "Oakmont Proves Need of Big Tournament Changes," *New York Sun*, 31 August 1919; William Everett Hicks, "Davidson Herron Wins National Golf Title at 22," *Brooklyn Daily Eagle*, 24 August 1919; Innis Brown, "Herron Takes Golf Title by Beating Jones," *New York Sun*, 24 August 1919; Hagen, "Losing Tournament Will Not Hurt Bob, Says Walter Hagen," *Atlanta Constitution*, 24 August 1919; Gibby, "The Morning Hatchet: Herron's Happy Win," *Pittsburgh Post*, 25 August 1919; E. Ellsworth Giles, "U.S.G.A., Not Oakmont Club, Responsible for Any Tourney Shortcomings, Writes Giles," *Pittsburgh Gazette Times*, 7 September 1919; Francis Ouimet, "Jones Showed His Gameness Even in Defeat," *Atlanta Georgian*, 24 August 1919; Perry Lewis, "Analysis of Play in 1919 National Golf Championship Pictures Herron Assisted to Throne by Fickle Goddess," *Philadelphia Inquirer*, 31 August 1919; "Flagrant Violation of Rules by Tourney Golf Officials Destroys Bob's Last Hope," *Atlanta Journal*, 24 August 1919; Grantland Rice, "Little 'Bob' Jones Is Defeated in Big Match," *Atlanta Journal*, 24 August 1919; Special to the *New York Times*, "Herron Takes National Golf Title, Defeating Jones in Final at Oakmont by 5 and 4," *New York Times*, 24 August 1919.

75. All other commentators besides Wilkes placed the bunker around twenty rather than fifty yards ahead of Jones's drive. Our evaluation of the available photographic evidence (an aerial photograph of all eighteen holes in 1925) suggests that twenty yards is the better estimate. Walter P. Wilkes, "Pittsburg Fans Acted Like Poor Sportsmen," *Atlanta Georgian*, 27 August, 1919.

76. Charles Doyle, "Herron Wins Amateur Golf Title, Beating Jones, 5–4," *Pittsburgh Gazette Times*, 24 August 1919.

77. Perry Lewis, "Analysis of Play in 1919 National Golf Championship," *Philadelphia Inquirer*, 31 August 1919.

78. Special to the *New York Times*, "Herron Takes National Golf Title, Defeating Jones in Final at Oakmont by 5 and 4," *New York Times*, 24 August 1919.

79. "Million-Dollar Shout Regretted by Costin; What about Gallery?" *Atlanta Constitution*, 8 September 1919.

80. Charles Doyle, "Herron Wins Amateur Golf Title, Beating Jones, 5–4," *Pittsburgh Gazette Times*, 24 August 1919.

81. D. J. McGuiness of the *Boston Globe* used the term "embedded" in his account, and said that Jones's efforts to extract his ball only made the situation worse. Given the frequent rains during the week and the recent building and sodding of new bunkers, we believe that this problem affected play throughout the week far more often than was reported in the press. See D. J. McGuiness, "Herron New Golf King," *Boston Globe*, 24 August 1919. Innis Brown also described the bunker as "a trap with a steep bank in front," and the Associated Press reported that Bob's ball "rested in grass on an upslope of the pit." Innis Brown, "Herron Takes Golf Title by Beating Jones," *New York Sun*, 24 August 1919; Associated Press, "Herron of Oakmont Club Is New Amateur Golf Champ," *Montgomery Advertiser*, 24 August 1919.

82. We are especially skeptical of Grantland Rice's report that Jones's ball lay in a heel print in the sand at the bottom of the bunker. No other reporter mentioned anything about a heel print, and it is hard to imagine that a "heel print"—presuming that Rice was physically close enough to the bunker to see the ball—would be inescapable for a player as strong as Bob Jones. We suspect Rice included this faux detail to bolster his larger claim that Jones only lost because he was "unlucky" and a victim of "fate." Grantland Rice, "Herron Smothers Jones in Final Round for National Amateur," *New York Tribune*, 24 August 1919.

83. Walter Hagen, "Losing Tournament Will Not Hurt Bob, Says Walter Hagen," *Atlanta Constitution*, 24 August 1919.

84. Associated Press, "Herron of Oakmont Club Is New Amateur Golf Champ: Pittsburg Man Defeats Youthful Bobby Jones of Atlanta in a Hard Fought Match on Oakmont Course for the Championship," *Montgomery Advertiser*, 24 August 1919; Francis Ouimet, "Jones Showed His Gameness Even in Defeat," *Atlanta Georgian*, 24 August 1919.

85. Grantland Rice, "Herron Smothers Jones in Final Round for National Amateur," *New York Tribune*, 24 August 1919; Special, "Jones Defeated in Game Battle for Golf Crown," *Atlanta Constitution*, 24 August 1919; "Flagrant Violation of Rules by Tourney Golf Officials Destroys Bob's Last Hope," *Atlanta Journal*, 24 August 1919.

86. Walter Hagen, "Losing Tournament Will Not Hurt Bob, Says Walter Hagen," *Atlanta Constitution*, 24 August 1919.

87. Grantland Rice, "Little 'Bob' Jones Is Defeated in Big Match," *Atlanta Journal*, 24 August 1919.

88. Walter P. Wilkes, "Pittsburg Fans Acted Like Poor Sportsmen," *Atlanta Georgian*, 27 August 1919.

89. "Flagrant Violation of Rules by Tourney Golf Officials Destroys Bob's Last Hope," *Atlanta Journal*, 24 August 1919.

90. E. Ellsworth Giles, "U.S.G.A., Not Oakmont Club, Responsible for Any Tourney Shortcomings, Writes Giles," *Pittsburgh Gazette Times*, 7 September 1919.

91. Innis Brown, "Herron Takes Golf Title by Beating Jones," *New York Sun*, 24 August 1919.

92. D. J. McGuiness, "Herron New Golf King," *Boston Sunday Globe*, 24 August 1919.

93. Perry Lewis, "Pittsburgh Player Captures Amateur Golf Title of Country," *Philadelphia Inquirer*, 24 August 1919.

94. Ralph Davis, "Herron Wins Golf Championship," *Pittsburgh Press*, 24 August 1919.

95. Perry Lewis, "Pittsburgh Player Captures Amateur Golf Title of Country," *Philadelphia Inquirer*, 24 August 1919.

96. William Everett Hicks, "Davidson Herron Wins National Golf Title at 22," *Brooklyn Daily Eagle*, 24 August 1919.

97. Special to the *New York Times*, "Herron Takes National Golf Title, Defeating Jones in Final at Oakmont by 5 and 4," *New York Times*, 24 August 1919.

98. Grantland Rice, "Little 'Bob' Jones Is Defeated in Big Match," *Atlanta Journal*, 24 August 1919.

99. "Flagrant Violation of Rules by Tourney Golf Officials Destroys Bob's Last Hope," *Atlanta Journal*, 24 August 1919.

100. Walter P. Wilkes, "Jones Tackles Herron for Golf Title Today," *Atlanta Georgian*, 23 August 1919.

101. Harry C. Smith, "Herron Made Real Clean-up in Tourney," *Pittsburgh Gazette Times*, 24 August 1919.

102. Innis Brown, "Herron Takes Golf Title by Beating Jones," *New York Sun*, 24 August 1919.

103. Special to the *New York Times*, "Herron Takes National Golf Title, Defeating Jones in Final at Oakmont by 5 and 4," *New York Times*, 24 August 1919.

104. Perry Lewis, "Pittsburgh Player Captures Amateur Golf Title of Country," *Philadelphia Inquirer*, 24 August 1919.

105. Grantland Rice, "Little 'Bob' Jones Is Defeated in Big Match," *Atlanta Journal*, 24 August 1919.

106. Paul Cervantes, *John J. McDermott and the 1971 U.S. Open: A Novel* (Jacksonville, Fla.: Movement Publishing, 2019).

107. O. B. Keeler, "Pittsburg Is Our Nemesis: No Sportsmanship in That City: Bob's Bad Shots Applauded," *Atlanta Georgian*, 26 August 1919.

108. Daniel, "High Lights and Shadow in All Spheres of Sport," *New York Sun*, 25 August 1919.

CHAPTER 16. THE BOY WONDERS GO HOME

1. Morgan Blake, "Sports Barrage," *Atlanta Journal*, 14 August 1919.

2. "Flagrant Violation of Rules by Tourney Golf Officials Destroys Bob's Last Hope," *Atlanta Journal*, 24 August 1919.

3. "Back in Atlanta, Bobby Prepares for South's Open," *Atlanta Constitution*, 26 August 1919.

4. It is important to clarify the timing of the inaugural Southern Open in 1919. Contrary to Mark Frost's account in *The Grand Slam*, the Southern Open was played in September 1919, not earlier in spring 1919 and not prior to the Southern Amateur. The Southern Open, not the U.S. Amateur, was Jones's final championship event of 1919, not his first. See Frost, *The Grand Slam*, 100. Curiously, even Bob Jones (and his coauthor, O. B. Keeler) got the sequence of events wrong in their landmark book, *Down the Fairway*. Jones and Keeler claimed that Jones played in the Southern Open immediately following the "international" tournaments in Canada, which is incorrect. Further muddying the chronological record is Keeler's 1931 biography, *The Boys' Life of Bobby Jones*. In this volume Keeler incorrectly claimed (just as Frost does in *The Grand Slam*) that Jones's first big tournament in 1919 was the Southern Open,

followed by the Southern Amateur. See Robert J. Jones Jr. and O. B. Keeler, *Down the Fairway* (London: A & C Black, 1990), 83–84; and O. B. Keeler, *The Boys' Life of Bobby Jones* (Canada: Sleeping Bear Press, 2002), 98–106.

5. Angus Perkerson, "Cups and Tees," *Atlanta Journal*, 3 August 1919.

6. Angus Perkerson, "Cups and Tees," *Atlanta Journal*, 27 August 1919.

7. Ibid.

8. During one of their rounds together Jones shot 68 to tie his own course record at East Lake. According to Stephen Lowe, Ogg "declared it 'the most phenomenal golf' he had ever seen." Stephen R. Lowe, *Sir Walter and Mr. Jones: Walter Hagen, Bobby Jones, and the Rise of American Golf* (Chelsea, Mich.: Sleeping Bear Press, 2000), 84.

9. Homer George, "Edgar Will Win," *Atlanta Constitution*, 10 September 1919.

10. "Tech Golfers Will Compete with Best College Material," *Atlanta Constitution*, 28 September 1919; "'Bob' Jones Lowers Own Court Record on East Lake Links," *Atlanta Constitution*, 19 September 1919; "Jones and Adair Again Victorious," *Atlanta Constitution*, 22 September 1919.

11. Charles Doyle, "Sharon Golf Title Falls to Dave Herron," *Pittsburgh Gazette Times*, 30 August 1919; "Herron Plays Great Golf at Sharon," *Pittsburgh Gazette Times*, 31 August 1919.

12. Doyle, "Sharon Golf Title Falls to Dave Herron," *Pittsburgh Gazette Times*, 30 August 1919; "Herron Plays Great Golf at Sharon," *Pittsburgh Gazette Times*, 31 August 1919.

13. Grantland Rice, "Herron Smothers Jones in Final Match for National Amateur Championship," *New York Tribune*, 24 August 1919.

14. Charles Doyle, "Herron and Peacock Win in Golf Trophy Playoff," *Pittsburgh Gazette Times*, 25 August 1919.

15. The only prior U.S. Amateur victor to win both the medal and match-play components of the championship was the Englishman Harold Hilton, who accomplished the feat at Apawamis Country Club in Westchester, New York, in 1911. E. Ellsworth Giles, "Giles Suggests Preserving the Tourney to Devotees by Making Movies of It," *Pittsburgh Gazette Times*, 14 August 1919.

16. E. Ellsworth Giles, "Herron Third National Champion Accredited to Oakmont Golf Club," *Pittsburgh Gazette Times*, 25 August 1919.

17. "Herron and Teammate Win American Golfer Trophy," *New York Evening World*, 25 August 1919.

18. Charles Doyle, "Herron and Peacock Win in Golf Trophy Playoff," *Pittsburgh Gazette Times*, 25 August 1919.

19. "Enters Sharon Tournament," *Pittsburgh Gazette Times*, 25 August 1919.

20. E. Ellsworth Giles, "Giles Replies to New York Critics Who Brand Herron Fluke Champion," *Pittsburgh Gazette Times*, 31 August 1919.

21. Charles Doyle, "Dave Herron Is Medalist in Sharon Golf Tourney," *Pittsburgh Gazette Times*, 28 August 1919.

22. "Banquet at Oakmont for Herron, New King," *Pittsburgh Gazette Times*, 7 September 1919; "Herron Testimonial Dinner Attended by Many Admirers," *Pittsburgh Sunday Post*, 14 September 1919.

23. "Two Priests Lead Field in Opening at Sharon Tourney," *Pittsburgh Post*, 27 August 1919.

24. Charles Doyle, "Dave Herron Is Medalist in Sharon Golf Tourney," *Pittsburgh Gazette Times*, 28 August 1919.

25. E. Ellsworth Giles, "Dave Herron's Victory at Oakmont 1919 Golf Feature," *Pittsburgh Gazette Times*, 28 December 1919.

CHAPTER 17. DAVE HERRON VERSUS THE PRESS

1. Grantland Rice, "Big Golf Match Was Decided On 12th Hole by Megaphone," *New York Tribune*, 25 August 1919.

2. Today, Pittsburgh is spelled definitively with an "h." But in 1919, both spellings, with and without an "h," were widely used and accepted. Therefore, we have chosen not to note further misspellings. "Sporting Editors Score Treatment Given Jones by Pittsburg Gallery," *Atlanta Constitution,* 27 August 1919.

3. "Million-Dollar Shout Regretted by Costin; What about Gallery? " *Atlanta Constitution,* 8 September 2021.

4. Wilkes, "Pittsburg Fans Acted Like Poor Sportsmen," *Atlanta Georgian*, 27 August 1919.

5. Brown was three and a half years younger than Rice and focused on football, where he was a star offensive guard and team captain in 1905. Rice—never a star and injured frequently—played on Vanderbilt's baseball team, basketball team, subvarsity football team and competed intermittently in track and field. William Arthur Harper, *How You Played the Game: The Life of Grantland Rice* (Columbia: University of Missouri Press, 1999), 45.

6. Ibid., 295.

7. Rice later wrote about this visit in his autobiography: "Those were interesting evenings. While Floncy [Rice's daughter] scampered about and Kit [Rice's wife] burst her buttons to entertain Bob and Perry, I'd bang away at the typewriter getting out my column. . . . How Kit, Floncy, and I relished their stay. One evening I took the entire brood to Coney Island—a great trip. We didn't miss a ride!" Grantland Rice, *The Tumult and the Shouting: My Life in Sport* (New York: A. S. Barnes, 1954), 79.

8. "Grantland Rice," *Pittsburgh Post*, 8 August 1920.

9. Grantland Rice, "Tales of a Wayside Tee," *New York Tribune*, 31 August 1919.

10. Grantland Rice, "The Sportlight," *New York Tribune*, 11 September 1919. Rice's comment regarding Herron's prowess from bunkers is a bit odd because in the championship match Jones hit into fairway and greenside bunkers far more often than Herron (see Appendix 3).

11. Grantland Rice, "The Sportlight," *New York Tribune*, 12 September 1919.

12. "Golf: Princeton Wins Intercollegiate. Herron '18 National Champion," *Princeton Alumni Weekly* 20, 1 (1 October 1919): 14.

13. The Runner-up, "Tri-state Golf Play Territory May Be Widened," *Pittsburgh Gazette Times*, 4 September 1919.

14. "Won't Do to Slur Herron's Winning of U.S. Golf Title," *Brooklyn Daily Eagle*, 5 September 1919.

15. E. Ellsworth Giles, "Giles Replies to New York Critics Who Brand Herron Fluke Champion," *Pittsburgh Gazette Times*, 31 August 1919.

16. Grantland Rice, "The Sportlight: The Big Four in Golf," *Indianapolis Star*, 4 September 1919.

17. Innis Brown, "Herron's Showing Is Not Impressive," *New York Sun*, 7 October 1919.

18. "Herron, Jones, Ouimet, Evans and Kirkby Lead in Golf Rating for Season in That Order," *New York Times*, 30 November 1919.

19. Ralph Davis, "Ralph Davis Column: Hopes Herron Will Silence Idol Worshipers," *Pittsburgh Press*, 29 August 1919.

20. E. Ellsworth Giles, "East vs. West in State Golf Championship," *Pittsburgh Gazette Times*, 12 September 1919.

21. "Won't Do to Slur Herron's Winning of U.S. Golf Title," *Brooklyn Daily Eagle*, 5 September 1919.

22. "Golfers Gather at Nassau Thursday," *New York Sun*, 22 September 1919.

23. Ibid.; Jean Portland, "The Lesley Cup Matches," *Golf Illustrated*, November 1919, 34.

24. Kirkby "was out in 38 and played the return holes in one under par." Portland, "The Lesley Cup Matches," *Golf Illustrated*, November 1919, 34.

25. "Herron Is Defeated by Kirkby in First Day of Lesley Cup Golf Tournament," *New York Times*, 4 October 1919.

26. Jean Portland, "The Lesley Cup Matches," *Golf Illustrated*, November 1919, 34.

27. "Herron Is Defeated by Kirkby in First Day of Lesley Cup Golf Tournament," *New York Times*, 4 October 1919.

28. Innis Brown, "Pennsylvania Golfers Score in Lesley Cup Match," *New York Sun*, 4 October 1919.

29. "Herron Is Defeated by Kirkby in First Day of Lesley Cup Golf Tournament," *New York Times*, 4 October 1919.

30. Innis Brown, "Pennsylvania Golfers Score in Lesley Cup Match," *New York Sun*, 4 October 1919.

31. Innis Brown, "Herron's Showing Is Not Impressive," *New York Sun*, 7 October 1919.

32. Jean Portland, "The Lesley Cup Matches," *Golf Illustrated*, November 1919, 34.

33. Ibid., 36.

34. Sandy McNiblick, "Percentage of Dave Herron Not Too High," *Philadelphia Public Ledger*, 6 October 1919.

35. Ibid.

36. Innis Brown, "Women Golfers in Title Tournament: Herron in Exhibition Match," *New York Sun*, 29 September 1919.

37. The *New York Evening World* reported that Dowling sank a ten-foot putt. The *New York Times* estimated fifteen feet, and the *Sun* said ten yards. "Hooks and Slices," *New York Evening World*, 6 October 1919; "Herron Has Gala Day at Scarsdale," *New York Times*, 6 October 1919; "Herron-Peacock Lose Golf Match," *New York Sun*, 6 October 1919.

38. "Herron Has Gala Day at Scarsdale," *New York Times*, 6 October 1919.

39. "Hooks and Slices," *New York Evening World*, 6 October 1919.

40. "Herron Has Gala Day at Scarsdale," *New York Times*, 6 October 1919.

41. Innis Brown, "Herron's Showing Is Not Impressive," *New York Sun*, 7 October 1919.

42. Ibid.

43. "Herron Is Piping Rock Medalist," *New York Times*, 9 October 1919; "Champion Herron Defeats Graham, 5 and 4, in Final Round of Piping Rock Tourney," *New York Times*, 12 October 1919.

44. "Herron Is Piping Rock Medalist," *New York Times*, 9 October 1919.

45. Innis Brown, "National Golf Champion Leads Field in Qualifying Round at Piping Rock Tourney: Piping Rock Golf Honors to Herron," *New York Sun*, 10 October 1919.

46. William Abbott, "Gleaned by the Golf Gallery," *New York Evening World*, 10 October 1919; Brown, "National Golf Champion Leads Field in Qualifying Round at Piping Rock Tourney," *New York Sun*, 10 October 1919.

47. Abbott, "Gleaned by the Golf Gallery," *New York Evening World*, 10 October 1919.

48. "Herron Is Piping Rock Medalist," *New York Times*, 9 October 1919.

49. William Abbott, "Gleaned by the Golf Gallery," *New York Evening World*, 10 October 1919.

50. Ibid.

51. "Herron Is Piping Rock Medalist," *New York Times*, 9 October 1919.

52. William Abbott, "Gleaned by the Golf Gallery," *New York Evening World*, 10 October 1919.

53. Innis Brown, "National Golf Champion Leads Field in Qualifying Round at Piping Rock Tourney," *New York Sun*, 10 October 1919.

54. Innis Brown, "National Golf Champion Again Shows Skill in Piping Rock Tourney: Herron Romps in Piping Rock Golf," *New York Sun*, 11 October 1919.

55. Ibid.

56. Ibid.

57. "Herron, White, Graham and Greenway Are Semi-finalists in Piping Rock Golf: Herron Advances in Golf Tourney," *New York Times*, 11 October 1919.

58. Ibid.

59. "Champion Herron Defeats Graham, 5 and 4, in Final Round of Piping Rock Tourney," *New York Times*, 12 October 1919.

60. "Herron, White, Graham and Greenway Are Semi-finalists in Piping Rock Golf: Herron Advances in Golf Tourney," *New York Times*, 11 October 1919.

61. Ibid.

62. Gibby, "Pride of Oakmont with 'Well-Digger' Startles Gallery," *Pittsburgh Post*, 14 October 1919.

63. "Champion Herron Defeats Graham, 5 and 4, in Final Round of Piping Rock Tourney," *New York Times*, 12 October 1919.

64. Innis Brown, "National Golf Champion Adds to Season's Laurels by Carrying off Honors in Piping Rock Invitation Tourney: Graham Easy Mark for 'Davy' Herron," *New York Sun*, 12 October 1919.

65. Ibid.

66. Gibby, "Pride of Oakmont with 'Well-Digger' Startles Gallery," *Pittsburgh Post*, 14 October 1919.

67. William Everett Hicks, "Champion Golfer Plays over House in Winning Final," *Brooklyn Daily Eagle*, 12 October 1919.

68. Ibid.

69. Gibby, "Pride of Oakmont with 'Well-Digger' Startles Gallery," *Pittsburgh Post*, 14 October 1919.

70. William Everett Hicks, "Champion Golfer Plays over House in Winning Final," *Brooklyn Daily Eagle*, 12 October 1919.

71. Ibid.; Innis Brown, "National Golf Champion Adds to Season's Laurels by Carrying off Honors in Piping Rock Invitation Tourney: Graham Easy Mark for 'Davy' Herron," *New York Sun*, 12 October 1919.

72. Hicks, "Champion Golfer Plays over House in Winning Final," *Brooklyn Daily Eagle*, 12 October 1919.

73. Gibby, "Pride of Oakmont with 'Well-Digger' Startles Gallery," *Pittsburgh Post*, 14 October 1919.

74. Innis Brown, "Herron Convinces of His Prowess," *New York Sun*, 13 October 1919; Gibby, "Pride of Oakmont with 'Well-Digger' Startles Gallery," *Pittsburgh Post*, 14 October 1919; William Everett Hicks, "Champion Golfer Plays over House in Winning Final," *Brooklyn Daily Eagle*, 12 October 1919.

75. Brown, "Herron Convinces of His Prowess," *New York Sun*, 13 October 1919.

76. "Comment on Current Events in Sports: Herron's Golf and the Critics," *New York Times*, 13 October 1919.

77. William Everett Hicks, "Champion Golfer Plays over House in Winning Final," *Brooklyn Daily Eagle*, 12 October 1919.

EPILOGUE. DAVE AND BOB: "TEN-TENTHS" THE HEROES OF PITTSBURGH AND ATLANTA

1. We borrow this evocative phrase from Herbert Warren Wind to apply equally to Dave Herron and Bob Jones in 1919 as authentic hometown golf heroes, in the same way Wind used it for Francis Ouimet in 1913. Herbert Warren Wind, *The Story of American Golf: 1888–1941* (New York: Callaway Editions, 2000), 72.

2. "Herron Jones Ouimet, [sic] Evans and Kirkby Lead in Golf Rating for Season in That Order," *New York Times*, 30 November 1919.

3. E. Ellsworth Giles, "Dave Herron's Victory at Oakmont 1919 Golf Feature: Pittsburgher Chief in Eyes of Linksmen," *Pittsburgh Gazette Times*, 28 December 1919.

INDEX

Page references in italics refer to figures, photographs, maps, or tables.

Abbott, William, 201, 268–69, 281–83
Adair, Forrest, 154
Adair, George: admiring of Merion Golf Club, 80–81; Atlanta Athletic Club (1915), 38; Birmingham Invitation (1915), 36; Cherokee Country Club (1916), 63; Druid Hills Invitation (1914), 27; illness of, 154; Montgomery Invitation (1915), 27–29; Montgomery Invitation (1916), 61; Southern Amateur (1915), 29, 34–35; as surrogate father to Bob Jones, xvii, 23, 27, 68, 74–76, 80, 101; U. S. Amateur at Merion (1916), 68–69; Western Amateur (1915), 35; Western Amateur (1917), 111
Adair, Perry, *32, 66, 169, 248*; Atlantic Athletic Club (1915), 37–38; Druid Hills Club, 35; Montgomery Invitation (1915), 27–29; nineteenth birthday, 312; postwar Red Cross exhibition matches, 119–23, *120*; Red Cross match (1917), 105–6, *107*, 110–11; rivalry with Bob Jones Jr., 23–36, 38–39, 60–70, *70*; Roebuck Club Invitation, 36–37; Southern Amateur (1914), 24–27, 29–32, *32*, 34; Southern Amateur (1917), 99, 101–3, 105; Southern Amateur (1919), 140; Southern Open (1919), 246, *248*; U. S. Amateur at Merion (1916), 71–73, 75, 78–79; U. S. Amateur at Oakmont (1919), 153, 156–57, 159, 167–68, *169*, 174; War Relief Fund tournament (1917), 111–13; wartime experience of, 99, 101–3, 105–6, *107*, 111–13
Aldredge, George, 69
Allegheny Country Club, 4, 20, 44, 54, 89, 94–95, 116, 137, 256
Allis, Edward P., III ("Ned"), 22, 47
Allison, Jack, 62
Altoona Country Club, 13–14, 19–22
A. M. Byers Company, 127

American Golfer, 25–26, 30–32, 68–70
American Golfer Trophy: 1914 competition, 46, 48; 1916 competition, 73, 251–53; 1919 competition, 169–71, 251
analysis of play: ball-striking in championship match, *285–86*; driving distance in championship match, *284*; hole-by-hole descriptions of Oakmont, *281–83*; most to least difficult holes at Oakmont, *211*; putting in championship match, *227*, 290–93, *290, 291, 292*; scoring averages by hole, Herron vs. Jones, *212–13*; scoring in championship match, compared to prior averages, *219, 287, 288*
Armstrong, Dwight, 58, 88, 94–96, 162, 175, 179, 254
Associated Press, 201, 210, 215, 222, 225, 228, 235
Atlanta Constitution, 24, 25–26, 30–34, 37–38, 62, 76–77, 80, 102, 110, 113, 118–20, 123, 139–41, 168, 175, 189–90, 194, 197, 199, 234, 248, 258–59
Atlanta Georgian, 65–69, *66*, 75–78, 80, 101–4, *107f*, 142–44, 154–155, 169, 173, 175, 184, 196, 221–22, 229–30, 233, 258–59
Atlanta Journal, 37, 67, 103, 153–54, 178, 195–97, 238, 243, 246, 258–59

Badham, William, 36–37
Barnes, Jim, 111, 143, 145, 245–50, *248*
Baxter, C. L., 30
Behr, Max, 47
Bendelow, Thomas, 273
Big Bob. *See* Jones, Robert P. ("Big Bob")
Birmingham Age-Herald, 36, 62, 101, 104
Birmingham News, 99, 101–2, 105
Blake, Morgan, 243
Blossom, Frank, 51, 86

341

Bodeker, Fred, 101–2
Boston Globe, 236
Bothamly, John, 245, 249
Brady, Mike, 124, 131, 249
Brae Burn Country Club, 121–24, 131, 174, 246
Brame, John, 28
Brand, Fred, 58
Brooklyn Daily Eagle, 201, *205,* 216, 223, 259, 261–62, 270
Brown, Innis: on Bob Jones, 206, 235; on Herron, 214, 224, 238–39, 262; on Herron at Scarsdale, 266–67; on Herron at the Lesley Cup, 262, 267; on Herron at the Piping Rock Invitation, 267–70, 271; on Herron at the 1919 U.S. Amateur, 262, 267, 270; on spectators at the 1919 U.S. Amateur, 201–3; taking the place of Grantland Rice, 259
Buhl, Franklin, 254
Bush, Reuben, 30, 36, 69, 81, 99, 101–3, 131, 139–41, 246, 249
Butler Country Club, 21, 138
Buxton, C. B., 22
Byers, Eben: Allegheny Invitation (1916), 55; Allegheny Invitation (1918), 116; Canadian Amateur match, 141–42; dual membership in Pittsburgh and New York clubs, 5, 90–91; East-West competition, Detroit (1914), 47; Field Club match (1917), 97; influence on Dave Herron, 8, 18, 23, 27, 40, 273; influence on Loeffler, 8; Lesley Cup (1916), 88; not competing during the war, 95; Oakmont Invitation (1913), 16, 17, 20; Pennsylvania State Amateur title match (1914), 22; Sharon Country Club (1919), 254; U.S. Amateur at Merion (1916), 71, 73, 75–76, 114; U.S. Amateur at Oakmont (1915), 47; U.S. Amateur at Oakmont (1919), 8, 134, 150, 167, 175; West Penn Amateur (1915), 45; West Penn Amateur (1916), 58; WGA rating, 44
Byers, J. Frederic, 5, 127, 171, 254

caddying: by Dave Herron, 7–9, 11, 22, 46, 47, 87, 127, 137, 252, 274; by Francis Ouimet, 132–33; by Jimmy West, 267; by Reuben Bush, 141
Canadian Open (1919), 142–45
Canon, Lawrence, 22, 86, 88
Carlton, O. S., 140–41

Carter, Philip, 14, 69, 73
championship match at the U.S. Amateur at Oakmont (1919), 200–240; aerial photograph of course, *217;* afternoon round, 220–37; course map, *205;* crowd control at, 202–4; loud noise at the twelfth hole on Jones's swing, 233–34; morning round, 204–11, 214–20; politics and factional bickering at, 201; press writers at, 200–203, 237–40, 258. *See also* analysis of play
Cherokee Country Club, 63–64
Chicago Daily Tribune, 105–6, 112
Chicago Tribune, 107, 226
"Church Pews" at Oakmont, 205, 330n47
Clark, Frank T., 32, 34
Cleary, Eddie, 179
"Colonel, The" (*American Golfer* correspondent), 25–26, 30–32, 69–70, 297–98n5
Corkran, D. C., *41,* 42–43, 85–88, 91, 163
Costin, W. G., 220, 233–36, 258
Crabbe, William, 4
Crawford, Joseph, 149
Crookston, J. B., 5, 13, 18, 44–45, 58–59, 88, 92, 116
Crowell, James R., 78
Culver, P. C., 201

Daniel (*New York Sun* columnist), 240
Darragh, R. H., 255
Davis, G. H., 25
Davis, H. K. B., 54
Davis, Joe, 106, 119, 124, 201, 226
Davis, Ralph, 184, 237, 262
Davis & Freeman Cup, 23, 35, 38, 63
Dean, Simpson, 252
Dexter, Charlie L., 30, 32, 69, 99
Diegel, Leo, 143, 249–50
"Dixie Kids," 123–24
Dowling, Jack, 113, 124, 263, 266–67
Down the Fairway (Jones Jr. and Keeler), 23, 29, 74, 78, 99, 119
Doyle, Charles, 225, 234
Druid Hills Club, 23, 27, 35, 38, 58, 63, 104, 143
Dyer, Franklin W., 51, 263

East Lake: 1912 competition, 23; 1919 competition, 245–50, *248*
East-West: 1914 competition, 46–50; 1919 competition, 131

Edgar, James Douglas, 143–45, *144*, 245–47, 250–51
Edgeworth Club junior golf tournament (1909), 9–11
Edwards, Kenneth, 118, 123
Egan, H. Chandler, 54, 77
Engineers Country Club, 249, 267
epidemic of 1918 and 1919, 148, 150, 170
Estabrook, "Bunny," 264
Evans, Charles, Jr. ("Chick"): dual victories in U.S. Open and U.S. Amateur (1916), 54, 69, 81; in Red Cross exhibition matches, 118; in U.S. Amateur at Merion (1916), 54, 69, 81; in U.S. Amateur at Oakmont (1919), 131–32, 150–51, 164, 166–67, 170, 174, 181–86
Evans, William H., 69, 72
Exmoor Country Club, 276

Flynn, William, 72, 85
Fownes, H. C., xvi, 9, *16*, 71, 93, 257
Fownes, H. C, II, 7, 252, 315n27
Fownes, W. C., Jr., *8, 52*; Allegheny Country Club (1916), 55; *American Golfer* Trophy (1915), 48; in Canadian International match (1919), 141–43; course operations at Oakmont, xi, xvi, 7, 15, 20, 44, 85, 88–89, 128, 130, 136, 156–57, 166; esteem for golfing ability of, xvii, 5, *8*, 71–72; Lesley Cup (1919), 52, *52*; as mentor to Herron, xvi, 9, 71, 134, 257; Oakmont Invitation (1913), 15–17, 20, 22; in steel manufacture, 127; U.S. Amateur at Detroit (1915), 47–50; U.S. Amateur at Merion (1916), 71–73; U.S. Amateur at Oakmont (1919), xvii, 150, 153, 160–62, 167, 175, 179, 193–98, *213*; U.S. Amateur at the Country Club (1910), xv, 5, 106; West Penn Amateur (1915), 44–45; West Penn Amateur (1916), 57–58; W. W. Flanegin Cup (1916), 56–57
French, Emmet, 113, 246
furrowed bunkers, 156–57, *156*

Gardner, Robert: *American Golfer* Trophy (1919), 171; *American Golfer* Trophy, Detroit (1915), 48, 50; in the military, 309n59; Red Cross benefit (1917), *107*; U.S. Amateur at Detroit (1915), 54; U.S. Amateur at Merion (1916), 69, 74, 76–79, 81; U.S. Amateur at Oakmont (1919), xiv–xv, 131, 141, 152, 157, 161, 167, 175, 178–80, 187–90, 197, *212, 213*, 234, 240, 259, 324n13; Western Amateur at Chicago (1917), 109
Gardner, W. Hamilton ("Ham"), 179
Gavin, Mrs. W. A., 111
Georgia State Amateur Championship, 64–68
Georgia Tech University, 126, 172, 177, 203, 245, 250–51
Gibby (*Pittsburgh Post* columnist), 202–3, 269–70, 271
Giles, E. Ellsworth, *52*; ball-striking and putting statistics, 328n19; on Bob Jones Jr., 196, 198, 206, 221; on Bob Jones, Sr., 236; on Dave Herron, 8, 115, 163, 198–99, 221, 232, 236, 253, 256, 261–62, 274; defense of Herron against press accusations, 261–62; on the Ouimet-Evans match, 181–84; playing in and covering the 1919 U. S. Amateur, 149, 151–52; on Robert Gardner, 161, 180; in the Sharon Country Club competition (1919), 255; in the Stanton Heights Invitation (1916), 59; on unruly spectators, 177, 220
Golf, 80–81
golf ball materials, 296n4
Graham, John, 116
Graham, Sam J., 270–71
Great Steel Strike of 1919, 148, 315n1
Greenway, G. C., 270
Guilford, Jesse, 51, 88, 109, 123, 124, 134, 161, 238

Hadden, John, 142
Hadley, S. H., 255
Hagen, Walter, 332n71
Haight, Richard, 252
Hall, Spick, 201
handicap ratings, xv, 43, 46, 54, 90–91, 96
Hayes, Mrs. Frank, 111
Hays, W. A., 10
Heard, Bryan ("The Commodore"), 28, 30–31, 34, 99, 102
Herron, Andrew, Jr., *4, 117*
Herron, Andrew, Sr., *6*
Herron, Louise Johnston, 275–76, *275*
Herron, Pomeroy, 3, *4*, 5, 9–12, 13, *41*, 42, 55, *117f*
Herron, Samuel Davidson ("Dave"; "Davie"; "Davy"), *4, 41, 117, 162, 192, 199, 238, 239, 252, 256, 275*; academic achievements, 89, 115; after the Oakmont championship match (1919), 54–55;

Herron, Samuel Davidson (*continued*)
Allegheny Invitation (1916), 54–55; Allegheny Invitation (1918), 116; *American Golfer* Trophy competition (1919), 171, 251–53; analysis of play in championship match, 211–13, 219, 227, 284–93; as an iron worker, xiv–xv, 127; caddying at Oakmont, 7, 9, 14, 22, 138, *252*; ceding the low-qualifier medal, 253–54; erratic early game, 58–59; Fownes as mentor to, 71; golf performance during the war, 94–95, 96, 111, 114, 116; Intercollegiate Championship, Greenwich (1915), 50–51; Intercollegiate Championship, Oakmont (1916), 85–87, 256; Lesley Cup (1916), 51–53, 88; Lesley Cup (1919), 262–63; loyalty to Oakmont, 89; in the Marines, 117, *117*; maturation at Princeton, 40–43, *41, 51–54, 52*; McCurdy-Trees "ringer" trophy (1914), 46; MGA rating of, 91; not competing in low-score medal at Oakmont, 252–53; Oakmont Invitation (1913; 1914), 17, 20; on Oakmont teams (1915), 44–45; Piping Rock Invitation Championship, 263, 267–71, *271*; playing other sports to get into shape, 115; postchampionship play to convince the press, 263–72; power of, 51, 55–56, 163, 208, 266, 269; President's Cup (1914), 40, 42; press criticism after the U.S. Amateur win, 258–72; as Princeton's "Best Natured" graduate, 115; quiet dignity and elite traditions of, 252, *252*; rejection from the armed services, 96; return to play at Princeton (1917), 96–97; Scarsdale Golf and Country Club, 124, 263, 266–67; Sharon Country Club competition (1919), 254–55, *255*; Southern Amateur, Roebuck (1917), 102; sustained mental stress and, 74–75; U.S. Amateur at Detroit (1915), 45–50; U.S. Amateur at Merion (1916), 54, 59, 73–75; U.S. Amateur at Oakmont (1919), 135–38, 161–63, *162*, 167, 175, 179, 187, 193, 196; weight gain, 94–96, 269. *See also* championship match at the U.S. Amateur at Oakmont (1919)

Herron, San D., 3

Hickey, Richard, 110, 111, 140, 153, 155, 157–58, 168, 175, 243, 247

Hickman, C. F., 28

Hicks, William Everett ("The Analyst"), 201, 216, 218, 223, 225, 230, 233, 237, 259, 270–71

Hoblitzel, E. S., 142

Hoffner, George, 190, 193

Hubbell, J. W., 87

Hunter, Paul M., 54

Hutchison, Jock, 246–47

influenza epidemic of 1918 and 1919, 148, 150, 170

Ingalls, J. H., 63

Inglis, John M., 36

Jacoby, Louis, 26, 61, 101, 103–5, *103*, 140–41, 164–65, 167, 178

James, R. L., 12, 18, 21, 138, 254–55

Jernigan, Harry, 28

jigger, 207, 224, 329n23

Jones, Robert P. ("Big Bob"), *32, 121*; friendship with Adairs, 23; golfing by, 27, 30–31, 36; on Jones Jr.'s twelfth hole at the championship match (1919), 234–35, 244; parenting by, xvii–xviii, 6–7, 23–24, 27–29; Southern Amateur (1917), 99, *100*, 101; Southern Amateur (1919), 140; writing as "The Colonel," 297–98n5

Jones, Robert T., Jr. ("Bob"; "Bobby"; "Bobbie"; "Little Bob"), *33, 37, 155, 188, 192*; analysis of play in championship match, 211–13, 219, 227, 284–93; in Canadian competitions (1919), 142–45; Chicago Red Cross match (1917), 105–6, *107*, 109–11; compared with Arnold Palmer, xiv; congratulating Herron after the championship match, 236, 244; on crowd noise, 203, 245; dependence on Stewart Maiden, 178, 243; *Down the Fairway*, 23, 29, 74, 78, 99, 119; as emotional player, 206; as a nationwide celebrity, 139, 141; peevishness of, 121–22, 160; postwar Red Cross exhibition matches, 118–23, *120, 121*, 124–25; as a prodigy, 37–38; rising celebrity, 60–70, 74–76, 78–80; rivalry with Perry Adair, 23–25, 27–39, *32, 33, 37*, 60–65, 67–70; Roebuck Club Invitation (1915), 36–37, *37*; shoe in a wheelbarrow incident, 139, 141, 314n9; Southern Amateur (1914), 29–34; Southern Amateur (1917), 99–106; Southern Amateur (1919), 139–41; Southern Open (1919), 245, 246–47, *248*; after Southern Open (1919), 250–51; temper of, 63–64, 76, 134–35,

159–60, 236, 244; U.S. Amateur at Merion (1916), xv, 72, 74–76, 78–80; U.S. Amateur at Oakmont (1919) arrival, 153; U.S. Amateur at Oakmont (1919) matches, 174, 177–78, 180, 181, 193–96; U.S. Amateur at Oakmont (1919) preparation, 134, 153, *155*, 157–61, 172; War Relief Fund tournament (1917), 112–14; wartime experience of, 99–106, *100*, 105–6, *107*, 109–14. *See also* championship match at the U.S. Amateur at Oakmont (1919)

Keck, Harry, 152–53, 186, 190–91, 195–96, 198, 220

Keeler, O. B.: on Adair, 69, 119; biographer of Jones, xvii, 303n48; coauthor of *Down the Fairway*, 23; on crowds, 203; on Edgar, 144–145; on Herron, 67, 113, 221; on Jones, 6, 67, 68, 69, 70, 76, 113, 119, 221, 240, 243; on Montgomery Invitation (1915), 61; not at Oakmont (1919), 316–17n18; on Perry Adair–Bob Jones match (1915), 61–62; on Southern Amateur (1917), 99

Keffer, Karl, 143

Kieran, John, 324n13, 328n19

Kirkby, Oswald, xiv, 47, 51, 53, 91, 131, 135, 141–42, 163, 168, 264

Knepper, Rudolph ("Rudy"), 190, 194–96, *212*, *213*

Knowles, Clarence ("Moose"), 31

Knowles, Ellis, 139–40

Knoxville Sentinel, 63–64

Lesley Cup, xv, 5, 42, 46–47, *47*, 328n19

Lewis, Perry, 201, 204, 231, 232–33, 237, 239

Liddell, L. C., 17, 20, 22, 56

Loeffler, Emil, Jr., *15*; in the army, 97–98, 126, 128; mentor of Herron, 8–9, 11, 273, 276; Oakmont greenkeeper, 15, 20, 55, 85, 88–89, 129–30, *156*, 157, 164, 166, 207, 234, 246; U.S. Amateur Open (1919) preparations, 128–30, 150, *156*, 157, 166, 234

Long, Richard C., 92, 95

Los Angeles Morning Tribune, 78

"lost hole of Oakmont," 216

Louisville Courier-Journal, 78–79

Lowe, Stephen, 118

Lowrie, William, 11, *41*, 85

low-scorer medal, 252–53, 255

Lyon, George, 142
Lyon, Seymour, 142

MacFarlane, Willie, ix
Maiden, Stewart ("Kiltie"): mentoring Adair, 168; mentoring Jones, xv, 39, 114, 125, 188, 243–44, 247, 250, 273; U.S. Amateur at Oakmont (1919), 153–55, *154*, 157–58, 172, 174, 178, 243–44
Manion, James ("Jimmy"), 175–76, 178, *213*, 253
Marston, Max, xix, 69, 91, 122, 124–25, 131, 141, 171, 175, 178, 187
Martin, H. B., 80, 252
Maxwell, Norman, *41*, 73, 112
McCurdy-Trees "ringer" trophy, 40
McDermott, John, 240
McDonald, C. B., 263
McGuiness, D. J., 201, 236
McLeod, Frank, 112–13, 246
McLuckie, W., 142
McNamara, Tom, 124, 263, 266
McNiblick, Sandy (pseudonym), 265
megaphone incident at Oakmont (1919), xiii–xvii, 233–36, 244, 260
Memphis Country Club, 24
Merion Golf Club, 68, 71, 72
Metropolitan Golf Association (MGA) handicap ranking, 90–91, 96
Miller, Johnny, 158
Montgomery Advertiser, 28–29
Montgomery Country Club, 28, 60
Morrison, R. G., 73
Morse, George E., 152
Mott, C. B., 29
Mudge, Dudley, 49–51, 54, 86
Munger, C. H., 30, 102
Murchie, John, *256*

National Golf Links, 14, 50, 90, 134, 150, 263–64, 266, 274
New Castle Country Club, 13, 14
New York Sun, 204, 222, 224, 240, 259, 263, 267
New York Times, 62, 77, 79, 108–13, 122, 124, 130, 133, 135, 142, 157, 161, 163, 165–66, 201, 203, 220, 222, 224–27, 231, 233–34, 235, 237–39, 262, 264, 266–69, 272, 274, 284
New York Tribune, 130, 201, 258–59
Nicholls, Gilbert, 112

Oakmont Country Club: caddie corps, 11, 17–18, 155, 165, 172, 273; course design and improvement, xvi, 44, 89, 93, 128, 153–54, 156–57, *156*, 166, 312–13n8; founding of, xvi, *16*, 93; interclub matches, 5, 18; Intercollegiate Golf Championship (1916), 85–87, 256; Oakmont Invitation (1913; 1914), 15–16, 17, 20; U.S. Amateur (1917), 90, 91–93; U.S. Amateur (1919) preparations, 128–30. *See also* U.S. Amateur at Oakmont (1919)

Ogg, Willie, 245–47, *248*, 250

O'Hara, Peter, 97

Ormiston, George, xv–xvi, 5, 8–9, 13, 16–18, 20, 22, 40, 42, 44–45, 47, *52*, 55, 58–59, 71, 73, 89–91, 94–95, 137

Ouimet, Francis, *185, 192*; illness during U.S. Amateur at Oakmont (1919), 170–71, 175, 179, 191; loss of amateur status for selling sporting goods, xiv; U.S. Amateur at Oakmont (1919), 133, 150–52, 163, 164–67, 181–86, *185*, 191–92, *192*, 201;

Palmer, Arnold, xiii–xiv

Paton, L. B., 69

Peacock, Grant A., 19, 42, 51, 96, 171, 175, 179, 240, 251–53, 263, 266, 269

Pearce, H. H., 255

Pennsylvania State Amateur Championship, 5, 21, 255, 275

Perkerson, Angus, 154, 174, 178, 180, 190, 194, 246

PGA (Professional Golf Association), 8, 111, 145, 249–50

Philadelphia Inquirer, 74–77, 79, 81, *156*, 204, 231–32, 237

Philadelphia Public Ledger, 69, 72, 77, 80, 265–66

Piping Rock Invitation Championship (1919), 263, 267–71, *271*

Pittsburgh Chronicle-Telegraph, 237

Pittsburgh Field Club, 9, 17, 22, 89, 92–95, 166

Pittsburgh Gazette Times, 20–21, 43, 45, 48, *52*, 53, 134, 149, 151–52, *155*, 163, 179–80, 184, 187, 190, 194, 198, 220, 222, 224–27, 232, 238, 253, *256*

Pittsburgh Post, 13, 17, 55, 57, 85, 87, 89, 95, 129–30, 134, 136–38, 163, 168–69, 184, 200, 203–4, 260, 269–70

Pittsburgh's first golf courses, 295n2

Pittsburgh Sunday Post, 71–72, 92–93, 96, 97–98, 167

Platt, J. Wood ("Woody"), 171, 186, 191–93, *192*, 196–97, *212*, 266

Portland, Jean, 264

Prescott, Tom, 110

President's Golf Trophy tournament (1913), 23

Preston, P. H., 59, 95

Princeton University, 4, 11, 17, 19, 40–44, 50–53, 85–87, 89, 93, 97

Probasco, Scott, 25, 36

Professional Golf Association (PGA), 8, 111, 145, 249–50

racial violence in 1919, 148, 315n2

Rainwater, C. V., 65, 99

Ray, Ted, xiv, xix, 45, 48, 81, 90, 97, 132, 148

Red Cross exhibitions, 118, 133, 174, 259, 263

Reekie, Willie, 263

Reid, Archie, 268

Reith, T. B., 142

Rice, Grantland: descriptions of Jones Jr., 63–64; friendship with Jones Jr., 260; on Gardner, 161; on Herron's playing, 190, 197–99, 224–24, 235, 238, 330n33, 332n71, 333n82; on the importance of the draw, 177–78; on Jones's ball in a heel print, 333n82; on the Jones-Gardner match, 188–89; knowing Jones as a child, 259–60; megaphone incident, 233, 258–59; on the Oakmont course, 100–101, 164–65, 168; on Ouimet's illness, 186; Southern connections, 259, 336n7; speculation on a Ouimet-Evans match, 320n16; on the U.S. Amateur win by Herron, 240, 258–60, 261; on weather at Oakmont (1919), 165, 173; writing as "The Judge," 297–98n5

Roebuck Golf and Automobile Club Birmingham Invitation, 36–38, 99, 101–5

Rose, J. B., 11, 16–17, 19, 42, 45, 94–95

Rosenthal, Elaine, 119–22, 125

Ross, Donald, 23, 55, 273

Rotan, George V., 24–25, 30

Rowan, Will H., 29, *32*

Rowe, Charlie, 8, 97, 160, 170, 215, 220, 246

Sarazen, Gene, xiii, 8, 21

Sargent, W. S., 19

Sawyer, Daniel E. ("Ned"), xiv, 46–48, 50, 54, 69, 71, 75, 97, 110, 131, 135
Scarsdale Golf and Country Club, 124, 263, 266–67
Schenley Park Golf Links, 4–5, 45, 129, 164, 254, 263
Schmidt, Heinrich, 109
Shady Side Academy, 3–7, 10, 11, 13, 19
Sharon Country Club, 10, 254–57
Simpson, G. O., 112
Smith, Harry C. ("The Runner-Up"), 201, 238
Smith, Horace, 246
Smith, MacDonald, 7
Smith, Victor R., 65
"Snake Mounds" at Oakmont, 223
Sockel, Albert, 47
Southern Amateur: 1914 tournament, 24–27, 297n3; 1915 tournament, 29–34; 1917 tournament, 99–106; 1919 tournament, 139–41
Southern Golf Association (SGA), 23, 102, 245–46
Southern Open, 245–50, 334–35n4
Spanish Flu epidemic (1918), 148
Spur, The, 78, 250
Standish, J. D., Jr., 54, 119
Stanton Heights Golf Club, 10–11, 59, 129, 254
State, E. J., 12
Stearns, J. S. ("Jack"), 187, *212*
Stirling, Alexa, 35, 68, 78, 119–23, *120*, 125, 273
Stitt, Bill, *15*
stymie/half-stymie, 12, 25, 61, 109, 181, 189, 206, 229, 270
Sullivan, John H., Jr., 108, 122
Sweetser, Jesse, 134, 167, 175, 177, 317–18n30
Swift, Allan, 47

Tellier, Louis, 124
Tewksbury, Paul, 174, 178, 253
Thompson, Charles, F., 12
Thompson, W. C., 12
Thomson, W. J., *212*
Thorn, Howard, *24*
Thornburg Country Club, 10
Travers, Jerome ("Jerry"), 132, 153, 167, 304n59
Travis, Walter J., 46–47, 49, 73, 80, 108, 121–22, 123, 251, 271
Turpin, G. H., 142

U.S. Amateur at Detroit (1915), 45–50
U.S Amateur at Merion (1916), xv, 54, 59, 68–69, 71–75, 76–81, 114
U.S. Amateur at Oakmont (1917), 91–93
U.S. Amateur at Oakmont (1919): *American Golfer* Trophy, 169–71; demographics of, 175–77; Herron vs. Platt, 193; Jones vs. Gardner rematch, 187–90; Jones vs. Knepper, 194–96; Oakmont preparations, 118–20, 168; Ouimet vs. Platt, 191–92, *192*; praise for Oakmont course, 152–53, 168–69, 170; preparation of players for, 131–38, 149–63, 164–72; press after Herron win, 237–40, *239*; press location, 177; press on upcoming Jones–Herron match, 196–99, *199*; press predictions for, 190–91; random draw for qualifier matches, 177–78, 261; USGA officials, 149; weather at, 170, 173–75, 180. *See also* championship match at the U.S. Amateur at Oakmont (1919)
U.S. Golf Association (USGA): founding of, 46; handicap ranking, xv, 46–47, 54; international match in Canada (1919), 140–41; officials late to the U.S. Amateur (1919), 46; suspension of championships during WWI, xvi, 91–93, 98; ; on the Spanish flu (1919), 148
U.S. Golf Association rules controversies: amateur status definition, 88, 106, 108, 132–33; splitting players into east and west, 54, 72; stymie, 109, 309n56; tee placement, 48–49

Vance, Henry, 99, 101, 104
Vardon, Harry, 45, 48, 77, 81, 97, 132

Waldo, C. G., 178
Walker, Cyril, 112
Walker Cup, 71, 194, 276
Ward, John Montgomery, 14, 152
War Relief Fund tournaments, 111–14, 118
Washburn, L. M., 42
West, Jimmy, 267
Western Amateur: 1915 championship, 35; 1917 championship, 111
Western Golf Association (WGA): amateur status, 108; handicap ranking, 43–44; Red Cross donations, 109; Red Cross exhibition matches, 118–19; stymie acceptance, 109; Western Amateur sponsor, 43; Western Open sponsor, 43

Western Open, 43, 143, 245, 249
Western Pennsylvania Golf Association (WPGA), 55–56, 90–92, 94
Western Pennsylvania Interscholastic Athletic League (WPIAL), 4
West Penn Amateur, xv, 11, 44–45, 55, 57–58, 94–95, 296n9
West Penn Open, 11, 58, 94–95
W. Flanegin Cup, 56–57
WGA. *See* Western Golf Association (WGA)
Wheeler, Frederic S., 251, 253
Wheelock, Thomas ("Tommie"), 103
White, Gardiner, 91
"White Faces" at Merion, 72
Whitney, Nelson, 26, 29–30, 46, 50, 54, 69, 75, 91, 99, 101–2, 131, 133–34, 139–41, 175, 178–79, 190, 193, 245, 246, 249
Whittemore, Arthur ("Buck"), 264–65
Wilkes, Walter, 155–59, 173, 178, 182, 184–86, 191–92, 194–97, 201, 221–22, 224, 229, 233, 235, 238, 258–59, 316n18
Wilson, Hugh, 71, 72, 85
Wind, Herbert Warren, xix, 317n21
women in War Relief Fund tournament (1917), 111
Wood, Warren K., 105, 118
Woodruff, Fuzzy, 103
WPIAL (Western Pennsylvania Interscholastic Athletic League), 4

www.ingramcontent.com/pod-product-compliance
Lightning Source LLC
Chambersburg PA
CBHW030749010525
25920CB00001B/1